When the Babe
Went Back to Bosto.

When the Babe
Went Back to Boston

Babe Ruth, Judge Fuchs
and the Hapless Braves of 1935

BOB LeMOINE

McFarland & Company, Inc., Publishers
Jefferson, North Carolina

Frontispiece: "No king, potentate or conquering hero was ever given a more enthusiastic welcome," James C. O'Leary wrote in the *Boston Globe* when Babe Ruth joined the Boston Braves. Ruth's tenure, however, was a short reign (*Saint Petersburg Times* via ZUMA Press; IMAGO via ZUMA Press).

LIBRARY OF CONGRESS CATALOGUING-IN-PUBLICATION DATA

Names: LeMoine, Bob, 1973– author.
Title: When the Babe went back to Boston : Babe Ruth, Judge Fuchs and the hapless Braves of 1935 / Bob LeMoine.
Description: Jefferson, North Carolina : McFarland & Company, Inc., Publishers, 2023 | Includes bibliographical references and index.
Identifiers: LCCN 2023004454 | ISBN 9781476685021 (paperback : acid free paper) ∞
ISBN 9781476648309 (ebook)
Subjects: LCSH: Ruth, Babe, 1895–1948. | Fuchs (Judge), 1878–1961. | Boston Braves (Baseball team)—History. | Baseball players—United States—Biography.
Classification: LCC GV865.R8 L46 2023 | DDC 796.357092 [B]—dc23/eng/20230207
LC record available at https://lccn.loc.gov/2023004454

BRITISH LIBRARY CATALOGUING DATA ARE AVAILABLE

ISBN (print) 978-1-4766-8502-1
ISBN (ebook) 978-1-4766-4830-9

Front cover: Boston Braves outfielder Babe Ruth in the dugout at Wrigley Field in May 1935 (*Chicago Sun-Times/Chicago Daily News* collection, Chicago History Museum)

Printed in the United States of America

McFarland & Company, Inc., Publishers
Box 611, Jefferson, North Carolina 28640
www.mcfarlandpub.com

To Melissa,
who heard me talk about this book
from the time we first met.
Yes, it's finally done.

To Mary and Anne,
my high school English teachers,
who encouraged me to read, write, and think.
I'm still working on these.

Table of Contents

Preface:
Why Another Babe Ruth Book?

Babe Ruth died over 70 years ago, yet the dozens of resources listed in the bibliography of this book make it clear that he will be a subject worth studying for all time. Of special note are the great biographers who have studied him, their names synonymous with Ruth himself: Robert Creamer, Marshall Smelser, Leigh Montville, and Jane Leavy. I consider each of these contributing to a Ruth canon which introduces not only Babe Ruth the baseball hero but also George Herman Ruth the man. I would throw in two recent authors on Ruth who have also influenced me. Thomas Barthel explored Ruth as the first celebrity athlete, and Edmund F. Wehrle examined how organized baseball shunned its greatest star after capitalizing on him for decades. I am indebted to the voluminous research conducted by these writers who have studied Ruth either from cradle to grave or from a specific angle.

Each of these works pulled Ruth from the throes of myth and fable which dominated the first half of the 20th century and presented a more accurate picture of who he truly was. Perhaps it was Roger Kahn's monumental 1959 article "The Real Babe Ruth" in *Esquire* which started us on the path to evaluating baseball's greatest celebrity with a critical eye.

> Just as good money drives out bad in economics, so heroic fancy drives out heroic fact and, in the case of heroes, we are often left standing in a forest of chopped-down cherry trees wondering what our man actually was like. The greater the hero, the more prevalent the fictions. Since Ruth was the most popular of all baseball heroes, movie companies, careless writers and glib storytellers have busied themselves with the obfuscation of fact.[1]

The cherry trees have been chopped down over the past 50 years and we have a clearer picture of who Ruth was. In the 21st century, we understand more of Ruth and his times every time an old newspaper is transformed from microfilm roll to computer screen. In the process, we discover a Ruth who says things we haven't heard him say before.

One facet of Ruth's life which has always intrigued me has never been explored in depth. In 1935, Ruth returned to Boston for a last hurrah with the Boston Braves. I've always wondered why. From 1935 until the end of his life, Ruth aspired to be a major league manager but was never given the opportunity. I've always wondered why. Ruth lived the rest of his days feeling unfulfilled, or so I thought, and cancer whittled him down to nothing. Who was this Ruth who faced failure, rejection, lone-liness, anxiety, and depression? This is the Ruth I wanted to know. He was not the heroic Ruth of old.

We know *that* Ruth. "Back in 1919," wrote Grantland Rice, "the Babe was about as robust as two atomic bombs. He was a young man of mighty appetites and unre-strained desires that were beyond all curbing. He was something the world of sport had never seen or known before. Big, rough, gentle, tough, powerful, kindly, gener-ous, natural, profane, he caught the fancy of the world."[2] Ruth rambled through the Roaring '20s, becoming the most popular man in the country.

Sportswriters followed his every move, from the home runs and the World Series titles to the cars, coats, feasts, and appearances. A lot has been written about this Ruth. I wanted to explore the Ruth of 1935–1948.

In 1935, Ruth was fat, slow, and past his prime. He stayed in at night and tired easily. He was desperate to hang on to a game that was passing him by. This Ruth had an identity crisis. He could not continue on the field since he was an embarrassment. He had frequent aches, pains, and colds. His body, which had so much energy in the 1920s, now was betraying him in the mid–1930s. What would he do without the game? What *could* he do? We can all relate to the Babe Ruth of angst.

I can't relate to the Babe Ruth of 714 home runs, but I can relate to 1,330 strikeouts.

I can't relate to being the most recognized person on the planet, but I can relate to the feeling that no one cares anymore.

I can't relate to Ruth's fame and stardom, but I can relate to wondering where the time has gone.

I can't relate to being the highest paid player in the game, but I can relate to being desperate for a job.

I can't relate to becoming a Hall of Famer, but I can relate to being plump, slow, and middle age. I can't relate to being a phenom, but I can relate to having your hopes dashed.

We can all relate, or at least will someday relate, to this Babe Ruth who was sub-ject to the passage of time and who watched his hopes and dreams disappear. It is a fearful thing to admit to yourself that you are not who you once were. He was used to being called the greatest of all time and couldn't relate to having to find him-self all over again. As Rice wrote, "So few can appreciate the shock that suddenly comes when all dreams and all illusions suddenly blow up—when one suddenly feels tired and old and out of date, bewildered and a trifle dazed, wondering what it is all about."[3]

This Babe Ruth, "a trifle dazed, wondering what it is all about," is worth explor-ing. This Ruth was desperate to hang on to the game in 1935. He spent the remainder of his life desperate for a manager position so he could still be connected to the game which discarded him. Think about it. Baseball's all-time great spent his later years listening to games on the radio, sending up pinch-hitters and bringing in relievers from the bullpen in his mind. Organized baseball, which became a big business because of him, had thrown him to the curb. He longed to return, as his fulfillment was dependent on putting on a major league uniform again. He finally found fulfillment, but in an out-of-the-way place. His final months were devoted to those who really cared about him and those he truly cared about. Through his weakness and constant pain, he nevertheless traveled the roads to visit, as Rice wrote, "those who might need help and inspiration." Rice concluded that Ruth was "greater nearing the trail's end of glory" than he ever was while slugging 714 home runs.[4] Ruth found his ultimate fulfillment.

That's the Ruth we need to explore.

In 1935, another man was desperate to stay in

Babe Ruth and Judge Emil Fuchs smoke cigars in celebration of Ruth's signing with the Boston Braves (courtesy Boston Public Library, Leslie Jones Collection).

the game. Boston Braves owner Judge Emil Fuchs, a successful lawyer, had struggled to maintain his second-division club since purchasing it in 1923. He was a baseball fan, not a businessman, by his own admission. He brought Sunday baseball to Boston, brought in movies and entertainment, children and ladies, radio broadcasts, and even tried managing the team himself on the assumption that if they were going to lose, why pay someone else to do it? Eventually, a perfect storm of the Great Depression, America's racing craze, and multimillionaire Tom Yawkey buying the Red Sox sent Fuchs reeling. The Judge was in debt and his club was floundering. He needed something, or someone, to attract fans to Braves Field when it was more attractive to go elsewhere. He was desperate to salvage the team for all New England, but time was running out.

He needed Babe Ruth.

It was a genius move on paper. Babe Ruth would return to the city he started in 21 years before. The Red Sox dominated baseball from 1915 to 1918, when Ruth was the dominant pitcher in the league. Three World Series titles resulted, something unheard-of in Boston again until the next century. Ruth was sold to the Yankees, and Boston's dynasty was over; the Yankees' dynasty began. Judge Fuchs could reverse history. Ruth returns to Boston, finds the fountain of youth, fans pour into Braves Field, and the Braves win the National League pennant. Actually, fourth place would be perfectly fine. Ruth could prove himself worthy of becoming a manager, and he would lead the Braves to success in years to come.

It has a great Hollywood feel to it, but of course reality was far from it. Judge Fuchs never found fulfillment in his baseball endeavors. But he had a lot of fun trying.

And so two desperate men who loved the game and would do anything to stay in it formed an unlikely partnership in 1935. Each one gave the other unrealistic promises. The Judge gave Ruth fancy titles which meant nothing. Ruth promised the Judge his heart and soul for the Braves. Neither could fulfill what they promised. I don't believe one double-crossed the other. It was a simple matter of putting two desperate baseball men together and hoping for success out of chaos.

The 1935 Braves were one of the worst teams of all time. This book is not about victory but about collapse. It is not about high achievement and amazement, but failure and bewilderment. How bad can it get? The 1935 Braves are a good answer to that question.

This is the story of a failing hero, a frantic owner, and a forfeited franchise. I believe it is a story worth telling.

Introduction

"Babe Ruth shouldn't have gone to Hawaii," Charles C. Alexander wrote in *Breaking the Slump: Baseball in the Depression Era*. Detroit Tigers president Frank Navin was seriously considering Ruth to manage his club at the end of the 1933 season, but Ruth headed to Hawaii for some exhibition games. Ruth assumed the offer would be there when he returned despite the warnings of others that if he wanted to manage, now was the opportunity. By the time Ruth phoned Navin, however, it was 2 a.m. Detroit time, and his potential employer was not impressed. Navin instead hired Mickey Cochrane.[1]

Alexander called the 1934–1935 seasons "New Deal Baseball." America had stabilized during the Depression years. The New Deal was helping pull the nation out of the worst of times, through the Federal Emergency Relief Administration, Civil Works Administration, and Civilian Conservation Corps. The National Recovery Act provided better working conditions, so people had time for recreational pleasures, such as baseball. Baseball had been losing attendance steadily since 1930: the American League dropped from 4.6 million in 1930 to 2.9 million in 1933; the National League attendance fell from 5.4 million to 3.1 million over that same time. In 1934, attendance rose in both leagues, a sign that better days were ahead.[2]

Ruth hobbled through one final season with the Yankees in 1934. He played in just 125 games and was often taken out of games to rest his creaky knees. The Yankees finished second behind Cochrane's Tigers, the job Ruth might have had. Yet the Bambino was confident another big-league managerial position awaited him. He had his eye on the Yankees job, since in his mind he could be a far better manager than Joe McCarthy. But Boston would be a fun place, too. Ruth announced that he was done as a full-time player, and the possibilities of where he might go were endless. Just as long as it wasn't in the minor leagues.

Ruth faced an identity crisis he had not experienced since he was a boy in Baltimore. Ruth was confident that, under the tutelage of Brother Matthias and others at St. Mary's Industrial School for Boys, he would have amounted to something. The Brothers took the boy who lived over a saloon and gave him a place to belong. If he hadn't become a ballplayer, Ruth once remarked, he would have been a shirt maker, and a damn good one at that. But baseball would become his identity, from his remarkable feats with the Baltimore Orioles, the Boston Red Sox, and then the

New York Yankees. His identity was that of the Bambino, the Sultan of Swat, the Big Bam, the Big Fellow, and so forth.

By the end of 1934, Ruth's popularity remained high, perhaps still the highest of anyone in his day, but his play on the field was slowing down. His glory days had passed, and he had hinted ever so slightly for the past few years about wanting to manage a team, preferably the Yankees. Owner Jacob Ruppert and GM Ed Barrow wanted nothing to do with Ruth as manager. Other clubs seemed like good possibilities, but none of them were willing to take the perceived risk of letting the Babe take charge of a team.

While Ruth was making shirts at St. Mary's, Emil Fuchs was building a law career in New York City. Fuchs was a child of the Lower East Side tenements, but by the time Ruth was a star pitcher for the Red Sox, Fuchs was a magistrate. "Judge," as he was forever called after his short time on the bench, was convinced by John McGraw to buy the Boston Braves. Winning ball games was not like winning court cases. While Ruth was breaking home run records and becoming perhaps the most recognized face in the country, Fuchs was struggling to keep his team alive. Ruth was swimming in a fortune; Fuchs was drowning in debt.

By the end of 1934, Fuchs also experienced an identity crisis. He could easily have sold the club long before that point and resumed his law career, but he wanted to succeed in baseball more than anything else in the world. When tapping into America's racing craze fizzled, Fuchs turned to the only possible attraction to draw folks to Braves Field: Babe Ruth.

The story of the 1935 Boston Braves includes the tale of two desperate men willing to try almost anything to remain in the game they loved. Even if Ruth was in decline, he could certainly help the Braves win more games and draw fans to Braves Field. The 1934 Braves finished 78–73, good enough for fourth place in the National League. Credit manager Bill McKechnie with finding ways to take castoffs from other teams and make them into a first-division club. To finish fourth was an accomplishment in that day, and a nice bonus for your players despite finishing 16 games behind and never seriously challenging for the pennant. There were high hopes the Braves could finish even higher with Babe Ruth's bat in the lineup next to Wally Berger's.

Boston went nuts to have Babe Ruth return to the city where his career began 21 years before. If anyone could save a franchise, it was the Great Bambino. All was right with the world.

No one could have imagined what was about to happen.

1

Babe Ruth

Hail & Farewell at Fenway
(August 12, 1934)

"I want to remain in baseball."—Babe Ruth

"St. Francis of Assisi didn't love birds as much as the Babe loved kids."
—Leigh Montville

The Tribute

He left the field that day to the resounding applause from the largest crowd that had ever gathered at Fenway Park. The quaintly shaped park squeezed in about 46,766 fans for what Paul H. Shannon of the *Boston Post* called "a farewell tribute to baseball's idol."[1] Their idol was once thin, or at least thinner, fast, and barreling. Now he was plump, slow, and sluggish. He was a fading contributor on the field, but still an idol off it. He was the aging star of the New York Yankees, and fans in Boston sensed that this was his last game in their city. It was the cycle of life, after all. He started there, starred there, then was unfairly sold to the Yankees, where he became bigger than the game itself. Now he was back for the final time, and they wanted to say goodbye.

"Who else," Shannon wondered, "upon such a cold and gloomy day, with showers imminent at all times, could have packed those ample stands and drawn to the Fenway such a cheering, enthusiastic assemblage?" No one else could because no one else was Babe Ruth. Boston was sending him off with a "Hail and Farewell" salute.[2] The large crowd, Shannon wrote, indicated that Boston fans "were all anxious to be in at the death, for even the one-time King of Swat himself has acknowledged that he is soon to pass out of the picture."[3] Another 20,000 fans were turned away at the gate. Some refused to miss the proceedings and clambered up nearby rooftops just to catch a glimpse of greatness they could one day tell their children about. Others scattered along Jersey Street, looking for a back way into the park.

The date was August 12, 1934. But perhaps Babe Ruth's mind was elsewhere. Maybe he was recalling an earlier day when he wasn't podgy and gray or have knee

The overflow crowd for Ruth's final games at Fenway Park, August 12, 1934 (courtesy Boston Public Library, Leslie Jones Collection).

trouble. Maybe some in the star-gazing crowd could also reminisce about Ruth's first appearance in the Hub 20 years before.

From Saloon to Fenway

It was Saturday, July 11, 1914. A lovely summer day with a high temperature of 80 greeted the crowd of 11,000 as they entered Fenway Park, just two years old. Fans took a streetcar either on the Ipswich Street or Beacon Street lines for a nickel. A few weeks later, a new incline was built, and the trolley would continue into what would become known as Kenmore Square.[4]

Fans may have chatted about the events of the day on the way to Fenway. The Reverend G.A. Rainville of St. Joseph's Church in Salem, Massachusetts, on vacation in Switzerland courtesy of a congregational gift, learned of the devastation in the Great Salem Fire. The blaze on June 25 destroyed 1,300 buildings, including the church, and left 18,000 people homeless. Rainville immediately set sail back to the United States aboard the *RMS Lusitania*, the British luxury liner. In less than a year, that ship would be destroyed by a German torpedo. The incident would lead to anti–German sentiment and pull the United States into World War I.[5]

Baseball provided a distraction from these horrors. The Boston sports pages provided intrigue and excitement over three new Red Sox players acquired for $25,000 from the Baltimore Orioles of the International League. The sale was called "one of the biggest deals of the baseball year" by R.E. McMillin of the *Boston Journal*.[6] Orioles owner Jack Dunn was short on cash but rich on talent, which he would sell for the right price to compete with the Baltimore club in the Federal League.[7] Red Sox owner John J. Lannin was glad to oblige, taking catcher Ben Egan, gangly pitcher Ernie Shore, and a pitcher he said was "the minor league sensation of the year," George Herman "Babe" Ruth.[8] The new sensational pitcher had only been with the Orioles a few months, but he had spent his life in Baltimore.

Jacob Ruth, the Babe's great-grandfather, emigrated from Germany with his brother Francis in 1832 and settled in the Fells Point waterfront area of Baltimore, a thriving city second only to Ellis Island as a destination for 19th-century German immigrants. Jacob was a cabinetmaker. He had six children. One of them, John Antone Ruth, became Babe Ruth's grandfather. John Antone married Mary Strodtman, and they lived in Ridgely's Delight, a neighborhood dubbed Pigtown, the picturesque nickname coming from the route pigs ran on the way to the slaughterhouse. Residents could race to their basement windows and "reach out and try to grab a passing, squealing Sunday dinner," Leigh Montville wrote.[9] Many African Americans settled in the area after being evicted from their homes to make room for the new Camden Station.

John Antone Ruth was in the lightning rod business on Frederick Avenue in the western part of town. His two sons, John Jr. and George Herman, worked in the lightning rod shop, which included a social club and saloon.[10] George Herman married Catherine "Katie" (Schamberger), daughter of Pius and Joanna Schamberger. On February 6, 1895, Katie gave birth to George Herman Ruth, Jr., in her parents' home at 216 Emory Street, a red brick row house which looked like all the others. It now serves as the home of the Babe Ruth Museum. Pius once ran a saloon near the Ruths' lightning rod shop. Perhaps Babe Ruth's parents met there.[11] John Antone Ruth died in 1897, leaving John Jr. and George Herman, Sr., to run the lightning rod business. The brothers moved to South Woodyear Street, a mostly German working-class neighborhood, and ran the lightning rod shop in their backyard.[12]

When George Herman Ruth, Jr., was six, the family moved to an apartment over his father's saloon at 426 West Camden Street.[13] It was gritty, smoky, and bustling.[14] The 1900 census described the neighborhood as "poor white," and Baltimore was known for being the largest unsewered city in the country.[15] "When I wasn't living over it," Babe recalled about his dad's saloon, "I was living in it, studying the rough talk of the longshoremen, merchant sailors, roustabouts, and water-front bums."[16] The new Camden Station and the B&O Railroad kept the area bustling. The B&O Warehouse stands today as the backdrop to Oriole Park at Camden Yards. There is a statue honoring the little boy who lived nearby over a saloon.

Young George saw a lot of tragedy in his early years. He knew a lot of death and depression. His siblings: Augustus (or Augusta), William, Anna, and Gussie, either died in infancy or just after their first birthdays. Only his sister Mamie survived childhood. Mamie claimed there were eight total siblings, not six, but only six are verified. Young George saw a lot of death, anyhow.[17] So is the reality of a painful childhood known more for chaos than compassion. Ruth spent the rest of his life seeking approval that he rarely received at home. "Parental abandonment would become the defining and unacknowledged biographical fact of his life," Jane Leavy wrote.[18] The pain was too much.

Growing up over a saloon was certainly a lousy environment, and children bereft of attention often act out until they find it. Even negative attention is better than none. His mother buried so many children. What was her mental and physical well-being? His parents spent long hours at the saloon, so what would a young boy do except get into trouble? Katie suffered physical ailments, developed a drinking problem, divorced George Sr., and died of exhaustion and lung disease in 1912.[19] It was a tragic story of a disconnected and grief-stricken family. No wonder Ruth referred to himself as "a bad kid." "They told him he was a bad boy, so he grew up thinking he was a bad boy," his daughter Julia remarked.[20]

George Sr. admitted George Jr. to St. Mary's Industrial School for Boys, a Catholic reform school. Ruth lived most of his life there from 1902 until he turned 19 in 1914. St. Mary's accepted boys the state deemed "incorrigible," but the label of "orphan" was not something Ruth embraced. George Sr. may have paid tuition for Babe to attend. "Some boys lived there simply because their parents couldn't afford to raise them," wrote Brian Martin. "Others, because the courts sent them."[21] St. Mary's wasn't an orphanage, but they would accept orphans. It was not a reform school, but many wayward youths *were* reformed. It was a religious school, but the curriculum exposed students to many disciplines without a religious emphasis. It was a catch-all for youth of many backgrounds: from parents who could afford tuition and wanted the best of academics for their child, to runaways with no place to go. It was an inclusive place. George Sr. was better at running a saloon than raising a son and probably recognized that. St. Mary's was the best place for young George. But he entered alone and abandoned.

"Get me right—I'm no orphan," Ruth told *The Sporting News* in 1931. "All these stories about my being an orphan kid, too tough for my aunts and uncles to handle, and about my being shoved into a reform school are a lot of baloney, just plain old applesauce and hooey. I was a pretty good kid when my old man decided I would be better off in St. Mary's Industrial Home." The Brothers could keep watch of him better than his father. "There's been a lot of talk about my being a hell-raiser in St. Mary's and that the brothers were glad to get rid of me, but you can put it down in your paper that some of the brothers cried when I left there. I'd been there so long. I didn't get in any more trouble than any other boy, although I didn't fall for all the rules and regulations, but nobody else did."[22]

The Ruth of Bob Considine's ghostwritten account, which Ruth sparingly contributed to, said: "I was listed as an incorrigible, and I guess I was. Looking back on my early boyhood, I honestly don't remember being aware of the difference between right and wrong."[23] Given the circumstances, Ruth had far more access to trouble than to nurture. Perhaps Ruth never pulled himself away from his own myth: the rags-to-riches, down-and-out "bad boy" of the streets who was rescued by holy men and became a home run king through good old-fashioned hard work.

He was, after all, constantly reminded of sin, fallenness, confession, salvation, and sacrifice at Mass. Ruth didn't really know his parents, and he didn't really know himself, either. No wonder Ruth connected with kids more than anyone else. He understood pain, confusion, and neglect. He listened to them because rarely did his parents take time to listen to him.

"I remember that Babe was a little rascal," recalled Harry C. Birmingham, the boyhood friend of George Sr., who was the cop on the beat in their neighborhood. Birmingham recalled 45 years later how George Sr. had asked him to escort Babe to St. Mary's. "He was not a bad boy—just mischievous, and no more so than other boys his age. He certainly never gave the police any trouble. But his father decided to send him to St. Mary's because he just couldn't make him mind at home. Babe had a will of his own and was never one to take orders."[24]

The cattle grazing in the lush pasturelands in the Victorian-style fortress made St. Mary's a safe environment, far from the grungy, violent world of a saloon.[25] The haven was everything West Camden Street lacked: structure, discipline, caring, and accountability. St. Mary's was a sanctuary for "any destitute white boy" like Ruth.[26] What was it like that first day when he entered St. Mary's? He was just one of two surviving siblings and was now surrounded by masses of children with equally bad or even worse circumstances. Their lives now had order as they slept row by row, and they had routines to follow.

The Xaverian Brothers ran a tight ship at St. Mary's. The Brothers (to this day) are a Catholic religious order established in Belgium in 1839. They are not priests but laymen who adhere to lives of poverty, chastity, and obedience in devotion "to the teaching and moral development of youth."[27] The boys would arise at 6 a.m. and head to the chapel for Mass, followed by a breakfast of oatmeal. Then off to class until noon. Everyone had a slate and chalk to do their assignments. Lunch was soup and homemade bread. After recess, it was back to class. Older students worked on trades: carpentry, tailoring, shoemaking, or playing in the band. The Brothers instilled values in the boys, providing a job and responsibilities to occupy their time. Ruth had a well-being he never had before. "They started to teach me to be a shirt-maker," he recalled, "and I'll bet you if I hadn't become a ball-player I would have been a darned good one."[28] With the money he made for making shirts, Ruth would buy a bunch of candy and distribute it to the littler kids who were orphans or had no family.[29] Even then, he had a heart for the kids. By mid-afternoon, it was baseball or other recreation. They would have a simple supper, often bread and soup again, but on Sundays they had special treats such as hot dogs and baloney. On Sunday, children would also have families visit and bring care packages and treats to eat.[30]

Ruth rarely had visitors. Ruth's classmate at St. Mary's, Louis "Fats" Leisman, wrote a short memoir in 1956, *I Was with Babe Ruth at St. Mary's*. Leisman recalled once sulking that he hadn't seen his mom in a couple of years. "You're lucky, Fats," Ruth responded. "It's been ten years since I have seen my father." After another Visitors' Sunday passed without any visitors, Ruth said, "I guess I'm too big and ugly for anyone to come see me. Maybe next time."[31] Guests one time brought candy to the children and neglected Ruth, his size making them believe he was one of the staff. Someone felt bad about that, and the next time gave Ruth his own box of candy. Instead of stashing it away like other kids did, Ruth opened his up and shared it with everyone. Marshall Smelser called Ruth's time at St. Mary's a "postponed childhood," on the heels of neglect in his first seven years at home. "The first seven years of neglect were survival years. We don't know what they may have done to the child deep down. The twelve years at St. Mary's brought out the kinds of traits we can see and describe."[32]

But this was still a school, and kids found it easy to pick on Ruth for his big ears and nostrils. With a dark complexion like his mother, he acquired a nickname: Nigger Lips, or Nig.[33]

Brother Matthias became the father figure Ruth never had. He was born Martin L. Boutlier in Cape Breton, Nova Scotia, Canada, in 1872, and his family moved to Boston in the 1880s.

Boutlier was first associated with the Xaverian Brothers in 1890, and by 1900 he was known as Brother Matthias, who vowed a life of poverty, chastity, obedience, and stability.[34] He was assigned to St. Mary's, where he taught and maintained discipline, helped by his husky, 6′6″ frame which earned the nicknames of "Big Matt" or "The Boss." He never needed to raise his voice despite his "shambling gait, and a quiet and diffident manner," said the *Boston Evening Transcript*.[35] Matthias meant a lot to Ruth. "It was at St. Mary's that I met and learned to love the greatest man I've ever known," Ruth said of Matthias. "He seldom raised his voice, a sharp contrast to what I had known at home and in my neighborhood. But when he spoke, he meant business."[36] Matthias took an interest in young Ruth, who "needed love and attention and thrived when he received it," wrote Brian Martin. A special, close bond came between the two. Ruth's future wife, Claire, wrote that at age 23 everyone loved the Babe, but at 13 only Brother Matthias did.[37]

Matthias recruited Ruth for one of the dozens of baseball teams at the school. Ruth was a rare left-handed catcher at one point but evolved into a pitcher. In one remarkable game, he beat St. Joe's and their star pitcher, Bill Morrisette (a future major leaguer), 6–0, with Ruth striking out 22. There was no doubt Ruth could find the seam on a baseball far better than he could on a shirt.

Enter Jack Dunn, on the lookout for standout players for his Orioles, who were

The young catcher (top row, center) at St. Mary's: George Herman Ruth (Wikimedia Commons).

competing for fandom with the Baltimore club of the renegade Federal League. On February 14, 1914, a week after Ruth turned 20, Dunn arrived at St. Mary's to see Brother Matthias.

"Can he pitch?" Dunn asked.

"Sure," Matthias replied. "He can do anything."

Ruth appeared in a pair of overalls. Dunn watched Ruth pitch and wrote out two contracts. One gave Ruth a $600-a-year salary; the other was for Dunn to become Ruth's legal guardian.[38]

"He was free," wrote Robert Creamer. "After all those years he was finally out of the cage, and nobody was ever going to get him into one again."[39]

"He would have been a very good tailor," Brother Clarence said at St. Mary's.[40]

Baltimore soon noticed the phenom. "The new Bird is George H. Ruth, a pitcher, who played with teams out the Frederick Road," reported the *Baltimore Sun*.[41] Ruth went to North Carolina for spring training and hit a home run farther than anyone there had ever seen.[42] The legend grew over the summer. "Jack Dunn's sensational southpaw," noted Jesse A. Linthicum, shut out Buffalo, 6–0, in his first professional start.[43] In July, C. Starr Matthews of the *Baltimore Sun* called Ruth a "big, powerful fellow, with a heart like a child and a left arm which during the last four months has made the whole baseball world and the thousands of fans who surround it sit up and pay attention."[44]

One of those paying attention was Red Sox owner Joseph J. Lannin. Ruth was on his way to Boston. "He simply loves baseball and will play all day if permitted," said the *Boston Herald* of the Red Sox's new acquisition.[45]

Becoming a Living Legend

Ruth's debut at Fenway Park was an eye-opening, "short, snappy contest" wrote Tim Murnane in the *Globe*. Ruth was "a strapping big fellow" with "an inexhaustible supply of stamina." The crowd was into the game from the opening pitch.[46] Ruth won his first game in a 4–3 decision over Cleveland, allowing eight hits and three earned runs in seven innings. Paul H. Shannon, present at Ruth's Fenway debut and at his finale, said he "gave a fine demonstration of control and smooth workmanship," notable since he was on a train all night from Baltimore.[47]

Ruth split time that season between the Red Sox and their farm team in Providence, which won the International League pennant. George Herman Ruth played for St. Mary's, two minor league clubs, and one major league club all in one season. He saw his first contract and first pennant. He also met his first girlfriend, maybe the first day he was in Boston. She was Helen Woodford, the 16-year-old waitress who served him breakfast. The 19-year-old Ruth had no family or friends in Boston, so a fresh face and smile served with bacon and eggs went a long way. Ruth was alone in this new world but now had someone to talk to. They were married at the end of the season.

Ruth went 18–8 for the Red Sox in 1915 with a 2.44 ERA on a team dominated by pitchers: himself, Rube Foster, Ernie Shore, Dutch Leonard, and Smoky Joe Wood. He batted .315 in the limited time he played in the outfield. The Red Sox beat the Phillies in the World Series without needing Ruth. But no one was better on the mound in 1916, when Ruth went 23–12 with a 1.75 ERA. The Red Sox beat Brooklyn for back-to-back World Series titles, with Ruth winning once. He dominated the mound in 1917 (24–13, 2.01 ERA) and batted .325. Ruth's .300 average with 11 home runs topped the league in 1918 while he remained a top pitcher (13–7, 2.22 ERA). The Red Sox won another World Series and wouldn't again until 2004.

Ruth didn't get along with Red Sox manager Ed Barrow, but nevertheless it was he who moved Ruth to the outfield so his slugger could play every day. He responded in 1919 with unheard-of numbers of 29 home runs and 113 RBI. Red Sox owner Harry Frazee saw Ruth more in terms of dollars than pennants and sold him to the New York Yankees. The destinies of two franchises changed from that time on.

Ruth was part of the Yankees dynasty which coincided with the Roaring 20s. No one dominated a sport like Ruth, often hitting more home runs himself than entire teams did. The Deadball Era, symbolized by Ty Cobb, died a sudden death. Fans wanted to see home runs, and Ruth provided seasons of 54, 59, 35, 41, 46, 25, 47, 60, 54, 46, 49, 46, and 41 between 1920 and 1932.

The Yankees won the World Series in 1923, 1927, 1928, and 1932, and the AL pennant 1921, 1922, and 1926. Ruth batted .356 and averaged 46 home runs a year over that time. The Red Sox went into baseball oblivion.

Ruth became the most recognizable person in the country during the 1920s and early 1930s. American was on the move, and no one seemed more mobile than Ruth. "The dirty-faced street urchin of myth morphed into a man of style, even elegance, and underappreciated dignity," Leavy wrote. "Winking, swinging, mincing, sliding, he seemed always to be going somewhere, doing something, usually over the speed limit."[48] Ruth was also the first athlete who was more famous for exploits *off* the field as *on* it.[49]

Society was moving at breakneck speed, and Ruth sprinted right along with it. American incomes were up, and consumers had cash to spend. Electricity, flush toilets, and washing machines were common in most American homes. Only 25 percent owned an automobile in 1920; by 1929 it was 60 percent.[50] Women won the right to vote, jazz greats were on the radio, and people found creative ways around Prohibition. Everything Ruth did was covered in newspapers (several editions a day) and newsreels, and a crowd followed wherever he went.

Ruth's agent, Christy Walsh, knew exactly where and when to showcase Ruth in this "dawn of hectic and hurry."[51] Walsh was the first true PR man and sports agent, ahead of his time, with Ruth one of a kind. Walsh handled everything from Ruth's taxes to his personal appearances, to investments and endorsements. Never had an athlete been so marketable. "There was a stormy excitement over baseball unknown before or since," Marshall Smelser wrote of the 1920–1932 period. "The public love of Ruth approached idolatry."[52]

"A born showman, Ruth allowed himself to be displayed to a greater extent than many famous people before him," wrote Thomas Barthel. "So long as there was a reporter with a note pad or a camera with film in it, he was known to wear any hat, put on any outfit, show up at any place, and sit on any animal, for he and his agent, Christy Walsh, knew there was money to be made. Ruth was not a reluctant celebrity. Amiable and accessible, Ruth knew he made good copy and because he did, the press looked after him."[53] Everyone wanted a piece of the Ruth brand.

Wherever you turned, the Babe was there:

There were both the Babe Ruth Baseball Scorer and Babe Ruth's Baseball Game by Milton Bradley.
The Babe Ruth Home Run Candy Bar (not to be confused with the Baby Ruth candy bar which profited off his name despite having no connection to him).
Babe Ruth on the cover of *Time, Vanity Fair, Liberty, Popular Science, American Boy,* and *Hardware Age.*[54]
Babe Ruth in early films: *Babe Comes Home, Headin' Home,* and *Speedy.*

Ruth became the pitchman for nearly every product imaginable: shoes, automobiles, clothes, hardware stores, cigars, bread, puffed wheat and puffed rice, biscuits, cola, chewing gum, ice cream, Girl Scout Cookies, and underwear.[55] "Few figures were sought after or as willing to endorse products as Babe Ruth," wrote Jules Tygiel. "Walsh combined the proper blend of honesty and chicanery that characterizes the best publicity men."[56]

Ruth was the biggest name on and off the field. By 1934, he was the all-time leader in home runs (708), which would last for four decades. His slugging percentage (.690) is still #1 all-time, as is his On-Base Plus Slugging Percentage (OPS). He walked more than any other hitter until 2001.

His 2,214 RBs were #1 until 1975. Ruth and the game were synonymous. "He was a national monument."[57]

And children loved him. Ruth visited orphanages and promised home runs to sick children. He barnstormed the country, so they had a chance to see him in rural areas and small towns. "Stories about the Babe and kids were sports page favorites," wrote Montville. "Walsh loved them. Writers loved them. People loved them. He appeared at events for kids. He sold a bunch of products to kids. St. Francis of Assisi didn't love birds as much as the Babe loved kids."[58]

He was oriented to children, wrote Smelser. "He was a hero to the whole world of children with whom he had a 'fine, soft touch.' He might sometimes be curt with elders, but he never protected his privacy and comfort from children. The kids liked him. When they learned his tough face masked real kindness they leaned toward him, not away."[59]

The Aging Bull

By 1934, society was mired in the Great Depression, far from the "hectic and hurry" days of the 1920s. Ruth was not the athletic person he once was. He still had the biggest name in sports, but the body had worn down. He had trouble even getting out of his own way. Throughout his career, Ruth would predict how many home runs he would hit that year; now he predicted how many games he *might* play that year. Maybe 100, he thought.[60] The 1934 season was painful for him physically and painful for fans to watch.

"He waddled and creaked and lumbered," Montville wrote, "an aging bull elephant left to roam in a right-field pasture. He huffed and puffed and still blew houses down, but simply not as many."[61] The once rambunctious Ruth now played a cautious game in the outfield, taking no chances of blowing out a knee or twisting an ankle. He was often replaced late in the game. The writing was on the wall. There was little left in the tank for Babe Ruth the player, beyond brief, spontaneous glimpses, often in the best of moments.

Starting in 1932, speculation arose about Ruth becoming a manager, maybe returning to the Red Sox. But Ruth wasn't done playing.[62] Maybe the Chicago White Sox, Cleveland, or St. Louis Browns were interested, but no serious discussions emerged. The most legitimate offer was from Detroit Tigers owner Frank Navin. Ruth dilly-dallied in returning Navin's phone call, and the offer was off the table.[63] The Yankees suggested Ruth manage their minor-league club in Newark, New Jersey. Not Babe Ruth. "To ask me, after twenty years of experience in the major leagues, to manage a club in the minors would be the same, I think, as to ask Colonel Ruppert [Yankees owner], one of the foremost brewers in the country, to run a soda fountain."[64]

Ruth hobbled through 125 games in 1934, batting .288 with 22 home runs, his worst numbers since his injury-shortened 1925 season. "My legs were giving me some bother," Ruth recalled. "In 1934 I couldn't get in there every day. I used to sit on the bench and hear the kids out in the left-field stands, where they were admitted free a couple of afternoons a week, yell, 'We want Ruth! We want Ruth!' Maybe you think it doesn't mean much to an old guy to hear a couple of thousand kids proving in that way what they think of him!"[65]

The highlight of the year was hitting his 700th home run. "I'm definitely through as a regular player at the end of this season," he said on August 10, two days before his return to Fenway. "I really don't know what the future holds for me—time alone will tell. I would like to remain in the game as a manager and perhaps do a little pinch-hitting on Saturdays and Sundays or days when I figured it would help the gate."[66] He hinted that he would like to return to Boston to finish his career as a part-time player. "I guess everybody will agree with me that I cannot go on as a regular, after this season. Age has slowed me up too much. I hope to get a place next season in one of the two major leagues as a manager."[67] He needed to convince club owners first.

"I don't know what I'll do next season, but I won't go hungry," he joked. "I have enough money now to keep the wolf from the door. I started at $600 per season and at the peak of my career I received $80,000—more than the President of the United States gets."[68] His salary in 1934 was cut to $35,000, and receiving a contract for 1935 was mere speculation.

On August 12, 1934, the "staid New England metropolis virtually turned itself inside and out to pay a fitting tribute," wrote John Drebinger.[69] Ropes were strung between the right-field foul line and the center field flagpole to accommodate the crowd. Thousands of cranky Bostonians were left outside, where they "stormed and fumed in the streets." The Boston Elevated Railway, the precursor to today's Massachusetts Bay Transit Authority (MBTA), sent 45 extra streetcars to Kenmore Square, where 20 extra police and 40 extra firefighters were on the scene.[70]

They packed Fenway to see the Red Sox–Yankees doubleheader. Ruth batted cleanup in the opener and went 2-for-5 with a double. His single in the first inning loaded the bases, and the Yankees went on to score two runs. The game was 3–3 in the bottom of the eighth. Billy Werber hit a low liner to left, where the tottering Ruth charged, but the ball went through him for a two-run triple. Boston fans, forsaking their team, hoped for a great catch by the Babe for a memorable finish. Ruth doubled into the right field roped-off area, where fans grasped for a souvenir. He drove in a run, but Boston prevailed, 6–4.

The late-afternoon contest was played under a periodic drizzle. Ruth walked twice to a chorus of boos from the frustrated Hub fans, who then stood for a mighty ovation as Ruth left the game.

The applause was "deafening," Burt Whitman wrote, watching the "big-bodied, small-legged, fat veteran … slower and below the amazing co-ordination he maintained when he was the overlord of all home run hitters."[71] Ruth was overwhelmed and left with tears in his eyes. The Yankees won, 7–1. "It was a sight I'll never forget," Ruth said. "Boston has always been kind to me, and I was a bit disappointed that I couldn't have hit a homer for that big mob."[72]

Ruth shuffled to the end of the 1934 season, starting only 24 of the final 47 games. He batted an impressive .309 with three home runs to bring his career total to 708. The Yankees went 28–19 over that stretch, but Detroit was a nose better at 30–16 and won the pennant by 2½ games. "I am getting too old for the game and know it," Ruth admitted to S.J. Woolf for a *New York Times Magazine* feature, "even if folks in the grand stand don't. The trouble with most players is that they don't get on to the fact until long after the guys in the bleachers are beginning to turn their thumbs down. There's nothing sadder than to see a fellow trotting around the diamond and hear his legs creaking for want of oil. If I kept playing much longer I'd be tripping over my whiskers or putting on a pair of specs to see the ball."[73]

Boston eliminated the Yankees from the pennant with a 5–0 victory at Yankee Stadium on September 24. Ruth had slugged the first home run there in 1923. In his finale, he drew a first-inning walk and left the game for a pinch-runner. The sparse 2,000 fans applauded their hero for a final time. Ruth's last game as a Yankee was in Washington, where he was lavishly presented a scroll signed by President Roosevelt and his Cabinet. The St. Mary's Industrial School Band performed. Ruth announced he planned to keep playing "as long as I can do anybody any good," hoping for a managerial position to turn up where he could let himself pinch-hit occasionally.[74]

At the end of the season, Ruth visited Jacob Ruppert to ask whether the owner was content with Joe McCarthy as manager. The Colonel was. "That's all I wanted to know," Ruth replied. He left to cover the Tigers-Cardinals World Series for the Christy Walsh news syndicate, with someone ghostwriting for him. His presence alone drew attention. "I want to remain in baseball, but I will not sign a player's contract next year with any club," he affirmed. "In view of Colonel Ruppert's decision, I will make my plans accordingly."[75]

After the World Series, Ruth joined a team of all-stars on a tour of Honolulu, Japan, Shanghai, and Manila, acting as baseball's ambassadors. Ruth's second wife, Claire, and daughter Julia accompanied him along with stars Lou Gehrig, Lefty Gomez, and Jimmie Foxx. The *Empress of Japan* set sail from Vancouver on October 20. Connie Mack, owner and manager of the Philadelphia A's since their founding in 1901, was official manager of the team but turned the duties over to Ruth.

Rumors spread that this was a managerial trial for Ruth.[76] Mack needed people in the seats.

Mack watched from the stands as Ruth's stars beat the Hawaiian All-Stars, 8–1. "Babe Ruth can do the worrying today," the old manager told the *Honolulu Advertiser*.[77] "If the price were not prohibitive, I would like nothing better than to have him on my bench."[78] Then Mack told the *Star-Bulletin*, "The only time that I'll quit, is when they cart me off the diamond."[79] Back in the states, Washington traded Joe Cronin to the Red Sox and hired Bucky Harris as manager, ending that rumored opportunity. "Ruth has never been regarded as a managerial possibility here by me, nor will he be so regarded," owner Clark Griffith stated. "I greatly respect the Babe as a man and for his great work in the game. He is of managerial timber, I believe. But he is definitely out of the picture so far as the management of my ball club is concerned."[80]

Ruppert and GM Ed Barrow were willing to give Ruth away for free.[81] In the back of their minds, Ruth would come back to haunt them on the field, so this "deal" was only for a club offering a managerial position. Ruppert hoped an American League club would take the risk, sparking a rivalry and gate receipts.[82] But who wanted Ruth, even for free? An anonymous owner said it was doubtful Ruth had the patience to build up a bad club, and a good club didn't need him.[83]

One team showed interest, far from the major leagues. The House of David independent barnstorming club offered Ruth $35,000 if he would play for them, a product of the religious commune which followed Biblical commands forbidding men to shave. Ruth didn't even need whiskers. Commercial opportunity superseded religious dogma.[84]

Ruth heard shouts of "Banzai! Banzai, Babe Ruth!" from 100,000 Japanese fans who lined the streets of Tokyo.[85] American ballplayers were celebrities and Ruth the biggest star of them all. Crowds of 65,000 watched their local stars get crushed by the Americans.[86] Ruth batted .408 with 13 home runs and 33 RBI as the Americans went 18–0 on the trip.[87] Back home, the Yankees had already moved on, signing 18-year-old Joe DiMaggio for $75,000.[88]

By the end of the trip, Mack wanted no part of Ruth as his manager. Claire Ruth seemed to make every decision for him while onboard. Mack had no place for an opinionated woman and told sportswriter Joe Williams she "would have been running the club in a month."[89] The all-stars played their final game in Manila on December 20 and boarded the *Empress of Canada* for home. The Ruths continued on a world cruise and wouldn't return to the United States until February. He believed a managerial job was forthcoming. "I don't care which one," he said while golfing in Manila. "I am not worrying about the future. I am having a good time."[90]

Ruth could have had a real fun time if he had accepted the $75,000 offer to join Zack Miller's 101 Ranch traveling circus show. The promoter envisioned crowds watching Ruth riding an elephant to the tune of "Take Me Out to the Ball Game" and hitting fly balls. "Ruth is free to join a circus or do anything he likes," Barrow said. Ruth wanted no part of a circus.[91]

He would soon find himself in one anyway.

The Braves Come Calling

Someone *did* want Ruth after all, someone just as desperate for a gate attraction as Ruth was for a job. "A baseball magnate is about as informative as an oyster on the half shelf," wrote John Lardner. "I don't believe the magnates are as dumb as they seem to be. But when they play shy, it's up to us gossip-cullers and canard-slingers to unfurl our own ears, talk to reliable people, and pass the secret along to the public in the hope that we are not more suckerish and wrong than usual." Lardner had the scoop.

"Ruth is slated to manage the Boston Braves."[92]

Since October, Judge Emil Fuchs, Boston Braves owner, had been denying that Ruth was coming to the Braves.[93] The team was nearing financial collapse as the #2 baseball team in Boston. But the Braves had one of the best managers in the game in Bill McKechnie, so where would Ruth fit?

If the Braves were a fit, that was fine with American League club owners, who discussed what to do with Ruth and avoid a PR disaster. "How do you get rid of a demigod who won't go quietly?" Smelser asked.[94] They discussed Ruth while National League club owners discussed Fuchs. Ruth was not Fuchs' first choice to resurrect the Braves.

His first choice was greyhound racing. How he got to that point is another story.

2

Judge Fuchs

All Good Wishes at Braves Field
(1923–1934)

"I felt I'd be happier trying to make a living from baseball than any other business I know."—Judge Fuchs

"If I didn't have confidence in you, I wouldn't join with you."—Charles F. Adams

Judge Fuchs' Day

Wednesday, April 16, 1935, was a chilly day in Boston, and you could feel snow in the air. Several inches fell in Boston that night, but that didn't derail the activities of John O'Malley of Newbury Street. A patrolman at the corner of Boylston Street and Massachusetts Avenue spotted "the jovial rotund Mr. O'Malley stalking through the storm—a nudist," said the *Boston Globe*. Madden shoved O'Malley, blue feet, shivering, and hair crusted with snow, into a cab. The *Globe* called O'Malley "Boston's pioneer nudist," and "he wasn't a very good-looking one at that."[1]

Opening Day at Braves Field was perfect "except the weather," wrote James C. O'Leary.[2] It was a perfect day for two baseball men desperate to stay in the game. The 40-year-old icon Babe Ruth, whose bat and personality had catapulted him to more fame and fortune than anyone before him, now hobbled around on bad knees. But he remained the biggest star in the game, and Boston fans hoped the Bambino had a little left in him. Ruth was discarded by the team he made famous and took the only offer on the table—the floundering Boston Braves.

Even more desperate was Judge Emil Fuchs, the cash-strapped owner of the Braves. Fuchs was the successful lawyer and impoverished baseball executive whose only hope of survival was in signing the broken-down Ruth. Perhaps Ruth had enough left in the tank to get the Braves out of their financial hole. Fans would stream through the turnstiles to see the icon, remembering the days of their youth. For Ruth, it was a welcome home; for Fuchs, it was a thank you. The day was, after all, designated "Judge Fuchs' Day."

Fuchs depended on financial assistance from the National League even to get the Braves to Opening Day. Everything from the spring training trip to Florida to bats and balls was provided by the National League. Fuchs organized the "Boston Braves Citizens Committee," which mobilized an advanced ticket sale campaign to generate enough cash flow to begin the season.

Opening Day was to honor Fuchs for his devotion to the team. "We want the people to realize what a real citizen Judge Fuchs is," said Boston Mayor Frederick Mansfield.[3] They presented Fuchs with a plaque signed by all New England governors and other dignitaries in a pregame ceremony.[4] The plaque read:

Presented
By the citizens of New England to
Hon Emil E. Fuchs
in commemoration of Judge Fuchs Day with their appreciation of his
unselfish services their affectionate regard
and all good wishes
Braves Field   April 16, 1935

Governor James Michael Curley presents a plaque to Judge Fuchs on Opening Day at Braves Field, April 16, 1935. The day was proclaimed "Judge Fuchs' Day" (courtesy Boston Public Library, Leslie Jones Collection).

The 65th home opener since the franchise began in 1871 was memorable, with Ruth's return and home run bringing snowflakes. "We started right and hope we keep on going," Ruth said. "It was simply wonderful," Fuchs said of his tribute, "and I simply cannot find words to describe how thoroughly I appreciate the consideration of my friends, who turned out in such numbers in such disagreeable weather."[5]

Years later Fuchs would say, "I felt I'd be happier trying to make a living from baseball than any other business I know."[6] "Happy" would not describe the Judge in the baseball *business* world. He had lost nearly everything he had as Braves owner, striving to make them a contender since 1923. His skills as a lawyer in the New York judicial system far surpassed his baseball business knowledge. Fuchs was a baseball fan, but his love for the game did not turn into dollar signs. His business losses didn't affect his overall pleasant demeanor. "He had a passion for baseball," Carolyn Fuchs, the Judge's granddaughter, recalled. "He wanted those fans to be happy. In a tale of two cities, he worked in New York as a successful lawyer and commuted to Boston when getting involved with the Braves. He not only loved his work in baseball but loved Boston as well."[7]

Fuchs tried to resurrect the franchise, marketing the game to female fans and children, tapping into the new medium of radio, and fighting for Sunday baseball against New England's staid Puritan culture. He saved money one season by naming himself the manager, since he could lose more cheaply. Since 1933, Fuchs had operated in the shadow of Tom Yawkey, the young and affluent Red Sox owner across town. Yawkey lavishly spent money on new stars and renovated Fenway Park. Fuchs ran a bargain basement team with a less desirable Braves Field. "Fuchs was a fan who tried hard to be an owner … a manager, a financier, and a public-relations man," wrote Harold Kaese. "He was successful as a public-relations man."[8]

Much like Babe Ruth, Judge Fuchs had a last gasp in the fall of 1934. Ruth tried to keep hold of a fading career, and Fuchs tried to hold onto a fading team. Both loved the game.

They needed each other.

"Judge Fuchs' Day" was a glorious day for the baseball magnate, the German immigrant who grew up in the tenements of Manhattan's Lower East Side.

A Jewish Youngster with a Dream

Emil Edwin Fuchs was born on April 17, 1878, in Bromberg, Germany, in what was the Province of Posen in the Kingdom of Prussia. His parents were Herman and Henrietta (Wollenberg) Fuchs, Orthodox Jews who immigrated to New York City. Herman, the son of Simon and Eitel (Kemiske) Fuchs, married Henrietta in 1875. Henrietta was the daughter of Jacob and Hanna (Plomska) Wollenberg.[9] Herman arrived in the United States in 1883, according to a later census. Nailing down specifics of his arrival are difficult. The best guess is an "H. Fuchs," of roughly the same age who arrived in New York City on May 4, 1883, on the steamship *Plantyn*. On June 14, 1884, Henrietta and her five sons, Benjamin, Oscar, William, Berthold, and Emil, arrived in Castle Garden, New York (Ellis Island had not yet opened), on the maiden voyage of the ship *EMS*.[10]

Herman had no formal schooling but worked in Europe as a compounder (one who mixes chemical ingredients and tests the results) for 25 years. His business failed, and he sought new opportunities in the U.S. In February of 1884, Herman answered an ad for a chemist position responsible for manufacturing essential oils and essences. His employer, Theodore Koerner, had been a jewelry box maker until his business partner wanted them to go into the chemicals business at a shop at 58 Liberty Street. Koerner had no background in chemicals, and when his partner departed, he was desperate for help. Fuchs applied and was given a one-year contract for $1,800 ($37.50 per week) to make essential oils, compound alcohol flavors, and mix extracts.

Herman was terminated after just five months. He pleaded to be rehired, but Koerner decided jewelry boxes were an easier endeavor. Fuchs sued over the loss of wages, and the case went before the Superior Court of the City of New York. Both sides produced witnesses. Some claimed Fuchs was incompetent with chemicals; others complimented his work. The jury sided with Herman Fuchs for $871.82.[11] He later worked as a chemist for the Eimer & Amend Company and ran his own syrup manufacturing business.[12]

The work Herman did with essential oils, flavoring extracts, and alcohol gives us some clues as to where the family lived in the 1880s and 1890s, although a definite address proves problematic. The Fuchs family lived on Manhattan's Lower East Side in the University Settlement housing, a place of refuge for the swelling immigrant population.[13] The 1884 New York City directory lists a Herman Fuchs working at 172 Chambers St. This was the H.F.A. Pinckney & Co, owned by Henry Pinckney, an importer of patented spices.[14] This Fuchs lived at 137 Ludlow. Later directories list a Herman Fuchs working in "oils" or "liquors," with addresses on Delancey and Norfolk streets in the Lower East Side. It was common in tenement life to move frequently to a better cramped apartment where the smell and noise were not quite *as* bad.

Emil Fuchs remembered those days on the crowded tenement streets, barefoot and playing a version of One Ol' Cat, an ancestor game to baseball.[15] It was here that "a Jewish youngster on the east side of New York had a dream," wrote Dan Daniel in the *New York World-Telegram*, himself the son of a Jewish immigrant on the Lower East Side.[16] "Drab tenements, with fire escapes festooned with firewood in the winter and mattresses in the summer," Daniel remembered, "were the backdrop of his little theater of make believe. His stage props were the steaming pavement of an east side summer, with the hokey-pokey vender and his rickety pushcart and the 'hot corn' purveyor on the corner appealing to empty pockets and spurring his ambition."[17]

One section of the Lower East Side was known as Kleindeutschland, "Little

Germany" or the "Jewish East Side." Historian Stanley Nadel described the area as "the first of the giant foreign-language settlements that came to typify American cities by the end of the nineteenth century. New York's Germans were the first group to face the problems of adaptation and innovation that have become characteristic shapers of the American immigrant experience"[18] Only Vienna and Berlin had more Germans than this one section of New York City between 1855 and 1880. While the German States were unified following the Franco-Prussian War in 1871, their distinct cultural traditions made unity an arduous process. "Cultural, religious, and linguistic boundaries cut across those of states, custom unions, and empires, dividing German Europe into a multitude of small cultural and linguistic regions," wrote Nadel. "These regions, and not a mythical German nation, were the source of the German emigration that created German New York."[19]

Kleindeutschland included Wards 11, 17, 13, and 10, which by 1875 were 64 percent German American.[20] The area bordered the Bowery to the west, East 14th Street to the north, Division Street to the south, and the East River. The Tenth Ward had become a German haven with those identifying themselves from Posen or Prussia.[21] By 1880, Prussians constituted half of the German population of the Tenth Ward.[22] The Lower East Side could be compared to "a veritable sardine can," wrote Percy Hutchison in the *New York Times* in 1936. "Entire families lived, slept, and cooked in a single room."[23]

By 1880, German immigrants began moving uptown, and Kleindeutschland started being referred to as the Lower East Side. Immigrant Jews moved into these vacated areas, crowding into the tenements, seeking jobs in the garment industry.[24] The area swelled in population, and by 1895 one section of the Lower East Side (south of Houston Street between Clinton and Columbia) housed 800 inhabitants per acre. It was the most populated area on the planet.[25]

An 1895 report of the Tenement House Committee of the New York State Legislature sheds light on the world Emil Fuchs grew up in. The Tenth Ward tenements were described as "the house, home or residence of three or more families living independently of one another, and doing their cooking upon the premises, or by more than two families upon a floor so living and cooking, but having a common right in the halls, stairways, yards, water-closets or privies, or some of them."[26] Children slept outside because the air was so bad inside. Squalor and overcrowding led to "the promiscuous mixing of all ages and sexes in a single room—thus breaking down the barriers of modesty and conducing to the corruption of the young."[27] The so-called "double-decker" houses were devoid of ventilation and natural light and were prone to disease and fires. The Tenth Ward averaged 57 tenants per house.[28]

In 1886, while the Fuchs family was still becoming accustomed to this new world, Amherst graduate Dr. Stanton Coit returned to the United States after visiting London's Toynbee Hall. Toynbee Hall was s settlement house and immersion experience for recent social work graduates to live and work in depressed areas. Coit created the Neighborhood Guild, the first settlement house in the U.S., in a building on Forsyth Street. Education, recreation, and social reform efforts benefited the neighborhood. The Guild became the University Settlement on Eldridge Street, where it remains to the present day.[29]

"The first problem," wrote Hutchison, "was to make Americans out of these thousands of hopelessly bewildered foreigners who poured endlessly into a small area of narrow streets and huddled in crowded and inadequate tenements." The Settlement was an oasis for the bewildered, exhausted, and lonely immigrant family looking for a new life on the Lower East Side. They could learn job skills and find countrymen who knew their songs and dances from the old country. The Settlement had a free library which circulated 28,000 volumes in 1894.[30] They could learn through lectures and classes. Teddy Roosevelt visited the Settlement in 1899. "Nothing is better than the way in which the Jew and Gentile, Catholic and Protestant, are striving together to accomplish just such things as this society set out to accomplish."[31]

Fuchs attended New York City Public Schools and had the opportunity to play baseball. The 13-year-old Fuchs became the catcher on the University Settlement team. He believes he would have been a major leaguer if it weren't for a wild pitch. "I was hit in the arm," he recalled in 1929. "It broke a small bone in my shoulder and ruined my throwing. Otherwise, I might have been a professional ball player. I didn't amount to much after that." Fuchs attempted a comeback, playing for the City College of New York and then the short-lived New Jersey State League in 1897.[32]

In 1898, Fuchs and 600 other boys from the University Settlement proposed a bill to allow baseball games on Sundays. "Emil Fuchs said it would be better to have the boys play ball than shoot craps." reported the *New York Times*.[33] Urban parks, such as Central Park, forbid ball playing, so the outskirts of Brooklyn and Queens were the places to be. Fuchs and the boys left the city on Sundays to play baseball in Maspeth, Queens.[34] These parks and picnic areas were like rural retreats for those in the crammed tenements. Grand Street Park in Maspeth attracted 3,000 fans or more on a given Sunday to watch the various local baseball games and frolic in the grass.[35]

The Fuchs family was more financially stable by the mid–1890s and moved away from the Lower East Side. According to the directories from 1894 to the turn of the 20th century, Herman Fuchs lived at 121 Clinton Place, with occupations listed as "liquors," "flavors," and "extracts."[36] Clinton Place, on the western side of Manhattan in Greenwich Village, later became Eighth Street, so their address changed to 49 West Eighth.[37]

After the turn of the century, they moved a couple of blocks south to 102 Waverly Place, overlooking Washington Square Park. Emil lived with his parents until getting married in 1909.[38] In 1913, Herman pled guilty to two counts of shipping adulterated and misbranded strawberry and vanilla extracts which contained imitation colors and flavors.[39] His business continued, and after his death in 1917, "the flavoring extract business of H. Fuchs, New York, has been incorporated as H. Fuchs, Inc. Oscar Fuchs, Henrietta Fuchs, Emil E. Fuchs; capitol [*sic*] stock, $7,000."[40]

Emil attended evening classes at New York University Law School and graduated in 1901 with a Bachelor of Laws. He served his old neighborhood in the East Branch of the Legal Aid Society with an office in the University Settlement building.[41] In 1901, Fuchs testified in a trial of New York City police captain John D. Herlihy, who was accused of failing to enforce the law in the "Red Light District" on the Lower East Side. Fuchs had toured the area between October of 1899 and November of 1900 as a member of the Legal Aid Society. The *New York Times* reported that Fuchs had "been solicited numerous times by women from the stoops and windows of houses, and upon two or three occasions by men who either ran the places or acted as 'lookouts' and 'pullers-in.'"[42] Fuchs' office was flooded with complaints by residents of the doings in some of the houses in the area. "Parents would come in and complain that their daughters had been abducted from their homes and taken to houses of ill fame to lead lives of shame," he said.[43]

By his early 20s, Fuchs was already busy in public service. In addition to the Legal Aid Society, Fuchs served as Deputy Elections Inspector, clerk for the Deputy Attorney General, and Deputy Attorney General, the last for nine years.[44] Fuchs' title of "judge" came from his one term of service as New York City Magistrate from 1917 to 1918.[45]

Emil Fuchs married Aurelia "Oretta" Marcovich on June 15, 1909. Oretta was the daughter of Henry and Rose (Trauber) Marcovich, immigrants from Jassy (also spelled Lassi or Lasi), a city in Eastern Romania. The newlyweds lived at 310 West 93rd Street on Manhattan's Upper West Side.[46] Fuchs maintained a law office at 320 Broadway and later 51 Chambers Street in Lower Manhattan. He was involved in many prominent law cases throughout the city in the first two decades of the 20th century.[47]

Legendary gambler and mob kingpin Arnold Rothstein was holding a high-stakes poker game in a New York City apartment with 19 other gamblers on January 19, 1919. There was a knock at the door as the police yelled, "Open up there!" Rothstein fired three shots at the door, injuring three officers who nevertheless managed to break the door down. By the time they entered, Rothstein was nowhere to be found. The other gamblers claimed he was never there. As the gamblers were being loaded into a paddy wagon, Rothstein was seen hiding on a fire escape. He was arrested and paid the bail for all 20 of them with a stack of $1,000 gold notes. The gang faced a grand jury but, to no one's surprise, the gamblers couldn't recall any details of the shooting. Fuchs represented Rothstein. There was no evidence that Rothstein fired the gun, and since no one testified against him, Fuchs called for dismissal. "The record is barren of any evidence tending directly or indirectly to connect the defendant with the commission of any crime."[48] Rothstein was freed, and Fuchs had successfully defended the man believed by many to have fixed the 1919 World Series, the Black Sox Scandal. Rothstein wasn't indicted for that, either. He is remembered as one of the most influential crime bosses of the 20th century. "The Judge represented the powerful and the powerless," Robert S. Fuchs, the Judge's son, wrote in 1998. "Saints and sinners, millionaires and misfits, toting up an enviable record. He was one of the world's most cosmopolitan men in the most cosmopolitan city on the face of the earth."[49]

Fuchs represented New York Governor Charles S. Whitman in a failed ballot recount in his 1918 re-election bid.[50] He also represented the New York Giants on several occasions, helping outfielder Benny Kauff to a non-guilty verdict in an automobile theft case. Kauff was still suspended from baseball for life by Commissioner Kenesaw Mountain Landis. Fuchs also represented Giants manager John McGraw, who in a drunken rage punched comedian John C. Slavin, fracturing his skull. Slavin decided not to prosecute.[51]

Buying the Braves

McGraw and Fuchs frequently socialized together at the Lambs Club, a popular New York City attraction.[52] On one occasion, they were joined by actor and songwriter George M. Cohan, famous for the World War I song "Over There," and noted concessions operator Harry M. Stevens, who made a fortune when he realized a hotdog at a ballgame was a winning idea.

"Why, there's George Washington Grant," McGraw exclaimed, pointing out the owner of the Boston Braves. "Did you know you can buy his ball club for half a million dollars?"[53] Grant was the "derby-wearing, cane-carrying," prosperous cinema owner who had owned the Braves since 1919.[54] Grant promoted theaters and motion pictures and was an early investor in the new fad of roller skating. But he had lost money on the Braves. Once asked about selling the club, he remarked, "I will sell anything I have but my family, if I get my price."[55] McGraw suggested that Fuchs buy the club. The Judge had one condition. He wanted Christy Mathewson to join him.

Mathewson, the legendary Giants pitching ace, won a remarkable 373 games in his career and compiled a devastating 0.97 ERA in 11 World Series games. He was retired and suffering from tuberculosis from gas exposure during World War I. He lived at Saranac Lake in upstate New York under the care of physicians. "I'd buy the Braves if I could continue my law practice and he'd [Mathewson] be general manager and president," Fuchs promised.[56]

Mathewson agreed and became club president and treasurer despite his doctors' warnings that it would shorten his life expectancy.[57] "I would rather spend another two or three years in the only occupation and vocation I know than to linger many years up in Saranac Lake," Mathewson said. The purchase price of the Braves was between $300,000–500,000.[58]

The biggest stockholder in the deal was Albert H. Powell, a millionaire in coal and real estate from New Haven, Connecticut. A baseball fan, Powell had previously owned the Worcester club of the Eastern League. The *Hartford Courant* noted

Powell's economic influence. "His financial interests are not confined to coal and baseball. He is a director in banks and corporations, a large holder of real estate and until a few years ago owned a river transportation company."[59] Powell worked his way up to create his own coal business, A.H. Powell & Co., and the Powell Building was the first skyscraper in New Haven. Powell's stock was worth $250,000, or 33 percent of the club.[60] Joining the group was James McDonough, a New York City banker.

Fuchs became vice president. He wanted Mathewson to have no financial burden in the deal in the hopes that Mathewson would one day buy him out. "I was always glad I did not permit him to assume that additional worry," Fuchs said.[61] Mathewson grabbed the headlines in the sale as he "charmed his small audience last night by his straightforward, manly, modest and highly conservative remarks," wrote Burt Whitman in the *Boston Herald*. "He stands for everything that is uplifting in baseball."[62] He overshadowed Fuchs, described as "a well-known lawyer who has appeared in a number of cases of great importance."[63] That was fine with the Judge.

Working with Matty

Ownership looked different, but the Braves did not, finishing 54–100 in 1923, 41½ games behind the Giants. There would be many seasons like this over the next 12 years. Fuchs and Mathewson tapped into the world of entertainment to make Braves Field a more popular venue. They signed a contract with Marcus Loew, motion picture entrepreneur and vaudeville magnate, to stage movies, concerts, fireworks, and vaudeville shows over the summer.[64] On June 25, a crowd of 8,000 enjoyed dancing and the movie *Trifling with Honor*. The Braves Field Exhibition Company was incorporated. The events continued throughout the summer of 1923 but were dropped, likely due to financial reasons.[65]

The duo also created Ladies' Day at Braves Field, admitting women free of charge on special days.[66] This would become a regular feature at both Braves Field and Fenway Park for years to come. Then they made one of the biggest trades the Braves had made in years, acquiring star shortstop Dave Bancroft from the New York Giants to be the Braves' player-manager.[67] But the 1924 Braves flopped again at 53–100.

The team improved to 70–83 in 1925. The first baseball game broadcast from Boston was heard on WBZ radio from Braves Field on Opening Day, April 14.[68] Many club owners hesitated at the new technology, but Fuchs saw the potential and paid for the broadcasts out of his own pocket.[69] Broadcasts were seen as competition to newspapers and as reducing attendance at the stadium. Fuchs also purchased the minor league club in Worcester, Massachusetts, and gave Casey Stengel his first managerial experience.[70]

Fuchs Becomes Club President

Mathewson's health continued to fail, and he died while Fuchs was at the 1925 World Series in Pittsburgh.[71] Fuchs was elected club president and Powell became vice president.[72] The club had two more lousy seasons in 1926–1927, finishing seventh both years (66–86 and 60–94).

At the end of August 1926, Powell sold his stock to Fuchs and returned to his coal endeavors. "Al Powell has had several years of baseball and probably is glad to get out of it," the "Sportsman" sarcastically noted in the *Globe*, "leaving to Judge Fuchs the work of rebuilding the Braves."[73] The Braves franchise had an estimated worth of $1 million.[74] Fuchs sold Powell's stock to James V. Giblin, an attorney who soon needed to sell out. Fuchs wanted the stock to stay in local hands. Wesley Preston of the *Boston Herald* introduced Fuchs to grocery chain magnate Charles Francis Adams, who was well known in the Boston business and sports scenes. Adams invited Fuchs to his office at 41 Milk Street and handed Fuchs $200,000 in cash without even asking for a receipt. "Buy him out," Adams told Fuchs. "If I didn't have confidence in you, I wouldn't join with you." This was the first of many times when Adams would hand over money to Fuchs in a crisis.[75]

Fuchs recalled the transaction in later years. "No one but a good sportsman would have handed me $200,000 without a receipt or an agreement and said: 'When you return with the ball club in three or four weeks, we can get together on the legal documents.' His object in taking up the interest of one of my former colleagues was his desire to give Boston a winning ball club."[76] Adams became vice president of the club, and two associates, V.C. Bruce Wetmore and Charles F. Farnsworth, joined him. Wetmore was the president of the Wetmore-Savage Electrical Supply Company. Farnsworth was president of the Quincy Market Cold Storage and Warehouse Company and would become president of First National Stores.[77] They had the money to invest in the Braves. "When the time comes to spend money for new players," Wetmore promised, "we will dig down and furnish it."[78]

The price of the stock Adams purchased was reported as $202,258.[79] Boston newspapers covered the transaction on their front pages next to stories of the "flying fool," Charles Lindbergh, who was preparing for the first transatlantic flight.[80] Adams would one day wonder if he was a flying fool for investing in this club. The story of Charles "C.F." Adams, the Vermont store clerk boy who became one of the biggest sports promoters in Boston sports history, will be discussed in Chapter 10.

The new ownership group included Adams, who bought into the Braves in May 1927. They signed Rogers Hornsby in early 1928, the first full season with this new ownership and the first opportunity to really make any changes. The $35,000 was "more money than any two non-managing Boston players ever received," wrote Whitman.[81] Expectations were Hornsby alone made the Braves a pennant contender. The Braves also hired a new manager: Jack Slattery, former Boston College coach.[82] It was a disaster. In spring training, Fuchs gave Hornsby a new three-year contract, for $40,600 a year plus $600 for being team captain. Only Babe Ruth was paid more, and the salary was three times that of Slattery.[83] Slattery clashed with Hornsby and resigned in May with the Braves in seventh place. Hornsby become manager.[84]

Fuchs also moved the fences in at Braves Field for more offense, since the dimensions (320 ft. to left field instead of 402; center field from 461 to 387; right field from 365 to 310) meant "outfielders needed motorcycles to retrieve drives between the outfielders," Fuchs said.[85] It backfired as visiting clubs slammed more home runs, and the *Herald* joked that the new slogan of Braves Field should be "Buy a 75-cent left field bleacher seat and get a baseball free."[86] Fuchs' first solution was a wire netting, and in July he moved the fences back.[87]

Hornsby could hit wherever the fences were. He won another batting title (.387, with a .487 OBP), but the Braves finished 50–103 in 1928. Hornsby said of Fuchs, "He wasn't the smartest baseball man around, but he took second place to nobody in the way he felt about the game."[88] Fuchs traded Hornsby to the Cubs in November for five forgotten players and $200,000, the most ever in a baseball deal at the time.

Sunday Ball

November was quite the month. Massachusetts was just one of eight states in the presidential election to vote for the losing Democratic candidate, Al Smith, who lost to Republican Herbert Hoover. Massachusetts voters also approved a referendum allowing professional sports to be played on Sunday.[89]

A 1692 law had restricted recreation on Sunday.[90] In 1920, the Massachusetts Legislature allowed amateur sports on Sundays if no admission was charged, games were not played within 1,000 feet of a church, and games were only played between 2–6 p.m.[91] Massachusetts law also required that voter-submitted petitions with 20,000 signatures be automatically reviewed by the legislature. Fuchs and Adams worked behind the scenes to get the necessary signatures.[92] Adams represented the Braves at the State House.[93]

The issue then had to go before the Boston City Council. Fuchs and Adams claimed they had been offered a bribe by a city councilman.[94] The Boston Finance Commission discovered that the Braves had contributed $30,000 to the Outdoor Recreation League, drawing a fine of $1,000.[95] Fuchs spent $200,000 towards the bill's passage, and the measure was approved. Just as he did as a kid on the Lower East Side, Fuchs fought for Sunday baseball.[96]

Fuchs decided to save money and name himself Braves manager in 1929. The Braves lost money in 1928 and drew only 227,001, over 150,000 fewer patrons than the Red Sox.[97] "These are the ingredients of the most sensational and most unusual baseball story which has broken in Boston in many and many a year," Whitman wrote in the *Herald*.[98] Fuchs surrounded himself with 1914 World Series heroes as his coaches: Johnny Evers, Rabbit Maranville, and Hank Gowdy.[99] By June 1, the Braves were 15–23, and Evers declined Fuchs' offer to manage the club.[100] The Braves finished eighth (56–98), but without Hornsby's salary. Fuchs discovered, "I can do it a lot more cheaply."[101] Attendance improved to 372,351, with one-quarter of that being Sunday games.

Fuchs quit managing and brought in Bill McKechnie in 1930.[102]

Deacon Bill Handed Lemons, Makes Lemonade

Born in Pennsylvania to Scottish immigrants, "Deacon Bill" McKechnie had been around the majors for two decades as a utility player, manager, and father figure. He managed the Pirates to a 1925 World Series championship and brought the Cardinals to the 1928 NL pennant. He was unceremoniously replaced in both places. He had far less to work with on the Braves. Yet McKechnie pieced together an improved 70–84 Braves team in 1930, led by rookie Wally Berger's 38 home runs. While the team stumbled in 1931 (64–90), a franchise-best 464,835 fans poured into Braves Field, helped by 2-for-1 Sunday doubleheader deals. It was a perfect deal to spend a day forgetting about the Great Depression.

The Braves finished 77–77 in 1932, the best record in the Fuchs era and team-best since 1921. McKechnie's pitching staff was second in the NL in ERA (3.53), the team's defensive efficiency (a measure of a team's defense by determining how often batters reached base on balls put in play) was second in NL, and their fielding percentage was a league-best .976 while committing the fewest errors. An attendance of 507,606 (half of which came on Sunday) saw the Braves only three games back of first place on August 11. But they ran out of gas. Fuchs hosted a "Jobless Carnival" at Braves Field which drew 22,000 and featured Amelia Earhart and boxer Jack Sharkey.[103] On August 1, the bearded men of the House of David team brought their portable lighting system to Braves Field and played the first-ever game by artificial light in Boston.[104]

Fuchs reported that the club had made $25,000–30,000 in 1932. In 1951, the House Judiciary Committee investigated Major League Baseball's exemption from anti-trust laws and reviewed the ledgers of every team. Fuchs made a profit in only four years: 1925, 1929, 1930, and 1932, for a grand total income of $118,522. The best season, financially, was 1925 ($62,440). Fuchs lost $383,563 over the other seven seasons, with the worst being 1933 (-$120,597).[105] Fuchs lost $265,041 between 1923 and 1933 according to these records.

In 1933, Fuchs increased the number of lowest-priced seats at Braves Field, and the 1,500-seat, 50-cent "Jury Box" section in right field was expanded to 5,200 seats. Both Fuchs and Red Sox owner Bob Quinn moved Ladies' Day Games to Saturday, since many women were working on the weekdays.[106]

Fuchs had to cut salaries, while the new Red Sox owner across town was spending like there was no tomorrow.[107]

Tom Yawkey had arrived.

Judge Fuchs (right) with Braves manager Bill McKechnie (courtesy Boston Public Library, Leslie Jones Collection).

The New Millionaire in Town

He was born Thomas J. Austin in Detroit in 1903 to Thomas J. Austin and Augusta Lydia Yawkey. Tom's father died before he was a year old, and his mother placed him under the care of her brother, Bill Yawkey. Tom changed his last name to become Thomas Austin Yawkey after his mother died in 1918. His uncle Bill inherited a $10 million lumber fortune from his father. A baseball fan, Bill bought the Detroit Tigers in 1904, and Tom grew up knowing Ty Cobb and other stars. Six months after his mother died, his uncle Bill also died, leaving behind a $40 million estate, with 50 percent designated for Tom Yawkey, who was then only 16. Yawkey would receive his inheritance when he turned 30.[108]

On his 30th birthday, Yawkey collected his inheritance and bought the Boston Red Sox from Bob Quinn for $1.5 million on February 25, 1933. The Red Sox, like the Braves, had been near the bottom of the league. Fenway Park needed renovations. By the end of the 1933 season, Fenway's attendance had nearly doubled, and Yawkey and GM Eddie Collins planned to renovate Fenway for $500,000. Fenway's wood facility was replaced with concrete, and a 37-foot-high wall in left field, later dubbed "The Green Monster," was erected. Seating capacity expanded to 38,000. The renovation was good news for unemployed Boston laborers.[109]

Other owners were selling; Yawkey was buying. He acquired new stars, notably Lefty Grove for $125,000 from Connie Mack. "Mr. Yawkey is making many good friends of the fans in Boston," wrote W.A. Whitcomb in the *Globe*, "he is using his check book to good effect, and presumably will continue to."[110] Fenway Park was now the place to be. Yawkey spent while Fuchs scraped.

Fuchs received an offer of $1,000,000 for the Braves. "There was a man by the name of Kennedy," Fuchs said to NL club owners. This was likely Joseph P. Kennedy, father of John F. Kennedy and head of the Kennedy family dynasty. "He turned out to be a restaurant keeper who had made his money in some—I would say questionable way, but it was with reference to liquor, at any rate, at the time when liquor was not legal."[111]

Fuchs turned down the offer, but his financial situation was deteriorating. He needed help from the National League. He went to New York to ask them for help.

The National League Meeting

It was a clear day in New York City on June 20, 1933, with a high temperature of 73 degrees on the day before summer officially began.[112] National League club owners met at the Commodore Hotel on East 42nd Street, an imposing structure in its day. Around the country, states were voting to repeal Prohibition while President Roosevelt was vacationing on Campobello Island.

Judge Fuchs' money issues had surfaced publicly in October of 1932. Fuchs surrendered his controlling interest of 7,000 shares of stock worth $189,000 to Adams, who legally became the new club president.[113] Adams avoided the report, wanting to stay behind the scenes. "I was and still am a silent partner in the Boston Braves."[114] Fuchs remained the public face of the club, but Adams held his shares. He tried to remain silent, but it became impossible as Fuchs continued to compile debt. "If circumstances had been different when he took over the Braves," wrote Al Hirshberg, "Adams undoubtedly would have spent tremendous chunks of money to build up the shaky structure of the ball club, just as he had built up his hockey team."[115]

Present at the meeting were John Heydler, NL President, Charles A. Stoneham and Leo J. Bondy of the New York Giants, Bill Veeck of the Chicago Cubs, Sam Breadon of the St. Louis Cardinals, Sidney Weil of the Cincinnati Reds, William Benswanger of the Pittsburgh Pirates, Stephen McKeever and Joseph Gilleaudeau of the Brooklyn Dodgers, and Gerald Nugent of the Philadelphia Phillies.[116]

The 7,000 shares Adams had acquired had been held in collateral by the National League. Fuchs had borrowed the money from Breadon and Stoneham out of desperation. To guarantee the loan, the 7,000 shares were held in collateral by the NL. On September 27, 1932, an emergency meeting of NL club owners was called to "relieve a very serious emergency." Fuchs was behind in payments. The Braves could have been taken over by the NL at that point due to Fuchs' indebtedness. But Adams again came to the rescue. He forwarded $189,000 to the NL, assumed that loan, and claimed all of Fuchs' stock.

Adams discovered that Fuchs held 2,000 shares of preferred stock which had not been accounted for in the Braves' financial records. Fuchs had received the stock from Powell and Mathewson. Fuchs never claimed any of the dividends and used part of these shares as collateral to obtain another loan. "While it was perfectly legitimate," Fuchs explained, "that was partly my fault that we never entered it into the minute books of our Board of Trustees."[117] The First National Bank of Boston held 450 shares of it as collateral on a $30,000 loan, and the other 1,550 shares were held by a private individual later revealed to be Frank Stevens, son of concessionaire Harry M. Stevens. Stevens loaned Fuchs $100,000 and claimed those shares.

Adams grew tired of giving Fuchs extra time to repay his loans and came into a meeting in February of 1933 to declare himself in charge of the club. Adams had been bailing out Fuchs from financial ruin for several years since Adams bought into the team.

In addition to his original $202,258 investment and the $189,000 for the NL loan, Adams detailed his other loans to Fuchs:

On December 22, 1927, Adams loaned Fuchs $12,500. On November 9, 1928, Adams loaned Fuchs $20,000. On November 26, 1928, Adams loaned Fuchs $30,000 for "special Sunday baseball expenses." Fuchs repaid him within six months. On June 4, 1929, Adams loaned Fuchs $50,000 through the Boston Professional Hockey Association. Fuchs now owed Adams $82,500 in total.[118]

Adding interest, Fuchs' indebtedness was nearly $300,000, and all his stock, the 7,656 majority shares, belonged to Adams, who held them in collateral. Adams had over $500,000 invested in a team he didn't want charge of. In today's dollars, Adams' holdings would be worth $9.5 million, and Fuchs would owe him $5.7 million.[119]

Fuchs offered to sell his stock to Adams for $60 a share, but Adams wanted nothing to do with pouring more money into the club. Adams had previously said, "I am neither all the way in this club nor all the way out," and he would gladly take $588,000—if someone wanted the club—and walk away.[120] Fuchs had to pay off his loans, or Adams threatened sell the club at public auction. This was disconcerting to the NL executives to say the least, imagining a baseball club which anyone off the street could purchase at auction.

Fuchs and Adams agreed to a plan on June 17. Fuchs would buy out the Adams-Wetmore stock after he paid off his debts.[121] Fuchs would rally his friends, encouraging them to buy bundles of 25, 50 or 100 shares of his stock at a time at the $60-per-share price (ranging from $1,500 to $6,000 investments). Adams would get paid, his friends would own stock, and Fuchs would buy it back from them over time. Adams set a deadline of July 20 to receive $100,000 and another deadline of August 6 to receive another $50,000. Fuchs' 2,000 shares of preferred stock would be available to stockholders for $65 a share (a $130,000 investment). After $150,000 was paid back, Fuchs had another year to pay off the remaining debt. "My aim is not to make any money," Fuchs said, "but to have enough money to pay my obligations."[122]

If Fuchs couldn't meet the deadlines, he would forfeit his stock. "My main hope, then," Fuchs said, "was to avoid anything, even if I walked out without a nickel and had the satisfaction of having the relationship, as I have in this organization, and my only regret being that I embarrassed some of my friends in it. But I figured I could go back to the practice of law and start all over again."[123] One of his friends was James "Jimmy" Roosevelt, President Franklin Delano Roosevelt's eldest son.[124]

"Mr. Adams is a very wealthy man," Fuchs said, noting that Adams' stock in his grocery business, First National Stores, had tripled. "The League by having him would have a man who would be to greater advantage to it from the money standpoint than I would be." A December report in the *Globe* stated that First National Stores had a 1.6 percent increase in sales for November and 4.6 percent for October, compared to the year prior. That resulted in nearly $8 million in sales, and the stock had risen from a low of 43 to a high of 70¾ that year.[125]

Adams had no interest in being majority owner of the Braves. He wanted out as soon as possible, as he stated in a letter to Fuchs a few days before the meeting.

> I wish to express the hope that you will be able to make the arrangements that you contemplate, so that you will again be the controlling owner of the Boston Club without the difficulties which you have been facing recently. In that case, it would mean my withdrawal from activity in the base ball world, but if this is to be the result, I want to say that I have enjoyed my association with you, and only regret that pressure of other affairs makes it inadvisable for me to continue active in this deal. I sincerely hope that your contemplated arrangements will be completed, and that the arrangement which we made today will be carried out in full, and that you will be able to retain your leadership in the club which owes so much to your efforts in the past.[126]

Fuchs requested $25,000 from the National League in case he was short on July 20 or August 6.[127] Breadon had reservations about the league handing money over to Fuchs. "I think you have done a wonderful job in Boston," he said. "We don't have to worry about the Boston Club because Adams with money up there will carry the Boston Club. It is just you that we have to worry about. As far as the League is concerned, from a cold-blooded, business standpoint, Boston is taken care of."[128] The National League voted to borrow $10,000 and buy that amount of stock if Fuchs raised $140,000.[129]

Saving the Judge

"It may safely be said that within a short time there will be a change in the financial setup which controls the Boston National League club," O'Leary wrote in the *Globe*.[130] Fuchs' friends came through, and Adams received $100,000 by July 20. Fuchs stated:

I have just made the first payment under an agreement with Charles F. Adams which will enable me to pay off my financial obligation to Mr. Adams. Mr. Adams has personally loaned me money and took over a loan that I had in New York, stating that he desired to have all the Boston baseball stock in Boston. His investment, through his purchase of stock and his loan to me, is very large and substantial. He has drawn neither salary nor expenses. I cannot close without expressing heartfelt gratitude to my friends and neighbors in Boston, for the devotion and love of the baseball writers of this city, and for the confidence placed in me, which I shall hope by my very action to deserve.[131]

Fuchs made further payments to Adams: $7,500 on August 2, $20,000 on August 7, $1,000 on August 9, and $21,500 on September 1. But Adams had to put another $100,000 into the club to maintain the team's credit rating on a $200,000 loan held by First National Bank.[132]

The Braves Field turnstiles in 1933 saw 517,803 fans watch the Braves hang around the pennant race until late August. With the Braves trailing the Giants by six games on August 31, fans packed Braves Field for a six-game series with the New Yorkers. A Friday doubleheader on September 1 saw 60,000 pennant-starved fans bring a new energy.[133] The Braves only mustered one win in the series and fell from the race. "The boys did their best," Fuchs said.[134]

Despite the disappointing finish in 1933, the Braves' 83 wins were the most in the franchise since 1916. It would also be their highest win total until 1947. Their attendance would not reach such heights again until 1946. This would also be the last season the Braves outdrew the Red Sox. It was a short-lived success.

The Braves of 1934 were competitive, finishing fourth (78–73), but attendance dropped dramatically to 303,205 (-214,598). The attendance at Fenway exploded from 268,715 to 610,640. "About this time in their history, more attention was being paid to Braves owners than to Braves players," wrote Harold Kaese. "It wasn't so much a question where the Braves would finish, but if they would finish."[135] They were a financial disaster at the end of 1934, losing over $40,000.[136]

New racing venues at Rockingham Park in New Hampshire and Narragansett Park in Rhode Island opened, causing a new competitor to the Braves. Pari-mutuel wagering on horses was a new craze. Suffolk Downs in East Boston (horses) and Wonderland Park in nearby Revere (greyhounds) would open in 1935. "If you were into sports, fashion, and a fast crowd during the late 1930s and 1940s," wrote T.D. Thornton, "then Suffolk Downs was the place to see and be seen in Boston."[137] "When the Red Sox were on the road," wrote Charlie Bevis, "it was an easy decision to skip the Braves games and head for the racetrack."[138]

Fuchs was left with few options at the end of 1934. So he too went to the dogs.

Source

Lionel Pincus and Princess Firyal Map Division, The New York Public Library. "Plate 13 [Map bounded by E. Houston St., Attorney St., Grand St., Bowery]" *The New York Public Library Digital Collections*. 1893. http://digitalcollections.nypl.org/items/a1ed0d43-d53a-e912-e040- e00a180645ad

3

Fuchs Barking Up the Wrong Tree
(November–December 1934)

"Baseball and dog racing are a different breed of cats."—Commissioner Kenesaw Mountain Landis

"Boston itself, with one or two exceptions, has been heartily behind me."—Judge Fuchs

"I've settled down now. All I want is a chance."—Babe Ruth

Fuchs Wanted to Let the Dogs Out

The 1933 season was the best chance the Boston Braves had for a pennant during Judge Fuchs' era. They were in their tightest pennant race in decades as they approached Labor Day weekend. The masses of fans pouring into Braves Field recognized the novelty of a pennant race. The first-place New York Giants were in town for six games, including two sets of doubleheaders. "He [Fuchs] had never seen response of this kind in Boston," W.A. Whitcomb wrote in the *Boston Globe*, "and it must have been most gratifying."[1] But the Braves managed to win only one game against the Giants, and their dreams ended. While Labor Day weekend saw the end of one race, another was just gearing up 30 miles north in Salem, New Hampshire.

Large crowds streamed into Rockingham Park over that weekend. Legalized pari-mutuel betting on horses had been legalized in the Granite State earlier that year. Pari-mutuel is a system whereby the payouts to winners are based on the pooling of all winners together, so no individual bettor is betting against the track, and more bettors can participate. The more bets which are made, the bigger the pool.[2] A crowd of 20,000 on Labor Day arrived despite less-than-ideal weather which created a muddy track.[3]

Racing fever gripped New England, putting yet another obstacle in Judge Fuchs' way to make the Braves a success. The *Portsmouth Herald* described Rockingham's successful opening earlier that year as "plenty of thrills, and every event was run off smoothly and well."[4] Fuchs had competed with Tom Yawkey's Red Sox for the sports fan's attention, and now was competing with the racing crowd. Fuchs

Crowds poured into Salem, New Hampshire, for pari-mutuel betting on horse races at Rockingham Park—crowds which weren't going to Braves Field (courtesy Boston Public Library, Leslie Jones Collection).

himself was a racing fan, and he, Mrs. Fuchs, and Boston Mayor James Michael Curley were among the 10,000 at Rockingham Park later that week.[5] Within a year, Rhode Island would also tap into the racing profits when Narragansett Park opened.

In November 1934, Massachusetts voters overwhelmingly passed a referendum to allow pari-mutuel betting in the Commonwealth.[6] A new racing commission was formed, while Fuchs and Vice President Charles F. Adams made plans for Braves Field to be a greyhound racing site. No horse racing track could legally come within a 15-mile radius of the Boston city limits, but there were no such restrictions on greyhounds.

"It would not interfere with baseball at all," Fuchs promised about the envisioned five-sixteenths-of-a-mile portable track which would run along the outer edges of the baseball field. "I have implicit faith in what engineers can do."[7] Baseball by day, racing by night. The Braves' Board of Directors (Fuchs, Adams, V.C. Bruce Wetmore, Charles H. Innis, and Leopold M. Goulson) submitted the application.[8]

The musical *Anything Goes* was set to debut on Broadway. For Fuchs, "anything goes" described his efforts to keep the Braves afloat. But there were major obstacles still: the National League club owners and baseball's commissioner, Kenesaw

Mountain Landis, were opposed to any mix of baseball and gambling, and Commonwealth Realty, which represented the Gaffney family, the owners of Braves Field.

Baseball Responds

"I'll quit! I'll quit!" Landis responded. "I am fond of Fuchs personally, like him as well as anybody in baseball, and would like to see him recoup his losses, but baseball and dog racing are a different breed of cats and they'll never be associated so long as I'm at the head of baseball."[9]

For dog racing to work, Adams planned to give Fuchs an option to acquire his Braves stock. Adams would run a separate organization for the dogs, and Fuchs would lease Fenway Park for Braves home games. Perhaps this disconnection was enough to convince Landis to approve the deal. Adams would soon become a director of the Eastern Racing Association, which soon erected the state's first thoroughbred track in East Boston, Suffolk Downs, outside the city limits.[10]

The Massachusetts Racing Commission opened for business on December 7, 1934. Fuchs and Adams applied for a permit, as did the Bay State Greyhound Association, which sought dog racing at Boston Garden.[11] "Absolutely preposterous," blasted Ford C. Frick, the National League president-elect.[12] "It is entirely at variance with the principles for which baseball has battled so strenuously…. Organized baseball has outlawed players for gambling, and it is ridiculous to conceive that baseball now could permit a sport founded on gambling to move into the same premises with it."[13]

The story created excitement as the National League winter meetings were held on December 11–13 in New York City. At the meetings, Frick officially succeeded John Heydler as NL President. Larry MacPhail sought approval for night games in Cincinnati. American League club owners were ready to discuss what should be done with Babe Ruth. But dog racing now moved to the top of the agenda. "It looks as though I've already talked too much," Fuchs said upon arriving at the meetings. "In Boston we have a proposition that looks very good to us and one that will in no way cast any reflections on baseball. But I am still confident that when other owners have heard my complete story, they will take another view of the situation."[14]

Victor O. Jones in the *Globe* wrote it would be inconsistent to

> throw the gamblers out of the right field pavilion in the afternoon and then invite them all into the grandstand for a whirl at the parimutuels in the evening. Baseball parks are rent out to boxing and wrestling promoters and have been for years. There are no parimutuels in connection with these two sports, but there is betting. Baseball has not suffered materially from its landlord connection with these less revered sports. It is quite possible that dog racing at one of the ball parks wouldn't in any way affect that reputation. On the other hand, there's some small chance that it might, and that chance is not worth taking.[15]

Burt Whitman in the *Boston Herald* pointed out that the Braves rented Braves Field for $40,000 a year from Commonwealth Realty and would require a sub-lease.[16]

Albert W. Keane of the *Hartford Courant* sympathized with Fuchs. "Barring 1933 the Boston Braves have been a financial flop for years," he wrote. "They know that Judge Fuchs has expended every nickel of his personal fortune to keep things going in Bean-town. They know that the Braves have not strengthened their team because money to purchase minor leaguers or season stars was not available. They see in dog racing a chance for the estimable Judge Fuchs to recoup some of his losses." Yet, Keane added, "every man connected with baseball turns away from the idea of having baseball men interested in gambling propositions."[17]

Besides dealing with the Black Sox Scandal, Landis had forced John McGraw and Charles Stoneham of the New York Giants to sell their interests in a racetrack in Cuba in 1921.[18] "The further baseball men keep away from racing and betting in all forms, the better it is for the diamond sport," Charles A. Barton wrote in the *Minneapolis Star Tribune*.[19]

The most outspoken Boston sportswriter was Bill Cunningham of the *Boston Post*. "I'm strictly, completely and irrevocably against it," he ranted, filling an entire page of newsprint. "It will bankrupt the entire community. You might as well close up everything in Boston except the newspapers and tip-sheets, for the dogs will close 'em up anyhow. There are comparatively few winners each day but a great many losers."[20] His sources told him that Al Capone, the legendary gangster in prison for tax evasion, was connected to the Boston racing interests. "Mr. Capone is supposed to have turned his extensive holdings over to certain gentlemen before he went away, and these gentlemen are now understood to be in Boston pulling every string possible toward getting a dog track or two or three before the general citizenry gets wise to just whom they are."[21] Was there any truth to this? Cunningham's suspicions may have been accurate.

Capone's Chicago was a hotbed of greyhound racing between 1927 and 1930. His gang "extended its control over speakeasies, bookie joints, gambling houses, brothels, nightclubs, distilleries and breweries, and later segued into labor racketing," wrote Steven A. Riess in his article, "When Chicago went to the dogs: Al Capone and Greyhound Racing in the Windy City, 1927–1933." Nearly $105 million was made in 1927 alone.[22] Capone invested in the Hawthorne Kennel Club (HKC), owned by "Easy Eddie" O'Hare. Capone was frequently seen at HKC with O'Hare, surrounded by bodyguards as bets were made. "If he (Capone) disagreed with the outcome of a race, he would walk over to the judges' stand and 'convince them' to reconsider," Riess wrote.[23]

In 1930, the Illinois Supreme Court outlawed pari-mutuel racing at dog tracks. Capone was on trial, and "Easy Eddie" squealed to authorities that Capone's people were paying off jurors and hiring hitmen. Capone was convicted, sent to federal prison, and transferred to the brand-new Alcatraz.[24] O'Hare made a fortune in Capone's absence, opening dog tracks in Miami and Boston, where he was known for the Dighton Dog Track in Taunton. "Easy Eddie" denied any connections to Capone, but he was always looking over his shoulder. On November 8, 1939,

O'Hare was assassinated on the streets of Chicago after being pursued by gunmen in his coupe with Massachusetts plates. The crime was never solved and, ironically, Capone was released from prison just a few days later. O'Hare's son, Butch, got a free ride to the U.S. Naval Academy for his dad's cooperation with the feds. Butch was killed in combat during World War II, and Chicago named an airport for him.[25]

"All the New England public at the moment is rated prime sucker No. 1," Cunningham concluded.[26]

The Winter Meetings

The baseball winter meetings were held at the sparkling Waldorf-Astoria Hotel in New York City, the largest hotel in the world in 1934. American League club owners gathered at the Commodore Hotel on East 42nd Street. After the leagues held separate meetings, they converged on December 13 for a joint meeting at the Roosevelt Hotel on East 45th.

Owners continued to reel from the Great Depression. In 1933, the real Gross National Product (all goods and services produced by Americans, domestic or abroad) was only 70 percent of what it was in 1929. Americans had less to spend on going to the ballgame, and sports dollars decreased by 29 percent. Spending on entertainment wouldn't reach 1929 levels until 1940. Both the American and National Leagues would return to profitability in 1935, but few envisioned such confidence at these winter meetings.[27] National League attendance in 1934 was 3.2 million, down from 5.4 million in 1930. The Braves' attendance declined 41 percent in 1934, thanks to Tom Yawkey, who saw a 127 percent increase at Fenway Park. Only New York and St. Louis made a profit in the NL in 1934.[28]

The first day of the winter meetings was quiet.[29] Cleveland was chosen for the 1935 All-Star Game, Frick became NL President, and night baseball was approved for Cincinnati. Fuchs realized, perhaps as he mingled with other owners, that he had no support for greyhound racing. He had already given up on the idea before the meeting started. Fuchs addressed the owners.[30]

Gentlemen, let me say once and for all that I have eliminated myself from any consideration for the reason that I believe that there comes a time even where friendships exist that you are in a position where your best friends say, "Now, you are up against it. Now, why don't you quit?"

And so, I have said to Mr. [Charles F.] Adams that I wanted to follow [in] my father's footsteps and pay everybody that I owed anything 100 cents on the dollar. I believe that I can work out my problem in a manner that would protect the league, and that there will be no further question of finance or anything else.

Boston itself, with one or two exceptions, has been heartily behind me. It has really been wonderful to think that I could get, without having anything of value, with all my securities gone and everything else, I raised almost a quarter of a million dollars and paid it into the hands of those gentlemen who had taken a loan on my stock. I have reduced it to such an extent now that I really think I am going to work out of it beautifully for everybody's edification. But that is my problem. So, I told Mr. Heydler if there was anybody that would come in so as to take over the Boston club and help the National League, I would be glad to step out.

Nothing will be done by me that will embarrass baseball or the National League. Under the constitution of the National League, betting, legal or otherwise, is prohibited in its ball parks where baseball is played. I have always and will abide by the constitution of the National League.

It was over just like that. The meetings ended without any true discussion of greyhounds. But Fuchs still believed dogs could run at Braves Field if the Braves played at Fenway Park. It would not embarrass the league. Would Yawkey even allow that?[31]

From Dogs to Babe

A day earlier on December 11, American League club owners debated what the Yankees should do with Babe Ruth.[32] Ruth could still draw the crowds but was worn down as a player. What would happen if Ruth was released and found revival in the National League? That would mean lost profits in the AL. Ruth wanted to manage, but who would be willing to give him a shot?

Would he manage a minor league club? It was a public relations nightmare to throw the game's greatest icon to the curb.

Eddie Collins, Red Sox GM and Yawkey crony, believed Ruth would likely go to the Braves. "The rumor is," Collins said, "because of this dog racing situation he [Fuchs] will retire as far as any connection with the Boston club goes, because he is well situated with the governor, has been admitted to the Massachusetts Bar, and…. McKechnie, who is very much in favor not only with Fuchs but with others, will step up into his place and Ruth will be McKechnie's successor as manager."

Clark Griffith of the Washington Senators said, "If you give Ruth permission to do as he pleases, I think your hands are perfectly clean. I say go ahead and let Ruth choose his job." Yawkey said Ruth would want to come to the Red Sox, but they had no place for him. "It was our idea to build an organization and put everything we could into it, and for that reason we did not consider him," he said. "If you are sort of trying to hold him up for your own personal interests you are apt to come in for more criticism than if you said to him, 'There is no situation here for you; you have a free hand to do whatever you can.'"

Sportswriter John Lardner was in the hotel lobby snooping for information. "What is going to happen to Babe Ruth?" he asked a man in a brown suit puffing a cigar. "Who cares?" was the reply. Lardner figured this was "just a man in a brown suit, plus cigar," or "an unemployed flute mender from Knoxville." Others must care, but Lardner had no luck in his quest. "The Babe's fate is supposed to be settled at this meeting," he wrote, "but the Babe is not a meek and strictly stable piece of goods. He has his own ideas." The trouble was, he added, that Ruth "does not understand business very well."[33] Philadelphia writers were still convinced Ruth would become Connie Mack's assistant. Others saw him managing in Cleveland.

Ruth was in Manila reading wire reports. "Whatever baseball does to me is all right with me. The game has been good to me. I'm ready to quit if there is no place for me." Tillinghast Huston, one-time part-owner of the Yankees, considered buying the Brooklyn Dodgers and installing Ruth as manager. "I hope it's true," Ruth said of the possible Brooklyn opening. But that never happened.[34]

Adams discussed Ruth with Colonel Jacob Ruppert, the Yankees owner, at the winter meetings. When the meetings wrapped up, Adams stayed in New York that night to watch his Bruins play the New York Americans at Madison Square Garden. "I had a short talk with Col. Ruppert," he affirmed. "Ruth's name was mentioned, but nothing of any importance about his coming to Boston was discussed." Ruppert denied even discussing Ruth with Adams. "I have not spoken with Mr. Adams or anybody connected with the Boston Braves today or any other day in connection with Ruth," he stated. "My stand on the Babe is just the same as it always has been. If any club wants him as manager, I will release him outright. So far not a single club has approached me with that idea in mind."[35]

Fuchs claimed to have no idea about Ruth. "Wherever did they dig that one up?" he asked.[36]

Adams revealed more the following day. "I told Mr. Ruppert that if he failed to find a place for Ruth in his own league, I was sure that manager Bill McKechnie of the Boston Braves would be glad to have him as his assistant. Mr. Ruppert expressed his thanks and that ended the matter."[37]

Writers and Fans Weigh In

Newspaper writers continued to speculate on Ruth's future throughout December. Besides the barnstorming, bearded House of David team offering Ruth a contract, Ruth was offered $50,000 to manage Syracuse of the International League.[38]

Ruth also refused to manage Newark, the Yankees' farm club, something Ruppert and GM Ed Barrow encouraged. Ruth had a long-standing distrust of Barrow from their Boston days.

Barrow "viewed Ruth essentially as a delinquent youth with the potential for unleashing significant disorder in baseball," wrote Edmund F. Wehrle. "Ruth may well have suspected a setup. If he failed in Newark, his prospects would be all but over."[39]

"Even now," wrote Edward J. Neil, "the Babe still lingers as the game's most perplexing problem. What to do with him, now that his playing days are over, may turn out to be as vexing a question as his managers faced in the days when he was the game's greatest star and at the same time baseball's greatest developer of grey hairs and headaches. Once more they can't let him go, and yet they can't keep him either."[40] "When it comes to a managership," an editorial in the *Dayton Herald* stated, "there may be doubts whether he can qualify because of a temperament which hardly could have been improved by years of pampering."[41]

"It is no secret," wrote Alan Gould, "that most major league magnates consider the Babe too big a gamble, as a manager, to justify the substantial investment required to signing him up." "The big question," said one baseball executive, "concerns Ruth's ability to maintain discipline."[42] Westbrook Pegler wrote of Ruth as a national treasure, "comparable to George Washington's false teeth, which are kept under glass at Mount Vernon." Who would come to the ballpark to see a manager? "The mere sight of any man," wrote Pegler, "including even the Babe, pondering whether to leave a pitcher in or take him out, is not the stuff that ovations and receipts are made of." Why pay Ruth $50,000 when someone else can do the job for $5,000?[43]

Would Babe Ruth make a good manager? Fans believed he would, at least those who were asked by the *New York Daily News*.[44]

"I am sure that Babe Ruth would make the most colorful playing manager that baseball ever had," said Dr. Herman Rosenbaum at his drug store in the Bronx.

"As a playing manager they [fans] will still flock to see his team play," said Fred T. Nash, a soda dispenser on Walton Avenue. "He will always be a great attraction."

"Over the season I think he will attract larger average crowds," said salesman "Speedy" Taub on E. 169th, "which is really what the baseball owners would like."

"Babe has a spot in the heart of every baseball fan," stenographer John L. Quann of Bathgate Ave. said. "Who else has the same drawing power?"

Al Schwartz, a pharmacist on Garfield Street, said, "The majority of baseball fans want Babe Ruth to continue in baseball, and they believe that he will make a good playing manager."

"To refuse him a manager's berth," said stenographer Edward Goldberg of the Bronx County Court House, "would be stupid and shortsighted."

"All I Want Is a Chance"

Colonel Ruppert saw it differently. Ruth made him a lot of money, and the Yankees became the most successful and profitable team for the past two decades. The Yankees lost money only in 1932 and 1933 (-$38,000 and -$126,000). Attendance dropped from 1.1 million in 1930 to 728,000 in 1933, while Ruth remained the highest-paid player in the game. Ruth made $80,000 per year in 1930–1931 and took a cut to $75,000 for 1932. "No sir," said Ruppert. "Never again will any player get that much a year, and that means the Babe. The peak of salaries for players has been reached with Ruth. We realize the Babe is a big asset, but he isn't the big drawing power of the Yankee club by a good long ways."[45] After a contract holdout in spring training, Ruth signed a one-year deal for $52,000 for 1933, his lowest salary since 1926.[46]

At the end of 1933, Ruth's skills were declining, and rumors of managerial jobs began. Some said Ruth had the maturity to manage, his reckless days behind him. "The Ruth of today is a different chap from the careless, boisterous, swaggering and unruly Playboy of the Western World of ten years ago," wrote John Kieran in the *New York Times*. "He stays home at nights now. He knows the value of money. He has quiet friends instead of loud followers."[47]

Ruth was still the highest-paid player in the game in 1934, despite a cut to $35,000.[48] He was a part-time player who had trouble getting out of his own way. "His roistering days were behind him," Jane Leavy wrote. "If not quite sedate, the Babe had become at least respectably middle-aged, especially around the middle."[49] Fans started to boo, and Yankees teammates felt they couldn't win the pennant with Ruth on the field. His 22 home runs were his lowest total since 1918, when he was still known as a pitcher. "The fans who journey to the Yankee Stadium under the hallucination that they are going to see the Sultan of Swat, the King of Klout, and all the things he used to be are doomed to disappointment," Richards Vidmer wrote in the *New York Herald-Tribune*. Fans were cheated, he wrote, because of Ruth's sluggishness "covering so little ground that the other outfielders must play out of position, blocking the base paths when there are fast youngsters trying to score behind him."[50]

Perhaps the harshest writer Ruth encountered was a kid writing a school paper. With a brown-bag lunch packed by his mom and a note from his teacher explaining the assignment, teenager Jhan Robbins rode the train from Brooklyn to Yankee Stadium. That boy, who would one day write biographies of Hollywood stars Jimmy Stewart and Jimmy Durante, wasn't afraid to ask the penetrating question asked by reporters his grandfather's age. "How can you manage the Yankees when you can't even manage yourself?"

It struck a nerve. "That's the trouble with you newspaper guys," he hollered at the adolescent. "You never forget the past. Maybe I lived it up in my time; but don't forget, I did the papers a favor—I gave you plenty to write about." Ruth confused Robbins for an inhabitant of the press box instead of the playground. It spoke volumes about Ruth's inner turmoil. "This was a man begging to be seen for who he had become and not for the image he so happily collaborated in constructing," Leavy wrote. "It figures he would reveal himself most fully to a fourteen-year-old boy reporter trying to play the role of an adult, but ironic, too, that he was pleading with a child to be seen as an adult."

"I've settled down now. All I want is a chance," Ruth said to Robbins.[51]

Ruth deserved at least a *chance* at managing. But he never escaped perception. Ruth, "who grew up an impoverished, castaway child in Baltimore and never enjoyed much education or refinement," wrote Wehrle, "remained forever an outsider to baseball's halls of power. The establishment essentially blackballed him for lack of sophistication and a supposed dearth of intelligence. Ruth's swagger, his self-confidence, his independence, and his demands all made him appear a dangerous apparition of a baseball world upside down."[52] It was politics and power, not maturity. But someone needed him.

Judge Fuchs, failing at dog racing and drowning in debt, needed a miracle. Who else but Ruth could make that happen? Ruth could save the franchise. But Fuchs had other issues to deal with first.

He needed money to send the Braves to spring training.

4

A Homeless Team
and Wandering Souls
(January–February 1935)

"My friends and the people of New England, generally, have responded so kindly and so enthusiastically to the proposed movement that I feel very hopeful."—Judge Fuchs

"Don't they know who I am?"—Babe Ruth in Paris

Happy New Year

Judge Fuchs and his family celebrated New Year's Eve 1934 at their home on 480 Jamaicaway in Jamaica Plain, one of Boston's well-to-do streetcar suburbs. Immigrant labor in the late–19th century created the large estates for the upper class in Boston's South End and Back Bay areas, as well as Roxbury, Milton, Dedham, and Jamaica Plain, which was annexed by Boston along with West Roxbury in 1874.[1] Fuchs gave up his New York home at the end of the 1932 season to live year-round at Jamaicaway. He was admitted to the Massachusetts Bar in 1934 and practiced law in both New York and the Commonwealth. Fuchs' home was described in a 1932 ad as a "luxurious gas-heated apartment in Duplex estate of Georgian Colonial architecture overlooking beautiful Jamaica Pond."[2] The duplex included three tiled baths, a tiled kitchen, laundry, parquet floors, an electrical refrigerator, and a three-car heated garage.

Fuchs entertained some prominent people from Boston's business, legal, and political sectors that night. Miss Eleanor Early was there to welcome the new year. The famed prolific author and journalist would one day write the *New England Cookbook,* a must-have in Yankee kitchens for decades. Former Braves manager Fred Mitchell and Traveling Secretary Ed Cunningham were there. But one guest topped them all and lived less than a half-mile up the road at 350 Jamaicaway: Governor-elect James Michael Curley.

Curley, involved in Massachusetts politics for most of the first half of the 20th century, was called "a near-mythic figure who symbolizes either the best or worst of

Boston politics to many people" by author Lawrence W. Kennedy. "He—more than anyone else, was responsible for shaping Boston from 1915 to the middle of the century."[3] Likening Curley to Robin Hood, Kennedy described him as having no issues with stealing from the rich and giving to the poor. He was a social reformer in his four stints as mayor of Boston in which he provided better hospitals, clinics, beaches, roads, and tunnels in low-income, ethnic neighborhoods. Sometimes his activities landed him in jail. "Curley was indeed a mayor of the poor," Kennedy wrote. Yet he nearly bankrupted the city in doing so. "Curley's objective was to win votes and his strategy worked: poorer residents in Boston had a champion in city hall."[4] How Curley paid for his Jamaicaway Georgian colonial mansion with its 18 rooms and shamrock shutters is a matter of speculation even decades later.[5]

Fuchs was connected to Curley and the political establishment in Massachusetts. In his "nearly sixty raucous years of public service," in the words of Charles H. Trout, "Curley was elected to the U.S. House of Representatives twice, mayor of Boston four times, Governor of Massachusetts twice, and he served two jail terms. Yet through it all, he increasingly became the center of all political alignments in Boston. Voter identification polarized on a pro–Curley and anti–Curley basis."[6]

Curley was born in the Irish tenements of Boston. His mother scrubbed floors for a living to help the family survive. "I have known what it is to be hungry," he said, "and I have known what it is to be cold, and if I have sometimes erred in response to the dictates of the heart rather than the head, perhaps I am not altogether to blame. My sympathies and purse have been ever freely given to those who stood shivering in the shadow of adversity."[7]

Curley's son Paul was named Braves Traveling Secretary in December of 1933. Paul suffered physical infirmities as a child and was prone to drinking and recklessness as he grew into an adult. He often embarrassed his father in social occasions. He dropped out of law school and bounced from job to job. Paul died in 1945 at age 32.[8]

Fuchs had once served as Curley's campaign manager. Now he depended on the power and connections Curley had to bail him out of his Braves' financial nightmare. Friends had come to his aid in the past, but now Fuchs depended on them to make sure the Braves actually made it to Opening Day 1935.

The Braves had a 25-game spring training schedule beginning March 9 and concluding with the annual exhibition games with the Red Sox in Boston on April 12 and 13. Players were due to report to St. Petersburg, Florida, by March 1.[9] Where they would play in Boston was another matter.

A Homeless Team

Charles F. Adams, a director of the Eastern Racing Association, filed an application with the Massachusetts Racing Commission for a license to run horses in East Boston. Construction of the proposed $2.5 million Suffolk Downs track would begin in March.[10] The Boston Kennel Club also applied to hold greyhound racing with pari-mutuel betting at Braves Field. Rumors circulated that the Braves had already relinquished their 11-year lease on Braves Field to the kennel club. Fuchs' dream to host greyhounds at Braves Field didn't materialize because of the protective National League. The Boston Kennel Club seized the opportunity.

Boston baseball fans having a morning coffee while glancing at the Sunday paper on a cold January 13, 1935, morning realized the Braves were now homeless.[11] The Boston Kennel Club never asked the National League for permission to use Braves Field.[12] Who had the final say? The National League governed the team. Commonwealth Real Estate Trust owned the lease to Braves Field. "There will be no dog racing in Braves Field without the permission of the National baseball league and commissioner Landis," NL President Ford Frick announced.[13]

Sheldon H. Fairbanks, president of the Boston Kennel Club, was the former general manager of the Boston Garden and owned a string of racehorses. Fairbanks envisioned a 20-foot-wide track which would require renovating Braves Field. The right field Jury Box seats would be removed along with the third-base dugout, and the center field bleachers would be shifted. Fuchs met Frick in New York as a cry for help. The Massachusetts Racing Commission members were in Florida, observing racing and pari-mutuel betting. No decision on who received a license to run dogs would be made until they returned in several weeks.[14]

"Tom Yawkey was most emphatic in stating that he did not care to share his field with the Braves," Red Sox GM Eddie Collins affirmed. "What the Braves have done concerning their field is their own business. Had their field burned down, we would have been glad to extend them the courtesy until such time as they were able to return to their own park. What the Braves will do now is strictly up to themselves and we are not interested."[15] An act of God would have sufficed, not an act of dog.

With Yawkey's denial, the Braves' only solution was playing all their games on the road. Otherwise, the National League would need to adjust to a seven-team league or move the team to a city wishing for a major league franchise, such as Baltimore or Montreal.[16]

"I have salvaged everything possible," Adams said, "both for the owners of the real estate and for the ball club. If I fail it is not because I have not tried."[17] Adams had been persuaded by banking associates to invest in the club and had been trying to get out with minimal loss ever since. He had reached the limits of his charity to Fuchs. Adams and V.C. Bruce Wetmore could have invested more to get the team out of this mess, but they wanted out of baseball *and* wanted their money back. "At any time within the past two years," wrote Paul H. Shannon in the *Boston Post*, "these men might have stepped in, taken advantage of the Judge's embarrassed condition and taken hold of the reigns themselves. That they have not already done so must indicate that they are weary of playing a losing game and willing for someone else to hold the bag."[18] "I am in hopes that the situation will, in time, be clarified,"

Adams said. "But try and figure out what happens when an irresistible force collides with an immovable object. It's a crossword puzzle. That's all."[19] It wasn't a crossword puzzle to Commonwealth Realty Trust. "We no longer consider the Braves as our tenant," said Arthur C. Wise, treasurer. "They have not lived up to the terms of their lease and we have declared it broken. We are now negotiating with the Boston Kennel Club, Inc., and a lease is in the process of being written."[20] The Braves were behind in rent, and greyhound racing would be more profitable tenants than the Braves.

While Adams viewed the Braves as a puzzle to solve, Fuchs was resigned to fate. "It was all in the hands of the gods," he helplessly said.[21] Their styles and outlooks clashed. "Personally," wrote Bill Cunningham in the *Boston Post*, "I think the Judge ought to get out of baseball. He openly parted company with its ideals and its valued place in the community when the State racing law came in. Furthermore, unwittingly or deliberately, he has now got the game into one of the worst jams in its history."[22]

January 18 Meeting

Ford Frick called an emergency meeting of National League club owners for Friday, January 18. Adams joined Fuchs for the meeting at the NL headquarters on the 19th Floor of the RCA Building at Rockefeller Center in midtown Manhattan, later dubbed "30 Rock." Henry Fonda, Katharine Hepburn, and Will Rogers were starring in various matinees around the city that day, and you could see Ginger Rogers perform on stage at Radio City Music Hall.[23] The National League put on its own 13-hour show that day, discussing dogs, back rent, leases, and a baseball team on the verge of collapse.[24]

"I have undergone a great deal of humiliation," Fuchs said in his opening remarks.

> And I have been the victim of a lot of innuendo and whispering. I came to Mr. Heydler [former National League President] not very long ago and said, "If I have been wearing out my welcome with my colleagues, tell me so, and in some way or other, I will find a way of getting out." I have been under this innuendo that has been going on, and I am going once and for all to settle it in no uncertain terms, because I have got to defend and protect three young children who are innocent and a lady who is not entitled to the kind of publicity that I have been getting.[25]

The "innuendo" probably referred to an article by Tommy Holmes in the *Brooklyn Daily Eagle* that morning. Holmes wrote of Fuchs:

> In his regime, the Braves have usually cost him money. Prominent in Massachusetts politics, closely connected with the newly elected Governor Curley, he suddenly sees an opportunity by which he can clear up any debts he might have incurred and get into smooth financial waters. He was a first-rate plugger—some say campaign manager—for Governor Curley. At

the same time Curley was elected, the resolution to legalize betting on dogs and horses was adopted. Fuchs was in a position to get in on the ground floor. It is estimated that the most popular dog track in Boston would see the passage of $10,000,000 through its pari-mutuel machines. As a promoter Fuchs probably could clean up a profit of $1,000,000 next summer.[26]

Others reported Fuchs surviving solely on the generosity of friends, while Bill McCullough in the *Times Union* in Brooklyn reported Fuchs' debt at $350,000.[27] "I know that I come here empty-handed," Fuchs admitted. "If I am given the proper opportunity, I will exonerate myself."[28] "If it is the judgment of any of you gentlemen that maybe it will be better for me to step out—Oh, I thought I would die in the game, but it will be all right, I will be glad to do it. All I ask is that I be given a fair opportunity to get something for all the interest I had, and not be deprived of a fair opportunity or getting enough to go out and start life anew."[29]

Allowing greyhounds at Braves Field was out of the question. A motion passed early and unanimously that day. The public statement read: "At a meeting of the National League this morning the club owners and representatives again went on record as being unalterably opposed to playing National League baseball games in any place or park where dog racing is held or permitted."[30] While not unexpected, the decision put Fuchs in a bind. The bank would have been more generous with another loan to Fuchs if the rent on Braves Field were split between baseball and dogs. Fuchs was on his last rope.

The Braves had not been able to afford the yearly rent ($45,000) the past two years, so under a gentleman's agreement they paid 8 percent of gross income in 1934 and would pay 9 percent in 1935. The now-revised rent was $25,000 in 1934, which the Braves were still in default of for $11,000. "This dog racing situation only developed because of a very serious emergency in Boston," Adams explained. "Judge Fuchs in his emergency and need felt that some concessions might be made by the League and by Judge Landis. For instance, racing after the baseball season was over."[31]

Fuchs didn't like the "poor judge" image Adams and newspaper writers portrayed, which he believed resulted in a loss of clients. Fuchs admitted:

> While I have been careless, nothing ever happened in the way of any publicity directly or indirectly affecting the National League or the Boston Club. I am president really by virtue of the men on that board tolerating me, although I am the majority stockholder, because other than the agreement I have made, I have no control, I have nothing. I have been very foolish, spent a lot of money I should not spend, but money does not mean anything to me today, if I had just enough to finish the education of my children, that is all. Mrs. Fuchs does not care about any splendor. But we do want peace, and the only way to get peace is to have this thing out.[32]

Adams and Wetmore could, "by a mere snap of their finger," borrow $50,000 from the bank to extend the team's credit, as Fuchs knew.

> They are fortunate to be in that position. But I can do this: If the credit that the club had is continued of $200,000 or the $205,000, I can raise within three days all the money that is needed to pay up our debts and to go to spring training. I want to get into the minds of you gentlemen that while a certain great act was done by Mr. Adams when he took the stock over, and God knows I appreciated it awfully much, but from the minute he took it, I have not had

any peace on earth, nor have I had any control. Either we can induce Mr. Adams and Mr. Wetmore to keep our credit and impose upon me a limited time in which I can work that out, for myself. If not, the League ought to get together with me and try to work a way out of it. I am willing to walk out, provided I get enough, much less than I am paying, for the only thing I have left in the world.[33]

Adams and Wetmore had no desire to pump more money into the club. "You must see what Adams' situation is," said Adams, speaking of himself in the third person, "and why he cannot do that, or at least he wouldn't consider, after what he has done in the past, that it is asking a little too much of Adams to do." Adams had "snapped his fingers" to bail Fuchs out numerous times in the past. Adams also had to forward almost $12,000 to Harriman Bank to maintain Fuchs' credit rating there.

I have offered extensions, extensions, extensions. I did not want to foreclose. I did not want the ball club. I have a business that won't give me the chance to give that ball club the time it needs and the thought it needs to run it successfully. I think it is hopeless. It is impossible and certainly to the extent that I am involved, would it seem reasonable or fair to me or to anybody in a similar position that I extend my own credit? It is extremely difficult for me with reduced income. My own salary has been reduced 40 per cent on my main job, which I voluntarily accepted. I have employees, personal employees, of whom I am their sole support.[34]

Fuchs *had* repaid Adams $210,000 of the $289,000 he owed, but there was still the $200,000 note at First National Bank which Adams contributed $100,000 towards to keep the team's credit whole. Fuchs also owed $100,000 to Frank Stevens and $50,000 to other friends. Back taxes on Braves Field equaled $11,000. Out of the 7,656 shares of stock Fuchs held in the club, Adams held 4,427 of it as collateral, and Harriman Bank held another 300 shares.[35]

The meeting passed lunch and dinner times, and the magnates canceled train reservations. After 13 hours, an agreement was reached around 11 p.m. "By this time," Paul Shannon wrote, "Steve ('Jedge') McKeever of the Brooklyn club was sound asleep in his chair. And a few of the others were in a state of partial coma."[36] Some were perturbed. "One or two of the fifteen representatives of the league who attended Friday's hot air endurance contest," wrote George Kenney of the *New York Daily News*, "are reported ready to sell their holdings, even, if necessary, at a slight loss, and give big time baseball the cold shoulder henceforth." The two unnamed club owners were disgruntled at being asked to rescue Fuchs "by digging into their own coffers to make up the Boston deficit." "If Fuchs and his fellow stockholders in Boston can't run their Braves profitably, it is not the fault of the other magnates."[37]

However, they voted unanimously for the National League to take over the lease on Braves Field:

"Resolved that the National League assume the lease on Braves Field for the balance of the term [1946], and that Mr. Adams be authorized to negotiate with the landlord to this end, and that an assignment or sub-lease be obtained running to the league, and further resolved that the president be authorized to sign in the name of the National League a guaranty of said lease."[38]

The lease was for $25,000 a year plus 6 percent interest on any Braves' gross income over $400,000. The interest rate would rise to 7 percent in 1936 and 8 percent after that until the lease expired at the end of the 1945 season. If the club defaulted, the NL would cover the deficit. If the NL defaulted, each of the other seven NL clubs would contribute 1/7 of the balance. Fuchs downplayed the whole affair. "This talk of our being homeless was silly. We have a lease on the field which runs until 1946, and it's still in force. The dog-racing people have no lease on the park, and they can't force us out without one."[39]

Cunningham took issue with Fuchs' "silly" comment. "The plot [dog racing] never did make sense and the finale leaves it screwier than ever." A Braves official told reporters the club *had* surrendered its lease, not a "silly" situation at all. "Somebody wanted it [the story] to stand," Cunningham wrote, "and wanted it to stand until the National League could, in distress, assemble. That somebody, whoever it was, wanted the National League to believe that either it would have to share its Boston field with the sad-eyed hounds so nightly disillusioned in their drive for the mechanical rabbit, or weep Tom Yawkey into taking the orphans into his park in the name of fair play, sportsmanship, good of the game, or something."[40]

More details would be sorted out at the National League's annual meeting on February 5.

Gathering Community Support

Adams and Fuchs returned to Boston to work out the arrangements of the lease. They met with minority stakeholders, including Gov. Curley and other interested parties, to generate ideas for increasing revenue.[41] On January 28, Fuchs and Adams, Curley, Boston Mayor Frederick Mansfield, state treasurer Charles F. Hurley, and Massachusetts Attorney General Paul A. Dever met at the State House.[42] The group devised an advance-ticket sale campaign allowing fans to purchase a $5 book of five tickets valid for any five games. The advanced sales would provide $50,000, enough to pay bills and send the club to spring training. The whole situation was stressful for Fuchs.

"My family, and no man ever had a finer one," Fuchs said, baring his soul to Bill Cunningham, "is living on the smallest budget it ever has known. That hurts me to be sure. I'm not exactly young anymore, but I've got a kick left. I'll tackle that problem after this one is out of the way." Fuchs never liked the dog racing plan but was desperate. "What are you going to do when you see what represents your life's savings slipping away from you?"[43] Fuchs' life was a tale of a "once wealthy man who's run into business reverses," wrote Cunningham, "who sees his considerable fortune melt away, who becomes entangled with mortgages and banks and loans finally called, who's finally reduced to a desperate fight to save even some part of what he's lost, who sees the ship sinking deeper and deeper, and finally, without actually giving up hope, is forced to recognize that the thing that just couldn't happen is now a looming possibility—that personal disaster is ahead, unless unforeseen help comes at once."[44]

"I have done my best," Fuchs said.

> I am still fighting, but if they [National League] can find anybody who can do better than I have or can, let them trot him out, and I will make it easy for him to get in.[45]
>
> I am willing to sacrifice my equity in the Boston club if by so doing I can save the other stockholders from any loss.[46]
>
> My friends and the people of New England, generally, have responded so kindly and so enthusiastically to the proposed movement that I feel very hopeful.[47]

Those friends of Fuchs established the Boston Braves Citizens Committee. They met on January 31 at Boston's Copley Plaza (where a generous manager provided free rent to the Braves in the winter months). By the end of the night, more than $28,000 was pledged, and Opening Day at Braves Field was designated "Judge Fuchs Day," a half-holiday for city workers. "I suppose when I see him privately, he will tell me I should not say this," Curley said of Fuchs, "but it shows the kind of man Judge Fuchs is—kindly, large hearted and generous to a fault, as the old saying goes."[48]

February 5 Meeting

A cold, clear day greeted the NL club owners as they gathered again at the Waldorf-Astoria. "I think, with me, you are all anxious to avoid another thirteen- or fourteen-hour session," Frick understated.[49] The Braves Citizens Committee was nearing its goal of raising $100,000.

Politicians forfeited their usual free tickets and were buying ticket books. A local printer provided 20,000 ticket books free of charge. The bank also granted a 60-day extension. "So, I say to you in conclusion, gentlemen," Fuchs said, "that I realize I have embarrassed you. I am trying to fight like hell to do the other things— to do the square thing, and I believe I will do anything in the world—sacrifice anything that I have, what I can, to stop this thing going into other hands that are not in the hands of the Boston people. I will play with anybody that helps."[50]

Adams didn't share such optimism. He felt the Fuchs plan of advance ticket sales was a mere band-aid on a festering wound. New capital was needed, otherwise the plan was not sustainable, like "plowing up the snow in front of you."[51] Adams demanded that if $50,000 was repaid to the bank, $50,000 must also be repaid to him as well.

Fuchs had also cut expenses by severing ties with their minor-league affiliate in Harrisburg, Pennsylvania, in the New York–Penn League. Fuchs had purchased the club in 1932 and ran it as a farm club, with his son Robert S. serving as the general manager. Harrisburg had the lowest attendance in the league, and Fuchs lost $9,000. He sold the club to Joe Cambria, a future legendary scout of Cuban players, who assumed its indebtedness.[52] Fuchs later created a working agreement with McKeesport of the Pennsylvania State League.[53]

Fuchs and Adams left the room as the magnates met in executive session. There were three options:

1. Deny any help to the Braves. "After all, the National League is not going around to underwrite ball clubs. This thing will have to go along through its natural course and you [Fuchs] will have to assume your liability."

2. Accept Fuchs' optimism, the 60-day bank extension, and "go along with Mr. Adams who calls this 'the rosy side' of the picture and pray that there is sunshine in Boston, and they have this tremendously large crowd, and that in the sixty days and up to the 5th of April, we will be able to work this thing out."

3. Provide new management for the Braves.[54]

Sam Breadon of the St. Louis Cardinals said, "I think Judge Fuchs is a terrible businessman. There is no question he has gone out and started a fire. He can cause a lot of trouble. When you get the Governor of the state, thirty of the mayors and the Mayor of Boston behind a professional baseball club, I think he had done a hell of a job. Unless he gets new capital, I don't think he is going to finish any better than he is today, but he has made this effort." The National League would look bad if Fuchs were displaced while the community rallied around him. "I didn't think the Judge could do it three weeks ago, but any man that can get these men behind him is entitled to have a chance to work it out."[55]

Thomas Conroy, the secretary/treasurer of the Cincinnati Reds, agreed. "The Judge, through his friends, has fanned the flames up to a point where he is in the martyr role."[56]

"I am not arguing against Judge Fuchs," Bob Quinn, from Brooklyn, said. "You can't take it away from him now. You have got to give him the sixty days, but in the meantime, should we sit idly by and let matters go?"[57] But what would happen if Fuchs could not pay his debts by April 5? Frick had to find potential buyers, but you can't sell the club until you are able to get these liabilities straight. Breadon was skeptical. "Is there anybody who thinks that adequate capital is going to be there on the 5th of April? I don't think there is a man here that expects that. Judge Fuchs personal indebtedness is no concern of this group of gentlemen."[58]

There was also the issue of the preferred stock given to Frank Stevens. "Adams takes the attitude that that preferred stock is illegal," Leo Bondy, attorney and executive with the Giants, said. "Fuchs, on the other hand, takes the attitude that that stock was properly issued. In their usual careless way, they kept no minutes. I checked it up one time and there were no records then of those things ever having taken place."[59]

"That has been going on for five, six, seven years," added Quinn. "I knew all that stuff. That's why I tried to keep out."[60]

If anyone understood the trials of Judge Fuchs, it was Quinn. His ownership of the Red Sox was sandwiched between the eras of Harry Frazee and Tom Yawkey. His ownership group bought the Red Sox from Frazee after it had floundered following the sale of Babe Ruth to the Yankees. Quinn survived on the deep pockets of Indiana glass bottle baron Palmer Winslow, part of his ownership team. Quinn spent $250,000 to acquire new players and revive the Sox, but none of his plans worked. Winslow died, and Quinn's deep pockets were gone, but he decided not to sell out. "His decision directly resulted in the most unsuccessful era in Red Sox history," Glenn Stout and Richard A. Johnson wrote, as the Red Sox became one of the worst teams in history. Both Quinn and Fuchs operated losing clubs through the 1920s. "Quinn had borrowed and bargained the franchise nearly into oblivion and now had little choice but to sell."[61] The same fate now faced Fuchs. Quinn found a savior in the wealthy Yawkey. Fuchs needed the same rider on a white horse. "It wouldn't be hard to interest people in any proposition to buy the Braves," Quinn said after the meeting.[62] Adams had approached Quinn about joining the Braves after selling out to Yawkey, but he declined, "although he didn't have a job," wrote Cunningham.[63]

Stevens offered to sell his shares of common stock and give the Braves a smaller cut of the advertising. The NL considered paying off $50,000 of the loan to Stevens over a period of years.[64] Fuchs sought a deal with First National Bank to borrow an additional $50,000 for three months to pay the back rent and taxes. "Bear in mind," Adams reminded everyone, "You can't start the team south without a little more than $50,000."[65]

The magnates voted unanimously to allow Frick to negotiate with new prospective buyers of the club. The National League became the new landlord for the Braves. Fuchs had sixty days to pay off the loan at the bank. The team might have enough money to go to spring training. And Fuchs' friends were still raising money. "We have been embarrassed a good deal with this Boston situation," Quinn said. "I think there should be as little publicity given to this as possible. We should say that the Judge has shown that he has done something in Boston, and that the League is going ahead with him." Frick agreed.[66]

"I hope that within sixty days you will be glad that you gave me the chance," Fuchs graciously responded, "and that I will dedicate my time and effort with everything I can do to deserve what you have done for me."[67] Fuchs put on a good face to the press.

"We have neither asked nor do we need outside help," he said, covering a multitude of woes. "We have had wonderful cooperation from the league, and I feel confident we have the full support of the baseball people in Boston in our attempt to put the Braves back firmly on their feet." Fuchs expressed confidence in manager Bill McKechnie, but when directly asked about Babe Ruth, Fuchs declined to say whether there was a place for Ruth in "any capacity."[68]

The Unknown Ruth in Paris

Babe Ruth and his family had been in Paris since the middle of January. Upon arriving, Ruth reaffirmed that he would accept only a player-manager contract and would not play full-time. If no positions were offered, he would take it easy, write a book on his world travels, and play some golf. Hardly an exciting headline. On the same page of the *Times Union* was the report of a five-hour standoff with the FBI at a farmhouse in Florida which led to the demise of the notorious Ma Barker and her son, Fred.[69]

It was quiet in Paris. Too quiet. Ruth was frustrated because no one recognized him. He was homesick, then perturbed when he saw his name listed in the unclaimed mail column in the *Paris Herald Tribune*. "Don't they know who I am?" he barked. "You know I've had letters follow me around the world with nothing on the envelopes but my picture."[70] He visited an American boys' school and found a lad willing to pitch to him so Ruth could knock a few fly balls. "Some of those American kids born over here never have seen a baseball game," Ruth said, "as if such misfortune was hardly conceivable," the Associated Press wrote of his shock.[71] Ruth couldn't understand it all.

"He found the streets of Paris indifferent fields of concrete," wrote Walter Gilhooly in the *Ottawa Journal*. "He walked along unnoticed and unknown, just another American tourist, taking in the town."[72]

Ruth hoped someone back in the States still remembered who he was.

5

Boston Invites the Babe to Dinner
(February 1935)

"He could be a player, coach or have a shiny mahogany desk in the front office on which to rest his pipe-stem legs while smoking those big, black cigars."—Judge Fuchs on Babe Ruth

"Gee, this is certainly some town."—Babe Ruth on Boston

Wicked with a Wicket

"I guess it's a better game than I thought," Babe Ruth said as he swung a cricket bat in the comfortable settings of London, England, his last stop on his world tour. In Paris, no one recognized him, but in jolly old England, he was happy to be a celebrity again. "But I think I will stick to baseball," he concluded as he drove the ball all over the grounds of a subterranean school under the Thames River. He couldn't master the proper cricket stance, so he reverted to his familiar batting stance. "I wish I could have him for a fortnight," his coach, Australian cricket star Alan Fairfax, said. "I could make one of the world's greatest batsmen out of him." But Cricket wasn't lucrative. "They tell me $40 a week is top pay for cricket," Ruth said. "I believe I had rather be a club owner than a player."[1] He swung and turned the wicket into a jumble of splinters.

"I wish they would let me use a bat as wide as this in baseball," he joked. "I'd be good for at least five more years and top Colonel Ruppert's payroll," Ruth added, thinking of his employment status. The locals started arguing whether a cricketer could throw faster than Walter Johnson or hit farther than a Ruth home run. Ruth couldn't be bothered. It was time for lunch with his wife Claire.[2] "Say, you haven't any traffic over here," he remarked as he left. "The cars in America would get you by the heels every time."[3]

Not since he was a confused, troubled boy under Brother Matthias' tutelage at St. Mary's had Babe Ruth experienced an identity crisis like this. He celebrated his 41st birthday, in his mind at least, since it was really his 40th. His sister Mamie later discovered the discrepancy researching the family. He was eager to get back home, but teams weren't exactly wrestling for his services.

Ruth liked London, but he cut his vacation short two weeks early. He would be back in New York on February 20. "I find I must get home earlier," Ruth said with urgency in his voice.[4] He worried what he would find waiting for him. "There's no danger of the Ruths being on the bread line," quipped Jack Cuddy in Brooklyn's *Times Union*, "because Babe has plenty of tomatoes. But it would pain George Herman to no end to be shunted out of baseball, even for a year."[5]

Ruth's agent, Christy Walsh, taught him the value of saving a buck. Ruth had so much green stashed away in annuities that without even touching the principle, he would be guaranteed $15,000 a year for life. The median income for an individual in 1935 was $830 a year.[6] After signing his two-year contract for $80,000 a year in 1930, he said that his days of wasting money were over. "At least $100,000 of that $160,000 salary will go right into a trust fund," Ruth promised. "I've got enough income now to live on. From here on out I'm going to save money in a big way. Even a guy like me don't remain a sucker all his life."[7] But money wasn't everything.

Money couldn't buy freedom, and baseball's reserve clause held Ruth to the owners' control until they figured out what to do with him.

"Just a Slave"

Over three decades later, Curt Flood of the St. Louis Cardinals challenged that reserve clause. He was asked by Howard Cosell about his $90,000 salary, "which isn't exactly slave wages." Flood responded, "A well-paid slave is nonetheless a slave." The reserve clause, he said, ensured that players were treated like cattle, or a commodity bought and sold in the marketplace.[8] Ruth felt the same way in 1935.

"You belong to your club, you know," he said to U.K. reporters following him around. "They buy you and they've got you. You do as they tell you, and if you get funny with 'em and walk out, they just blackball you and that's the end of it."[9] Such comments were rarely, if ever, spoken in the United States at the time. Clifford Webb of London's *Daily Herald* said Ruth had "travelled 21,000 miles around the world since last October to try and forget the game which brought him in nearly £20,000 a year for an awfully long time."[10]

"I'm on my first real holiday," the despondent Ruth told David Walker of London's *Daily Mirror*, comparing himself to "a man on the way to the gallows." Ruth felt he was just a pawn of the Yankees. "I'm their property—that's all," he bemoaned. "They bought me for $125,000 and I guess I'm theirs now. Bought outright. Just a slave." If only he had lived long enough to have a chat with Curt Flood.

"Will you become their manager when you retire?" he was asked.

Ruth shrugged. "How can I tell? They own me. They can scrap me or keep me. I'm merely a pawn. I'm a slave, that's what I am—just a slave."[11] Yet Ruth desperately wanted to stay in that institution which treated him as a piece of merchandise to attract cash-paying customers.

On his own, who was he?

"I'd Be Lost Without the Game."

On Wednesday, February 20, the luxury liner S.S. *Manhattan* docked at Pier 60 in New York City. Also arriving to little fanfare was English actor Clive Brook, famous for portraying Sherlock Holmes in three films.[12] The crowd stirred as an orchestra launched into "Take Me Out to the Ballgame" when Babe Ruth and family stepped back onto United States soil after four months. Rud Rennie in the *New York Tribune* called him "a portly ruler without a throne and without definite plans."[13] Ruth made his way down to the lounge on the promenade deck. The whiskey was on him, he announced as he gave "indefinite answers to definite questions" to the reporters swarming him.[14]

"I don't want to leave baseball," Ruth said. "I'd be lost without the game. I want to get back into a uniform. It's hard to stay away from the game after being in it so long. I think I'm entitled to a manager's job, or a try at it anyhow. I don't think I should be asked to sign as a player and sit on a bench waiting for a chance to pinch-hit maybe once in seven days."[15] Claire Ruth was afraid of "sitting out in the grandstand every day with clenched fists," watching Babe play. "He was hurt three times last season and I want no more of that," she said. But she also acknowledged, "I realize he can't be happy unless he is playing baseball."[16] The Yankees' provisional $1-a-year complimentary contract was waiting in his mailbox at home.[17]

What about the Braves? "I thought they made a dog track out of that," he joked. "Seems to me I heard something about that. But about managing there? No, nobody even talked to me about that, ever."[18]

Others had talked about it. Back in Boston, Judge Fuchs and Yankees owner Jacob Ruppert had met while Ruth was at sea. Their plan would satisfy everyone: Ruppert would place Ruth on waivers, knowing no team was interested in claiming him as a player. After clearing waivers, Ruth could sign with the Braves with an offer to be assistant manager, a second vice president, and play as much as possible. Maybe he could manage the Braves in 1936. "We would welcome Ruth with a brass band," Fuchs said. "He could be a player, coach or have a shiny mahogany desk in the front office on which to rest his pipe-stem legs while smoking those big, black cigars. We would be able to pay him as much as Col. Ruppert has offered, which I understand is $20,000." Lou Gehrig ($31,000) was now the highest-paid player in the game, but Ruth's salary still ranked among the highest in the game. How could one of the poorest teams afford that? Fuchs claimed "several wealthy local men" were prepared to finance the deal if Ruth was brought in. It was now up to Ruth.[19]

Ruth wasn't in a hurry. He went home, spent Thursday unpacking, and later met with Ruppert one more time. Ruppert assured him Joe McCarthy was secure as Yankees manager, but there was a possibility with the Braves. On Friday, Ruth went golfing in Vermont, not realizing the snow was too deep.[20] Sometime on Friday, Fuchs talked to Ruth by phone and laid out the plan. Fuchs followed it up with a letter on Saturday, February 23:

My Dear George:

In order that we may have a complete understanding, I am putting in the form of a letter the situation affecting our long-distance conversation of yesterday.

The Boston Braves offer you the following inducements, under the terms and conditions herein set forth, in order to have you sign a uniform contract plus an additional contract which will further protect you, both contracts to be filed.

    1. The Boston club offers you a straight salary contract.
    2. They offer you an official executive position as an officer of the corporation.
    3. The Boston club offers you also the position, for 1935, of assistant manager.
    4. They offer you a share of the profits during the term of this contract.
    5. They offer you an option to purchase, at a reasonable figure, some of the stock of the club.
    6. The details of the amounts agreed upon will be the basis of a separate contract which shall be a personal one between you and the club, and, as the case may be, with the individual officials and stockholders of the club.

In consideration of this offer, the Boston club naturally will expect you to do everything in your power for the welfare and interest of the club and will expect that you will endeavor to play in the games whenever possible, as well as carry out the duties above specified.

May I also give you the picture as I see it, which, in my opinion, will terminate to the best and mutual interest of all concerned.

You have been a great asset to all baseball, especially to the American League, but nowhere in the land are you more admired than in the territory of New England that has always claimed you as its own and where you started your career to fame.

The fans of New England have a great deal of affection for you, and from my personal experience with them are the most appreciative men and women in America, providing, of course, that you keep faith, continue your generous cooperation in helping civically and being a source of consolation to the children, as well as to the needy, who look up to you as a shining example of what the great athletes and public figures of America should be.

I say frankly, from my experience of forty years interest in baseball, that your greatest value to a ball club would be your personal appearance on the field, and particularly your participation in the active playing of exhibition games, on the ball field in championship games, as well as the master-minding and psychology of the game, in which you would participate as assistant manager.

As a player, I have observed and admired your baseball intelligence, for during your entire career I have never seen you make a wrong play or throw a ball to the wrong base, which leads us to your ability to manage a major league baseball club. In this respect we both are fortunate in having so great a character as Bill McKechnie, our present manager of the club, who has given so much to baseball and whom I count among my closest friends. Bill McKechnie's entire desire would be for the success of the Braves, especially financially, as he is one of the most unselfish, devoted friends that a man can have.

That spirit of McKechnie's is entirely returned by me, and I know by my colleagues in the ball club. They feel, as I do, that nothing would ever be done until we have amply rewarded Manager Bill McKechnie for his loyalty, his ability and sincerity, which means this, George, that if it was determined, after your affiliation with the ball club in 1935, that it was for the mutual interest of the club for you to take up the active management on the field, there would be absolutely no handicap in having you so appointed.

It may be that you will want to devote your future years to becoming an owner or part owner of a major league ball club. It may be that you may discover that what the people are really looking forward to and appreciate in you is the color and activity that you give to the game by virtue of your hitting and playing and that you would rather have someone else, accustomed to the hardships and drudgery of managing a ballclub, continue that task.

So that if we could enter into the spirit of that agreement, such understanding might go on indefinitely, always having in mind that we owe a duty to the public of New England that I have personally learned to love for its sense of fairness and loyalty, and it is also in this spirit that I hope we may be able to jot down a few figures of record that will prove satisfactory to all concerned.

                    Sincerely yours,
                    Emil E. Fuchs, President[21]

Most notable in the letter is Fuchs' expectations of Ruth's "active playing of exhibition games" and doing "everything in your power for the welfare and interest of the club." Fuchs needed a mere Ruth appearance to assure strong attendance and bail out the franchise. Fuchs wasn't looking for a baseball star, although those Ruthian home runs wouldn't hurt. Yet, how would "do everything in your power for the welfare of the club" be evaluated? With references to Ruth's civic endeavors of "helping civically and being a source of consolation to the children, as well as to the needy, who look up to you as a shining example of what the great athletes and public figures of America should be," Fuchs needed the larger-than-life hero. Fuchs may as well have been asking for a Messiah to lead Boston to the Promised Land.

Ruth had gone hunting, so it's unknown when he read the letter.[22] It was a brief trip, though, as on Sunday night the 24th, Fuchs met Ruth for dinner. Fuchs hyped what Ruth's many roles would be. "I was to have more titles than an incurable lodge joiner," Ruth later said to ghostwriter Bob Considine. "I didn't realize it at the time, but Fuchs, like [Harry] Frazee of the old Red Sox, had bought the Braves largely on speculation and was heavily extended. He hoped that by capitalizing on my popularity and by exhibiting me in the National League he could get himself out of the red."[23]

This was not the first time Fuchs had asked Ruth for a favor. The Bambino held out in a contract squabble with Ruppert in 1930, and his absence in the Yankees' lineup would have financially hurt Fuchs in a spring training game. Ruth and Ruppert were close to a contract. Ruth left their meeting and ran into Fuchs, hanging around the hotel lobby.

"Did you sign?" Fuchs asked. "No," Ruth replied.

"Too bad. I was hoping you'd sign. We'd have a good crowd tomorrow. Without you, there won't be anyone there. Say, will you do me a favor? Even though you haven't signed, will you play tomorrow ... your first appearance ... for a couple of innings ... it would help a lot."

"Sure," Babe said enthusiastically. "I'll play if it will help you."

Ruth went home and relayed the news to Claire. He had rejected the Yankees offer of $80,000 for one year. Ruth wanted two years for $160,000. But he felt good about playing the exhibition game anyway, to help the Judge. Claire wanted nothing to do with it. "Suppose you get hurt tomorrow. Suppose you break a leg. Do you think the Yankees are going to give you $80,000 a year with a broken leg?"

"Oh boy!" Ruth exclaimed. He had never even thought of that.

He quickly went back to Ruppert, and within the hour agreed to the two-year contract.[24] The deal served Fuchs well. A crowd of 4,500 was the largest crowd to attend a spring contest in St. Petersburg, Florida, Ruth being the draw.[25]

Five years later, both men needed each other again. Fuchs still needed a gate attraction, and Ruth needed a place to feel wanted.[26] Ruth felt wanted with the showering of fancy titles, although no one knew what a second vice-president or assistant manager actually did. Some would say Fuchs was deceiving Ruth with the offer, but Marshall Smelser may have the best explanation. "The letter is not evidence of ill will," he wrote, "it is just the work of the inexact and foggy mind of a desperate man who hopes that things will turn out well and that nobody will be angry."[27]

A meeting was held between Fuchs and Ruppert on Monday, February 25, at Ruppert's brewery. The meeting flew under the radar of newspaper reporters. In the meantime, Ruth delivered a motivational speech to a group of 800 homeless men in Orange County, New York, near his hunting site. They were at Camp Greycourt, an experimental agricultural farm created to get homeless men off the streets and into jobs picking potatoes, sweet corn, and tomatoes. Ruth was considering a pay cut to come to the Braves for $25,000 a year. These down-and-outers were making $6 a day, but they were the first to hear Ruth declare he was still a player. Ruth said he "definitely decided to play baseball for several more years because games I played in Japan demonstrated I am good for several more years. A decision about my future will be made and probably announced in the next day or two."[28]

A letter from Fuchs to Ruppert dated February 25 summarized the deal.

My dear Colonel Ruppert: The following are the opportunities which we offer Babe Ruth if you are still inclined to give him the chance which he requests—namely, to join with us of the Braves:

1. *Straight salary contract.*
2. *An official executive position—namely, vice president of the club.*
3. *Assistant manager of the club.*
4. *Share of profits.*
5. *An option to purchase stock.*
6. *An opportunity to become a part owner.*

Men in any walk of life who are as fair and generous as you have been in these dealings with me and who have been as loyal and kind as you have been with Babe Ruth are very rare, and everybody joins me in appreciation.

Sincerely, Emil E. Fuchs,
President[29]

Ruth cleared waivers, no other team taking a chance on him. "You are free to sign with the Braves if that is your desire," the Colonel said.[30] The greatest celebrity the game had ever seen was given away for nothing, costing Ruppert only $47.50 in long-distance calls.[31] "Do you think I would sell this man?" said Ruppert. "It just happens we cannot satisfy him this time, and if he can better himself somewhere, the New York Yankees are not standing in his way."[32]

Fuchs beamed. "I am perfectly willing to make you an executive vice-president of the club where you will continue to be connected with the Braves when your playing days are over. As to your suggestion of assistant manager, I will be glad to announce that position with the understanding that the circumstances which compelled Colonel Ruppert to deny you the position of manager have changed, in which event I will not stand in your way if you can qualify as a big-league manager."[33]

Fuchs reaffirmed that Bill McKechnie was manager, but his letter dangled the carrot of *ifs* for 1936. To Ruth, *if* meant *will*. In a best-case-scenario, Ruth would succeed, Fuchs would save the Braves, money would flow in through the clicking turnstiles, and everyone would have a smile on their face. Ruth would become manager

Ruth's legendary Yankees career came to an end when owner Jacob Ruppert (right) placed Ruth on waivers, allowing him to sign with the Braves. His new boss was Judge Fuchs (left) (courtesy Boston Public Library, Leslie Jones Collection).

in 1936 by popular choice, Braves Field would become the House that Ruth Saved, and McKechnie would graciously step aside for his old pal, Ruth. It felt like an afternoon matinee. Reality was far from Hollywood. The $25,000 contract offered to Ruth was "a last hurrah in the face of extinction," in the words of Robert S. Fuchs and Wayne Soini. "Both [Ruth and Fuchs] looked for a second wind, a rebirth, a miracle at Braves Field in 1935."[34]

Ruppert was desperate to part ways with his icon while avoiding any negative publicity. Ruth was no longer desperate. "Don't you think I ought to get a percentage of the exhibition games?" he boldly asked.

The question pierced Fuchs to his core, and he remembered it decades later. He offered everything he could muster, and still Ruth wanted more. "I don't want you to invest any money in the Braves," the Judge told him. "But I will set aside a substantial lot of stock so that if you bring the Braves up to a paying proposition, you will reap the benefits of it in addition to your salary and share of the exhibition games." The deal was solely "an opportunity to save Babe Ruth for baseball while he saved the Braves for the Judge." Lost in all this was McKechnie, who was never consulted.[35]

A deal was put in place and "Ruppert thus got rid of his demigod in a seemingly dignified way," Smelser wrote, while "Fuchs satisfied the whim of Governor Curley, chief of his ticket-sellers. And it was faintly possible that Fuchs could still squeeze some profit out of Ruth's popularity."[36] Ruth received a three-year contract as a player, assistant manager, and second vice president.

"If he wants my position as first vice president, he can have it," a snarky Adams said to reporters the next day.[37]

A press conference was called for February 26 at Ruppert's brewery.

The Press Conference

Ruth sent a letter to Fuchs dated February 26.

> *My dear Judge: The generosity of Colonel Ruppert enables me to accept the attractive offer and opportunity of the Boston Braves as contained in your kind letter of Feb. 23.*
>
> *I join with you in the sentiments as well as the spirit expressed in that letter. I shall always remember with tender recollection and appreciation the farewell testimonial accorded me at Fenway Park.*
>
> *Mrs. Ruth and our daughter join me in the expression of our joy in again being with the kindly and fair people of Boston and its surroundings.*
>
> *I am mindful of the great battle and sacrifice you have made to give Boston a good ball club and a winner. I shall fight shoulder to shoulder with you, our associates, Charles F. Adams, and Bruce Wetmore; and that great character, my friend Bill McKechnie, and my old pal Rabbit Maranville—we being the last of the two Mohicans—in giving the best I have in me, to the end that the great sportsmanship of Boston and New England may be deservedly rewarded for their loyalty and support.*
>
> *In the spirit of the memory of Christy Mathewson, that we both hold sacred, and who came to Boston almost fourteen years ago, the culmination of my long friendship with you, I pledge to you and to the people of New England that we shall keep the faith.*
>
> *I shall give to the National League the same measure of allegiance, loyalty, and effort that I gave in the past to the American League.*
>
> > *Sincerely, your friend.*
> > *Babe Ruthe Ruth*[38]

Fuchs wrote a follow-up letter to Ruth verifying the terms. "If the terms and conditions contained in the uniform contract," he wrote, "as well as in the letter dated February 23rd, are lived up to and conformed with, you have the choice and right to be the manager of the Boston National League Baseball Club for the season of 1936 and 1937." Ruth felt becoming Braves manager was just a matter of time as he ignored the ambiguous and unmeasurable expectations.

Nevertheless, he would receive 15 percent of all gate receipts over and above the average net gate receipts from 1929 to 1934. Three of those years had been net losses.[39] Ruth declined to purchase stock, probably the smartest decision he made. He would receive 25 percent of all the net profits from exhibition games.[40]

The press conference was "acclaimed over foaming steins of beer that vanished miraculously down the Ruthian gullet," wrote George Dixon in the *New York Daily News*. "With a beaker of suds in one hand and a half-chewed cigar in the other, Ruth pledged allegiance to Judge Emil Fuchs, his new boss, who stood beaming beside his new acquisition."[41] Ruppert was perhaps the happiest of them all. "Today I hand Ruth his unconditional release," he beamed, accentuating *his* generosity.

> I get not a penny in return, not a promise, nothing. Ruth is a free man. Ruth has always been a credit to baseball, and it has always been a pleasure to have had him with us. We regret that our long association is ending. We will miss him, but his future is of paramount importance. Baseball needs Ruth, just as Ruth needs baseball, and in giving him his release I offer him my heartiest congratulations and hope sincerely he will continue the success that has been his for so long a time.[42]

What about McKechnie? Fuchs unconvincingly said, "Babe will assist him, but in addition Babe will be vice president. They will get along very well together. They will share authority." How could Ruth assist a man called "one of the brainiest managers in baseball" by Jack Barnwell in the *Boston Post*, who "has done more with 10-cent material than any manager in the business?"[43] "No ball club can have two managers," McKechnie said, already at spring training in Florida.[44] "Unless he dons a uniform and is able to take part in the game, he wouldn't be worth a nickel to any club. He is a popular hero, but baseball fans are fickle."[45]

What does a second vice president do? "Why, a vice-president signs checks," Ruppert stammered. "Everybody knows that." "That's right," Fuchs seconded. "I'll give him a check now if he'll sign it."[46]

They were off to a great start.

"I'm sorry to leave New York," Ruth said, "but I'm glad to be going back to Boston. This is just the kind of spot I wanted."[47] Ruth estimated he would play in 100 games. "I'm in good shape and I've got a lot of baseball still left in me," he boasted.[48] And reporters ate it all up.

James C. O'Leary in the *Globe* called the signing "a masterful stroke of business" and said Ruth "still is a powerful box-office attraction, and probably will be for some time."[49] *Globe* writer Hy Hurwitz called Ruth "the greatest individual performer the national pastime has ever known."[50] Grantland Rice wrote that Ruth "no longer is a Babe lost in the woods. He's heading home again."[51] Burt Whitman of the *Boston Herald* wrote, "the Yankees have given away, to the Boston Braves, the most colorful figure baseball has ever seen."[52] At least one oddsmaker, Tom Kearney in St. Louis, increased the odds of the Braves winning the pennant from 40–1 to 10–1.[53]

Not every writer was thrilled. Pat Robinson of the *Worcester Evening Gazette* wrote, "He (Ruth) also becomes vice-president and assistant manager—whatever that may mean—and an option to purchase stock in a club already sunk in the red." Ruth was like "an old fire horse which has outlived its usefulness between the shafts," only to "pass his declining days in the pasture of the Boston Braves."[54] "Color does not win ball games," said the *Herald*, "but it makes the turnstiles click merrily."[55]

Bill Cunningham of the *Boston Post* wrote, "Babe Ruth is nothing but a sentimental problem. If he were what he is, and broke, the case would be tantamount to a national issue. Far from broke, he's so well fixed with a fool proof financial arrangement that if the country holds together and anybody's money's any good, he can pent-house it from here to the end of his days if those days run on into the 21st century. No tears are in order."[56]

There were no tears as Ruth and Fuchs left the press conference around 3 p.m. Children flocked to Ruth and were disappointed when their hero said he signed with Boston. Ruth continued signing autographs long after Fuchs hurried off to his 4 p.m. train.[57] Fuchs had preparations to make for a welcome home banquet on Thursday night, February 28.

Back in New York, Ruth went to the Customs House to pick up his knick knacks from Japan. "I'll be assistant manager for a while," he promised, "but I'm to become the real manager. I have a definite agreement to replace Bill McKechnie as manager of the 1936 season."[58] "But I want it made clear that first I must be assured that Bill McKechnie, a great fellow and a rare manager, is fully taken care of if I take his place."[59]

"Ruth to Lead Braves in 1936" was a *Globe* headline the next day.[60] Many expected it to happen before 1936, with McKechnie moving up to the front office.[61]

"What would I do in an office?" McKechnie wanted to know.[62]

A Banquet for the Babe

Ruth bundled up in his bulky overcoat and donned his cap, both keepsakes from London, to enter the train with Claire at Grand Central Station. A crowd in the hundreds was waiting for him, including youngsters seeking autographs. A policeman escorted him through the spectacle. Ruth spoke, signed, and waved. Ruth waved farewell and entered the train, followed by reporters. Ruth entertained them with stories of his world travels. He talked to them with gusto while devouring broiled scrod, baked beans, and brown bread. "We're on our way to become real Bostonians again," he chuckled. The passengers were surprisingly polite, not mobbing him for autographs. One lady tapped him on the shoulder and said, "I do hope you make a lot of touchdowns, Mr. Ruth!"[63]

The train stopped in Providence, Rhode Island. Hundreds of fans were pressed against the gate to catch a glimpse. Judge Fuchs got on board and posed for pictures with Babe and Claire on the steps. Off they went, holding an unofficial press conference. A larger crowd formed at the New Haven, Connecticut, station, and Boston newspaper reporters jumped on board. "Besides newspaper reporters, there was a crew from a Boston radio station," Fuchs recalled. "Once we got within range of the city, they had the Babe speak to the fans. It was said to be the first time a broadcast had been made from a moving train."[64]

It was a spectacle on that cold night in Boston as Babe Ruth stepped off the train at Back Bay Station at 5:40 p.m. A huge crowd at the platform breathlessly awaited his arrival.

James C. O'Leary wrote, "No king, potentate or conquering hero was ever given a more enthusiastic welcome."[65] Jack Barnwell in the *Post* wrote, "No greater manifestation of hero worship has ever been tendered in the history of the city."[66] As the train "rolled into the murky Back Bay Station, the roar of welcome burst forth from the throats of thousands of admirers to drown out the last, lusty puffs of the giant locomotive that dragged the celebrated Bambino here in palatial fashion."[67] Ruth could look out the train windows and see a crowd estimated at 8,000. He said it was even greater than the bobsled ride he took in Switzerland.[68]

Police fought the mob to clear a path while Ruth chomped on a fat cigar and was already noticeably perspiring. Claire, decked out in a silk black frock and mink coat, was presented a bouquet. They cleared the first mass of humanity and made it up the stairs to the street level. Another crowd was waiting for them. "Tears of emotion could be seen creeping into the eyes of the Babe as he stood motionless before that vast assembly," Barnwell wrote. "He was struck in such a manner that he seemed powerless to take another step."[69] In France, he felt lonely and unnoticed. In Boston, he was exhausted. Everyone wanted to greet him.

Babe and Claire Ruth arrive at Boston's Back Bay train station. Judge Fuchs is directly between the couple. Charles F. Adams is standing in the back on the right in a dark hat (courtesy Boston Public Library, Leslie Jones Collection).

A cab was waiting for him. "Naw," Babe waved off the offer. "I know where the Copley Plaza is. It's only a few steps. Let's walk."[70] With the crowd, it took 30 minutes to get to the Dartmouth Street entrance.[71] Ruth bumped his way through the revolving doors and leaned against the wall, his hand trembling from all the handshakes, sweat pouring down his face. "Boy, oh, boy," he wheezed, "I didn't get any the better of that."[72]

Flash bulbs popped nonstop. The police couldn't get Ruth to his suite, so they took him up a half-light of stairs to the Braves' little two-room office. Soon the door pushed open, and the room was cramped with reporters. They obeyed Fuchs' pleas to let Ruth retire to his suite upstairs. After a shower, Ruth remarked, "Gee, this is certainly some town. There's a great gang here. This is home to me. I suppose I'll have to go through it all again tonight, but I can still take another shower."[73] He would never have time.

Ruth made his way down to a suite Fuchs reserved for the contract signing. "No less than 35 cameras were there to greet him," Barnwell wrote. Ruth sat down behind a long table with Fuchs and Adams. He quickly signed contracts as the cameras flashed. "Gee, kid," Ruth said, "there are more bulbs in this room now than there are on Broadway."[74] Ruth again retired to his suite to rest up for the official banquet in the Swiss Room. Nearly everybody in the Boston political, business, and newspaper worlds were there.[75]

The ceremony began. "Babe," Fuchs said in a rambling opening introduction which almost seemed apologetic, "we are mighty glad to have you with us in Boston. I've given my word to Bill McKechnie that he is to stay as manager this season, and I won't go back on it. I would rather walk out of here without a nickel than to violate my word of honor. Babe and Bill will work together, and the Babe has a chance to become the manager in 1936 and '37."[76]

"You are the hero of the children of the state," proclaimed Lieutenant Governor Joseph Leo Hurley, "and that is why we are glad to have you back in Boston. You are the best sportsman in a generation."[77]

"I'm going to call you my friends," Ruth said glowingly, "and want to say that it hurt me worse to leave you 15 years ago than it did you. New York has been wonderful to me, but my first love, without a doubt, is Boston." He spoke kindly of McKechnie. "I will obey him to the limit," he promised, "If he asks me for advice, I will give it to him gladly."[78] Cameras flashed so much that Ruth asked for a pair of sunglasses. "Say, aren't you out of bulbs yet?"[79]

"I can't play forever," Ruth admitted. "Somebody has got to fill my shoes sometime. But you can bet your sweet life I won't play until I drop, although I will play until I nearly drop."[80]

Adams gave the final speech of the night, and Fuchs, hailing him in an introduction, likely had no idea what C.F. had in store. Ruth figured it was a done deal, while Fuchs painted an optimistic picture. But the grocery store entrepreneur who cut his teeth on results and bottom lines showed no hint of such fervor. Adams stated

Ruth signs with the Braves between Charles F. Adams (left) and Judge Fuchs (courtesy Boston Public Library, Leslie Jones Collection).

that Ruth would become manager in 1936 *only* if he proved capable to do so and had any interest in it by then.

> I certainly hope that the Babe realizes his ambition and that he will merit the position he has so much desired. He has much to learn in the next few months. To succeed he must gain the confidence of the public, press and owners of the Boston club. He must learn to be a good soldier if he is not one already. He must, by his own example, create loyalty and respect within and without the club. This having been established, there is little doubt but that the Babe will merit the best the club has to offer."[81]

Adams mentioned the great complexities in choosing personnel from the top of the organization down to the bat boy and dealing with the constant irritation of second-guessers. "No one can ever be fit to give orders until he has learned to take orders," Adams said, giving advice based on running a grocery business. "Once having the responsibilities of riding a bucking broncho—a big league baseball club—though the Babe can whether the gale, many the time he will say to himself, 'I was happier as a lieutenant to Bill than as a boss without him.'"[82] He added, to stab more

Ruth shaking hands with his new manager, Bill McKechnie (courtesy Boston Public Library, Leslie Jones Collection).

plans with a dagger, "Judging from Ruth's past career, we can hardly consider him of managerial caliber now."[83]

What about Bill McKechnie? "If he so elects," Adams said, "Bill McKechnie will become my personal representative, speak and act for me in the Braves organization, have my unqualified proxy to carry on whatever official responsibility and authority I properly should shoulder."[84] Imagine the awkwardness of Fuchs vs. Adams, the fan vs. the businessman, optimism vs skepticism. Ruth was still glowing from the flash bulbs, but the true attention should have been focused on a confused ownership.

Little attention was paid to the table where Claire Ruth, Oretta Fuchs, and other women dined. Fortunately, Grace Davidson of the *Boston Post* reported on the female perspective of the event. The hectic evening was just one of many for Claire, as taking care of the Babe was a fulltime job. She had been constantly packing and unpacking on their trip around the world, only to come back to the States and do it again for this harried Boston excursion. "You have no idea what it is to look after the Babe," she told Davidson. "Not that he isn't most helpful, thoughtful, but the work

Babe and Claire have a few minutes to relax at the Copley Plaza Hotel (courtesy Boston Public Library, Leslie Jones Collection).

he has to do is so tremendous that all the details of looking after him fall to me. There isn't a day that there isn't 15 to 20 telegrams to write." Claire had been stepped on by a fan rushing through the crowd on the way to the hotel. "He just couldn't get to the Babe fast enough," she said, showing a permanent heel print left on her stockings. "I didn't take anything along but an overnight case for the train, and so I will have to wear this pair of stockings tonight."[85]

The role of Claire Ruth shouldn't go overlooked. The tamed Ruth of the mid–1930s was a direct contrast to the rambunctious Ruth of the 1920s. Claire was a major reason for the difference. "With Claire's help," wrote Smelser, "he (Ruth) struggled successfully to order his life. Babe became more than a friendly, loudmouthed adolescent who happened to be catlike on the baseball field. He became a respected person."[86] Claire put boundaries on his diet and spending and accompanied him on road trips to make sure he wasn't out all night. "Isn't it reasonable to suggest," asked Robert Creamer, "that Claire, who for all her physical and social attractiveness was sometimes a nag, became his mother?" Babe's alienation from his own parents led to

Claire Ruth (second from left) with Oretta Fuchs (at her left) at the welcoming banquet in Boston (courtesy Boston Public Library, Leslie Jones Collection).

a man who "demanded the attention and affection of the world," and "he was forever seeking approval and gratification."[87]

That dependency may have cost him a managerial career. The good ol' boys club controlling the game had a gentleman's agreement not to sign players of color, and neither did they have time for the opinions of a woman. "Claire Ruth remained a stumbling point for many in the baseball establishment," wrote Edmund F. Wehrle. "Opinionated and enthralled by the business of baseball, she was no silent partner. Claire operated outspokenly in an almost exclusively male world; it was noticed and resented."[88] Perhaps Ruppert and Ed Barrow had the same qualms as Connie Mack did. With Claire's guidance and his mellowing over time, Ruth learned to manage himself better. Perhaps the baseball establishment feared Ruth not handling a team and a woman having a say. Davidson alone reminded readers, "the real work falls on Mrs. Babe Ruth, even though she doesn't swing her husband's mighty bat."[89]

The evening dragged on. After dinner, Ruth and Fuchs re-enacted, the contract signing for the newsreel. Then more autographs. The party moved on to another suite, with more reporters waiting. Ruth autographed six dozen baseballs while

Ruth addressing the banquet attendees at Boston's Copley Plaza Hotel (courtesy Boston Public Library, Leslie Jones Collection).

Claire and Oretta Fuchs chatted the evening away. Babe tired out first and impatiently called to her that it was time to leave.

They made their way to Back Bay Station for the midnight train to New York. Fans recognized him at the station and wanted autographs. A fan asked him what would happen if a baseball runner was hit on the head with a batted ball and died instantly. Who was out? Ruth wasn't sure, probably because of the pounding in his own head.

The train arrived and the Ruths waved goodbye. "See you in April," Claire said merrily. "It'll take me two days to recuperate," the Babe said.[90]

6

The Babe Goes to Spring Training
(March 1935)

"Whatever his athletic possibilities may be, his attractiveness to the fans is beyond question. He is that rare thing, a living tradition. Folks love to look at him, talk about him, think of the times he was mighty. They will still pay for the privilege of watching him bat 'em to the outfield in the pregame practice."[1]—*Boston Herald* on Babe Ruth

"When you quit bothering me to sign autographs, then I'll know I'm through. Slip me the old apple and a pen. And tell 'em to keep on bothering me."—Babe Ruth

On to the Sunshine State

Babe and Claire Ruth arrived at Penn Station on March 3 and prepared to step aboard the Orange Blossom Special. The famous Pullman train, which would have a fiddle tune named for it, brought northeast residents to their Florida winter excursions in style. Wealthy tourists and shrewd businessmen were part of a steady population boom in Florida. Ruth was dressed all in brown from his cap to his shoes. "Say, there ought to be a lot of fun down in St. Pete," he promised. "Won't our spring series with the Yanks pack 'em in?" Two little boys on the platform, ages seven and five, told Ruth they had swung their allegiances from the Yankees to the Braves. "I can sock a ball, too," the littlest one boasted. Ruth chuckled. "That's right, son, keep your eye on that ball!"[2]

The Seaboard Air Line train pulled out at 12:35 p.m. on March 3 with a scheduled St. Petersburg arrival at 5:40 p.m. on March 4. As soon as the conductor yelled, "All aboard!" Ruth realized he had forgotten his golf clubs. A train official said he would arrange for them to be picked up and sent on the next train.

"It's still like a dream to me," Ruth said. "I can't quite realize I won't trot out into the Yankee Stadium for the opening game next month. But I'm tickled to death with the switch. It's a break for me and I certainly hope it's going to mean I can help the Braves go places this year." He brushed off a question about Bill McKechnie. "All I ask is that they let Bill and me alone. I'm satisfied to let next year take care of itself."[3] The train pulled into a stop at Wildwood, Florida. A crowd of boys saw Ruth

Babe Ruth, with his back against a car, is mobbed by 3,000 fans upon arriving in St. Petersburg, Florida (Saint Petersburg Times via ZUMA Press; IMAGO via ZUMA Press).

in the window and rushed the train, seeking autographs. The train was delayed several minutes, but Ruth didn't mind. Nearly every stop had an impromptu welcoming of the Babe.[4]

Fans began gathering at the St. Petersburg station an hour before the train's arrival to see "still the brightest star in the baseball constellation," as Paul H. Shannon wrote in the *Boston Post*.[5] At least 3,000 fans greeted Ruth as he exited the train. "From the tops of parked cars, unused freight trains, freight platforms, scrapped cars and letterboxes others hung, yelling their vociferous welcome when the brown-clad, bulky figure of Ruth, perspiring and protesting good-naturedly, stepped down the train steps," reported the *New York Times*.[6] The crowd packed the station "to get a close-up of the perspiring but delighted veteran," wrote Alan Gould of the Associated Press.[7]

"It sure makes a fellow feel good to know that so many people are interested in him," Ruth said with a grin.[8] One of those there to greet him was Al Lang.

Albert Fielding Lang was a Pittsburgh businessman whose respiratory problems led him to the fresh air of Florida. He moved to tiny St. Petersburg in 1910 and in just a few years put it on the baseball map. Club owners at the time were skeptical of sending their teams all the way to Florida for spring training. Lang became a successful realtor who built a baseball stadium to entice the Browns (1914) and Phillies (1915) to the spring training facilities. Lang became mayor and was later known as the "Mr. Baseball" of Florida. The Braves moved to St. Petersburg in 1922, and a January ad in the *Boston Globe* that year invited readers to come enjoy the Braves in the nice 76-degree weather. St. Petersburg became a baseball hub when the Yankees made the city their home in 1925. Fans in the Northeast now learned of the city where Babe Ruth was galivanting around. Now Ruth would play against his old team and bring nationwide attention to Lang and his city.[9]

"Where's Bill McKechnie?" Ruth asked.[10] Deacon Bill was somewhere in the crowd, but it would be much easier to meet in a less chaotic setting. They needed to get Ruth to Billy DeBeck's car. DeBeck was the famous cartoonist of the era known for his creation of the *Barney Google* comic strip and his colorful use of the English language. DeBeck brought "Sweet Mama," "heebie jeebies," "balls o' fire" and "times a' wastin'" to the American lexicon.[11] Time was a wastin' as it took police 15 minutes to push Ruth, Claire, and Lang into DeBeck's car.

Finally, McKechnie and coach Hank Gowdy made their way to shake Ruth's hand through the car window. The vehicle couldn't go forward because of the crowd, so they backed up through the freight terminal. DeBeck whisked the Ruths away to their temporary home: a bungalow at 346 16th Avenue NE. McKechnie and Gowdy met him there later.

They posed for pictures. "What time do you practice in the morning, Bill? 10:45. Whoa, I'll have to get an alarm clock, I guess," Ruth said. "Leave us alone and we'll get along great," he said about his new manager. He was interested in playing first base like he did in Japan to save on his feet. "My weight's OK," he assured them, "but don't forget I've been loafing since the Orient trip and have done very little exercising. That's the trouble."[12] Reporters had to ask him what he was eating for supper.

"Aw, I'm not a heavy eater anymore," he said. "I'll have some of those stone crabs before I leave, but not as many as I used to stack away." He called to Claire, his secretary, homemaker, and nutritionist all rolled into one, who popped out to the doorway to clarify his menu. "He'll be lucky to get scrambled eggs and bacon tonight," she said. "And after supper he's going to stay in and help me unpack. He's going to have all his meals at home both here and in Boston." And early to bed, so the Babe was done for the day. "See all you guys at the ballpark in the morning," he waved.[13]

Training Camp Begins

A scorching sun was over Waterfront Park as Babe Ruth officially joined his new team. Billy DeBeck dropped him off at 10:15 a.m., a half-hour before practice. There were already 5,000 fans gathered outside the park, waiting for him. "He is still the greatest drawing card of them all," wrote Alan Gould.[14] The first to greet him was fellow geriatric Rabbit Maranville, three years Ruth's senior but, at 5'5" and 155 pounds, overshadowed by the 6'2" and 230-something-pound Ruth. Ruth and Maranville gave the Braves two legends who starred in Boston 21 years before. "Both sowed plenty of wild oats along the way and reformed in time to make sensational comebacks," said the *Boston Herald*. "Now, at the age when most of their contemporaries have taken to the rocking chair, they are still at it."[15]

"Hello, you big ape," Rabbit teased. "How are you?"

"Great, you little punk," Ruth fired back as the two pretended to box.[16]

Walter James Vincent Maranville was born in Springfield, Massachusetts, on November 11, 1891. He failed as a pipefitter apprentice because he was more focused on bats and balls. At 19, he was playing for the New Bedford Whalers of the New England League. He claimed that a seven-year-old girl gave him the nickname of "Rabbit" because she liked to watch him hop and jump around the field. He was known for making vest-pocket catches by holding his glove at his belly button. Antics and clowning made Rabbit Maranville a legend.[17]

Maranville played a key role in the 1914 "Miracle Braves" World Series championship. He stayed with the Braves through 1921, then moved on to Pittsburgh, the Cubs, Dodgers, and Cardinals before returning to the Braves in 1929. Sabermetrics guru Bill James lists him as the #4 defensive shortstop of all time.[18] "He made a mockery of the game and he was so good that he got by with it," James wrote.[19] Maranville missed all of 1934 after breaking his leg in spring training and was still limping around.[20] Two of baseball's biggest personalities were now teammates.

Ruth's uniform hadn't arrived, so he wore two flannel shirts, borrowed a pair of catcher Shanty Hogan's socks, and wore Hank Gowdy's pants, his derriere barely squeezing into them with the help of elastic V inserts. The team met in the middle of the diamond for McKechnie's regular morning briefing. He invited Ruth to speak.

"Well, fellers," he said, "I didn't come here to talk. But I think this is a wonderful opportunity for all of us this year. I believe that if we all hustle and cooperate with Bill McKechnie, we have pennant possibilities. Anyway, we can give them all hell. So, let's go."[21] He posed for a picture giving Maranville a bearhug. "The two most colorful figures in baseball," Shannon wrote. "It's going to be a lot of fun to play on the same team with that little devil," Ruth said. "I hope that I have as much pep as he's got when I'm his age."[22]

Ruth went up to bat against 32-year-old Ben Cantwell, one of McKechnie's intelligent, dependable pitchers. Cantwell, born in Milan, Tennessee, to a telegraph operator, had started and relieved throughout his eight seasons, winning 20 games in 1933. Ruth fouled off the first two pitches, then smashed the third pitch over the right-field fence and onto a hotel porch, to the delight of the huge crowd. "If we have crowds like that for our exhibition games," Ruth said, "it would give us a real nice start."[23] DeBeck picked up Ruth an hour later, and the two spent the afternoon golfing. Ruth shot an 82.[24]

Crowds followed Ruth everywhere. The following day, March 6, he slammed a home run off 23-year-old Bob Brown. Ruth was "dead tired" and took it easy on

Braves players, from left: OF Tommy Thompson, SS Billy Urbanski, P Bob Smith, P Leo Mangum, 2B Rabbit Maranville, P Flint Rhem, coach Duffy Lewis, P Fred Frankhouse, OF Wally Berger (courtesy Boston Public Library, Leslie Jones Collection).

Friday, resting up for the first exhibition games against Cincinnati over the weekend.[25] He stood behind the batting cage watching Hogan, the man they called the "Babe Ruth of Catchers." Ruth and Hogan took good-natured jabs at each other's weight.

James Francis "Shanty" Hogan, from Somerville, Massachusetts, would turn 29 in a couple of weeks. His bulk made him a stand-in for Ruth, reportedly weighing 280 one season. Harold Kaese of the *Globe* remembered Hogan's "size, slowness and jolly disposition."[26] Hogan was in his second stint with the Braves and had made himself into a valuable catcher. On this day, players feared for his life.

Hogan collapsed after being beaned behind the left ear by Brown. Ruth ran for the clubhouse to get trainer Jimmy Neary as other players raced to Hogan's side. Maranville took Hogan to Mound Park Hospital with a slight concussion.[27]

The Braves played an intra-squad game on March 7, the Yannigans (young players fighting to make the team) versus the regulars. Ruth did not play but slammed two balls over the fence in practice. He watched an inning, then left to visit the Florida Military Academy. He was presented with the title of Honorary Battalion Commander as the band paraded. He spoke words of encouragement to the young cadets. "There's something about a soldier," he said.[28]

A crowd of 5,000 turned out for the free seven-inning game and overflowed the stadium. Just the chance to see Ruth was enough of a draw. The highlight of the game was a home run by Joe Coscarart, whom they called "Coffee Joe."

Joseph Marvin Coscarart and his brothers, Pete and Steve, from Escondido, California, were dubbed "ball playing fools." Their father came from the Basque area of the Pyrenees Mountains of France. Pete had a nine-year major league career. "Coffee Joe" completed six seasons in the minors and now tried to stick with the Braves as an infielder. His home run was inside-the-park, and Coscarart streaked around the bases "as though the sheriff were after him for non-payment of taxes," wrote John Drohan in the *Herald*.[29] The Yannigans won, 2–0.

The Games Begin

On Friday, Wally Berger surrendered his uniform #3 to Ruth and switched to #4. Ruth would make his spring debut at Tampa's Plant Field against Cincinnati. On that same field on April 4, 1919, a thinner and younger Ruth hit one of the longest home runs anyone had ever seen. It cleared the fence, racetrack, and another fence in one swoop. Unofficially, it traveled 587 feet. Burt Whitman in the *Herald* wrote that the ball, "but for the fence would have rolled along to the Gulf of Mexico."[30] The ball was retrieved, and Ruth autographed it for Billy Sunday, the former baseball player turned evangelist, who was holding an old-fashioned revival meeting.[31]

Sixteen years later, Ruth needed a revival. He worked out on Friday and was dripping wet in the clubhouse. "I can truthfully say," he boasted, "that I haven't an ache or pain in my arms or legs, which has been something unusual for me at this stage in the game."[32]

A crowd of 3,500 came out on Saturday, March 9, a larger crowd than anyone could remember for a spring training game. Ruth, despite the new uniform, resembled "the same old Babe in all his portly glory."[33] Children were sitting on the grass in front of the bleachers. They gave Ruth ovation after ovation, even when he merely fouled pitches off. In his first at-bat, Ruth lined a single which scored Billy Urbanski. He moved to second but wasn't swift enough to avoid a Pinky Whitney grounder which caromed off his shuffling legs. "The same old portly Bambino on a pair of toothpick legs," wrote Red Newton in the *Tampa Tribune*.[34]

In the third inning, he hit a high foul popup and immediately started rubbing his arm. "It's nothing," he said later. "I start out swinging too hard. My legs stood up and that's all that's worrying me."[35] He took another mighty swing at Danny MacFayden's curveball, missing it by six inches and turning himself into a pretzel. He finished 1-for-4, had three putouts at first base, and the Braves won, 5–3. With the scores of reporters covering the game, an estimated 30,000 words about Ruth were sent through Western Union telegrams to newspapers around the country.[36]

The Reds blasted the Braves, 12–1, on Sunday, with a 22-hit barrage. Ruth went 0-for-3 but slammed three home runs onto the center field racetrack during batting practice to excite the crowd. "I am not forgetting that I am growing older and that I must expect more or less trouble with my legs in the season ahead," Ruth wrote in Christy Walsh syndicate column.[37]

Ace pitcher Dizzy Dean and his Cardinals made their way to St. Petersburg. When Ruth signed with the Braves, Dean made headlines by questioning his salary. "I don't believe he was ever worth $80,000 a year," Dizzy said. "I don't think I am worth it, and I don't believe there ever will be a player entitled to that much money for playing one season. He made all his money in the American League, so why not stay there? I resent Ruth coming to the National [League] and I think practically every player in the league will feel the same way about it."[38]

Dean's tune changed with a handshake and chat before the photographers. "The newspapers got me wrong," Dean said. "I meant that it was a dirty shame that the American League let you get away."

"That's okay, kid," Ruth replied.

"You're going to mean money in my pocket," Dean continued. "You're going to draw thousands and thousands through the turnstiles. Well, I just wanted to apologize. I didn't want any hard feelings between us."

"That's okay, kid."[39]

Most of the week of March 11 was spent focusing on fundamentals, with the anticipated Saturday game against the Yankees. This was the first of nine meetings for bragging rights of St. Petersburg. Ruth's arm was still sore, and he decided to rest. The press wanted details. "Every time I stub my toe nowadays some wise guy sends out the report that I'm hurted," he said.[40] "I want to stay off the hot sand as long as possible."[41]

Ruth spent time with a punching bag and went golfing several times. "That makes three days off in a row," Gerry Moore wrote in the *Globe*. Meanwhile, creaky Maranville was running laps, skipping rope, and mentoring Coscarart. While Ruth teed off, Rabbit went to the chiropractor. For 25 minutes, Moore wrote, the doctor performed "yanks, twists and turns of 'Rabs' slender leg through 15 of the most agonizing minutes you'd ever want to sit through."[42]

Hogan returned after his beaning. Reporters were busy trying to get McKechnie to comment about whether Ruth, who was barely around the field, would be the manager in 1936. Ruth wrote in his column, "I said last fall that I was prepared to retire from baseball permanently unless I could get a job as manager for 1935. I am glad I did not stick too closely to that. I feel now I would have missed something."[43] The Yannigans played the regulars again, but Ruth was away at a luncheon in Tampa. "According to the second vice-president and assistant manager," grumbled Drohan, "one can't let practice interfere with one's social obligations."[44] The regulars won, 11–1, on the strength of two home runs by Billy Urbanski.

The 31-year-old William Michael Urbanski had spent six seasons in the minors before breaking in with the Braves in 1931. Urbanski and Maranville gave them a solid middle infield from 1932 to 1933, helping the Braves' pitchers to the second- and third-best team ERAs.

Ruth was rested and ready to go by Friday, blasting home runs in practice, one time reaching First Street, hitting a house on a hop. He also swung and missed, grimacing as he felt a twinge in his elbow. Ruth received the six new bats he had ordered, 38-ounce sticks of wood instead of the 54-ounce models he swung 20 years before. If he was going to walk as loudly as the Ruth of old, he was going to carry a smaller stick.[45]

Waterfront Park was packed on Saturday, March 16, and the Chamber of Commerce raised temporary bleachers. Ruth was penciled in to play right field, with the Braves regular first baseman, Buck Jordan, at first. Jordan's wife was sitting in the right-field bleachers when a Ruth line drive came whistling towards her and struck her in the foot. She had a noticeable limp afterwards but said receiving an autographed ball from Ruth made it worthwhile.[46]

In Germany, Adolf Hitler rejected the Treaty of Versailles, which had limited Germany's military after World War I. Hitler announced that the Reich would be rearmed and a mandatory army would exceed 500,000 men. Britain, France, Italy, and the League of Nations denounced him, but it wasn't until Germany invaded Poland four years later that anyone realized what had happened on March 16, 1935.[47] People were focusing on far more trivial events, like a ballgame in St. Petersburg, Florida.

It was a perfect day with a warm sun and no wind for the packed house of 4,726. In attendance was Colonel Ruppert, NL President Ford C. Frick, and of course, Al Lang.[48] It was a star-studded game for a meaningless exhibition in March. Every seat was filled, and chairs were placed on the field, where they were roped off, creating altered ground rules.

The game was scoreless through four innings. In the bottom of the fifth, Frankie Crosetti led off with a walk. Joe Glenn hit a little pop fly to Ruth in right field. The Bambino trudged along and reached down for a shoestring catch, but the ball bounced through his legs as he took a tumble. By the time Wally Berger tracked it down, Crosetti scored, and Glenn was at third. Glenn later scored and the Yankees led, 2–0. "It doesn't appear at this reading," scoffed Shannon, "as though the daily golf game had appreciably strengthened his legs."[49]

Ruth atoned for himself in the sixth with a single over Lou Gehrig's head at first base. There the long-time teammates stood, Gehrig finally out of his Ruthian shadow. Ruth's day was done, and 24-year-old, versatile outfielder Tommy Thompson came in to run for him. "I have forgotten the circumstances of most of the home runs I have hit," Ruth said of the moment, "but I think I will always remember that single."[50]

Ruth sat in the stands smoking a pipe and autographing balls while watching the Braves tie the score. The Braves won, 3–2.[51] The fans had come to see Ruth, but the Yankees' new #3 put on a show. George Selkirk, his replacement, made four nice catches in the outfield and covered twice as much ground. He even launched a triple over Ruth's head for good measure.

"There is no doubt but that Babe drew the cash customers in," Shannon wrote. "Yet he didn't do much toward getting the Yankees out."[52] "The Prince of Wales, himself, wouldn't have drawn a bigger throng nor a greater volume of cheers," Cunningham wrote. "Every move the Babe made, every word he spoke, every fold and wrinkle of his uniform were minutely described." Despite his lack of agility, "he was out there and that's all that seemed to matter."[53] That's all the Braves needed.

Sunday the 17th was St. Patrick's Day, and a small crowd of 1,500 attended.[54] Ruth singled and scored in a three-run Braves first inning, reached on a fielder's choice in the second, and scored on a single. The Braves won, 9–4. "It might have been St. Patrick's Day in South Boston," Drohan mused, "but it was just another hot day down here."[55] The Braves went from swinging shillelaghs on Sunday to battling beards on Monday. The House of David had arrived.

The House of David religious community was founded in Benton Harbor, Michigan, by Benjamin Purnell, a self-proclaimed "prophet of God," in 1903. The community longed for the second coming of Christ and abstained from sex, tobacco, alcohol, and meat while sharing their earthly possessions with one another. Purnell was later accused of raping several minors in the commune, and the group splintered into factions. None of this affected their barnstorming baseball team, which competed for decades and recruited major leaguers. But you had to have a beard, based on a command in the Book of Leviticus forbidding men to shave. Major leaguers like Grover Cleveland Alexander wore fake beards to fit in.[56]

There were a sparse 1,000 fans who showed up, people Drohan said "evidently had no place to go."[57] Berger unloaded a grand slam in the six-run first inning. They added six more in the second. Janesco, the bearded warrior pitcher, couldn't get anybody out, so he decided to start lobbing in cricket pitches to Ruth. Babe got a hold of one and rocketed it over the right-field fence, but just foul. The Braves won, 17–6.[58]

The Yankees returned on March 19. Ruth smashed two long drives off Lefty Gomez, but Ben Chapman caught up to both. The game was knotted, 1–1, in the fifth inning when Tony Lazzeri lined a pitch to right. Ruth hustled and knelt to keep the ball in front of him, but the ball took a bad hop and bounced right over his hands, rolling all the way to the fence. Lazzeri sprinted around the bases and the Yankees led, 2–1. The play was scored an error even though Ruth made no contact with the ball. "New York writers in the press box had something to do with the scoring," wrote Whitman.[59] Ruth singled and called it a day. The Yankees won, 4–1.

The Yankees started rumors that Ruth had suffered a heart attack and was in weakened health. "I'll make the guy sorry who started that story," Ruth furiously said. "Do you think I'd be playing baseball and golf and do so much active work as I do if there was anything the matter with my heart?" Yankees players said Ruth was taking medicine for a bad heart, but it was really soda pop.[60] The story soon fizzled. Then Dizzy Dean arrived.[61]

The March 20 contest drew national interest, and Al Lang prepared for another huge crowd. Dean promised to do all he could to strike the big fella out. It was light-hearted fun considering that in other parts of the world, Nazis were practicing nightly bombing raids. Back in the U.S., Harlem, with unemployment at 50 percent, burned in a Race Riot.[62] St. Petersburg was a world away, and another record crowd of 6,467 jammed Waterfront Park with temperatures in the 90s. Ruth launched a 400-foot drive to right-center which would have been out of most major league parks. Gene Moore raced back and caught the thing as fans scrambled out of his way.

"That one was right in there, kid!" Ruth yelled to Dean, "and I should have clouted it out of the park."

"I know," Dean acknowledged.[63]

Matching zeroes with Dean was Boston's 38-year-old Huck Betts. Betts, from Millsboro, Delaware, had three separate careers. He began as a young reliever with the Phillies, then spouted off to management and had a second career in the minors. He discovered a third life as one of Boston's best starting pitchers from 1932 to 1934.

Ruth made the grand performance of the day. In the second inning, Ducky Medwick sliced a line drive down the right-field line. Ruth raced over, leaped, and saw the ball tick off his glove. "The great man then tumbled head over heels into the crowd," Moore wrote.[64] Ruth lay there out of sight for several seconds. McKechnie raced out as Ruth got up limping. The Cardinals won, 5–4.

A record crowd of 3,120 came out to Adair Field, later known as Henley Field, which still stands in Lakeland as of 2022.[65] Crowds meant profits, and the Braves had already made more money in spring training than they had in all of 1934.[66] On the other hand, the Yankees attracted only 364 people for a game against the Reds.[67] Still, Yankees players were glad Ruth was gone, according to reports. "Gone is the mighty Babe Ruth," Stuart Cameron reported in the *Brooklyn Times Union*, "and it is nothing in the way to say that everybody at the Yanks' camp here is glad that this is so. The pitching will be more dependable. Ruth's tendency to drop flies and put his moundsmen on the spot is responsible. The club has discipline. This was lacking when Ruth was around."[68]

Ruth bungled a fly ball in the second inning. "His hands went this way and that and the ball bubbled through and to the ground," wrote Whitman. Ruth went 0-for-3 in the 5–4 loss, but the crowd oohed and ahhed over his towering 400-foot fly ball. "That's what I came for," an elderly fan said, "to see Babe Ruth hit one, and he certainly hit that, even if it was caught."[69] The deep drive to right-center was another which would have been out of most major league parks. Whitman joked the spacious outfield was because land was so cheap in Florida.

Berger smashed two singles, a triple, and a double which brought in the go-ahead run. Berger slammed 34 home runs with 121 RBI in 1934. The 29-year-old was one of the few offensive threats for a pitiful Braves offense in the 1930s, which always ranked near the bottom. No one hit more home runs in the history of the Boston Braves than Berger. Teamed with Ruth, fans expected a power display.

Berger was born in Chicago in 1905 to German immigrants. Anton Berger, his father, ran a saloon where young Wally heard stories of the old White Sox. The family moved to San Francisco, and Wally dropped out of school to support the family. He signed with the San Francisco Seals of the Pacific Coast League in 1926. He displayed massive power in three minor league seasons, and he was brought to the Braves in 1930. His record 38 home runs as a rookie stood until broken by Mark McGwire in 1987.[70]

The Braves and Red Sox squared off on Friday, March 22 under a scorching sun. Ruth struck out twice in a 6–5 loss, disappointing a crowd of 1,387. On Saturday, the Braves lost to the Yankees, 7–2. Ruth didn't play because he had food poisoning. He showed up at the clubhouse as usual but suddenly ran home. Claire gave her husband castor oil. "I must certainly have been sick to have been able to take that stuff," Ruth said.[71] The Braves lost their fifth in a row.[72]

Ruth's intestinal issues were brief, and he legged out a triple on Sunday as the Braves lost again to the Yankees, 7–3. Most chose church or the beach instead of the Braves as Ruth was doubtful to play.[73] Prior to the game, Ruth was interviewed by Grantland Rice, who penned columns for the *New York Tribune* for decades. Rice coined the phrase "it's not whether you win or lose, but how you play the game." "When I sat down with him (Ruth) and saw him inhale a platter of stone crabs," Rice wrote, "and, later on, slash a triple to left center that he took at a jog, I knew it was the same old Babe."[74]

"I was never happier in my life," Ruth said about being a Brave. "It's keyed me up and given me a fresh target. I feel better than I have felt in four years. My legs haven't bothered me a bit. Bill McKechnie is a great guy to work for, and I am going to give him and Boston everything I have." The pair walked down the street, and a fan immediately approached Ruth, requesting that he autograph his ball. "You can bother me to autograph anything you want," Ruth replied, finding a sense of purpose. "When you quit bothering me to sign autographs, then I'll know I'm through. Slip me the old apple and a pen. And tell 'em to keep on bothering me."[75]

Ruth's digestive issues were tame compared to arriving at the park in Sarasota on March 25 to learn that he was dead. "Slightly exaggerated," Ruth said of the rumor circulating the East Coast newspapers, "as my old friend Mark Twain used to say." That night, Ruth called Pete Norton of the *Tampa Bay Times*. "What's all this I hear about my being dead?" he squawked. "I sound pretty much alive, don't I?" Norton said, "someone had started a report as far north as Washington that the Bambino had gone to his eternal reward."[76]

As if this wasn't enough of a circus, the Ringling Brothers were in town. Several German "little people" came over from the circus to get Ruth's autograph, providing further evidence that he was not dead. Since he was now a learned world traveler, Ruth asked them, "You speaka der Dutch?"

"Yah," they replied.[77]

Another crowd nearing 1,000 came out for the game on March 25. "This Babe thing is really and truly getting terrific, stupendous, callosal [sic] !" wrote Cunningham. "The Babe may lose the Braves' pitchers some of their ball games but he may have the Braves' treasurer dipping his pen in the black ink bottle, and won't that be something for a change?"[78]

The Braves lost their seventh in a row, 7–2. The Red Sox swept the six Florida games between the two Hub teams. The game was less exciting than the ride back to St. Petersburg. Long before interstate highways and the Sunshine Skyway Bridge, the fastest route from Sarasota to St. Petersburg was the Bee Line Ferry out of Bradenton. The trip from Sarasota to Bradenton is only 25 miles, but in 1935 only a two-lane highway could get you there, and once you approached Piney Point Road, you could sit in a half-mile of traffic to get on the ferry. To get on the 5:40 p.m. ferry, Ruth had to step on it.

Manatee County traffic officer Sam Murphy pulled over an irritated Ruth, who was traveling at 70 mph through Bradenton. "He threatened to get my job," Murphy said of the incident. "Mrs. Ruth told me they usually had a police escort through towns. Babe said he had planned great things for this section [of Florida], but he was through with Florida after this." Ruth said he wasn't prepared for a cash bond, and Murphy let him go on to the ferry anyway. Only Ruth, coach Duffy Lewis, and team treasurer Oscar Horton were able to make the ferry since they traveled by car. The rest of the team were on a bus and missed the boat. "A darn shame," Ruth said of the incident in which he was not speeding but "hurrying to catch a boat."[79]

The Braves finally won, 4–3. Ruth sent another behemoth drive to left-center caught in the wide-open spaces.[80] The pitching star of the game was Flint Rhem, a veteran trying to hang on in the game. If he didn't drink himself to death first.

Charles Flint Rhem was born in 1901 in Rhems, South Carolina, named for his ancestors. His father ran a store which sold everything from cotton to real estate. Flint studied engineering at Clemson, but his pitching soon took precedence. He was signed by the St. Louis Cardinals and won 20 games in 1926. But forever after he faced fines, suspensions, and a demotion to the minors because of his drinking. He even concocted a kidnapping story, claiming he was forced to drink, as cover for not showing up for a game.[81] He was with the Braves in 1934 and finished a decent 8–8.

Rhem was hoping for a comeback, one of six players in camp playing without a contract. The others were pitcher Leo Mangum, three outfielders: Hal Lee, Joe Mowry, and Tommy Thompson, and first baseman Buck Jordan. Jordan, the Braves' only .300 hitter in 1934 (.311), was seeking a $2,000 raise; Fuchs offered a $500 raise. Fuchs told Jordan he needed to pay his own expenses to stay at the team hotel, so Jordan left for home in Salisbury, North Carolina. Baseball was Jordan's escape from the mines he was working at as a 16-year-old. He was now 28, a solid contact hitter

Pitcher Ed Brandt (right) with Lefty Grove of the Red Sox (courtesy Boston Public Library, Leslie Jones Collection).

and slick fielder.[82] In his absence, Ruth would get experience at first base, which he did against the Reds on March 28.

The Braves beat the Reds, 5–2. Ruth grounded out his only two times at the plate but was enthusiastic in a letter to Fuchs. "I am trying harder than ever. I consider it a real privilege to be connected with you and your organization and to work with Bill McKechnie and Rabbit Maranville. And do not feel concerned because we lost all those games in a row. It was the result of a natural let-down, as the club was playing daily in the terrific heat without a single break. We will snap out of it and win a lot of games." Ruth said the Judge deserved his own day on Opening Day. "You deserve this great tribute as a reward for your fairness to the players, for keeping faith with the fans and for the many sacrifices you have made to give Boston the kind of baseball it is entitled to. We are all rooting for you."[83]

The Braves lost to the Tigers, 5–0, on Friday, March 29 and were defeated on Saturday by the Yankees, 7–3. Ruth looked sluggish, Whitman said, "as a result of this heat, which persists day in and day out, and also at night. He's not getting down for ground balls, not moving around the way you expect a big leaguer to move."[84] Ruth was hitless on March 30 and spent most of the game in the stands, fanning himself next to Rabbit Maranville, who had not played in an exhibition game.[85] Rabbit was optimistic that he and Ruth, both long in the tooth, would contribute. "I never felt better in my life," the confident Rabbit said, "and I expect this to be one of my banner seasons."[86]

The Braves finished March with another loss to the Yankees on Sunday the 31st, 7–3. The Yankees pounded 37-year-old Larry Benton, a discarded journeyman in a tryout. Ruth made a nice stop on a grounder to first but then fell on top of the ball trying to pick it up. "The Babe will hardly do at first base," quipped O'Leary.[87]

It was unsettling for the Braves as spring camp wound down. They lost three in a row and went 5–11 for the month. Ruth's knees made him a defensive liability, even at first base, and he batted a paltry .171 (7-for-41).

Heading North

Burt Whitman wrote in 1927 that Charles F. Adams "seems to have had a gift of making a success of everything which he touched."[88] He had a point. Adams became a millionaire in the grocery industry, became a major influence in creating the Boston Garden, and founded the Boston Bruins when he brought hockey to the United States. On March 31, while the Braves were winding down spring training, the Bruins were losing to the Toronto Maple Leafs in the Stanley Cup semifinals. Fans expected success from the Bruins, who had already given them a Stanley Cup championship in their brief existence. With hockey winding up, Boston fans set their sights on their two baseball teams heading north. But another sport, another of Adams' successes, was on the horizon.

Anticipation grew as the Massachusetts Racing Commission would soon grant a license to the Eastern Racing Association to conduct races at the Suffolk Downs track in East Boston. Bostonians didn't need to travel to New Hampshire or Rhode Island to bet on the races. The country was in a race craze, and Adams, an Eastern Racing Association director, was ready to capitalize. Plans were also underway to open a greyhound racing track in Revere, Massachusetts, Wonderland Park. That was the vision Adams and Fuchs had for Braves Field.[89]

Adams had yet to see success with one thing: the Braves. He held most of the stock but wanted out of the baseball business. Unless the broken-down, 40-year-old icon could still have drawing power.

Fans came to Ruth in the Florida heat. Would they come to see him in the Boston cold?

7

The Bambino Is Back in Boston
(April 1935)

"Babe Ruth, the Pied Piper of baseball whom the boys follow with almost religious fervor."—Burt Whitman, *Boston Herald*

"Mayor Mansfield, occupying the box with me, turned to me as the ball went over the fence and said, 'Judge, your problems are over!' So it seemed."—Judge Fuchs

Fish Stories

Babe Ruth got lost in the Gulf of Mexico while he was at spring training in 1935. He was with a fishing party which included newspapermen Charley Segar and Marshall Hunt. Because of a broken compass, the three were missing for six hours. Claire Ruth called the Coast Guard to find them. Segar was little help. He pointed to the setting sun and asked if that was west. "If it ain't," he was told, "you got yourself one hell of a story."[1]

The Boston Braves prepared to leave Florida, but they were just as clueless about what direction they were going in. They finished March with much fanfare but little substance. Babe Ruth's presence was supposed to be a jolt to their anemic offense, but most were reminded of the Bambino's bad knees with their aches and pains. He gave numerous excuses. It was too hot. He was a slow starter. It was only spring training. The Braves needed Ruth, not to win the pennant but to save a debt-ridden franchise. There were big expectations back in Boston for his climactic return.

Ruth was fishing on April Fools' Day with Flint Rhem and "Handy" Randy Moore. They hauled in 233 pounds of kingfish. Maybe someone uttered, "Holy mackerel!" Rhem had a 45-minute tussle with a shark which hitched a ride on a kingfish. Ruth shot at it with a .22 caliber rifle. "He took off with a jerk," Ruth said, "carrying with him all of Flint's line and equipment. Flint didn't think it was funny."[2] Wally Berger and Hal Lee were at the beach, burning to a crisp "like two kids at the seashore on the first day of their summer vacation," Burt Whitman wrote in the *Boston Herald*.[3]

An exhibition game versus Toronto of the International League on April 3 was

91

cancelled. Bill McKechnie thought rest was a higher priority. Games were scheduled along the train ride back to Boston, and Ruth was like a politician making campaign stops. The Braves hoped for strong gate receipts.[4] The final Florida game was against the Yankees on April 2. Ruth booted a grounder at first base which allowed a run to score. So much for that spring experiment. Berger slammed a three-run-homer in the seventh inning to put the Braves ahead, 5–4. Leo Mangum came in from the bullpen.

Leo Allen Mangum was 37 years old and the eighth-oldest player in the National League, joining his teammates Ruth, Rabbit Maranville, Bob Smith, and Huck Betts as four of the oldest players in the league. At least the Braves dominated *one* category. Mangum had made his major-league debut with the White Sox in 1924 and surrendered a home run to Babe Ruth before he even knew where the showers were. Mangum signed with the Braves in 1932, his 13th different club but with only 82 games played. "I was shipped back to the minors so much I was always two days ahead of my trunk," Mangum joked in his retirement years. "Train conductors and I became quite familiar." His southern drawl and fiddling on the ukulele and guitar earned him the nickname of "banjo."[5] Mangum allowed three runs, and the Braves fell again.[6]

An Education

Crowds cheered the Braves as they boarded the 9 p.m. train bound to Savannah, Georgia. Ruth finally hit a home run in a Braves uniform the following day. That's if you consider the South Georgia Teachers' College actual competition. "The lads who are trying to play ball while they learn to teach school," wrote Whitman, "were no better than any small high school team would be in greater Boston."[7]

A crowd of 2,000 came to Municipal Stadium, still standing as Grayson Stadium in 2022, wanting to see a Ruth home run and caring little about their local team. "Boston Braves Beat Teachers," was the headline of *The George-Anne*, the student newspaper of the college which would one day become Georgia Southern University.[8] "They yelled their heads off," James C. O'Leary wrote in the *Boston Globe*, "when Ruth bumped the ball into the bleachers in the right-field corner of the lot."[9] It was satisfying for Ruth nevertheless as he tipped his cap to thunderous applause. The author of the Sportsman column in the *Globe* wrote that the pitcher/teacher was "at least half scared to death by the great man."[10] The Braves won, 15–1, over the future educators.

The Braves journeyed north to Fayetteville, North Carolina, for a matchup with North Carolina State on Friday, April 5. It was a homecoming of sorts for Ruth. Like all superheroes, he had an origin story, and it took place in Fayetteville in 1914.

Fayetteville, 1914

George Herman Ruth said goodbye to St. Mary's Industrial School in Baltimore on a Friday. He spent one last weekend with his father before becoming a professional ballplayer. Jack Dunn, manager of the International League's Baltimore Orioles, spotted the talented Bambino and signed the 19-year-old to a contract. The train was scheduled to depart for spring training in Fayetteville on Monday, March 2. A Nor'easter slammed the coast on Sunday and Monday, and the streets of Baltimore looked like a "shelled city," the *Baltimore Sun* reported. "Scattered on all sides were tin roofs, shutters, awnings, bricks, plaster and every other material used in building." High winds and severe cold hampered efforts to assist those in need. Trains were halted.[11] Despite the blizzard, Ruth and several Orioles left Baltimore's Union Station on Monday night and made it to Fayetteville the following morning. It was Ruth's first train ride.[12] Ice and snow gave way to the warm 75 degrees in North Carolina.

"Looks like a promising twirler," the *Baltimore Sun* remarked of the young Ruth.[13] On Saturday, the kid "picked off the lots of Baltimore" did something the locals never forgot. The team was split between "Sparrows" and "Buzzards," and a few hundred people came out to watch. Ruth launched the longest home run the locals had ever seen, topping even a memorable home run Jim Thorpe hit there a few years earlier. A historical marker remains on that spot over 100 years later. "The ball went far over Morrisett's head and landed in a cornfield."[14] Rodger Pippen, Baltimore sportswriter, wrote it was "a hit that will live in the memory of all who saw it."[15] The legend was born.

His teammates had already been ribbing the green, sheltered Ruth, who was out on his own for the first time. They called him "Dunn's newest babe" or "Dunn's baby." It was an appropriate nickname since Ruth saw his first elevator and couldn't resist going up and down in it like a child. Fortunately, a teammate told him to duck his head back inside when the elevator was rising, otherwise there would have been no story at all. Ruth felt at home with neighborhood boys who let him ride their bikes around town. "He really was an overgrown child," Robert Creamer wrote. By the end of the month, newspaper reporters no longer called him George. He was Babe Ruth. And it all happened in Fayetteville.[16]

Fayetteville, 1935

It seemed like everyone in Fayetteville in 1935 knew who Ruth was. Fans surged the hotel "insistent upon an audience with baseball's popular czar," wrote Paul H. Shannon in the *Boston Post*.[17] Ruth obliged, and soon autographs and handshakes had him heavily perspiring. He was too exhausted to continue. So fans sprinted to the ballpark.

There were at least 7,000 fans at the park waiting for Ruth, and 2,000 more had jumped the fence and spread out all over the field. That was more than half the town's population. Some thought the left-field fence would collapse with the fans sitting on it. Fans sat in a ring around the baseball diamond. Fewer than 5,000 paid to get in, but even so, with adults at $1 and kids at 50 cents, "the Braves derived plenty of financial nourishment from the contest as the Boston club was given just 70 per cent of the gross," wrote Shannon.[18] Small boys were in harm's way sitting in front of the backstop. Maranville entertained kids with magic tricks. It was a half-holiday, and the local newspaper ran a late extra afternoon edition, not done since Lindbergh flew to Paris.[19]

Boston won, 6–2, but that mattered little. They only managed seven hits, likely out of fear of hitting fans sitting on the field. Fans hoped for another historic Ruth home run like they heard about from 21 years before. Instead, they saw a college kid named Olney Ray "Lefty" Freeman, whose nervousness was obvious as he nearly beaned Ruth. Freeman came back to get two strikes, then threw an overhand curveball which Ruth whiffed at.

N.C. State may have defeated the Braves if they hadn't run out of baseballs. Every batted ball was a potential souvenir. The Braves brought 40 balls, N.C. State a dozen, and the Chamber of Commerce four dozen. The supply dwindled to four, and a call went out to find any available baseballs in town. "The Chamber of Commerce wanted everyone to have a good time," Anthony J. McKevlin in *News and Observer* noted, "but it hadn't reckoned with the number of fouls or the number of fair balls to be hit among fans." Mason Bugg, a reserve on the N.C. State team, sat in the bleachers collecting souvenirs for Ruth to autograph. Ironically, he was up pinch-hitting when there were no baseballs left. He wanted a souvenir instead of an at-bat.

Freeman lived to the age of 98 and told his story 75 years later. He was likely the last man living who could say he struck out Babe Ruth.[20]

On to Newark

The team arrived in a rainy Norfolk, Virginia, Saturday morning, and their game with the Norfolk Tars of the Piedmont League was cancelled. The weather didn't stop the children who surrounded the train at a water tower stop in Virginia. They chanted for the sleeping Ruth to appear. He soon "appeared in his brilliant Japanese silk pajamas, waved to the kids, boys and girls, who apparently had walked a long way in the early morning, and signed their inevitable autograph books," wrote Whitman. "The Babe rarely turns down youngsters."[21]

When asked who would play in the World Series, Ruth said the Yankees and Giants. "You might see the Braves in there in 1936," he added, believing he would be managing the club.[22] W.N. Cox of Norfolk's *Virginian-Pilot* wrote that the Braves "positively can not be a factor in the first division this year. The Babe will not help them much in the matter of attack. The angle on Ruth seems to me to be not what can he do this year, rather what success will he have as the guiding hand in building the Braves into a championship contender later on. He will need more than the cheers of thousands of fans to win that battle."[23] Grantland Rice predicted a fifth-place finish for the Braves but said Ruth's "big bat should win more games than his fading legs will lose."[24]

The Braves needed those "cheers of thousands" to save the franchise. The new Babe Ruth–Jordan Marsh Club for Boys was established with this in mind. All boys in New England were eligible to register at Jordan Marsh in Boston's Downtown Crossing and receive a membership card and button which would allow them to attend weekly meetings featuring Ruth and other players.[25]

Judge Emil Fuchs was anticipating Ruth and a profitable Opening Day. He was also dealing with a lawsuit. In 1926, J.V. Giblin had purchased the 1,550 shares of Braves stock held by Albert H. Powell for $175,000. Shortly before Giblin's purchase, Fuchs and Powell issued $230,000 of special shares other stockholders were unaware of. As revealed at the National League meetings, the status of these special shares was in doubt since they were off the books and mismanaged. Giblin claimed he was entitled to 42 percent of those special shares, or $96,600, even though he sold his shares to Charles F. Adams in 1927. A Suffolk County Superior Court judge threw out the case.[26] Fuchs also won favor with the bank. The $200,000 loan to First National Bank of Boston, which held his stock as collateral, was due April 5. The bank granted an extension since the addition of Ruth "convinced the bankers that happier days were ahead for the sorely distressed baseball magnate."[27] Fuchs certainly hoped so.

On a chilly Sunday, April 7, the Braves defeated the Newark Bears of the International League, a Yankees farm team, 10–8. Rabbit Maranville was back on the field and not limping. The 10,000 fans "witnessed a real old-fashioned Ruthian field day," in the words of Louis Effrat of the *New York Times*. Ruth looked 20 years younger playing first base. He hit two home runs. The first was a line drive to right off a knuckleballer. The second was the longest hit anyone had ever seen at Ruppert Stadium. "The ball sailed over the heads of the bleacherites," Effrat wrote, "clearing the farthest corner in right field by fifty feet and landing in the street behind the park." His home run was estimated at over 500 feet.[28] He also showed fancy footwork at first base.[29]

Ruth spent the night in New York City to savor his day. Monday was an off-day, and the Tuesday game against the Washington Senators was cancelled due to ice and snow. Larry Benton received a contract and came north with the Braves.[30]

In Boston at Last

The Braves arrived back in Boston on Tuesday night, settling in at the Hotel Touraine. They took Wednesday off, and poor Boston weather forced them to work

out in the Briggs Memorial Cage at Harvard on Thursday.[31] The Red Sox–Braves contests on Friday and Saturday were rained out. Ruth joined his fellow Braves at the Harvard cage.[32] The Harvard campus was a rowdy place with anti-war protests that included a Hitler impersonator and stink bombs.[33]

The weather cleared for one Braves–Red Sox game on a raw Sunday, April 14. A bundled 10,648 fans showed up to get their first look at Babe the Brave. Players in the dugouts were covered in blankets, and Claire Ruth arrived in a mink coat, blue hat, and two white gardenias.[34] Boston streets were also filled with palm wavers—it was Palm Sunday, the beginning of Holy Week.

Protestant and Catholic worshippers recalled the story of Jesus entering Jerusalem on a donkey as the crowd laid palm branches along his route. Some of these Boston worshippers probably left church and made their way to Fenway Park to welcome Babe Ruth.[35]

Ruth with Red Sox manager Joe Cronin (left) and Braves manager Bill McKechnie before the Red Sox–Braves exhibition game at Fenway Park (courtesy Boston Public Library, Leslie Jones Collection).

Opposite, top: Poor April weather in Boston forced Ruth and the Braves to practice inside at the Harvard batting cage (courtesy Boston Public Library, Leslie Jones Collection). *Opposite, bottom:* Ruth at the Harvard cage joined by (from left) Buck Jordan, Tommy Thompson, Les Mallon, and Hal Lee (courtesy Boston Public Library, Leslie Jones Collection).

Ruth shaking hands with Worcester (MA) Mayor John Mahoney prior to an exhibition game with Holy Cross. Visible players behind Mahoney and Ruth (from left) are OF Wally Berger (gripping the bats), OF Johnnie Tyler (holding his hat), 1B Buck Jordan, OF Tommy Thompson, coach Duffy Lewis, and coach Hank Gowdy to Ruth's left (courtesy Boston Public Library, Leslie Jones Collection).

The rain held off in Boston while Midwesterners were experiencing "Black Sunday," one of the worst dust storms in history during the era of the Dust Bowl. The cloud of dust and dirt bore down on the Plains for 1,000 miles, turning a bright sunny sky soon into a dark haze of dust and dirt.[36]

Ruth failed to please the crowd, going 0-for-3 and dropping a throw to first.[37] Most of the small crowd had departed when Ruth did and never saw the single by Wally Berger to give the Braves the victory. One final exhibition game remained on Monday. The Braves traveled to Worcester, Massachusetts, to play Holy Cross.

A crowd between 10,000–15,000 packed into Fitton Field on the Holy Cross campus. Thousands of kids mobbed Ruth for autographs as if he were the "Pied Piper of baseball whom the boys follow with almost religious fervor," Burt Whitman wrote. People were standing on the nearby football field in right center since they couldn't get a seat near the baseball diamond. Ruth needed police assistance at first base when youngsters sprinted onto the field for autographs. In between innings, Ruth sat down with the Holy Cross band and pretended to play a horn.

"Everything he did, all these little things, delighted the crowd," Whitman

Babe Ruth signing autographs for enthusiastic youngsters at an exhibition game against Holy Cross at Worcester, Massachusetts (courtesy Boston Public Library, Leslie Jones Collection).

wrote.[38] Ruth failed to produce a home run. He walked twice and grounded out. Worcester mayor John T. Mahoney presented Ruth and McKechnie with keys to the city. The Braves rallied for a 5–2 win.[39] The games would count from here on out.

Opening Day

The Boston Braves Citizens Committee honored Judge Fuchs for bringing Babe Ruth back and keeping the franchise afloat, proving "that 13 years of earnest and unremitting effort by Judge Fuchs have been sincerely appreciated," Paul Shannon wrote. Ruth looked like the star they had dreamed of. "Age may have slowed him up a trifle, the old spring in his stride may be missing, perhaps, critics have labeled him 'damaged goods' and envious club officials questioned the wisdom of adding him to the Tribal roster, but Babe still reigns unopposed."[40]

April 16, 1935, was the 65th Opening Day for the Boston National League team, which started in 1871, and its 60th as a member of the National League. Present was 88-year-old George Wright, the last surviving connection to that original 1871 team. The game was much different when the pioneering Wright started for Boston at the old South End Grounds. But Wright called Ruth an "inspirational genius."[41] The Braves franchise capped their 150 years of continuous play by winning the World Series in 2021.

The Braves faced Bill Terry's New York Giants, favorites to win the National League pennant. In Terry's first two years as player-manager, the Giants won the 1933 World Series over Washington and finished a close second to St. Louis in 1934. Terry, outfielder Mel Ott, third baseman Travis Jackson, and pitcher Carl Hubbell were future members of the Baseball Hall of Fame. The left-hander, Hubbell, was 21–12 with a league-best 2.30 ERA in 1934, his second of five straight seasons of 20 or more victories. His screwball made him one of the greatest pitchers in baseball history. Hubbell struck out five straight legends, including Ruth, at the 1934 All-Star Game.

McKechnie chose lefty Ed Brandt, who was 16–14 for the Braves in 1934 with a 3.53 ERA. Dutch Brandt was from Spokane, Washington. His early career bounced up and down like a yo-yo until McKechnie told him he might end up back in a sawmill or tin shop. The motivation worked, and Brandt saw success. By 1935, he was considered second only to Hubbell among left-handed National League starters.[42]

The Massachusetts Senate closed early so members could get to Braves Field.[43] While 40,000 were expected, the raw weather kept folks away and only 22,000 arrived. Other fans stayed home and listened to the game on WNAC Radio. Patrolmen kept watch of the streets around Braves Field as extra train cars rumbled along. The governors of Maine, New Hampshire, and Rhode Island joined Massachusetts Governor James M. Curley, who threw out the ceremonial first ball. They joined a procession to the flagpole as the 101st Field Artillery gave a 15-shot canon salute. "Everyone in it and within a half mile of Braves Field trembled for 15 minutes afterward," wrote Arthur Siegel in the *Herald*.[44]

Three airplanes flew overhead and dropped good luck messages to the Braves. Fuchs was presented a plaque. No one could hear Curley's speech, and some kept yelling, "Play ball!"[45] Ruth was presented a floral arrangement by seven-year-old Dick Cresse of Medford, the first member of the Babe Ruth–Jordan Marsh Club. "Cannons boomed, airplanes overhead roared, martial strains filled the air, and the tread of military feet furrowed the grass in perhaps the greatest inaugural ceremonies Braves Field has ever held," wrote James P. Dawson of the *New York Times*.[46] Ruth took his place in left field.

In the bottom of the first inning, Billy Urbanski led off with a single and Les Mallon bunted him to second. Ruth walked to the plate to a standing ovation. He sharply singled to right, and Urbanski scampered home with the first run of the season. Ruth moved to third after singles by Berger and Pinky Whitney. Buck Jordan singled to left, and Ruth trotted home. Five hits in the inning brought two runs against the great Hubbell. As Opening Days go, Braves fans immediately started envisioning the Braves in the World Series. The falling snowflakes during the game did nothing to diminish their October fantasy.

Brandt held the Giants to one hit through four innings. In the top of the fifth, Hubbell hit a looper into short left. It took a second for Ruth to get his motor running, but once he did, he was a runaway locomotive, "exerting speed and energy which critics have claimed he doesn't possess anymore," Gerry Moore commented in the *Globe*.[47] Ruth "chugged along like a coasting truck," reached out, and made the catch just before hitting the foul line. "From the deep pasture," wrote Bill Cunningham in the *Boston Post*, "somewhere, with a speed never believed to be in those ancient legs, the old Babe came racing. It looked impossible, but onward he roared. Forward, at top stride, he stuck out his glove hand. The ball struck it, kersmack! And stuck!"[48] Ruth kept right on running to the dugout with the catch of the day. Fans were jubilant, and the best was still to come.[49]

In the bottom of the fifth, Urbanski reached with his third single and Mallon sacrificed him to second. Hubbell, who had struck Ruth out in the second inning, tried sneaking in a screwball which didn't break but stayed letter-high. Ruth crushed it to right field over the fence and onto the runway between the Jury Box seats and the first base pavilion. Ott in right field turned, looked, shrugged his shoulders, and just walked away. Ruth made his way around the bases with career home run #709. "The crowd went positively woozy," Moore wrote. Ruth doffed his cap and disappeared in the Braves dugout. "That's one for the old lady," Ruth said in honor of Claire on the eve of their anniversary. She and stepdaughter Julia were looking on from behind the Braves' dugout. "I can hardly express my delight," Claire beamed, "for I know that Babe was just as thrilled that his Braves start should be so successful."[50]

Ruth struck out in the seventh inning and was replaced by Tommy Thompson. Brandt went all the way for the complete-game victory, 4–2. Ruth went 2-for-4 with three RBI. It was the Ruthian debut fans had dreamed about. "The one and only Bambino made every mother's son and daughter in that huge gathering completely forget the cold with his storybook deeds," Moore wrote.[51] "Babe is the happiest man in Boston," Dawson wrote, "if not in baseball, because he was able to deliver when he knew every eye was upon him."[52]

Even Ruth was surprised. "I didn't even dream I'd get off to such a start," he said.[53] "We started right, and I hope we keep on going."[54] "On his first appearance he seemed to fulfill our fondest hopes," Judge Fuchs said years later. "Mayor Mansfield, occupying the box with me, turned to me as the ball went over the fence and said, 'Judge, your problems are over!' So it seemed."[55]

Paul Gallico wrote that the day reminded him "of the day you bought an expensive used car, a big, shiny model that had been used for many years by some fine old family and finally disposed of one day. And then you splurged and bought it and all the friends and neighbors came around the day of delivery to inspect the new arrival. And some one always said, 'It looks all right, but will it run?'" How long Ruth would have the new-car smell was anyone's guess. "Perhaps tomorrow or the next day the bearings will work loose a trifle," Gallico continued, "and strange noises may develop, but today he was truly as good as new."[56]

Ruth with fellow outfielders Wally Berger (center) and Hal Lee (courtesy Boston Public Library, Leslie Jones Collection).

The Braves hoped more fans would take a ride in that shiny used car with a lot of mileage. How much longer until he broke down on the side of the road? All they knew was that Opening Day was a sweet ride.

Dodgers Come to Town

Bad weather wiped out the Wednesday and Thursday games with the Giants. Ruth was antsy watching the rain and snow. "I'd liked to have had another crack at those Giants," he said. "I feel fit as a fiddle! The way I feel now, I'll play in 154 games this year."[57] April 19 was the Patriots Day holiday, the 39th annual running of the Boston Marathon, and Good Friday. There was a morning reenactment to honor the 160th anniversary of the ride of Paul Revere, when the Revolutionary hero galloped through "every Middlesex village and farm," in Longfellow's reflection, to warn residents the British were coming.[58]

The Dodgers were coming for a doubleheader. They had split their first two games in Philadelphia. After losing the 1920 World Series, the Dodgers spent the next 14 years mostly finishing fifth or sixth. They hoped their fortunes would change under their flamboyant manager, Casey Stengel, who naturally had a Ruth story from a generation before.

"I'll never forget the first time I ever suspected he could hit," Stengel recalled. "That was at least 20 years ago when I played centerfield for the Dodgers and the Babe was a gawky left-handed pitching recruit for the Red Sox. We met the Red Sox in an exhibition game somewhere down South and when Ruth came to bat the first time, I played him no differently than I would for any other big pitcher. He bopped one over my skull for a long hit." Brooklyn manager Wilbert Robinson let Stengel have it. "He climbed up and down my family tree and insinuated that no Stengel in generations had any brains. He was so hot that he made me hot, too. I was burning still when Ruth came at bat. I turned my back on the plate and walked out 50 feet. I'd show Robbie up. What I did was show myself up, for the Babe belted another over my bean although I was practically in another county."[59]

Huck Betts took the mound for Boston before the 10:30 a.m. crowd of 4,000. He left trailing, 4–1, and the ageless Bob Smith finished the game with six scoreless innings of relief. Ruth managed a couple of singles. He walked in the eighth inning, and Johnnie Tyler went in to run for him.

The 28-year-old Tyler was born to Polish immigrants, and baseball saved him from Pennsylvania's coal mines. He was so fast he once competed against Jesse Owens in a pregame race. Tyler played for eight minor league teams in five years before being signed by the Braves in 1934. He would play only 16 games in the major leagues, then another decade back in the minors. But when he settled back in coal country as a short-order cook, he could tell customers he once pinch-ran for Babe Ruth.[60]

The Dodgers won, 4–2, in a contest over in one hour and 32 minutes. Fans had time to catch the end of the marathon. They joined the 300,000 who packed the streets to watch Johnny Kelley win his first Boston Marathon. Kelley would win the race again 10 years later and compete for the 61st time in 1992 at the age of 84.[61] Kelley was on the ground while Amelia Earhart was in the air to Mexico. Hitler declared the death penalty as punishment for pacifism during times of war, and the U.S. House of Representatives passed the Social Security bill, 372–33.[62]

An estimated 17 percent of U.S. working Americans were unemployed in April of 1935, down from a high of 25.5 percent in May of 1933.[63] The bill was debated in the early months of 1935. "The cry of 'socialism' reverberated throughout the hearing rooms," wrote historian Robert S. McElvaine, "and business leaders predicted the end of initiative, thrift, and the American way of life. It was mildly entertaining theater, but actually the bill was sufficiently conservative so that all but a few Republicans finally voted for it." The bill would provide relief for the aged, unemployed, disabled, and poor, but not the *most* destitute. Farm and domestic workers were excluded, catering to Southern fears. "The average Mississippian" the *Jackson Daily News* declared, "can't imagine himself chipping in to pay pensions for able-bodied Negroes to sit around in idleness on front galleries supporting their kinfolks on pensions, while cotton and crops are crying for workers to get them out of the grass." The bill became law in August, helping "to win back for Roosevelt the allegiance of the forgotten man."[64]

Ruth was far from being forgotten, but the Braves barely showed for the second game. Rhem was the victim of sloppy Braves fielding. Two errors and a single in the first inning loaded the bases, and Danny Taylor launched a grand slam for a 4–2 win. Ruth went 0-for-4 before the crowd of 23,000 and struck out three times against Johnny Babich. He also grounded out to second, where Tony Cuccinello played in short right field in a Stengel shift. The "ol Perfessor" had paced the Kenmore Hotel lobby late at night, scribbling diagrams on a clipboard for positioning against Ruth.[65]

On Saturday morning, Ruth spoke at the Boston Arena to thousands of youngsters at the first Babe Ruth–Jordan Marsh Club for Boys meeting. "You can't be a ball player by just owning a glove or a bat," he bellowed, "you got to get out and hustle and play all you can."[66] Kids showed great hustle in swarming Ruth as the meeting ended. "2000 boys came over to have a closer look at their hero," said the *Globe*. "They swarmed up, sneaking under the arms of attendants and in general assaulted the platform. For five or ten minutes the place was in an uproar." Ruth made his way to the street, but the boys streamed behind him. The Babe looked unhappy as he was guided into a car "into the comparative safety of the Saturday traffic."[67]

The event almost didn't happen, according to Fuchs, revealed decades later. Fuchs needed Ruth's personal appearances to build up positive press, something as vice-president he was contracted to do. But photo ops quickly became a bone of contention between the two. Jordan Marsh was a key business which had purchased blocks of tickets for Braves games for a guarantee of a personal appearance by Ruth. Claire Ruth wanted to know what was in it for them. Babe approached Fuchs and asked for a $2,000 speaking fee, which Claire suggested, shocking the Judge. Fuchs felt betrayed. Ruth had already agreed to the event, and breaking the hearts of children was unthinkable. Ruth already found the role of goodwill ambassador tiring.[68]

Ben Cantwell pitched Saturday's game. A 33-year-old, tall right-hander, Benjamin Caldwell Cantwell was the youngest of 12 children of a Civil War veteran in western Tennessee. This was Cantwell's ninth season in the majors, his eighth with the Braves. Cantwell won 20 games with a 2.62 ERA in 1933 but suffered a down year in 1934 due to bone spurs.[69]

Cantwell dueled with Brooklyn's ace of the 1930s, Van Lingle Mungo. The crowd of 10,000 included the youngsters of the "Knot-Hole Gang," a group created by Fuchs and Christy Mathewson in 1924 to "reward good conduct and merit among youngsters holding membership in Greater Boston welfare organizations." Youngsters received free admission in the third base pavilion seats if they honored their pledge of good sportsmanship. They cheered Ruth's every move.[70] The game was tied, 1–1, in the sixth inning when Mallon walked, and Ruth singled to right.

Berger singled to left to score Mallon, but Ruth turned his ankle on his way to second base. He gingerly walked back to the dugout. The Braves cruised to a 7–1 win with Cantwell (1–0) pitching a complete game. He wouldn't win again until July 22, and the 2–2 Braves would never be .500 again in 1935.

April 21 was Easter Sunday, and the magnolia trees, blossoms, and lilies created a "brilliancy to the sidewalk gardens," according to the *Globe*. Spring was in the air, and residents were decked out in their Sunday best.[71] A crowd of 20,000 "went slightly daffy," wrote Moore, when Ruth hit a line drive home run to left, six rows into the bleachers, in the first inning, his second and career #710.[72] That was all the Braves managed in an 8–1 loss.

On to New York

Monday morning at 8:30, the Braves caught a train for Albany for an exhibition game. They would stay in New York for the next week, having three games each against the Giants at the Polo Grounds and the Dodgers at Ebbets Field in Brooklyn.

"Don't try to convince any fan who was at Hawkins Stadium yesterday afternoon that Babe Ruth is through as a hitter," boasted Con Heffernan of the *Albany Times-Union*. An energetic crowd of 4,000 watched his Braves beat Albany, 10–4. Ruth doubled his first two times at bat. The first blasted a light tower 400 feet away, and the second hit the scoreboard in center. He played first base and collided with Hack Wilson. Like Ruth, Wilson was an old home-run-hitting legend past his prime and trying to hang on. Ruth received a bruised knee which bothered him for several weeks. He was scheduled to appear at a local playground, but the team was late arriving. He was mobbed at the stadium by so many young autograph seekers that he had to withdraw.[73]

The stage was set for Ruth's return to the Big Apple. "Sure," he said, "I'm keyed up. I want to make good. I want to see the Braves win 'em all, and this is just another ball game so far as they are concerned. I'd like to hit a home run or a half dozen of 'em. I'm not feeling as well as I'd like to. I've picked up a cold that's bothering me some, but I expect to be in there trying. I don't know much about the Polo Grounds, but I guess if you hit one right there it'll go into the bleachers. I hope I can bust one hard enough to find out."[74]

The game wasn't "just another ball game." All Polo Grounds reserved seats had been sold out for a week by those who wanted "to see for themselves whether Ruth is a broken-down player," wrote Siegel, "tottering in his vulnerability, glorified only by the glamour of his past, or whether he is still a personage in active baseball."[75] Victor Jones described the scene as "the return of the conquering hero to the scene of his greatest triumphs."[76] He would not add to those triumphs.

Ruth's bumbling in right field likely cost the Braves a victory in front of a massive crowd of 47,009, reported as the largest Opening Day crowd in the city's history. "From the $2.20 boxes to the 55-cent planks they were jammed in shoulder to shoulder and knee to knee," Cunningham wrote. "Caesar returning from Gaul, victorious doughboy battalions home at last from the Rhine were never given fuller throated nor warmer hearted reception."[77]

The crowd stood in awe "waiting, with tense restraint, the slightest opportunity to shout with glee and adoration over his exploits." Celebrities were everywhere, including New York City Mayor Fiorello LaGuardia, Yankees owner Jacob Ruppert, boxer Jack Dempsey, and entertainer Jimmy Durante with his trademark "schnozzola" in the middle of his face.[78]

Betts took the hill for the Braves, and after two pitches he trailed, 2–0. Shanty Hogan slammed a home run for the Braves, but the Giants countered. Bill Terry lofted a pop fly to right. Ruth hustled in but overran the ball and it bounced 10 feet behind him. Berger chased it down and threw to relay man Les Mallon, who dropped it. Terry came all the way around to score a Keystone Cops version of an inside-the-park home run. In the fourth inning, a single became a double as the trudging Ruth was slow tracking it down. "Sentiment and romance took it on the chin," Siegel wrote of Ruth's pathetic performance on a day when many expected a triumph.[79] The Giants led, 4–1.

After two weak groundouts, Ruth drew a walk and scored on Whitney's home run in the sixth. He was replaced by Joe Mowry in the eighth. Buck Jordan homered in the ninth to tie the game, 5–5. Ott drove home the winning run in the 11th inning on a single past the diving Mallon, and the Giants won, 6–5, to "a thunderous roar and a shower of hats, programs and torn papers," James Dawson wrote in the *New York Times*.[80]

Ruth was even overshadowed by other 40-somethings that day. Bob Smith, who turned 40 the previous day, pitched a strong 6⅔ innings of relief for the Braves, while 44-year-old Cuban Dolf Luque pitched the last 2⅔ innings for the Giants, earning his 194th and final career victory. Luque debuted with the Braves in May of 1914, two months before Ruth. But the story of the game was that little pop fly which Ruth bungled into a home run.

"I've got a cold," Ruth said on Wednesday after batting practice. He took himself out of the lineup to rest his sniffles and bum knee. The crowd was verbally displeased, and Ruth asked youngsters to bring self-addressed postcards so he could sign and mail them later. When the game started, Ruth was lying in the Braves bullpen catching some sun to dry out his sniffles. He sent the clubhouse boy for a ham and swiss sandwich and a bottle of beer, perhaps good for what ailed him. He eventually returned to the dugout surrounded by cheers from 11,572 fans.

McKechnie sent Ruth up to pinch hit against Hal Schumacher, who had stymied the Braves all afternoon. Ruth weakly fouled off a couple of pitches, then took a strike right down the middle as "the ump swung the wicked words like Hitler's headsman swinging the axe." The crowd was stunned. "They all looked the other way as he waddled gloomily back to the dimness of the dugout," Cunningham wrote. "It was the kind of thing the church congregation does when the Easter soloist's voice breaks on high C. They all felt sorry for him without being able to do much about it."[81] The Giants won, 3–1.[82]

Thursday's game was more of the same as Roy Parmelee outdueled Cantwell for a 2—1 Giants win. Mel Ott's two-run home run was the only blemish on Cantwell for the day. The crowd was disappointed, expecting Ruth to pinch-hit in the eighth inning, but instead it was Randy Moore. Ruth was home in bed. Claire called the doctor for a house call and ordered Ruth to bed and "argyrol, or something, was being dropped up the schnozzle," Jones wrote in the *Globe*.[83]

Ruth was determined to play in Friday's opener, his first appearance at Ebbets Field. A crowd of 18,000 didn't know Ruth was home sniffling. The doctor feared his cold could lead to pneumonia if he didn't rest. It was unfair to the fans not to announce this, Jones wrote. "Those who prefer to see a movie or listen to a symphony concert rather than watch the Ruthless Braves would have a chance to stay away from the ball park."[84] The Dodgers won their fifth straight, 5–4, and the Braves had lost five in a row. Fred Frankhouse (0–1) took the loss, a victim of three unearned runs. The Braves rallied from a 5–1 deficit to cut the lead to 5–4, but Moore grounded out as a pinch-hitter with two men on base, the at-bat Ruth would have had.[85]

One Brooklyn fan noticed Ruth's absence when Moore made a nice running catch in the eighth inning. "Yes, it's too bad Babe didn't play today," the fan said. "We'd have got three bags on that one." The Ruth jokes had already begun. Would this final season tarnish Ruth's magnificent legacy? "It is painful," wrote Ed Hughes in the *Brooklyn Daily Eagle*, "to see a once great athlete blemish a brilliant record, become a mere caricature of a once redoubtable figure. Ruth is still a mighty hero with the general run of fans. But I wonder whether the tide of feeling will turn against him should his playing sink to the pitiable stage. Human sympathy runs out of gas."[86] Tommy Holmes called Ruth "The largest elephant in the Boston traveling circus."[87]

Ruth was on the bench, bundled up like an Eskimo, for Saturday's game with 28,000 fans on hand. He looked haggard but still launched a drive into the street in batting practice, breaking a window. He started in left field and was 0-for-3 at the plate, barely connecting on a little dribbler out in front of the plate. He drew a walk to load the bases in the sixth inning. Berger doubled down the left-field line, scoring two runs, and Ruth mustered up the energy to slide into third. Moore grounded to second, and an ambitious Ruth took off for home. He was thrown out "reminiscent of the climax of the game of ring-around-the-rosy," wrote Siegel.[88] Fans applauded him, Bill McCullough wrote in the *Brooklyn Times Union*, "because they knew he was trying."[89] Mallon cracked a double to score both Berger and Moore as the Braves scored four runs on four hits. Brandt's (2–1) masterful pitching led the Braves to a 4–2 win.

Ruth looked stronger on Sunday, April 28, shattering another window in batting practice. In the third inning, he cracked one deep over the wall in right, but it was just foul. Frustrated, he struck out for the second time. In the fifth, he hit the ball sharply and would have had a single if Tony Cuccinello hadn't again been playing that Stengel shift, 30 feet back on the grass. "What does a man have to do to get a base hit in this league?" Ruth whined after the game.[90]

He drew a walk in the seventh inning. Hal Lee went in to run for him and scored from first on Pinky Whitney's double. Ruth would never have made it. The Braves won again, 5–3, and Smith (1–1) gutted out the victory despite allowing six walks.[91] Ruth only had one putout in left field in the two games, a mark of genius strategy, according to Holmes. Braves pitchers jammed lefties inside and threw outside junk to righties since, the idea, Holmes wrote, "is to keep batted balls away from left field where the portly Mr. Babe Ruth lumbers around."[92]

Back to Boston

The Braves returned home for a homestand lasting through the middle of May. A sparse, shivering crowd of 2,000 greeted them as they hosted the Philadelphia Phillies. From 1920–1934, the Phillies finished as high as fourth only once and finished eighth seven times, helping the Braves avoid the cellar on a regular basis. The Phils finished 56–93 in 1934 under player-manager Jimmie Wilson and were already off to a 2–8 start. Starter Bucky Walters faced Betts.

Ruth started in left field and walked three times, scoring once. A windy day made Ruth's already perilous fielding acumen even more problematic. Betts enjoyed a 3–1 lead, but in the fifth inning, he allowed a single, a walk, and hit Jimmie Wilson in the head to load the bases. The stubborn, dazed catcher refused to leave the field. Mickey Haslin launched a high fly ball into the swirling wind over Ruth. He misjudged it, and it sailed over his head. Haslin had a double, and all three runners scored. The Phillies added another run for a 5–3 lead.

Walters was wild in the fifth inning and walked three (including Ruth). He threw a wild pitch to make the score 5–4. Joe Bowman came in and issued a bases-loaded walk to Shanty Hogan, Ruth scoring the tying run and calling it a day. The Braves won, 7–5, with Larry Benton (1–0) pitching four scoreless innings.[93]

The April 30 game was rained out. The three postponements were tough for a team needing gate receipts early. The Braves' six home games drew an average of just over 12,000 fans; road games against the Giants averaged just over 21,000, with 23,000 at Brooklyn. Many came to see Ruth, but the Bambino only played in 10 games with 25 at-bats. He batted .240 for the month with two home runs. His nine walks gave him a strong on-base-percentage (OBP) of .441, but already he had not performed the early magic the Braves were hoping for.

NL Standings thru April 1935

Team	W	L	Pct.	GB
Brooklyn	9	4	.692	---
New York	7	3	.700	.5
Chicago	8	5	.615	1.0
Cincinnati	7	7	.500	2.5
St. Louis	6	7	.462	3.0
Pittsburgh	6	8	.429	3.5
Boston	5	7	.417	3.5
Philadelphia	2	9	.182	6.0

The player with the hot hand was Shanty Hogan. He led the National League in batting (minimum 10 games played) at .448 with an OBP of .515.[94] The rest of the Braves compiled a league-worst .234 batting average for the month. Ruth's walks kept their OBP from being last.

April 1935 National League Team Batting Statistics, Sorted by Batting Average

Team	BA	OBP	SLG	R	H	HR	BB	SO	SB
NYG	.288	.342	.417	56	130	12	33	35	2
BRO	.286	.371	.437	82	131	11	60	38	5
PIT	.276	.361	.376	58	136	5	61	43	5
CHI	.274	.309	.389	54	128	9	22	56	1
CIN	.255	.331	.382	67	124	7	51	79	12
PHI	.252	.308	.361	60	120	15	34	59	1
STL	.245	.291	.351	53	113	5	29	46	5
BOS	.234	.301	.335	43	93	7	34	37	1

McKechnie's pitching staff was able to keep the Braves competitive with the lowest team ERA in the NL, and they were tied for the fewest hits allowed.

April 1935 National League Team Pitching Statistics, Sorted by Earned Run Average

Team	ERA	ER	BB	SO	H	HR	WHIP
BOS	2.87	34	38	35	105	7	1.34
CIN	2.99	43	42	52	132	2	1.83
BRO	3.09	40	32	47	105	8	1.17
CHI	3.38	45	48	61	118	9	1.38
STL	3.54	46	38	43	123	6	1.37
PIT	4.20	58	35	68	126	9	1.29
NYG	4.26	54	26	49	111	16	1.20
PHI	5.07	67	65	38	153	14	1.83

"If you drag a whale up here out of that water," a reporter told Bill Cunningham, "you could charge a quarter to see it and a lot of people would pay it. But the whale would only lie there. It couldn't do anything. That's Ruth."[95] Ruth started hot out of the gate, but his sniffles, the Boston weather, and cancelled games put this experiment in jeopardy. He was still an attraction, however, and NL club owners pleaded with Fuchs to keep Ruth around long enough to visit their ballparks at least once. "Going through the motions as an active combatant is undoubtedly a chore and a hard one to the venerable war hoss," Cunningham wrote. "One gathers that he [Ruth] isn't particularly delighted with his present portfolio as a sort of guest outfielder with a team that seems to have a lot of carbon in its valves."[96]

Fuchs hoped the long May homestand would be a smoother ride.

8

Babe Ruth's Last Hurrah
(May 1935)

"The Babe, God love him, can't see himself as he is. He still sees himself as he was. By that I mean he can't realize that he's rich, elderly, fat and failing."—Bill Cunningham, *Boston Post*

"I am hopeful that I may be able to carry out the ambition that actuated my coming here some 14 years ago and bring to New England eventually a championship ball club. If I could accomplish this, I would die happy."
—Judge Fuchs

"If I'm through I'm all through, and it looks like I'm all through, kid."
—Babe Ruth

His Last At-Bats in Boston

May began where April ended, with three straight weather postponements. Claire Ruth didn't mind because she needed to keep the Babe home in bed to shake his lingering cold. Pinky Whitney, Ed Brandt, and Hal Lee were also under the weather. Reports of friction between Ruth and manager Bill McKechnie surfaced. "There is no foundation for any such report," Deacon Bill responded. "We get along and there is absolutely no friction. Ruth is loyally supporting me in every way, and is just as anxious for us to win ball games as I am. We will keep plugging along and do the best we can."[1]

The weather finally cleared on Saturday, May 4, and the world champion St. Louis Cardinals were in town. The "Gas House Gang" led the National League in batting average, runs, and stolen bases in 1934 through their hard-nosed, rough-and-tumble style. Frankie Frisch sent Bill Walker to the mound against Ben Cantwell.

Walker's slow, sweeping curveballs dominated the Braves from start to finish, while Cantwell stymied the Cards, and the game was scoreless through six innings before 6,000 at Braves Field. Three singles gave the Cards a run in the seventh, and Ruth bobbled a grounder to score another. Besides the error, he walked and struck out twice. The Cardinals prevailed, 3–0.

Sunday, May 5, was a highly anticipated "meeting of these two most colorful of all big-league athletes," wrote Burt Whitman in the *Boston Herald* of the Dizzy Dean vs. Ruth matchup.[2] Dean had won 30 games for the 1934 champions and was 2–2 in 1935. The largest crowd at Braves Field all season, 31,000, turned out on a bright, sunshiny day but had little to cheer for.

The Cardinals pounded 10 hits, seven of them in an explosive second inning, making short work of Ed Brandt. Terry Moore slammed one to left which Ruth watched sail into the bleachers, and Dean slammed a home run of his own as he "ran loosely and happily around the bases to the tune of cheers," Whitman remarked. Dean sailed to a 7–0 victory. The Braves had 10 hits but stranded 12 runners. Ruth managed just a walk with a strikeout and groundout and was now in an 0-for-15 slump with seven strikeouts. He swung and missed so hard at Dean's first pitch in the fourth inning that he spun himself all the way around, bringing a laugh from both competitors. The Braves were 5–9.

Next up were the Pittsburgh Pirates, who finished fifth (74–76) in 1934 but boasted a powerful lineup including shortstop Arky Vaughan and the Waner brothers: Paul and Lloyd. The Pirates were 8–9 as they came to Boston. Ruth sat out with his cold. The Pirates blasted Flint Rhem for five runs in two innings, but the Braves scored five against Ralph Birkofer. Larry Benton came on and held the Pirates to two hits in six innings. The Braves rallied in the seventh inning for a 6–5 lead, but Benton faltered in the ninth and an error led to three runs. Pittsburgh won, 8–6.

Was Ruth better off *on* or *off* the field? Bill King of the Associated Press called Ruth an innocent pawn on a chess board "placed right in the middle of the Boston Braves' muddled affairs." If it were impossible for Ruth to play, the loss of gate receipts would mean Judge Fuchs would never be able to buy back his stock held in collateral by Charles F. Adams. Adams would take over the club and appoint Ruth as manager. But if Ruth continued playing, drawing the fans in and being a success, Fuchs would rebuild his finances, regain full control of the club, and Ruth would never manage. Ruth's success could be his downfall. Fuchs had until August 1 to keep the franchise.[3]

Fuchs had until May 13 to make a smaller payment to Adams, and the August 1 deadline was considered doable "unless the Babe's drawing power falls off tremendously or the position of the Braves in the pennant race savagely cuts down gate receipts," the *Herald* reported.[4] Fuchs already had a backup plan, as Governor James Michael Curley had offered him a judgeship.[5] "I have been offered a life appointment," Fuchs said, "but I am hopeful that I may be able to carry out the ambition that actuated my coming here some 14 years ago and bring to New England eventually a championship ball club. If I could accomplish this, I would die happy."[6]

Ruth denied any dissension among the Braves. "Judge Fuchs has kept faith with me," he said. "I have been trying to play ball with the most severe cold I have ever had when I should have been in bed. If I had been in better health, I know I would have done better for him and for the ball club. After my treatments are concluded I will demonstrate that I am far from through."[7] But patience was running out.

The May 7 game against Pittsburgh was rained out. Ruth was still home in bed on May 8, the series finale. There was a rare ray of sunshine at Braves Field for the meager crowd of 2,000. The Braves fell behind, 3–1. but Randy Moore's bases-loaded triple keyed a four-run inning, and the Braves won a laugher, 12–3.

Claire served as Babe's busy secretary for the thousands of fan letters requesting everything from autographs to money for medical bills. "She efficiently sees to it that all those who have no real business with the Babe never get beyond stating their purpose to her," wrote Janet Jones in the *Boston Globe*. "I jotted down, just for fun," Claire said, "the amount of money asked for. With a $5,000 here and $50 there, it added up to $35,000!" Claire had to wrap up each autographed response and take it to the post office to send it registered mail, costing $2.[8]

Ruth felt well enough to get into the May 9 game against the Chicago Cubs and Tex Carleton. "Tex is tall, thin and seldom smiles," Whitman wrote, "except when he hears from his manager that he is to pitch against the Boston Braves."[9] Carleton won six games against the Braves in 1934 while pitching for the Cardinals. He dominated them again in a 5–1 win, allowing only Berger's first home run. Rabbit Maranville entered to a hearty ovation in his first regular-season game since 1933. He singled in the eighth inning, and Ruth came to the plate representing the tying run. Ruth lofted a deep drive to right that was caught in front of the wall. Friday's game was rained out.

On Saturday, a crowd of 10,000 included 5,000 youngsters with free admission as part of the *Boston Herald's* Baseball School held that morning. McKechnie, Berger, Ruth and Maranville joined with several Cubs to teach the youngsters.[10] "The afternoon was one of the sweetest of the spring to date," wrote Whitman, "and so was the crowd."[11] The game certainly wasn't. Bob Smith walked the leadoff man, and Billy Herman doubled to left on a ball "a more agile suburbanite might have caught," had it not been Ruth. The Cubs scored five runs in the first inning, but the Braves rallied with three of their own. Ruth walked and scored on a sacrifice fly.

The baseball lads sat in left field cheering their hero's every move, but Ruth was tuckered chasing down extra-base hits. He hit a high fly to right, and the kiddos roared thinking it would sail for a home run. Chuck Klein had the ball bounce off his glove. Ruth was safe at second on the error, and the kids had something to cheer. But the Cubs clobbered Braves pitching, 14–7. The Braves had lost five of six games. "If it isn't one thing, it's several others with the Braves these days" wrote Gerry Moore in the *Globe*.[12]

At some point in early May, Ruth and Fuchs squabbled over Ruth not appearing at a clothing store opening. The angered store owner returned the 500 tickets he purchased in return for Ruth's appearance. Fuchs threw a tirade at Ruth, who responded, "You attend to your end of the business, and I'll attend to mine. Mine is on the field."[13] Both would shortly be arguing opposite sides of that issue.

May 12 was Mother's Day, and 11,500 fans were treated to a tight pitching contest between Ed Brandt and Lon Warneke, whose overhand curveball struck Ruth out twice. The Cubs won, 4–1.[14] After his second strikeout, Ruth dejectedly yelled in the dugout, "I've played my last inning of baseball. I'm through." On Monday, Ruth went to Fuchs and offered to place himself on the voluntarily retired list, which would keep him off the field but in the front office. Fuchs wanted no part of it as the potential loss of revenue on the upcoming road trip would be catastrophic.[15] "By now Babe was aware that the man he thought was going to give him the managership he coveted was merely giving him the business," Claire Ruth wrote. "The season was only a few weeks old, but the end was near."[16]

The 6–13 Braves next faced the Cincinnati Reds, who had lost four straight games. The Reds finished dead last in offense in 1934 and were 8–13. Jack Ryder of the *Cincinnati Enquirer* wrote that the Reds finally "found an outfit that they could beat," as Ruth "sat on the bench nursing a cold and with pains in his aged props."[17] Ruth was becoming more secluded from his teammates, part of the Braves only by laundry. "He wanted a day or two rest," wrote Whitman in the *Herald*, "and when he does not want to play, he does not play."[18] A dismal 1,381 fans ventured out on Monday to see the two floundering clubs.

Si Johnson, a country boy from an Illinois farm, was a good pitcher on a bad team.[19] The game was a 1–1 tie in the seventh inning when McKechnie decided not to send Ruth up to pinch-hit for the pitcher. Cantwell (1–3) pitched a solid game, but the Reds won, 3–1, as the Braves' offense "curled up like a piece of burnt birchbark," wrote James C. O'Leary in the *Globe*.[20]

Fuchs threw a fit near the hot dog stand in the right field pavilion. The Judge "got a little out of hand," Victor O. Jones commented of the tirade, "and talked and acted like most of the other fans."[21] "I'm going to tell the boys something tomorrow," he fumed, "and that goes for Bill McKechnie and Babe Ruth, too. I'm disgusted, like everyone else." He noted that old war horses Benton and Smith made a fraction of the salaries his struggling headline pitchers were making. "I realize, of course, that the setup here hasn't been exactly perfect," he added, "and that applies to my status, too."[22]

Fuchs made his May 13 payment to Charles F. Adams while writers still commented on dissension in the clubhouse. "It's a fairly safe guess," Jones wrote, "that there's been dissatisfaction and lack of morale somewhere along the line. Contented cows give good milk and contented ball players are apt to play good ball. Maybe the boys don't like the Ruth-McKechnie arrangement, whatever that arrangement may be. As nearly as I have been able to find out, McKechnie is boss, except that he can't tell Ruth a thing. Nobody, it appears, can do that."[23] Reports swirled of Ruth's demise. He was hitless in his last 20 at-bats and was batting .171. "The Babe always will be popular on account of his likeable personality," Ryder surmised, "but it is quite apparent that his day as a regular player and a big drawing card is over."[24]

Fuchs went into the Braves clubhouse around noon on May 14 and gave the Braves his "verbal shakedown," Melville E. Webb wrote, "telling them as they left on their western trip that if they did not make a better showing on the road there was likely to be some changes in the team's roster before they returned to Boston."[25] The elephant in the room was Ruth and the awkwardness McKechnie had in holding the team together, since Ruth was technically *his* boss.[26]

The Braves drew 134,381 fans to their first 14 home games in 1935, an average of 9,598 per game. Eight games were postponed, cutting off needed revenue. On the road, they drew 136,081 in the six games at the Polo Grounds and Ebbets Field, an average of 22,680 per game. Ruth had at least drawn more fans to Braves Field. In their first 14 home games in 1934, the Braves drew only 7,750 per game. The Red Sox controlled the town, drawing 14,360 per game in their first five games at Fenway Park.

The next game was another rainout. The Wednesday, May 15 game had already been cancelled. McKechnie wanted the club to get an early start on their trek west. It was also the opening of the racing season at Rockingham Park in New Hampshire. Some Braves fans considered the game's cancellation was "serving only to help one of baseball's big competitors."[27] No doubt, would-be Braves fans flocked to the races via the $1 Rockingham Racer out of North Station to the new home for pari-mutuel betting. "Today's a very significant day in New England," wrote Victor O. Jones, "betting on horse racing becomes legal. All the ladies and gents who have been laying it on the line with the illegal bookies, can now proceed to lay it on the till of the strictly legal pari-mutuel sills. What a difference a little law, judiciously applied, can make!"[28] Construction on Suffolk Downs would also soon be completed, providing a shorter trip to the tracks. "New England is gambling crazy," said the "Sportsman" column in the *Globe*. "When folks are in that mood, tracks prosper."[29]

The Braves wouldn't return home until May 31 after a 15-game road trip to St. Louis, Chicago, Pittsburgh, Cincinnati, and Philadelphia. Ruth would never play another game in Boston. "Ruth has been telling friends," Whitman reported, "that he is disappointed in the way he has been playing in the game. He says that he wants to help the Braves and Judge Fuchs all he can. Yet he has not been feeling well and strong. The Babe has intimated several times within the last two weeks that he has felt like quitting the active game. But he said yesterday that he would stick it out and give all he had to further the best interests of the team and of Judge Fuchs." Ruth went west with the club.

The Braves had until May 15 to trim their roster to 23 players, a cost-cutting practice during the Depression. Pitcher Leo Mangum and catcher Bill Lewis were sent to Montreal. Mangum never pitched again in the major leagues.[30]

Wednesday, May 15, was a cool afternoon as 25,000 made their way to Rockingham Park and poured $325,310 into the pari-mutuel machines. Governor Curley joined Fuchs, Adams, and Braves catcher Shanty Hogan, laid up with a broken finger. "It's the luck of the Irish," he joked, showing his winning ticket.[31]

Fans on the Rockingham Racer likely read the newspaper reports that Ruth was quitting.

"It Looks Like I'm All Through, Kid."

Ruth spent the off-days back in New York and was at the train station waiting to go to St. Louis. Bill Corum of the International News Service spotted the "tired, bitterly disappointed, half sick old guy," who was "on his way to St. Louis and at the end of the trail."[32] It was an illuminating encounter with the Babe.

"What's the use, kid?" Ruth asked. "I'm all washed up. I don't want to play baseball anymore." "Wouldn't you want to manage the Braves if you got the chance?" Corum asked.

"I don't even know about that," he replied.

> I guess they don't like me much up there in Boston. Fuchs is all right and McKechnie has been swell. There's been no trouble of any kind between us. You can make that plain. But the fans are on me and the newspaper boys, too. I don't know what I ever did to those fellows, except make pretty headlines when I was hitting home runs. I've been sick ever since the season started with the worst cold I ever had. I can't seem to shake it.
> But I guess it doesn't make much difference as far as baseball goes. I always said I'd know when I was through, kid. Well, I'm through as a player and I know it. What's the use of my getting out there and making a monkey out of myself?[33]

He reflected on his brief time in Boston. "I thought maybe that even at forty I could have one more good year with the stick for 'em. But I couldn't get going and neither could the team. Now they blame me for that, too." He continued to insist he didn't need the money and would just as well have time to golf and hunt, but Fuchs "begged me to go on this trip" with the potential of gate revenue, especially in locales he had never played in before: Cincinnati and Pittsburgh.

"I don't want to throw Judge Fuchs and Bill McKechnie down," he said, "but I guess this is the last one, the last swing around the loop, kid. I'm too old to be a sucker for a few extra bucks that I can get along without. If I'm through I'm all through, and it looks like I'm all through, kid."[34]

Corum saw that train ride for Ruth as "that long, that inevitable, that weary road that leads us all to the last turning" as he gazed at the sunset of his career. Ruth's road was "ineluctable and universal," and he was "so desolate that you might have thought someone near and dear to him was riding out the trip with the bats and uniforms in the baggage car ahead. And, come to think of it, something near and dear to him was—his youth. And it wasn't coming back on the train from St. Louis, or any other train."[35]

"He Still Sees Himself as He Was"

"Everything hinges on the western trip," Judge Fuchs acknowledged. "If it is true that he [Ruth] will quit, I for one, shall be awfully sorry. I would much rather see him retiring when he is back at the top or as near the top as possible. I hoped that Babe would make this homecoming to Boston a glorious one, and I tried to give Boston and the National League the color and benefit of the game's greatest athlete."[36]

Ruth immediately denied his quitting comments when he arrived in St. Louis. "There is nothing to it," he blurted, puffing on a black cigar at the Kings-Way Hotel.[37] "I haven't talked with anyone about my plans. I don't even know them myself. All that I can say is that as long as I feel able to get out there on the ball field and play, I'll play. I owe the people of Cincinnati and Pittsburgh, for example, something of a debut. Baseball has been good to me and I'm not anxious to quit it."[38]

"As long as the fans come out to see me and the club owners want me, you will see 'The Old Babe' out there," but, "unless I am able to shake the present cold that has severely handicapped me for several weeks, there is a possibility I will ask to be put on the voluntarily retired list." Ruth disputed Corum's article. "Where the New York writer got his information about the Boston fans 'riding me' I do not know, as I can truthfully say I never heard an unkind remark from a Boston fan. They have always given me a most cordial welcome and the writers not only in Boston but all over the country have been exceptionally kind to me."[39] The idealistic Ruth had returned.

This was normal for Ruth, Whitman noted. "During his past two seasons with the Yankees, he was known for 'dark, dismal moods, into which he had been plunged by protracted batting slumps, and that then he would state he was 'all through,' and 'all washed up.' Writers knew better and resisted rushing to their typewriters to break the story since Ruth would hit a home run the next day and all was forgotten."[40] But this time seemed different.

"The Babe, God love him, can't see himself as he is," wrote Bill Cunningham in the *Boston Post*.

> He still sees himself as he was. By that I mean he can't realize that he's rich, elderly, fat and failing. He's been in the money so long that even that isn't a novelty any more. It never changed him much anyhow. He still wears a country boy cap and prefers hot dogs to caviar. He can't see anything anomalous about a part-time outfielder with a near-cellar ball club living in a hotel suite which costs him $22 per day and riding around in his spare time in a limousine better than most of our bankers own.[41]

McKechnie put a positive spin on Ruth's struggles. "The Babe will quit talking about leaving the game after he cracks out a few homers, which he will do shortly because the weather is sure to warm up and put everybody in better spirits. I think our ball club is just as good and probably better than last season."[42]

A Final Matchup with Dizzy Dean

A strong weekday crowd of around 4,000 arrived at Sportsman's Park in St. Louis on May 17 for Ruth's first appearance. About 1,300 of the St. Louis Knot-Hole Gang youngsters cheered Ruth from the left field bleachers. There was more commotion *outside* the park. Stadium employees who were union workers were boy-cotting Cardinals games until Leo "The Lip" Durocher apologized. Union members of his wife's employer, the Forest City Manufacturing Co., went on strike in February, and she crossed the picket lines. Durocher mocked the picketers as he dropped his wife off at work. One lady jumped on his car and gave him lip right back. Durocher had backtracked on his anti-union remarks. "I have nothing against the union," he said. "I buy union-made clothing and eat union-made bread."[43]

Inside the park, the Braves pounded rookie Ed Heusser, making his first major-league start, and pulled off a surprising 7–1 win. Berger went 3-for-5 and Fred Frankhouse allowed just seven hits. Ruth singled down the right-field line in the fifth, his first hit in nearly a month, and finished 1-for-4.[44] The Braves ended their four-game skid.

A Ladies' Day game on Saturday, May 18, brought fans 12,750 to the park. Bill Walker again had his way with the Braves, throwing a two-hit shutout through eight innings, and the Cards won, 6–2.

Ruth struck out, walked, and grounded out before leaving in the sixth inning. Rhem fell to 0–3 on the overcast day. "I thought I'd sure get some sun when I came to St. Louis," Ruth muttered, "but I guess everybody's having a bad spring."[45]

Sunday's weather was not any better. It was chilly with rain in the forecast. That morning's *St. Louis Globe-Democrat* had a 2/3-page advertisement for boys and girls to send in box tops of Quaker Puffed Wheat or Rice to receive free gifts from Babe Ruth.[46] A crowd of 12,000 braved the elements to witness a Ruth vs. Dizzy Dean matchup. Huck Betts took the mound for the Braves.

Dean fooled Ruth and struck him out on a curveball. Randy Moore hit a towering home run, and the Braves led, 2–0. St. Louis quickly tied the score on a Pepper Martin walk, Jack Rothrock's double, and Frankie Frisch's single. Ripper Collins hit a towering drive to left-center. Ruth raced hard to his left, leaped, speared the drive, and "made the skeptics look very foolish," wrote Ray J. Gillespie in the *St. Louis Star and Times*. The crowd gave ooohs and ahhs after the catch "reminiscent of the kind Babe used to make in his heyday as a star," Gillespie wrote. "The play brought down the house in thunderous applause" as Ruth made his way to the dugout.[47] It was a good day for the Babe only with the glove. At the plate, he struck out, lined into a double play, hit a weak grounder back to Dean, and fouled out to third. As Ruth departed, "the fans paid him a fine tribute by clapping and yelling until their larynxes were about to bounce out onto the lawn."[48] The Cardinals won, 7–3.

"I'm sure glad Babe Ruth is going to stick in the Boston lineup," Dean wrote in his syndicated column. "It looked for a spell like I was gonna chase all the vice presidents right out of their uniforms. But he come along to St. Louis, and if he stays in there and is a good little out, I'll give him a nice fat one to hit a country mile sometime—sometime when we're 10 runs in front."[49]

The Braves left on the midnight train to Chicago.

A Final Visit to Wrigley Field

On May 20, Ruth returned to Wrigley Field, the home of his famous "Called Shot" in the 1932 World Series. It seemed a lifetime ago, and now his age and diminished skills were the focus of attention. "Braves Bring Old Babe Ruth to Town Today," headlined the *Chicago Tribune*.[50] A huge crowd was anticipated but only 6,000 turned out on Monday with a raw wind blowing off Lake Michigan. In batting practice, Ruth was looking spry for someone "whose obituaries already have been rushed in print," wrote Herbert Simons in the *Chicago Daily Times* and slammed a couple of home runs to right field. "He looked none of the 'dying gladiator' role his .155 batting average and his wheezing performances afield, to date, make him out to be."[51] But that was only batting practice.

Marvin McCarthy in the *Daily Times* wrote of the "rheumy, wheezy old gent" coming to Chicago, "worn out and ready to sit in the first wheel chair which some thoughtful soul trundles into position." Ruth couldn't hit a home run, McCarthy quipped, "if someone strung up the ball like a Halloween apple and left it hanging over home plate. Furthermore, he could not catch the ball if it floated out of the heavens into his outfield, stayed and supported by a parachute." But McCarthy also warned that Ruth had fooled them before. "Watch your steps carefully, Cubs, Old Man Babe River comes around to your door."[52]

Bill Lee, an emerging pitching ace for the Cubs, was dubbed "handsome Bill" for his dark hair and eyes.[53] Lee was 3–2 so far in 1935, with a 2.08 ERA. Ruth received warm ovations but never got the ball out of the infield. He drew a walk, popped up, and lined into a double play to end a Braves rally. The Cubs jumped on top early against Ed Brandt. Phil Cavarretta and Gabby Hartnett singled, Billy Jurges doubled, and Billy Herman singled. Throw in a sacrifice fly and the Cubs led, 3–0. In the third inning, Kiki Cuyler tripled when Randy Moore missed a shoestring catch and the ball rolled on by. Cuyler scored on Cavarretta's single, which dropped in front of the wheezing Ruth. The Cubs won, 5–0.[54]

The Braves were 7–17, a half-game behind the Phillies, who leaped over them into seventh place. The Braves were in the National League cellar and would remain so for the rest of the season.

Fred Frankhouse, coming off his stellar performance in St. Louis, took the mound for Boston against Tex Carleton on May 21. Ruth received more stirring ovations, but his deep fly to left was caught at the wall in the first inning. He did make two nice running catches and doffed his cap on his way to the bench.[55] The game was scoreless until Billy Urbanski doubled home two runs in the fifth inning, and the Braves led, 2–0.

Ruth led off the sixth inning. He smashed a pitch far and deep to right which cleared the bleachers and hit a building on the other side of Sheffield Avenue. He "romped around the bases to the tumult of cheers," Ralph Clifford wrote in the *Boston Herald*. "Even though he is an alien, the crowds have been rooting for him to hit a homer every time he comes to bat." Ruth gave the fans what they craved. Old Man River had fooled them again.

Moore deposited his own home run into the right field bleachers. Suddenly, the Braves looked like a powerhouse. Tex Carleton had won seven in a row against the Braves, but Frankhouse, Ruth, and the Braves bested him, 4–1. The last game of the series on May 22 was rained out, so Chicago's last memory of Ruth was a home run out of Wrigley Field.

The Steel City Awaits

The Braves left for Pittsburgh, and reporters were ready. Rumors of Ruth's imminent retirement were everywhere. It was a bleak day in the Steel City. "Come on, Mr. Sun," Ruth pleaded as he overlooked Forbes Field from his suite at the Hotel Schenley. The turn-of-the-century hotel was the classiest in all Pittsburgh, and its Oakland neighborhood became a center of health, academics, and culture. Called the "Waldorf of Pittsburgh," it stands today as the William Pitt Union building at the University of Pittsburgh.

Ruth was more concerned about Forbes Field, the Pirates' home since 1909. The concrete and steel structure was built on farmland three miles from downtown. The triple-decked grandstand was one-of-a-kind. Forbes was spacious: 365 feet to left field, 457 to left-center, and 435 to dead center. In 1925, the right field fence was cut from 376 feet to 300 with a double-decker grandstand behind it, a gargantuan target for left-handed hitters. To prevent cheap home runs, a 14½-foot screen was added to the 9½-foot wall in 1932.[56] Ruth had his eyes on that wall.

"That darned wind is blowing in toward home plate again," Ruth vented. "An hour ago, it was blowing out toward the right-field stands. Ever see anything like that? And doesn't it ever get hot in Pittsburgh? Never saw such weather. Why, on Opening Day in Boston we played three innings in snow. Our whole ballclub is sick with colds. I'm just shaking off a beauty myself, but I do wish it would get hot." While waiting for the sun, he rummaged through the pile of mail on his desk. "I'm getting more fan mail than I ever did before in my life," he said.[57]

Ruth publicly denied any retirement plans. "I feel I am in better condition at the present time than I have been in the last few years," he assured them. "My legs feel better, and I am getting rid of that troublesome cold."[58] He started in right field on Thursday afternoon, May 23, before a crowd of 10,000, half of them courtesy of the free Ladies' Day admission. "There is still some of the historic power running through his system," Havey J. Boyle remarked in the Post-Gazette, "but only a man of his past would be tolerated in the outfield."[59]

Ruth's first appearance at Forbes Field was 14 years earlier when the Yankees came for an exhibition game. It was a sweltering July day, and the stadium could barely contain the 18,000 in attendance. "I was on the field as a bat boy," recalled

Art McKennan, who later had a four-decade career as the Pirates' public address announcer. "The stands were filled, and more people were standing on the field."[60] They were disappointed when the young star Ruth failed to connect. William A. White wrote in the *Pittsburgh Post* of the "dejected multitude" filing out like "the look of a youngster who has just seen a fine piece of apple pie fall out of his hand and into the dust of the street."[61] No doubt some of those youngsters in 1921 returned in 1935 in hopes of a better outcome.

Ruth put on a show in batting practice. He slammed a ball which clanged off the roof of the right field stands and reportedly sent a pigeon, two robins, and a host of sparrows scurrying. Someone must have been bird watching. Ruth looked appreciably better at the bat and returned to the dugout. He sat on the bench and took a pinch of tobacco from the tin in his pocket. "Do they hit over the top of that thing very often?" he asked a reporter. No, he was told, but he was reminded of one he hit in nearly the same spot during the 1927 World Series.[62]

The game got underway with Bill Swift taking on Ben Cantwell. Ruth struck out in the first inning. The Pirates jumped on top when Arky Vaughan doubled home Paul Waner. Cantwell was knocked around in the fourth inning. Waner tripled off the right field screen, and Ruth was running in circles trying to play the carom. "There were creaks and groans that were almost audible," Chester Smith wrote in the *Pittsburgh Press* of the right fielder. Pep Young doubled and Gus Suhr tripled to right, and Ruth stumbled around again. "He was in his prime a very good fielder," wrote Harvey J. Boyle in the *Post-Gazette*, "but now with his baseball beard flowing about his knees he has difficulties."[63] It was painful. The Braves lost, 7–1.

The crowd longed for a Ruth home run and almost had one. In the sixth inning, he launched a drive to deep right. Paul Waner "sprang above the soil and accomplished a spectacular one-hand catch with the back of his mitt touching the concrete," wrote Edward F. Balinger in the *Post-Gazette*.[64] Waner and Ruth passed each other on the field. "You're an awful little guy," Ruth growled, "to be such a big thief."[65]

Rabbit Maranville pinch-hit in the ninth inning and received a warm ovation from the city where he had made so many memories from 1921 to 1924. Besides the hoopla for Ruth's return, Pittsburgh held a celebration honoring their lovable shortstop. Prior to the game, Maranville was called to home plate and presented with a set of golf clubs. He was honored at a banquet that night at the Hotel Schenley.[66] It was a memorable scene.

Judge John P. Egan, law professor at Duquesne University, gave a stirring speech. Egan praised the game for character-making of "the poor unfortunates who may not have any other way to turn." The speech seemed to touch Ruth. "Maybe the Babe was thinking of some of the unfortunate lads whom he had seen in his own childhood," Charles J. Doyle of the *Sun-Telegram* suggested. Ruth took the podium and "exhorted youngsters to take up the great diamond pastime as a means of staying out of trouble." Ruth may have pondered where he would have been but for the game

Pitchers Ben Cantwell (left) and Bob Brown with the Braves in 1933 (courtesy Boston Public Library, Leslie Jones Collection).

and wondered where he would go if the game was gone. The audience sat in stunned silence as the great Bambino wiped away tears. "I love him like a brother," he said of Rabbit Maranville, then choked through his words. "Dammit," he grunted. Maranville was also choked up. There was hardly a dry eye in the place and the audience stood and applauded. The band played something lively. Ruth sensed the passing of their era. He composed himself and continued, but that moment had already spoken volumes.[67] Robert Creamer called Ruth's speech his "lament for his lost youth."[68]

Chester L. Smith reported that Ruth would retire when the Braves returned to Boston. Smith claimed, "some who are in closer touch with the situation" said Fuchs was looking to cash in whatever assets the Braves had, mainly Wally Berger, to pay off his debts.[69]

On May 24, the Pirates sent Big Jim Weaver (6'6") to the mound against Brandt, and Ruth started in right field. Brandt never got on track as the Waner brothers and Arky Vaughan pounced on him, and he fell behind 2–0 after one inning. The Pirates extended the lead to 5–0, Brandt was done, and Bob Smith did his usual mop-up work. The Braves put together four hits in the fourth inning, one of them a single by Ruth, and scored two runs. The Braves trailed, 7–2, entering the ninth. Tommy Thompson hit a grand slam to cut the lead to 7–6. But the Braves' rally came up short. Brandt fell to 2–5, and the Braves were 8–19.

Ruth was again robbed of a home run by Paul Waner, in nearly the same spot as the day before. The drive was about 400 feet, and Waner again leaped against the concrete and pulled back the ball that seemed destined to travel out. Ruth stood at first base, staring in astonishment. Even when he connected, he couldn't catch a break. Ruth made a highlight-reel catch of his own, diving head-first and robbing Pep Young of a hit.[70]

That night, the Reds played the Phillies before 20,000 curious fans under the lights in the first official major league night game. President Franklin D. Roosevelt threw a switch from the White House at 8:30 p.m., and on came the lights at Crosley Field in Cincinnati.[71] The Reds played six more evening games in 1935. Babe Ruth would have been quite an evening attraction. He never got the chance.

The Great Man of Baseball

Pittsburgh residents who were at Forbes Field on May 25, 1935, had a story to tell for the rest of their lives. Some were still telling them into the 21st century. The morning began with Ruth meeting a group of newsboys who were invited to Forbes Field by the *Sun-Telegraph*. Fifteen youngsters won an autographed ball. Ruth autographed another one for a sick boy in McKeesport, which he sent someone to deliver.[72]

Another youngster was selling newspapers and peanuts outside the stadium. He lived in the Oakland section of Pittsburgh just blocks from Forbes Field. Each day of the series with the Braves, the boy waited for Ruth to arrive at the players' entrance. "Babe came in with his wife," he recalled 71 years later. "I got his autograph. I had nothing but an old scorecard." Ruth signed another scorecard on Friday. "On the third day, he passed out business cards with his name stamped on them and didn't sign for anyone."[73]

The boy was 12-year-old Paul Warhola. He would attend Pirates games with his brothers, John and Andy. Andy had little interest in baseball and was more consumed with drawing pictures. Later in life, Andy would drop the "a" from his last name and become Andy Warhol.

Red Lucas took the mound for Pittsburgh. A dependable starter, Lucas was in his second year with the Pirates after eight years in Cincinnati. Lucas was making his second start of the season, having pitched a strong, complete-game victory against the Giants five days before. He would never forget this day.

Ruth came up in the first inning with Billy Urbanski on second. Lucas threw a changeup, and Ruth lined it into the lower right field stands for career home run #712. "The Babe's hard to fool," Lucas said. "I knew the instant he took a cut at that ball that she was going to travel."[74] When asked about the home run in 1973, he said, "Well, I can't say exactly, except I know it was something inside. I for sure wasn't going to throw the ball to him where he might line it back through the pitcher's box. Ruth hit my pitch into the right field stands, just over a screen we had out there."[75] The ball was caught by 20-year-old Emmett Cavanagh, who had ridden the trolley to the ballpark that day.

Berger and Moore both singled, and the day was over for Lucas. In came Guy Bush from the bullpen. Ruth had a history with the "Mississippi Mudcat."

Bush had pitched for the Cubs the previous 12 years. The two faced off in the 1932 World Series. Game Three was at Wrigley Field before "a hostile crowd which booed him [Ruth] vigorously," wrote Richards Vidmer of the *New York Herald Tribune*. Charley Root hurled pitches to Ruth from the mound while Bush and other Cubs were hurled insults at him from the top step of the dugout. In the first inning, Ruth shut them up by slamming a three-run homer. Ruth faced "a bellowing of boos, hisses and jeers" when he batted in the fifth inning of a 4–4 game. This was "the most famous and meticulously analyzed at-bat in the history of baseball," wrote Thomas Wolf.[76] The crowd cheered as Root threw two strikes to the Babe. Ruth grinned and held up his bat with his left hand while pointing two fingers with his right hand, fingers which have forever been the stuff of legend. Ruth and Root jawed back and forth. Ruth swung, and the ball sailed out near the center field flagpole, the deepest part of Wrigley Field. Ruth had called his shot. Or he didn't. It depends on whom you ask. But the Yankees crushed the Cubs and swept the Series. "I never had so much fun in all my life," Ruth said.

In Game Four, Bush made a lasting memory by hitting Ruth in the arm with a fastball. "Hey lop ears!" Ruth shouted to Bush, "Was that your fastball you hit me with? I couldn't feel it. I thought it was one of those gnats flying around here."[77]

It was three years later. Ruth and Bush faced each other again. The Bambino launched his second home run of the day and career #713 into the second deck in right field. Ruth added a single in the fifth inning, then batted again in the seventh. Bush was still on the mound.

"It seems as if the 10,000 wanted a homer regardless of the cost," Doyle wrote, as Ruth "touched the sportsmanship strings" of any fan. The *Boston Globe* referred to Ruth, "his body reaching the stage of senility and his glorious major league career in the sunset stage."[78] Another homer would add to the majesty of the day. Bush was throwing Ruth slow stuff to keep him off-balance. On a three-and-one pitch, "Babe had all his beautiful power rhythm and follow through," wrote Doyle, "and the fans came out of their seats as they heard a sharp report that started the rocket soaring towards the roof."[79]

"No one before the Great Man," wrote Volney Walsh, capturing the moment in the *Pittsburgh Press*, "ever had been able to hit a ball over that stand since it was erected in 1925." It was a moment for baseball history. "The Great Man," Walsh continued, "unloosened his bat, took a tremendous swing and the ball traveled high and far toward the right-field stands. Pirate players stood in their tracks to watch the flight of the ball. It was a home run all the way and when the ball disappeared behind the stands, there was a mighty roar from the crowd of 10,000." The Great Bambino "convinced one and all that he is the mightiest of them all."[80]

In 1974, Guy Bush recalled those two Ruth home runs. The 72-year-old was tending to his soybeans on his Mississippi farm. "He hit a ball on the handle," Bush said of home run #713, "and he pulled it about eight or 10 feet fair and it just fell into the stands. Just a short fly ball was all it was. Well, it made me so mad that I thought to myself, 'Is that the kind of home runs he's been getting?'" Bush thought he was better prepared for Ruth in the seventh. "I said, coming out of the dugout, 'Well, that jackass who hit the little blooper home run before will be up again this inning. I'm going to throw three fastballs (contradicting reports of his slow stuff) right by that jackass and see what this crowd will do and get my laugh on him." Bush watched the ball sail over the roof. "It was the longest cockeyed ball I ever saw in my life. That poor fellow, he'd gotten to where he could hardly hobble along. I ain't mad no more."[81]

Ruth came around to home plate with a broad smile on his face and a tip of his cap. "I just look over there at him," Bush recalled, "and he kind of looked at me. I tipped my cap just to say, 'I've seen everything now, Babe.' He just looked at me and kind of saluted and smiled, and that's the last home run he ever hit. He was the greatest."[82]

"I'll never forget him smiling when he rounded third," Lucas recalled. "I can hear him puffing along and sort of grunting, 'Man, that one felt pretty good.'"[83]

Players were quoted after the game.

"Babe proved to everyone that none can compare with him," Pirates manager Pie Traynor commented.

"Who said the old Babe can't smack 'em anymore?" asked Paul Waner.

"Did you see those balls going?" asked Lloyd Waner. "They couldn't have gone any faster or further if they were shot out of a canon."

"He's the greatest hitter of all time," said Pirates legend Honus Wagner.

"I never thought anyone would ever put a ball over the top of the stands in a regular game," commented Gus Suhr, "but then, I never figured on the Babe."[84]

Phil Coyne was a teenager in the stands that day. "The first two home runs we really didn't pay attention to," he said. "We just run around a lot. But the third one we paid attention to. A miracle happened. That was a good, good, ways up there." Ruth's home run left the park, but Coyne remained. He became an usher at Forbes Field in 1936 and became a Pittsburgh institution. He remained at his post for the next 81 years, giving fans his "irreplaceable and effervescent smile," wrote Jason Mackey in the *Post-Gazette*. He finally retired in 2017 at the age of 99, eight decades after he saw that Ruth home run. Coyne was 102 when he died in 2021.[85]

Ruth made his way to the Pirates' dugout, which had the only entrance to the Braves' clubhouse. He sat down at the end of the bench next to rookie pitcher Mace

Brown, who made his major league debut earlier that week. "Boy, that last one felt good," Ruth said to the awestruck 26-year-old. They sat together for a few minutes. "That was a thrill just seeing Ruth," Brown said 60 years later. "Then to have him come in and sit right down beside me … that's something I've always remembered." Mace's wife Sue watched the game in the upper deck with a movie camera. Unfortunately, the film didn't survive. "It just wasn't any good at all," Brown said. "We had enough that we could see it and we showed it a few times. It just deteriorated over the years, and we threw it away."[86] Ruth's final home run survived only in the memories of those who were there that day.

Caleb "Socko" McCarey, clubhouse attendant and future Red Sox scout, attended to Ruth after he left the game. "I opened the clubhouse door for him," Socko recalled. "He wanted some hot dogs. I had to go get him some. I think I brought six. Or three. Three, six, it don't make no difference."[87]

Ruth's historic day overshadowed the Braves ineptness in losing, 11–7. Huck Betts had a 4–0 lead but left with a 7–5 deficit. The Braves tied the game, 7–7, in the seventh inning, but the Pirates touched Ben Cantwell (1–5) with three runs in the seventh and went on to victory.

Far more interesting is what became of the #714 baseball after it cleared the Forbes Field roof. Like Ruth himself, it is a fascinating tale mixed with myth and fact. Gus Miller, Forbes Field head usher, investigated and concluded that the ball traveled 600 feet, which could not be verified. Some said the ball bounced off a roof on Bouquet Street, but that house was in foul territory, parallel to the stadium. Others said it hit the roof of 334 Joncaire Street and bounced onto Bouquet Street. Yet another account stated that the ball landed in a backyard on Joncaire that was filled with construction materials. There it was picked up by Henry "Wiggy" DeOrio. Or maybe it was 51 Boundary Street. DeOrio lived in Panther Hollow, an Italian neighborhood of Oakland. Wherever he found it, DeOrio and his pals brought the ball to the Hotel Schenley for Ruth to sign. DeOrio kept the ball in a drawer and later donated it to Commissioner Happy Chandler, and it now rests in the Baseball Hall of Fame.[88] That ball was not only Babe Ruth's last home run, but also his last hit in the major leagues.

Thirteen-year-old Sam Sciullo of Castle Shannon, Pennsylvania, waited for autographs as players exited Forbes Field. "Babe comes out," he remembered 71 years later. "He was wearing a light camel hair coat, with a collar around his neck and a cap. He was looking straight ahead. He was the original sad sack. Kids started running up. He doesn't say a word. He was not rude, he didn't push anybody. He just put his head down and walked." The great highs of the day for Ruth now became great lows as he thought of his future. "He was going back to the Schenley Hotel. I caught up and walked with him, begging for his autograph, but he didn't say a word. He was not a well man that day. He was depressed and glad to get out of Pittsburgh."[89]

Emmett Cavanagh, who caught home run #712, did get Ruth to sign his ball at the Hotel Schenley. In 2008, his family auctioned off the coal-stained ball for

$172,500. "Truth be told," said his great-nephew, Jim Englert, "it was probably just wrapped in an old rag hidden somewhere in his coal cellar and surrounded by coal dust."[90]

Duffy Lewis, Braves coach, urged Ruth to retire after this glorious day, as did Claire. "This was the moment to quit, if ever there was such a moment," she wrote. "I told him that and he said, 'I thought of it going around the bases the third time.' Christy Walsh called from New York. 'You're going to quit, Babe. Do it now. Bow out on the notes you just struck.'"[91]

"I can't" he griped. "I promised that son of a bitch [Fuchs] I'd play in all the towns on this trip."[92] He later regretted not listening to those around him. "I wish I had had enough sense to call it a career after this grand and glorious day," Ruth said in Bob Considine's account. "I wanted to, but Fuchs again talked me out of it and told me to stick for the Decoration Day [(Memorial Day] games against Philadelphia. He had advertised me. I should never have listened to him."[93]

Babe Ruth Day in Cincinnati

Babe Ruth had little left in the tank as the Braves arrived in Cincinnati. His first appearance at Crosley Field was "Babe Ruth Day." He was swamped with autograph requests and signed everything but scorecards. "There are too many of those around," he said. A crowd of 24,361 on Sunday, May 26, arrived hoping Ruth could duplicate that magic at Forbes Field they read about in the morning paper.

Si Johnson, who had mastered the Braves in Boston, took the hill again. Fred Frankhouse, Boston's best pitcher so far, brought his 3–1 record and 1.26 ERA to the mound. The Reds had won three in a row and were 13–16. Boston was 8–20.

Ruth took a called third strike in the first inning. He was on the move in left field, chasing down a single and a double. "He got quite a workout," Jack Ryder wrote. The Braves trailed, 2–0, in the third inning. Ruth came up with the tying run in scoring position but popped up, then struck out twice. The Braves fell, 6–3. Ruth striking out was just as entertaining, according to Ryder. "Next to watching him swat one over the garden wall, the rooters like to see him indulge in a whiffing bee, with all the tremendous power of his swings accomplishing nothing more than to stir up the balmy spring atmosphere."[94]

That was the only complete game Ruth played in 1935. He took Monday's game off, giving no reason "other than to say he didn't feel like playing," Ralph Clifford wrote in the *Herald*.[95] He pinch-hit in the ninth inning and drew a walk in a 9–5 loss, the Braves' fifth straight.

Tuesday was Ladies Day at Crosley Field, and 12,000 came for their last glimpse of Ruth in left field. McKechnie started Flint Rhem, and the Reds slammed out 18 hits. It seems every one of them was hit to left field, where "Babe Ruth hoisted the white flag," said the *Globe*, and "sought the cooling refreshment of the showers."

The crowd cheered Ruth at the plate, but in the field you could hear "a good many snickers when he floundered around the pasture in trying to make plays on the hard drives belted out in his direction," wrote Ryder.[96] Ruth walked and scored on Randy Moore's triple in the first inning, then grounded out in his other two at-bats. The Reds won, 13–4, and the Braves got out of Cincinnati on the 6:10 p.m. train.[97]

A Fond Farewell in Philadelphia

The City of Brotherly Love was awaiting Ruth's arrival, not realizing that this was where he would last set foot on a major league field as a player. The Baker Bowl and its short porch in right field—280 feet down the line with a 40-foot wall—was a left-handed hitter's dream. It was Ruth's first appearance in the cigar box since he pinch-hit in his first World Series appearance for the Red Sox 20 years before. He was swarmed upon arriving at the Bellevue Stratford Hotel. Before the game, he was presented a baseball-shaped bouquet of flowers on a tripod of three bats. He gave a short speech.

The Braves knocked out rookie pitcher Orville Jorgens in the first inning. Urbanski doubled, Thompson and Ruth walked, Berger singled to score two runs, and Jorgens was pulled. The Braves loaded the bases against Tommy Thomas in the second. After throwing a ball to Ruth, he was pulled in favor of "Chief" Euel Moore, a member of the Chickasaw Nation. Ruth drew a bases-loaded walk for his final RBI. Berger smashed a grand slam to put the Braves up, 7–0, but Brandt's comfortable lead disappeared as the Phillies scored six runs. Bob Smith came in to hold the lead and the Braves won, 8–6. Ruth struck out twice in his next two at-bats.[98] But he impressed in the field.

His "work in the field was a revelation," wrote Stan Baumgartner in the *Philadelphia Inquirer.* "Without the aid of crutches, a perambulator, a kiddie car or a wheel chair, he made two scintillating running catches." Ruth said he felt good. "I feel better and am in better shape than I have been for the past three years," he said. "I hope to hit at least 25 home runs this year—and it is a cinch I will not hit them sitting on the bench watching someone else swing a bat."[99] Publicly, he was confident. It was a mirage.

Memorial (Decoration) Day, May 30, was a doubleheader. The city paid homage that morning to those who paid the ultimate sacrifice. Most residents didn't remember the days the 65 Civil War veterans remembered from 70 years before. They were a "little group of blue-clad, enfeebled men," wrote John M. McCullough of the *Philadelphia Inquirer,* "who had once stood on the battlefields of Chancellorsville, Antietam, and Gettysburg when the game was still an amateur sport."[100] In 1938, 2,000 veterans attended the 75th, and final, reunion at Gettysburg.[101] Their days were nearing an end, and so was Babe Ruth's career.

Ruth played in his final major league game on that day before 15,122 fans who had no idea they were watching his feeble finale. Rookie pitcher Jim "Slim" Bivin was on the mound for the Phillies. Frankhouse hurled for the Braves. Imagine the fanfare had everyone known what the day would mean.

With Urbanski on base, Ruth grounded out to bulky-armed first baseman Dolph Camilli, who gobbled up the grounder and took it to the bag himself. And there it was. Babe Ruth batted for the final time. "I remember facing the big boy," Bivin remembered in 1952. "Never realized I was the last pitcher to face him until he died and the papers carried a story about it."[102]

The reason was due to what happened next. "The big Bambino limped out into left field to start the first game," Baumgartner wrote.[103] He was still feeling the effects of banging his knee into the wall in Cincinnati. With two out, Johnny Moore singled and Camilli walked. Mickey Haslin doubled them both in for a 2–0 lead. Lou Chiozza sent an opposite-field drive to left field. Ruth raced over, stumbled, and bobbled the ball. Chiozza kept on racing to the plate. Ruth finally got a hold of the thing and relayed the ball to Pinky Whitney, who threw to Al Spohrer, and Chiozza was out at the plate. Ironically, the last play of Ruth's career was an assist. But he was hurt, again. He later described it as a charley horse. The crowd was disappointed to see him exit "to the clubhouse to pet his creaking joints" when the inning ended. The crowd chanted for him to appear in the second game, but the Bambino had walked off the field for the final time.[104] The Braves dropped both games of the doubleheader, 11–6 and 9–3. At the end of the day, the Phillies were 11–22; the Braves were 9–25.

Ruth and the Braves returned home, where he wanted to announce his retirement.

Back in Boston

McKechnie told Fuchs that Ruth simply could not continue. He even described a mutiny among his pitchers who were threatening not to take the hill if Ruth was playing in the outfield. McKechnie was told to get the complaints of Cantwell, Frankhouse, and Betts in writing before Fuchs confronted Ruth.

The Braves played a doubleheader with the Giants on May 31 to make up the rainout of April 17. Ruth sat on the bench, nursing his never-ending cold. The Braves were drowning. Flint Rhem (0–5) lasted seven innings, allowed 13 hits, and left trailing, 8–2. It would be his last game as a Brave, as he was shipped to Syracuse of the International League. Benton was crushed for seven more runs, and Hal Schumacher had an easy win, 15–3. The crowd of 7,000 hoped for better times in the nightcap.

The Braves figured out how to hit Carl Hubbell by slashing 12 hits, but 11 were only singles. The Braves stranded 12 runners. Ray Mueller, the Braves' rookie catcher, launched a home run into the empty left field bleachers for his first major league hit.

The Giants won, 4–2, and they were 5½ games up in first place at 26–9. The Braves were 9–27.

"It is indeed pathetic," David B. Miller, a Braves fan in Ludlow, Massachusetts, told the *Boston Globe*. "It is time the owners of the Braves realized that no team can be built up from players in the neighborhood of 40 years old. Look at your roster."[105]

Paul Shannon in the *Boston Post* called the Braves "an outfit that seems really dying of dry rot." They used excuses of cold weather, aches and pains, and the sniffles. "A spirit of unrest that has seemed to affect them ever since the team left the training camp still endures, and a major operation on the entire outfit looks like the only logical remedy."[106]

A Mighty Fine Ship

On May 29, the 80,000-ton ocean liner hailed as the "Queen of the Seven Seas," S.S. *Normandie*, shipped out on its maiden voyage from France to New York. The luxury liner would set a new standard for size, speed, and style. The bright upholstery, sparkling chandeliers, and spacious state rooms made the ship its own destination point as opposed to a mere vessel bringing you elsewhere. Take in a show, frolic in the garden, or take a dip in the pool. "Almost any view of the ship commands admiration," boasted *Popular Mechanics*. "All the usual comparisons seem vain. Her power plant alone would supply electricity for a city of 300,000. If you were 'stranded' for life on this floating island there is scarcely a thing you would miss, for this ship provides food, shelter, medical care, libraries, theaters, gymnasiums, swimming pools, newspapers, radio reception, barber shop, hairdresser, tailors, art galleries, and dozens of amusements." With 1,000 passengers and just as many crew on board, the sounds of hammers and drills could be heard as workmen were still completing parts of the interior.[107]

The great ship was expected to break the transatlantic speed record, and a crowd of 200,000 was expected in New York Harbor to witness its arrival on June 3. There would be dinner and dancing on the majestic vessel that evening, and Babe Ruth was invited. He desperately wanted to go to "represent baseball" instead of sitting on the bench of a losing team nursing his aches and pains. He asked Judge Fuchs for permission to attend, but the Judge, who once desired Ruth for the off-the-field publicity he could garner, would have none of it.

He thought Babe Ruth's ship had already sailed.

9

We All Strike Out Sometime
(June 1935)

"So few can appreciate the shock that suddenly comes when all dreams and all illusions suddenly blow up, when one suddenly feels tired and old and out of date, bewildered and a trifle dazed, wondering what it is all about."—Grantland Rice

"I knew from the first that this arrangement would not work out." —Claire Ruth

"I'll be driving back to New York for good tomorrow."—Babe Ruth

The first day of June looked like many others early in the Braves' 1935 season: it was raining. Yet another game was postponed. Judge Fuchs and Bill McKechnie discussed their beleaguered pitching staff. "I'm going to fairly camp on the long-distance telephone for some hours now and see if I can get some pitching talent to help us out," McKechnie said. In the meantime, Dr. M.E. McGarty announced that Ruth had fluid on the knee and a strained ligament, recommending rest for a few of days.[1] Fuchs prepared a letter to be sent to Ruth on Sunday, June 2, asking for the legend to resign.

Ruth never saw the letter.

The Braves were playing the Giants on Sunday. They had an exhibition scheduled in Haverhill, Massachusetts, on Monday. Ruth wanted to at least make an appearance at the exhibition game but knew he couldn't play against the Dodgers on Tuesday and Wednesday. He wanted to go on the voluntary retired list, which would take him off the active roster. Since he couldn't play for a few days, he asked Fuchs for permission to travel to New York and take part in the *Normandie* festivities. Fuchs was still steaming about Ruth not playing at all in Friday's doubleheader. "Nothing doing!" the Judge said to either the voluntary retirement or the *Normandie* trip requests.[2] From that point forward, the day was filled with "unprecedented confusion and a storm of contradictions," aptly described by Gerry Moore in the *Boston Globe*. Fuchs once wanted Ruth's publicity, but *Ruth* just wanted to play. Now, Ruth wanted publicity and *Fuchs* wanted him to play.

June 2, 1935: A Series of Hectic Events

Before Sunday's game, Ruth called Fuchs to ask again about the *Normandie* excursion and received the same response. That was it for Ruth. He called together his Braves teammates and said his time with the team was over and he was placing himself on the voluntary retired list. "There was an ominous silence," McKechnie recalled of the moment, "and you know that silence is golden. Then all the players rushed him for signatures and autographs."[3] They sensed the finality of the moment and sought a collector's item before he left. The Braves went out and played one of their best games of the year, a "great game to watch" according to James C. O'Leary in the *Boston Globe*.[4] And that was rare. About 7,000 fans showed up to Braves Field, many likely hoping to see a Ruth appearance, unaware of what was happening behind closed doors.

While the 40-year-old Ruth watched his last game as a major leaguer, two other elder statesmen, Bob Smith and Rabbit Maranville, led the Braves to victory. The Giants had won seven in a row entering play, and their starting pitcher, Slick Castleman, had won five straight starts. Smith kept the Giants off the scoreboard and showed craftiness in the sixth inning after Bill Terry tripled with one out. Smith forced Mel Ott to foul out to the catcher and Hank Leiber to fly out. Smith held a 2–0 lead in the eighth inning. Jo-Jo Moore lined a shot off Smith's arm. McKechnie and trainer Jimmy Neary raced out to attend to him. The stinging stopped, and Smith watched a ground ball by Mark Koenig take a bad hop and get away from Maranville. Terry singled and Ott walked to load the bases. Sore wing and all, Smith battled back to force Leiber to loft an easy fly out to get out of the jam. Smith threw an impressive shutout, the only time a Braves pitcher had done so that season and the only time the Giants had been shut out. But all was soon forgotten with what happened in the clubhouse.

Fuchs sent a statement to reporters in the press box, acknowledging that he no longer had the financial means to sustain the franchise. He was following McKechnie's recommendations despite "a very slight difference of opinion between us," Fuchs admitted. "I shall follow his recommendations, knowing that they are based on heart interest, sincerity, and the long experience of over 25 years in baseball." The reality had arrived. "I am unable to provide such capital," the Judge admitted, "as I have exhausted every personal financial means. My heart and soul is [*sic*] for Boston and New England. They deserve the best, and it occurred to me that it may be my situation, just described, that is handicapping that course."[5]

Fuchs was willing to surrender the Braves if a good "sportsman" was willing to take over the team.[6] Fuchs wanted to leave without selling off a single asset so he wouldn't disappoint his friends and stockholders. About 280 miles away in Prospertown, New Jersey, Amelia Earhart was leaping off a 115-foot tower to test parachutes.[7] Fuchs could have used one of them.

Ruth called up to the press box, inviting Boston and New York writers to a press conference in the clubhouse after the game. He later changed his mind and told them to meet him there in the eighth inning. They rushed to the clubhouse, leaving tele- graph operators to keep track of the game. Ruth herded them off to a side room used by trainer Jimmy Neary. Sportswriter Tom Meany remembered the day as "an unhe- roic passing for a figure who had contributed so much drama to the game." Ruth sat on a stool smoking a cigar in the corner, bundled up in a windbreaker, despite the warm day.[8]

"I hate like Hell to do this and say this," Ruth said, "but I'm going to go on the voluntary retired list." He hoped the Pittsburgh game would be a sign of things to come, but then came the injury in Cincinnati.

> I was invited to be a guest on the *Normandie* tomorrow night. I wanted to go. I thought that I'd not play again until Thursday, anyhow, so I saw no reason why it would not be a good thing for me to represent the club at that dinner in New York. So, I called up Judge Fuchs and asked him and he said: "Nothing doing." Now you fellows know me and what I've done. I just do not have to stand for that sort of treatment.[9]
>
> It's the first time I have ever been turned down on any request since I first joined the Yan- kee team. That refusal made me sore.[10]
>
> I'll be tickled to continue to play baseball. But I'm leaving the club after the game at Haver- hill tomorrow. I'll go to New York. My immediate plans are uncertain.[11]

"They've advertised me," he said of the Haverhill game, "and I do not want to disap- point the crowd." What about his vice-president position? "Oh, that vice-president's job is just a joke," he said. "You can take that job and throw it out the window. I never did find out what it was all about, anyway."[12]

"He's a double-crosser," Ruth said of Fuchs. He was asked in what way.

"Well, lots of ways. He told me he had two million bucks sunk in this club. Huh! If he's got two million bucks, I'd like to see some of it."[13]

"Have you any trouble with Bill McKechnie?"

"No, Bill and I get along fine. He's a great fellow and all this stuff about me try- ing to get his job is bunk. I never tried to get anybody's job."[14]

"Bill and I are the best of friends. We never had the slightest disagreement. Of course, I had privileges that some of the other players didn't enjoy. I left the game when I felt that I was unable to continue, but there was never the slightest objection on his part."[15]

"I'll not come back to the Braves so long as Fuchs has control of the club," he promised, holding out possibility of a return.

> I hate to leave the club. The players are fine. I never knew a better bunch of players. And McKechnie has been fine to me. I want you fellows to thank the fans for their fine treat- ment of me.[16] I am in a receptive mood, and if the opportunity presents itself to manage some big-league club, I may accept it. I love baseball. It is my life work. I intend to stay in it till the end. If things should shape up so that Judge Fuchs would quit, and the people here want me back I will be glad to come. But under present conditions, this is impossible.[17]

Paul Gallico wrote that Ruth's "pop off in the dressing room was truly Ruth- ian and splendid. He called Judge Fuchs a double-crosser and a liar and went out in a blaze of fine expletive, most of it beautifully unprintable."[18] George Dixon of the *New York Daily News* said Ruth's claim of being double-crossed by Fuchs was taken as gospel. Fuchs was "the same man who, a few months earlier, had won the sympathy of fans by his revelation that he had sunk a fortune in the Braves. They didn't know what Babe meant exactly, but since the Babe said he's been double-crossed, well, that was enough for them. They believed him."[19]

Claire Ruth was waiting outside the door. "I knew from the first that this arrangement would not work out," she said in hindsight. "The Babe made a mistake in coming here," she added, "playing many days when he didn't feel like it."[20] "I want Babe to be happy, and he certainly hasn't been happy up here. He told me what he intended to do today, and I told him it was his job and he could do whatever he wanted with it. I didn't try to advise him one way or the other."[21]

Ruth dressed into street clothes and left Neary's room for the larger conference room, where the victorious Braves gathered. Rabbit Maranville was fussin' and cussin' about an error charged to him. McKechnie sat at the table, writing the lineup for the Haverhill game. He denied that Ruth caused any discipline problems and that he had asked Ruth to resign.[22]

Vice-President Charles F. Adams said he didn't even know all of this was going on until he read about it in the papers. "Knowing Bill McKechnie as I do, I don't think Bill would make any suggestion one way or another about 'Babe's' resigning."[23] Contradictions were everywhere.

Was Fuchs putting words in McKechnie's mouth to justify his actions?

Reporters sought out the Judge for comment. Fuchs said he and McKechnie discussed this over two days and decided the most professional thing to do was give Ruth the opportunity to voluntarily resign. "It was not a matter of dollars and cents," Fuchs said, "but rather a question of baseball. What I wanted of him was the best possible physical condition which would enable him to go out and play the best ball of which he was capable. I am very sorry that Babe is not more of a sportsman," he added about the *Normandie* affair. "He can do his most for baseball right out there on the playing field."[24]

Fuchs contacted National League President Ford Frick and that night announced Ruth's release. Portions of the statement read:

> I have given Babe Ruth his unconditional release as a player and he is through with the Braves in every way.
> Ruth will be dropped as vice president at once. He never had any financial interest in the club, so there is nothing to be straightened out there.
> Two days ago, I refused a request of Manager Bill McKechnie that Ruth be released. Matters on the club had reached a state that the manager felt that no progress could be made in getting together a winning club with him as a member. I wanted to keep Ruth, as I felt the fans still desired him in the lineup.
> His statement that I "double-crossed" him is hard to understand. He blames me for writing a letter in which I said I had lost a large sum of money with the Braves so far this year. That was the truth, and I told him that if he thought I had double-crossed him by writing the truth, it would have to stand.

I cannot see where Ruth has any complaint over his treatment. He had an agreement with me which would have been carried out and placed him in charge of the club. He knew he would have to work for this reward and wait for it, but he would not go along like a good soldier. For the sake of discipline, we could not give him the extra privileges he asked for.[25]

I had an appointment with him [Ruth] in this office at 12:30 today. He failed to keep it. I was intending then to ask for his resignation, but as he didn't show up, I made up my mind to write him a letter to that effect. I understand that he has made the assertion that I have double-crossed him. I will not enter into any argument with him here. Facts speak for themselves."[26]

McKechnie sympathized with Ruth. "I think that the Babe should have retired so that he wouldn't get hurt," he told the *New York Times*. "I asked him recently to write his resignation" when the club returned home. "I told Judge Fuchs that Ruth couldn't go on and that some action should be taken regarding his status."[27]

The day began with Fuchs preparing a letter asking Ruth to resign. Those plans were interrupted by Ruth stating that he was retiring. The day ended with Fuchs firing Ruth outright, "the climax of a series of hectic events," Burt Whitman wrote.[28] Fuchs sent Ruth a telegram informing him of his release and forbidding him from playing in Haverhill. Ruth immediately called newspapers in Haverhill, telling them he would not be there, so they should spread the word as to why. Then he called New York newspapermen. "I'll be driving back to New York for good tomorrow," he declared.[29]

June 3: A Confetti Shower

On June 3, Ruth and the family packed their belongings for New York. Austen Lake of the *Boston-American* was there. "Hell, kid," Ruth said to him, "we all strike out sometime."[30] He held nothing back about Fuchs. "I'm so disgusted with that guy that I don't know whether to laugh at him or be sore at him. It's all so ridiculous that it makes me laugh, but then when I think it over, I burn up again. Judge Fuchs said Bill McKechnie said one thing and Bill says he said another."[31]

Ruth departed the luxurious Myles Standish Hotel, where he enjoyed the views of Kenmore Square. The hotel still stands as part of the Boston University campus and, as legend has it, Martin Luther King met the love of his life, Coretta Scott, in that very place.[32]

An anxious wedding party showered Ruth with rice and confetti, anticipating the bridal couple. "This is the first time anybody has ever been showered this way after being fired," he joked.[33] No one might have seen him leave otherwise. Quite the opposite to the thousands who arrived on that frigid February evening to welcome him back to the Hub. "To one who was present on both occasions," Hy Hurwitz of the *Globe* wrote, "it was a pathetic contrast."[34] Ruth shook the confetti from his hair and waited for Bill McKechnie. His big brown sedan was loaded, with aluminum pots and pans visible in the back.[35]

McKechnie was the only member of the Braves to see him off. "If I had actually done what I was charged by Fuchs with doing, I don't think McKechnie would have come down here to say goodbye," Ruth said. "I'd like to come back, and I'd like to come back right here in Boston, providing, of course, that Judge Fuchs is no longer associated with the team. I feel that I've disappointed lots of my friends here and I'd like to make up for it. I have nothing against the Boston fans and the press."[36]

"I'm sorry to see you go, Babe," McKechnie told him, "but I guess it had to come. I wish you all the luck in the world."

"I know you do," Ruth replied.[37]

They drove off, and just like that, Babe Ruth's Boston adventure was over.

McKechnie met with Fuchs and then left for Haverhill. Soon after, a statement was released which seemed out of place for Deacon Bill. Paul Shannon of the *Boston Post* wrote that the statement "could have been made with better effect at the very time that the Babe handed his notice of release." The timing was indeed odd. McKechnie had not uttered a critical word of Ruth, but now came a statement signed by him casting blame on Ruth for his lack of discipline. The statement from McKechnie read:

> I must state publicly that in justice to the action of Judge Fuchs with reference to Babe Ruth, on Friday and Saturday of last week I pointed out to Judge Fuchs that the main trouble with the ball club was that they were not able to function properly with Babe Ruth playing the outfield.
>
> I frankly stated that certain actions of Ruth, while with the ball club, which I would absolutely forbid with any other member of the club, were responsible for the lack of discipline, and that unless Judge Fuchs could convince Babe Ruth to retire, I was unable to get any real baseball discipline or proper spirit as manifested by the club previous to the acquisition of Ruth.
>
> The pitching staff complained continuously, to the end that Judge Fuchs promised me that he would have a talk with Ruth and endeavor to show him the impossibility of the situation; that if Ruth could not join in the spirit of these suggestions, which were made for his benefit as well as the decorum of the club, he would ask Ruth, in order to preserve his reputation, to retire, and we would make his parting as commendable and pleasant as possible.[38]

McKechnie took the blame for releasing Ruth. However, the statement didn't sound like McKechnie at all. This was also the first time that discipline problems were ever mentioned regarding Ruth. McKechnie's statement to the *New York Times* the previous evening was simply one of concern for Ruth's health, not a reprimand for disrupting the team. Who really wrote that statement?

Back in New York

"There's no basis for that at all," Ruth steamed after being shown McKechnie's statement. He had just pulled his sedan up to his home at 345 West 88th Street and was surrounded by children at the entrance. The Ruths owned the entire seventh floor of the Upper West Side building and had 11 rooms for a maid and cook to tend to.[39] "How could he say a thing like that? Anyway, I'm all washed up with the outfit and I'm not going to carry on any more arguments. I won't talk. I'm going to play a lot of golf."[40]

But carry on he did. "McKechnie told me he was not responsible for my release," Ruth said. "He made that statement to me and for the benefit of the newspapermen. Judge Fuchs double-crossed me. That's just what he's doing to McKechnie. He's making Bill take the rap which he should be taking himself." Fuchs said asking Ruth to retire was based on McKechnie's recommendation. "What's more," the Judge added, "whatever Ruth says from now on doesn't mean a thing to me." McKechnie was always a square shooter who would never be known as two-faced. Yet he was still owed $18,000 from the club and was "forced into the middle."[41]

"Well, you can believe it, if you want to," wrote a highly skeptical Victor O. Jones in the *Globe*. "The statement rapping the Babe, issued over McKechnie's signature, doesn't sound like Bill, either in point of content or literary style. On the other hand, it has all the characteristics of a typical Fuchs statement." The whole thing smelled fishy. McKechnie, Jones continued, "doesn't strike me as the kind of man who would see Babe Ruth off—the only Braves official to do so—shake his hand, and wish him well, and then voluntarily rush to the Braves office to dictate a statement blaming the Babe for all the Braves' troubles. No, it just won't do." Fuchs was to be blamed for the meaningless job titles given to Ruth. The portrayal of McKechnie wanting Ruth gone despite Fuchs' objections and Fuchs being regarded as "just a luvvable [*sic*] character trying to be a big-hearted brother to the New England baseball fans," Jones added, "purely and simply as an individual, is…. Nuts!"[42]

"The statement was type written and Bill's written signature wasn't on either of the two copies I saw," pointed out Bill Cunningham in the *Boston Post*.[43] George Carens in the *Boston Evening Transcript* wrote that the statement was "a friendly gesture on the part of Bill to alleviate the extreme embarrassment of his boss" for "Fuchs to put himself in a better light with the Boston public."[44]

"I didn't want to sign with Judge Fuchs in the first place," Ruth now complained.

> The negotiations were on and the proposition appealed to me. But I hesitated. I let him talk me into it. I guess the profits didn't come as he expected, and he couldn't see his way clear to paying me that $25,000 a year for three years. If he had come to me frankly and told me that he couldn't afford to pay me and asked me to quit, I would have obliged him. But, instead, he took the other way round and tried to get rid of me. Well, I quit.[45]
>
> Bill McKechnie was great to me from the day he met me at St. Petersburg until the time I was leaving Boston. He was on hand to say goodbye and good luck, and anybody who knows Bill McKechnie knows he means what he says. I don't pay any attention to statements credited to him. Bill is in a tough spot, but better days are coming for him, I hope.[46]

Ruth never saw Fuchs' resignation request letter, and Ruth claimed he invited the Judge to his press conference, but Fuchs didn't show. Ruth hated disappointing the promoter of the Haverhill exhibition game, who had already sent Fuchs $600. Ruth was entitled to 25 percent of gate receipts for exhibitions. "He [Fuchs] owes me some money for earlier exhibitions," Ruth pointed out. "I suppose I'll get that by mail."[47] Ruth was still bitter about a clothing store appearance and the owner who bought the 500 tickets expecting Ruth to sign them all. Ruth felt ill and wanted to do it at another time, but the owner was already refunded. So Ruth conceded. But what did he get from all of that?

Some writers blasted Ruth for the ordeal. "Babe is through," wrote Whitman, "except on some gala occasion, such as an Old Timers' Day or an informal picnic type of exhibition. He's a tremendous eater and is not going to lose that tummy of his, even if he plays 36 holes of golf a day for a month." Players were glad to see Ruth go.[48]

Bill Cunningham often criticized the Braves' ownership, but he too found room to defend the team and condemn Ruth. "The fact that he [Ruth] blew up to the point of quitting and departing permanently for New York over the matter of a banquet he wanted to attend, shows how far he has deviated from the ideas of a working ball player. He sounds like a spoiled boy, not the brawny hero of the bleacherites."[49]

Cunningham elsewhere wrote that Ruth was no longer the "big, easy going, 'Hi feller' type of ball player who liked to take his beef stew off a lunch counter stool, scribble his autograph for any kid with tousled hair and sit in with the boys at any athletic smoker." Instead, Ruth became "a temperamental celebrity completely dominated by a shrewd and managing wife who did all the talking and whose first question invariably was 'How much is there in it for us'?"[50]

Paul Gallico wrote, "Poor Babe. He wanted to go to a party to which all the other kids were going."[51]

No controversy in 1935 could ever pass without a comment or two from Dizzy Dean. "All I can say to all this is, what is baseball comin' to when a guy can't get a day off to see a boat?"[52]

Minus their star attraction, the Braves attracted 3,000 fans in Haverhill for the exhibition game. Al Blanche, a slender Providence College star, was their starting pitcher. McKechnie had allowed the Somerville, Massachusetts, native to throw batting practice during the season. Blanche took advantage of the opportunity, allowing just two hits in defeating the Pentucket League All-Stars, 9–4.[53]

The Dreams Pass Away

"So few can appreciate the shock that suddenly comes when all dreams and all illusions suddenly blow up," Grantland Rice elegantly wrote, "when one suddenly feels tired and old and out of date, bewildered and a trifle dazed, wondering what it is all about."[54] Beyond Ruth's declining physical skills was his mental makeup. How would the great Bambino recover from this 28-game embarrassment? He could blame Fuchs all he wanted, but the images of him bundled up on the bench, fighting sniffles, looking foolish at the plate, and bumbling in the outfield were not going away.

"Yes, I'm low now," Ruth admitted to Rice, "mentally and physically. My leg is still bad, but I still think that in shape I could do some good, here and there. I know I can build up and handle a big-league ball club. If I didn't think I could make good, I'd never take the chance. It's one of those dreams I've had for a long time." That dream was fading. "Baseball made me, and no one can know the love I have for that game."[55]

The issue wasn't the *Normandie* incident, said the *New York Times*. "The crisis might have come when Ruth asked for leave to attend a session of the American Philosophical Society. A breaking point is never out of reach for people who want to break."[56]

John Kieran called Ruth, Fuchs, and McKechnie "three men on a lame horse, headed for trouble all the time." Fuchs held the reigns but was clueless where the horse was going. McKechnie was in the middle, "a thin man with a weak stomach sandwiched between two stout men who finally got around to fighting." Ruth was on the end, barely hanging on. "The pieces of this puzzle picture didn't fit together at all."[57]

Ruth was trying to put his own pieces together, waiting for a call to manage and believing he had something left. A poll taken by club owners revealed that half of them wouldn't take Ruth for free. National League President Ford Frick said, "I would like to see the Babe get a break, but I do not know of any further opportunity for him now. He failed to take advantage of the chance given him in Boston." Others said the same.

"If the Babe still is valuable," said Alva Bradley, owner of the Cleveland Indians, "I guess the Yanks would have kept him."

"We haven't anything to offer Ruth," Bob Quinn in Brooklyn said.

"Don't want him," Sam Breadon said in St. Louis.[58]

No possibilities seemed to exist anywhere

Ruth found a captive audience aboard the *Normandie*, where the gathering was giddy and the wine plenteous. "That man Fuchs' big heartedness is too much for me," he said sarcastically of receiving his home Braves uniform. "You notice he didn't offer also the traveling suit. Nerts to him. And I don't want anything around to remind me of that two-timer."[59]

Ruth received offers for employment which were more entertaining than sustainable. He was contacted by Tom Baird, an executive with the Kansas City Monarchs of the Negro Leagues and manager of the House of David Barnstorming team. The bearded men of the religious community devoted to scripture offered Ruth $20,000 to finish their season. "No, we won't require the Babe to grow any foliage on that famous map unless he wants to," Baird said. And Ruth could visit as many boats as he wanted, Baird promised. "We'd make arrangements to have the boat dockings delayed."[60] Ruth never replied to the offer. He also received a telegram:

BABE RUTH
BOSTON MASS

WOULD YOU CONSIDER PROPOSITION MANAGEMENT NUTTING BALL TEAM SALINAS LETTUCE LEAGUE.[61]

Another packing company team in the highly competitive lettuce league also wanted him. But Ruth was certainly not in his "salad days." A semipro team in Chicago offered $10,000. The Farmers of Glendale offered Ruth a position and invited him to watch their upcoming doubleheader against the Pittsburgh Crawfords. A promoter of midget auto racing offered Ruth $20,000 to try to squeeze into a tiny car and zip around the track. He was offered to umpire an all-star college game on Manhattan Beach. A girls basketball team asked if he would wear a wig and bloomers and play for them.[62] Ed "Strangler" Lewis said Ruth should become a wrestler.[63]

The gutsy Westbrook Pegler believed Ruth should use his plentiful bank account to assist children in poverty. Ruth did not fit as an executive in the "group of soulless corporations which compose the industry," Pegler wrote.

> It has never been written that he ever gave a dollar of his earnings or devoted an hour of his time except as a momentary whim to the assistance of the kids. If the Babe is looking for a future one is open to him in the hospitals and boys clubs of the slums, both urban and rural. Now he may indulge his love of kids, if it is all it has been said to be, to his great big heart's content. There will be no money in it, but he has income and earning capacity to meet his wants. The question is whether he loves kids as much as he is supposed to love them or merely likes to pat them on the head in passing by.[64]

In the modern day, Ruth could have occupied a community/public relations role with a club and done just that. But not in 1935.

"Baseball owes you nothing, eh?" *New York Sun* columnist H.I. Phillips wrote in an "open letter to Babe Ruth." "Okay. Then racing owes nothing to Man o' War, the steel industry owes nothing to Bessemer, Rome owes nothing to Caesar, art owes nothing to Michelangelo, music doesn't owe a thing to Chopin, aviation owes nothing to the Wright brothers and the Greatest Show on Earth doesn't owe a dime to the elephant!" Shutting Ruth out of this game would be the equivalent to letting "the Washington Monument topple because of its age, all right to shoot a lifeguard because he slept late after a rescue, and okay to slay Santa Claus because somebody found a bottle of beer in his sleigh."[65]

Fuchs' Damage Control Back in Boston

The clock was ticking on Judge Fuchs, "unless a miracle comes to pass and it starts raining gold from heaven on a day when Judge Fuchs is out cruising in a topless, 10-ton truck," Cunningham joked. Fuchs failed with the dogs, the team was nearly homeless, but he was saved by a "pathetic effort to put the Braves on a par with an orphanage or a hospital, a public subscription campaign, which, in my humble opinion, sadly cheapened the name of the sport in a grand baseball town. His best bet would seem to be to leave now before he does any more harm."[66] Cunningham received various opinions from his readers, long before the days of Twitter:

"You can't run the Babe, Bill, because you are merely making an ass of yourself. So lay off."

"I am a staunch Red Sox rooter, and always was, but now I'm rooting my head off for the Braves, also. If I knew Ruth's New York address, I would send him a baby's nipple. His name, Babe, fits him to perfection."

"History will sing the praises of Babe Ruth when you sports writers are all forgotten."

"You recently established yourself as a strong candidate for the position of inmate in some local asylum by an article in which you blasted Judge Landis and numerous others for allowing Babe Ruth to get into such a predicament. Why in the dickens should the blame fall anywhere but upon the shoulders of the infernal skinflints that are running the Braves? I leave Boston (forever) with the firm conviction that it is the most unanimously repulsive city in the United States. If I can find a worse, I'll write and exonerate your beloved town."[67]

Victor O. Jones called the Ruth experiment "one of the costliest mistakes baseball ever made. Ruth's own actions have tarnished his fame and made it even more unlikely that he will ever be entrusted with the management of a major league team."[68]

"I did my utmost to protect him," Fuchs said, "but apparently he does not appreciate this fact." Ruth had blamed fans, writers, ownership, and finances of the club at various times. "I wish that the last word had already been spoken in the Ruth matter."[69]

Bob Quinn, GM of the Dodgers, was ready with a bundle of cash if Fuchs and McKechnie were planning on a fire sale. Quinn wanted Ed Brandt and Wally Berger. Fuchs backed down, saying he may as well close Braves Field if Berger and Brandt were gone.[70] The previous day, it was announced that the Braves had a net loss of $44,308 in 1934, even with the reduced rent on Braves Field (from $40,000 to $36,667). The franchise was valued at $201,000 but had debts of $205,000, with player contracts valued at $98,534.[71] No trades were made by the June 15 deadline, but Fuchs went cheap and acquired Danny MacFayden, a 10-year veteran pitcher, on waivers from Cincinnati.

The Braves' post–Ruth era began with a doubleheader with the Dodgers on June 5. This was the first of 11 doubleheaders in June because of all the rainouts. Van Lingle Mungo shut out the Braves on five hits in a 3–0 win in the first game. The Braves cruised in the second game, 10–2, as Berger's home run smashed into the signboard behind the left field bleachers.[72] Only 500 spectators appeared for the first game, and barely 1,000 for the second. Fred Frankhouse (4–3) had an easy win to bring the Braves to 11–28. They traveled to the Polo Grounds to face the first-place Giants.

Ben Cantwell had amazing stuff, allowing only seven hits in 9⅔ innings, but even that wasn't good enough. Mel Ott homered into the upper deck to tie the score in the ninth inning, and Bill Terry singled in the winning run in the tenth to give the Giants a 3–2 win. The Giants were 28–11 and 5½ games in front of St. Louis in the National League. Cantwell fell to 1–7 and had not won since April 20. Urbanski was carted off after hurting his back, and Joe Coscarart would start 21 games at shortstop in his absence. The game on June 8 was yet another rainout to be made up in August.

Sunday's game was played under threatening skies, and a small Sunday crowd of 6,000 included Babe Ruth, who sat behind the Giants' dugout with Claire and daughter Julia. "I can't stay away from ball games," he said, waving to players who were his teammates just days before. Fans surrounded him "with pleas to autograph everything from a score sheet to a hot dog," wrote Dixon, but Ruth had ushers blocking their path.[73] "I can't watch what's going on with pens shoved under my kisser every few seconds. I love this game and if I can't play it, I'll still be a fan. Please tell everybody I'm not going high hat. Come around after the game and I'll autograph your hatband or a dozen eggs if you want it."[74]

Ruth watched his old club do what they did best: lose. The Braves jumped to an early 3–0 lead, but the Giants batted around in the first inning against Bob Smith and tied the game. The Giants won, 5–4.

The Braves returned to Boston, only to be washed out of a charity game on June 10 in Randolph and the first game of a series against St. Louis on June 11.[75] A double-header on June 12 drew 5,000 fans who watched the Braves drop both games, blowing the lead in each. In the opener, Ed Brandt took a 4–2 lead into the sixth inning. Ripper Collins launched a three-run homer to put the Cardinals ahead, 6–4. The Braves tied the game in the bottom of the eighth. Dizzy Dean was summoned from the bullpen and blanked the Braves from then on while the battered Brandt (2–7) surrendered two runs in the ninth for the 8–6 St. Louis win.

Fred Frankhouse held the Cards hitless through five innings in the nightcap. With two on, Ernie Orsatti's bat knocked Braves catcher Al Spohrer on the side of his head. Spohrer later wobbled to the dugout and collapsed on the bench. Club physician Dr. Michael E. McGarty sent Spohrer to the hospital with a concussion. Frankhouse fell apart from then on, and the Cardinals took the lead, 4–2. The Braves, down 5–2, mustered a rally in the ninth inning but fell short, 5–4.[76] The Braves had now lost four in a row, and Spohrer was out for two weeks. Their fortunes turned around the next day as newly acquired Danny MacFayden looked like an ace on the mound.

MacFayden was born on Cape Cod in 1905 and grew up in Somerville, Massachusetts. He once struck out 32 batters in a 17-inning game in high school. Often referred to as "bespeckled" in the newspapers, MacFayden was the first pitcher in the American League to wear glasses on the mound. He went 52–78 with a 4.23 ERA in seven years with the Red Sox, then went to the Yankees for three years, but never met their expectations. The Yankees conditionally traded him to Cincinnati, who would pay his entire salary if they kept him after June 1. The Reds preferred to save money, so they sent him back, and the Yankees placed him on waivers. He was a bargain-basement deal perfect for Fuchs. MacFayden was a curveball specialist who could fool hitters with a sidearm motion.[77]

"Bespectacled Daniel," as the *Globe* called him, allowed nine hits and a run to the Cardinals. The Braves trailed Daffy Dean, Dizzy's brother, 1–0, in the bottom of the seventh inning. Joe Coscarart's bases-loaded single scored two runs, and MacFayden drove in another as the Braves prevailed, 3–1, before a satisfied 2,500 fans.[78]

Catcher Shanty Hogan (left) with new Braves pitcher Danny MacFayden (courtesy Boston Public Library, Leslie Jones Collection).

These were the "rejuvenated Braves," Gerry Moore wrote, as they finally showed a little fight. The Braves had outscored their opponents, 31–27, so far in June, a major victory after being outscored, 165–92, in May. The two clubs played a doubleheader on Friday, June 14, drawing 10,000 to Braves Field. In the first game, they trailed, 4–2, in the seventh inning when Berger launched a three-run-homer, his eighth of the season, three-quarters of the way up the bleachers. The Braves won again, 5–4.

Dizzy Dean faced them in Game Two. Berger remained hot, remained hot, the Braves leading 4–1 in the sixth. Huck Betts ran out of gas, allowing four singles, a walk and a sacrifice fly, and exited with a 4–3 lead. Bob Smith allowed three inherited runners to score, and the Braves trailed, 6–4. But Joe Mowry's bases-loaded pinch single and a sacrifice fly gave the Braves a 7–6 lead. The Cardinals tied the score in the eighth. Dean pitched all 13 innings as the Cards prevailed, 8–7.[79] The Cardinals were 30–20, four games behind the Giants.

The sixth-place Reds, 20–29, came to Boston. The opener was rained out, and a doubleheader on June 16 drew 15,000 customers. The Braves trailed, 7–3, in the bottom of the seventh inning. With two on, Berger smashed a home run that completely left Braves Field. "It appeared to be as long a home run as the oldest Allston inhabitant can recall," Burt Whitman wrote in the *Herald*. "It must have cleared the four

"Handy Randy" Moore was always ready to play whatever position was needed (courtesy Boston Public Library, Leslie Jones Collection).

regular tracks on the Boston & Albany Railroad right of way, and the mathematical sharps of the press coop decided it landed 500 feet from home plate."[80] The Braves fell short, 7–6. Berger went 4-for-4 in the second game, part of a Braves 15-hit attack, in a 7–4 victory.

There was a sparse holiday crowd of 4,000 at Braves Field on Bunker Hill Day. It was the 160th anniversary of the famous battle during the American Revolution, forever remembered by one of Boston's most notable landmarks. To this day, a parade is held annually on June 17 or on the Sunday prior. In 1935, the parade with 12,000 participants included a few Civil War Veterans in their 90s, and youngsters wearing red, white, and blue. An estimated crowd of 250,000 baked on the streets of Charlestown under a scorching sun.[81]

The Braves swept the doubleheader against Cincinnati, one of only two times they accomplished this, both times against the lowly Reds. Berger hit his 10th and 11th home runs with five RBI, and the Braves prevailed in the opener, 8–3. In the nightcap, MacFayden spun another gem and won his second complete game, 5–1.

The Braves played the postponed charity game at Stetson Field in Randolph on June 18 before 5,000 fans. The opponent was the ball team of the Arthur Fisher Shoe Company. Proceeds went to the Randolph Milk Fund for needy children. The shoe workers beat the Braves, 6–3, pounding 10 hits off Al Blanche. A group of 300 attended a banquet after the game. Brother Gilbert, from St. Mary's since the time of Babe Ruth, spoke. Considering events that month, one wonders what was said of Ruth that night.[82]

The Chicago Cubs came to Boston at 27–23, 8½ games back of the Giants. Only 1,500 people came out on the cold, rainy day. "The weather conditions were brutal," wrote O'Leary in the *Globe*, "yet, two better games in a single day have rarely been played."[83] The opener was a tight pitching duel between Bob Smith and Lon Warneke. Smith held a 2–1 lead but ran out of gas in the ninth inning. Chuck Klein lined a single to right which headed for the wall. He turned and motored to second, but Randy Moore fired a bullet to Maranville, who tagged Klein out.

The crowd was still cheering when Phil Cavarretta lined another one to right. Moore "flung himself over toward the foul line and in and made an elegant shoe-string catch of this drive." "Handy Randy" saved the day, and the Braves had their best winning streak of the season with their fourth straight, 2–1.[84] Their streak ended quickly in the nightcap as Bill Lee shut out the Braves, 3–0, in a game lasting just one hour and 25 minutes. Huck Betts fell to 0–4.

The weather didn't deter the 19,000 fans heading to Narragansett Park in Pawtucket, Rhode Island, who wagered $350,000 at the opening of thoroughbred racing. Two days later, Seabiscuit would win his first race and equal the five-furlong track record, beginning his legendary career as a champion and symbol of hope during the Great Depression.[85]

The Braves were rained out on June 20, then were hammered 11–3 the following day. Pinch-hitter Ed Moriarty, a star at Holy Cross who signed with the Braves the previous day, singled in his first major league at-bat. Soon, newspapers focused all their attention on this phenom for the rest of June. He had possibly the most colorful career in baseball history for someone who only played 14 games.

The Strange Case of Ed Moriarty

Edward Jerome Moriarty was born in nearby Holyoke, Massachusetts, in 1912. He played baseball for the Sacred Heart Schools and enrolled at the College of Holy Cross in Worcester in 1931. In 1934, he slammed a 490-foot home run off Lefty Grove of the Red Sox in an exhibition game at Fitton Field. It is still recognized as the longest ever hit there.[86] The *Globe* labeled Moriarty "the most dangerous hitter in college baseball" in his senior year of 1935. Moriarty batted .483 and led the 22–1 Crusaders. His final college game was on Tuesday, June 18, under the watchful eye of Bill McKechnie, who liked what he saw, and Judge Fuchs signed him on Thursday.

After Friday's loss, the Braves found an easier opponent that night. They played Sacred Heart, a semi-pro club in the Suburban Twilight League, at Pearl Street

Rookie Ed Moriarty looked like a star in his first two weeks. Then he left the Braves for a higher calling (courtesy Boston Public Library, Leslie Jones Collection).

Stadium in nearby Malden. The game was played for the benefit of The Malden Lodge of Elks' Christmas Basket Fund. The Braves won, 11–2.[87]

In Saturday's doubleheader, Moriarty went 2-for-5 (double, single) in the opener and 3-for-4 (two singles and the only home run of his career) in the nightcap. The Braves lost both, 7–4 and 5–3, before 7,500 fans who stirred when Moriarty came to bat. "The crowd nearly forgot the score in both games," wrote Moore, "as they concentrated on cheering young Moriarty."[88] He was 6-for-11 in his first three games. A fanbase desperate for hope was quick in exaggeration. "He shapes up as the best natural hitter to break into Boston big league ball in years and years," Whitman wrote.[89]

The third-place Pirates (34–26) came to Boston for a Sunday doubleheader on June 23, drawing 15,000 fans. Some of them may have arrived via the newly opened Sagamore and Bourne bridges connecting Cape Cod to the mainland. Over 30,000 cars traveled these bridges over the weekend.[90] The Pirates grabbed the lead, 1–0, when Moriarty misjudged a pop fly which resulted in a double. The Braves took the lead, 2–1, in the bottom of the seventh inning, Moriarty scoring on Berger's sac fly. The Braves lost, 4–3, and while Moriarty was 2-for-5, he looked lost at second base. The Pirates blasted Smith in the nightcap, 7–4. Moriarty went 0-for-5 and committed an error.

On Monday, the two teams hopped the train north for an exhibition game in Portland, Maine. The game was part of the St. John's Day celebration sponsored by the Knights Templars (Freemasons) who had gathered from across New England. They paraded in the city and sat down to a lobster dinner at the Portland Exposition Building. The game was played at Richardson Field (now Hadlock Field, home of the Portland Sea Dogs). Bobby Brown shut out the Pirates through seven innings, but the Pirates rallied for a 7–5 win.[91]

The clubs returned to Boston, and the Braves won on June 25, 7–2, ending their six-game skid. MacFayden pitched his third complete-game victory in four starts. Moriarty had a single, a triple, and a run scored and was batting .385. More attention was paid to the Joe Louis knockout of Primo Carnera at Yankee Stadium, which drew 57,000 fans and pocketed promoters $340,000.[92]

The Braves lost the June 26 opener, 4–2. Cantwell was victimized by a controversial call. Pep Young knocked a line drive down the left field line which nearly everyone in the park saw curl foul by six feet, except third base umpire George Magerkurth. The grumpy ump, who sportswriter Arthur Daley said "had bulldog features and disposition to match," waved his arms to signal a home run. Magerkurth, "the most vociferous, gaudy and pugnacious of all the men in blue," said the *New York Times*, was always prepared for a fight.[93] Deacon Bill McKechnie charged the bulldog. "When McKechnie cast aspersions on Magerkurth's veracity the latter banished the Braves manager for the rest of the afternoon."[94] Berger hit his 14th home run, the highlight for the Braves, but Cantwell fell to 1–9.

Maranville managed the second game, and the team was lackluster against Bill Swift (8–2) in a 5–1 loss dropping Huck Betts to 0–5. A crowd of 3,000 watched their Braves lose their eighth game out of their last nine. Moriarty went 1-for-8 in the doubleheader. Then he said he was quitting the game.

"I conferred recently with advisors and came to a definite decision this morning that I would start immediately preparing for examinations to enter the Grand Seminary in Montreal," Moriarty said.[95] There was a mass exodus of reporters to Moriarty's house in Holyoke. "I do not like professional baseball," he said, "and I intend to obtain a higher education." Moriarty was told he had many fans cheering for him, but he said he "didn't care for the publicity." He refused the signing bonus, stating that he hadn't made up his mind but agreed to play simply for the generosity Fuchs had shown Holy Cross.[96]

"I can truthfully say that I could think of no greater satisfaction for myself than to have a son of mine come to me and tell me that he was going to enter the ministry," Deacon Bill McKechnie said. "In this day and time, it seems to be that a young man attains high honor for himself in making a decision to study for the priesthood. He is a splendid young man, very conscientious and the cleanest living lad imaginable."[97] Just like that, the Braves' phenom left for a higher calling.

The Braves finished the month with six games against the Phillies (22–36), beginning with a doubleheader. The Braves exploded for an 11–1 win in Game One.

Berger launched a mammoth grand slam, the 15th for the newly named All-Star. His 15 jacks were second-best in the National League. Ed Brandt (4–8) went the distance for the Braves, limiting the Phillies to five hits. The Phillies found their hitting stroke in the second game against Bobby Brown and built a 7–0 lead. Their own inept pitching kept the Braves in the game. The Braves laced 12 hits off rookie Jim Bivin and tied the game. Johnny Vergez homered off Smith in the ninth inning, and the Phillies held on, 8–7.

Local newspapers didn't record the doubleheader attendance, but it was far less than the 30,000 who packed Fenway Park that night to watch Danno O'Mahoney become the recognized world wrestling champion, beating the "Golden Greek," Jim Londos. O'Mahoney won the match in one hour and 16 minutes, finishing off his opponent with a flying body scissors.[98]

The month of June had not been a good one for wearing wrestling trunks. It was one of the coldest in Boston in 63 years, according to weather data at the time. Two-and-a-half more inches of rain fell than normal, and the average temperature was 64, the lowest for the month since 1918. On June 28, however, the Hub's temperature soared to 85 degrees, and people sought beaches and pools. The Braves heated up as well. Tommy Thompson's 450-foot, two-run home run tied the game in the bottom of the ninth inning. But Smith allowed a 10th-inning home run to Dolph Camilli, and the Braves lost, 4–2.[99]

Curt Davis outdueled Danny MacFayden in the hot sun on June 29, 3–1. The Braves and Phillies closed out the month with a doubleheader which drew 7,000 fans impatient with the team and the heat. The Braves won the opener handily, 9–3, with Ed Brandt (5–8) getting the win and Berger smashing his 16th home run. In the nightcap, the Phillies pounded 23 hits off four Braves pitchers, including 10 off Cantwell (1–10). Trailing 7–3 in the fifth inning, Hal Lee singled, and Moore doubled. McKechnie held up Lee at third even though he would have likely scored. Moore kept running, and both men were left staring at each other at third base. Moore was out, and McKechnie was showered in a chorus of boos. The game was a mess as the Phillies won, 15–5. "It was a field day for the Phils," wrote Whitman.[100]

June ended with the Braves losing four of six and 12 of 15. "That cannot be blamed on 'Babe' Ruth," noted Moore. But their 11–19 record for the month was their best all season. They almost broke even on the month, allowing 137 runs while scoring 133.

National League Standings Thru June 30

Team	W	L	GB
New York	44	18	----
Pittsburgh	39	30	8.5
Chicago	36	28	9
St. Louis	36	29	9.5
Brooklyn	29	34	15.5

Team	W	L	GB
Cincinnati	29	36	16.5
Philadelphia	26	38	19
Boston	20	46	26

Buyers Beware

The lingering question was: who wanted to buy this team? Reports were bubbling that the Braves could be purchased free and clear for $500,000, or one could become a controlling partner for $350,000. Fuchs' August 1 deadline loomed, and if no buyer emerged, the National League would reluctantly take over. Cunningham referred to the club as the "greatest bargain in history" and "probably as luscious an opportunity as the business world affords in any quarter at the moment." "Instead of being broke, disorganized, bankrupt and bogged down" he explained, "the team has actually made money all along. These profits, however, have been spent for more ball players and for other expenses that can't be traced in the books, the books, incidentally, being very carelessly kept with expenditures frequently lumped under such headings as 'expenses,' 'back debts,' and other unelucidated items." With proper management, he asserted, the Braves could thrive.[101]

Names of potential owners looking for a bargain appeared in newspapers throughout the month. One name was George Preston Marshall.

Marshall made a fortune from his father's laundry business in Washington, D.C. and his creative slogan, "Long Live Linen." In 1932, Marshall got into professional football, paying $5,000 for a one-fifth interest in the Boston Braves' National Football League franchise. He eventually became sole owner and renamed the club the Redskins. "They asked me if I would take over the Braves," he said, "and I told them, 'Yes, if I am given the club.' But I'm not putting any money into baseball and I'm sure the Braves' owners won't present the club to me. Buying the Braves would be a gamble, I believe."[102]

A second name was Francis P. Murphy, New Hampshire entrepreneur and gubernatorial candidate (he would serve two terms as New Hampshire Governor from 1937 to 1941). Murphy owned 300 shares ($40,000) of Braves stock and wanted controlling interest "if certain conditions were met," the *Nashua Telegraph* reported. Murphy owned the J.F. McElwain Shoe Company, which had just announced the purchase of a new mill in Manchester.[103] Murphy later helped found WMUR radio and television stations in New Hampshire. "Maj Murphy is a great sportsman and a keen baseball man," Fuchs boasted. "He should be ideal to head the Braves."[104] Murphy partnered with James Campbell, president of the Goodall Worsted Textile Mill of Sanford, Maine, which produced the Palm Beach Mills clothing brand. Fuchs persuaded Campbell during a fishing expedition on Moosehead Lake, deep in the Maine woods.[105]

Charles Joseph O'Malley, hailed as "the dean of Boston advertising men," was also interested.[106] O'Malley came to the U.S. from Ireland with $12 in his pocket in 1883. In just six years, he was managing the *Detroit Free Press*. He came to Boston in 1905 and established the O'Malley Advertising and Selling Company. He traveled the world and documented his travels by movie camera, thrilling audiences back home.[107] His sons, Charles D., and Louis J., were his associates. "We're interested strictly as a business proposition if we can get the club at our price and without entanglements," Charles D. said. They announced that they were offering $250,000 for Fuchs' holdings and they wanted Ruth as manager.[108]

Reporters saw Ruth entering his Manhattan apartment. They called and asked him about managing. Claire answered.

"Mr. Ruth isn't in." Then she changed her mind.

"Mr. Ruth has retired, and he won't have, hasn't, any statement to make. Mr. Ruth doesn't know anything about that report."[109]

Joe E. Brown, "the bandy-legged comedian with a rubbery mouth and squeaky voice" whose career as an actor and comedian lasted from the circus to vaudeville, from burlesque to movies, and finally to night clubs over 60 years, was part of a syndicate interested in buying the Braves. Brown was part-owner of the Kansas City Blues of the American Association. His son would one day become GM of the Pittsburgh Pirates. Brown is most remembered for portraying Osgood Fielding III in the classic 1959 film *Some Like It Hot*, starring Marilyn Monroe, Tony Curtis, and Jack Lemmon.[110] "I'm definitely interested in the Braves," the comedian said, "and I'm crazy about baseball. Should Judge Fuchs decide to sell to us, I'd be willing to spend three months of my time in the East every year to look after the club's affairs."[111]

Brown was disillusioned that the NL would financially help him. "Every new owner needs help, especially when his club is down and out. The other owners should cooperate for the good of the game. If I buy the Braves, I'll try to give them as much color as possible. That's what the public pays for—entertainment."[112]

A fifth name was Joseph P. Kennedy, Sr. The patriarch of the Kennedy political dynasty was chairman of the Securities and Exchange Commission. The leaders of his family dynasty were still at home. John F. Kennedy graduated from high school that month; Robert Kennedy was nine; Ted Kennedy was three. If he bought the team as part of a syndicate, he was expected to install his father-in-law, John Fitzgerald, as team president. Fitzgerald, known as "Honey Fitz," was Rose Kennedy's father and had been involved with Boston baseball since the 19th century. He threw out the first ball at the opening of Fenway Park in 1912.[113]

By the last week of June, the plot thickened. Brown attended a Giants-Cubs game with Ford Frick. Fuchs met Marshall in Washington, D.C. "I'd get a kick out of out of owning the Boston National League team," Marshall said. Fuchs also met with a "mystery" investor, perhaps Kennedy.[114]

Back to the House He Built

Babe Ruth was growing accustomed to his newfound freedom. "He rises when he pleases," wrote Eddie Breitz of the Associated Press. "He eats what he likes for breakfast. He lights a cigar and spends a half hour with the papers. He reads the box scores closely, particularly those of the Yankee games. He pays little or no attention to the doings of the Braves. Almost any afternoon finds the Bambino shooting in the low 80's on one of a half dozen Long Island courses. Then he motors back to West 88th Street, eats what he pleases for dinner and spends the evening at cards or the movies."[115]

On the last day of June, Ruth made his return to Yankee Stadium to see the Yankees play the Senators. Ruth made his way to his seat with Claire and Julia, while acknowledging the cheers of 12,500 fans. He was dressed in a white suit, striking against his sun-browned skin after so many rounds of golf. He was protected by a policeman who kept autograph seekers away.[116]

Ruth planned to attend the All-Star Game in Cleveland on July 9. Ford Frick called a special meeting of NL club owners while they were there to discuss the Braves' finances. The hope was that one of the potential buyers would have committed by then.

Time was running out for Fuchs.[117]

10

The Judge's Swan Song
(July 1935)

"Fame hasn't any brains."—Babe Ruth

"I am anxious, now, to get rid of the club."—Judge Fuchs

"Someone is going to be bankrupt. It is either going to be the Boston Baseball Club or it is going to be the National League, and, by the grace of God, it isn't going to be the National League."—Ford C. Frick

Adams: The Grocery Store Genius

Charles Francis Adams was called the nation's #1 sports promoter in 1935 by the *Boston Globe*. His estimated profits were $2.6 million at the time.[1] His Boston Braves investment was said to be worth $600,000; the Boston Bruins and soon-to-open Suffolk Downs racetrack were valued at $1 million each. These were his sporting ventures, the hobbies he could afford because he had the means to do so through his success in the grocery business, which he had been running for 20 years.

Charles F. Adams learned about hard work and the value of a dollar at an early age. He was born to Frank Weston and Lizzie (Benoit) Adams on October 18, 1876, in Newport, Orleans County, in the Northeast Kingdom of Vermont on Canada's border. Charles was the oldest of four children, his siblings being Vernon, Glen, and Josephine. Lumber drove the local economy, and Lake Memphremagog was choked with logs awaiting the sawmill. The Prouty Miller Lumber Company occupied the area for well over a century. Frank Adams owned a sawmill. He was one of 16 children born to Abial and Irene (Gray) Adams, who were among the earliest settlers of the area. Young Charles helped his family by working at a corner grocery so he could buy logs for the mill.

Charles attended business school, then moved to Springfield, Massachusetts, working as a grocery clerk for $2 a week for his uncle, Oscar D. Adams. Oscar had started in the flour and produce business, then shifted to maple products. He created the Vermont Farmers' Company on Worthington Street in Springfield. His life was so prominent in Springfield that his death in 1925 was front-page news. In his 80s, Oscar knit sweaters for soldiers in the trenches in World War I.

Charles sold maple, tobacco, and other products from New England to Virginia to Chicago for his Uncle Oscar. On Sundays, he pursued overdue accounts. One of those sales calls proved to be of great personal investment. He met Lillias Mae Woollard, originally from Ontario, who was visiting her sister in Vermont. In 1901, Charles and Mae were married. In 1904, they were living on Spring Street in Springfield when they welcomed their son Weston, the future president of the Boston Bruins, into the world.

As Adams prospered in Boston's business world, newspapers often confused him with another prominent Charles Francis Adams. This Vermont Charles Francis Adams was referred to as "C.F." The other was secretary of the Navy, Mayor of Quincy, Massachusetts, and a grandson of President John Quincy Adams.[2]

C.F. soon managed the Vermont Farmers' Company for his uncle. He, Mae, and Weston moved to Cambridge, Massachusetts, and C.F. became treasurer of the New England Maple Syrup Company. In 1906, Adams consolidated both the farmers and maple companies.[3] He briefly left the produce world and became a broker for Fitzgerald, Hubbard & Co. There he met grocery magnate John T. Connor, who wasn't interested in what C.F. was selling. Connor was an innovator in the grocery chain business dating back to the late 1890s. Connor encouraged Adams to invest in *his* business, so Adams went to work for Connor and in 1914 bought the company. C.F. became president and treasurer of the John T. Connor grocery chain of 124 stores, known as Brookside.[4]

By 1919, the John T. Connor company reached $8.5 million in sales through its 210 stores. By 1923, there were 350 Brookside stores. By late 1925, after 10 years with Adams at the helm, there were 600 stores with the slogan "Always a safe place to economize."[5] Adams praised his employees. "Our vitality and growth is [*sic*] accounted for by this group," he beamed. "There can be but one end for such ideals and loyalty and cooperation as you give the company, and that end is success for us all."[6] One innovation was a deal Adams made with Vermont farmers to ship their milk directly to Brookside stores via the railroad, eliminating the middleman. Prominent investors in the company included Calvin Coolidge. The milk department alone made $1 million in sales its first year.[7]

"He's a youngish man, and humorous and frank," wrote Fred B. Barton in a 1924 article for the journal *Business*. Brookside stores dotted the landscape of a 60-mile radius around Boston.

Adams was opening one new store in Boston and two in the suburbs every week. Stores were often placed just outside of the city to save on rent, but were attractive on main roads leading to the city. Every store had fresh coffee on site. It cost Adams $65,000 for each of his 425 stores to have it, but it easily paid for itself.[8]

Adams expanded again in 1925 by purchasing two rival grocers, O'Keefe's Inc. and the Ginter Company, creating a megachain of over 1,500 stores with $50 million in annual sales. Adams assumed the role of treasurer in the new company, now called First National Stores, based in Somerville, Massachusetts. The company made a net profit of $1.7 million in 1925.[9] Adams expanded First National in 1926 when they merged with the Arthur E. Dorr meat company, which had grossed $6 million in 1925.[10] "In a natural and sensible way," Adams told Barton, who returned in 1926 for an interview for *Chain Store Age*, "we pooled our interests so that the First National Stores will continue to be in New England for a long time to come."[11] Adams was right on in his prediction. First National Stores had grown to 2,700 stores by its tenth anniversary in 1935, with 14,000 employees, 9,000 stockholders, and $28 million in annual sales.[12] First National continued through the 1970s until they merged with Pick-N-Pay grocers in 1978, when suburban shopping malls became the norm.[13]

Boston's No. 1 Sports Promoter

Adams was enamored with sports since he was a young boy who traveled to Canada to see professional hockey. In 1912, he managed the amateur Crescent Hockey Association club, which played at the old Boston Arena.[14] His "unbounded enthusiasm was contagious," Fred Hoey, future Braves broadcaster, said of Adams. C.F. earned the nickname "Pops" for his generosity to young players who couldn't afford equipment or supper after practice.[15]

Adams was one of several area businessmen who funded the rebuilding of the Boston Arena after it was partially destroyed by fire in 1918. Adams became a managing director of the new arena, which stands today as Matthews Arena. Hockey was prominent at the arena. Several Boston amateur clubs belonged to the United States Amateur Hockey Association. Fans tired of amateur hockey after a game-fixing scandal. The professional National Hockey League in Canada seemed a logical league to join. Montreal promoter Thomas Duggan purchased franchise options for both New York and Boston. Adams watched the Stanley Cup playoffs across the border and was determined to bring pro hockey to Boston. He formed an alliance with Duggan and persuaded Boston Arena directors to bring in professional hockey.[16]

Despite viewing hockey as a hobby, Adams purchased a new NHL franchise for $15,000. The Boston Bruins played Montreal at the Boston Arena in the first pro hockey game in the United States on December 1, 1924. There were small crowds that inaugural season, but Adams had the foresight to broadcast the games on WBZ radio and built a fanbase. He lost nearly $75,000 that first year, and finding talent was a daunting task. But Adams was undeterred. He bought the entire Western Hockey League, the NHL's competitor, for $300,000.[17] Adams acquired the player inventory to sell players to other U.S. teams and keep seven players for his Bruins, wisely choosing future legend Eddie Shore.[18] "I daresay," wrote Victor O. Jones in retrospect of Adams in 1967, "ole C.F. remains unique as the only man who ever bought a whole league to get a few players for himself."[19]

The Boston Arena was not a permanent home, however. The Bruins needed a new ice arena, so Adams joined other investors in building the Boston Garden in 1928. C.F. invested $500,000 to guarantee rental fees. Adams joined the Garden board of directors, and the Bruins won their first Stanley Cup championship in 1929.[20]

C.F. Adams loved horses, and he bred them on his Wedgemere Farm in Framingham.[21] He helped form the Eastern Racing Association by investing $500,000 into the construction of Suffolk Downs racetrack and spent over $2.5 million by the time it opened.[22] Adams and his business partner, V.C. Bruce Wetmore, were called "prime movers and main financial cogs in the enterprise" by the *Boston Globe*. Suffolk Downs was, in the *Globe's* view, "the finest racing establishment in New England, if not the world." The grandstand seated 16,000, and three trains transported fans there. "We intend that this track shall be included among the outstanding tracks of this country," Adams said.[23] "Suffolk Downs stands today resembling a bit of scenery snatched from another part of the world," wrote C. Joseph Harvey in the *Globe,* "in a magical transformation that has caused even the neighbors in East Boston to rub their eyes in pleasant amazement."[24] Burt Whitman of the *Boston Herald* wrote that Adams "seems to have had a gift of making a success of everything which he touched."[25]

Well, not *everything*. The Boston Braves also needed a miraculous transformation. Despite his applauded business acumen, Adams could not find a solution to keeping the NL Hub baseball team solvent. Adams had spent the previous decade handing money over to Judge Fuchs, from his original $200,000 investment to other bailouts over the years. The Braves were a losing and costly venture. Adams needed someone else to perform *this* miracle. He just wanted to get his money back and get out.

So did the National League.

The Road to the All-Star Game

The Braves played 21 of 28 July games on the road. It was a long month, and the team wasn't making itself attractive to a potential buyer. Time was ticking down on Judge Fuchs to sell his holdings by August 1, and Adams had run out of patience. The National League again had to intervene in the Braves' affairs. "Manager Bill McKechnie must be suffering a lot of mental torture when he looks back over this much of the season," wrote Ralph Clifford in the *Boston Herald*, "but so far he hasn't let out a word of criticism or of self-pity."[26] "I am confident," McKechnie said, "that the team will emerge from this rut."[27]

Judge Fuchs was on his way to Washington to meet George Preston Marshall. "I am anxious, now, to get rid of the club," he confessed. "I am tired and want the matter straightened out at the earliest possible moment." The O'Malley family was meeting with Adams.[28] Very little else of the Braves made front-page news, other

C.F. Adams (left) believed he had a new owner of the Braves in Boston Redskins football owner George Preston Marshall (courtesy Boston Public Library, Leslie Jones Collection).

than former rookie phenom Ed Moriarty passing his seminary entrance exams.[29] The Braves could have used whatever divine connections Moriarty had.

The Dodgers wanted to see the annual New York vs. Brooklyn sportswriters game and postponed their July 1 game with the Braves.[30] The Braves were shut out, 5–0, on July 2 by Ray Benge, who had survived the chicken pox.[31] On Wednesday, Hal Lee had four hits to raise his average to .327, but Braves pitchers allowed 18 hits in a 13–6 drubbing. A more important "game" was the one behind closed doors.

Fuchs invited NL President Ford Frick to Boston to meet the O'Malleys. Frick met with Adams and Fuchs separately, since the two cordial partners were no longer on speaking terms. Frick also met with an anonymous group. Perhaps Joseph P. Kennedy?[32] Comedian Joe E. Brown was not a serious buyer, Frick said, since he didn't have the cash to make an offer.[33]

Brown was busy horsing around, anyway, at Narragansett Park. He placed a claim for $5,500 on Captain Argo, a four-year-old bay gelding owned by Mary Hirsch, the first female horse trainer to receive a license by the Jockey Club. Captain Argo lost the race, but Brown acquired the horse, which won a Labor Day race. "I fell in love with Captain Argo," Brown wrote in his autobiography, *Laughter is a Wonderful Thing*, "and I think he became fond of me. I spent hours in the stable talking to that horse, and he would nudge me and whinny and carry on as though he understood every word."[34] Brown never mentioned the Braves, since he said even owning a minor league club had given him "plenty of headaches."[35]

Frick met with Fuchs and others, but the real meeting was at 101 Milk Street in Boston's Financial District. There, in a steel safe in C.F. Adams' office, sat 65 percent of the 15,000 shares of Boston Braves stock. The shares were purchased for $60 each, but Adams would gladly take $35 or even $30 a share from the National League, or someone could pay $250,000 for all 9,750 of his shares. "If any group is interested in purchasing the Braves," Adams told Frick, "it must do business with me, for I am the only one empowered to sell the club." A buyer could purchase Adams' shares for $250,000, and an additional $200,000 would satisfy Fuchs' debts with the bank and the Stevens family, the Braves Field concessionaires who had loaned the team $121,000. A half-million bucks could give one a ballclub.[36]

Bill Cunningham of the *Boston Post* visited Adams. "He's spiritually, mentally, and financially prepared to write it all off to wry experience," he wrote. Adams anticipated a loss of $100,000 but considered it a necessary loss since it was money invested before the Crash of '29, and he would have lost it one way or another.

"What happens if Fuchs doesn't come through?" Cunningham asked.

"What do we do with a grocery store that doesn't pay expenses?" he responded. "We close it up."

"Do you mean you'd close up the Braves?"

"Certainly. I'm not a baseball man. That's an entire business in itself. I haven't time to run it, nor even to watch the man who does."

"Under no circumstances will you carry it on?" Cunningham clarified.

"Under absolutely none. Gentlemen, I'm through." Adams told Frick, "If you find a real purchaser, if he really has money and is really interested in buying, I'll be glad to talk with him, but I'm too busy to bother with movie actors or other gentlemen primarily interested in publicity. I've had enough of hot air artists for one lifetime."[37]

Around 200,000 enthusiastic Boston residents witnessed a Fourth of July parade with flags, firecrackers, floats, drums, spirited music, and Moose. The parade was sponsored by the Loyal Order of Moose holding a convention. Meanwhile, 12,000 watched the Giants parade around the bases in a doubleheader. Ben Cantwell dropped to 1–11 in a 10–8 loss. In the nightcap, Fred Frankhouse was scorched for 13 hits and 10 runs as the Braves were clobbered, 12–3. "Those loud reports in the vicinity of Braves Field yesterday," wrote Gerry Moore in the *Globe*, "did not issue from any of those bootleg giant firecrackers. They merely were the constant clatter of the bats of the mighty New York Giants."[38]

A holiday parade was also held at the Westchester Country Club in Rye, New York, under a blazing sun. The Benedicts, a ball team of married men, many of them Wall Street brokers, appeared in full Navy admiral uniforms. Opposing them were the unmarried Bachelors' club, decked all in Army white. There were so many of the Bachelors, a ball could hardly fall in the outfield without hitting somebody. The

Benedicts had bigger waistlines and far more perspiration than the Bachelors. Joining the married men was George Herman Ruth.

Babe and Claire made the trip for the social affair, and she sat alongside other well-to-do ladies. A chubby waiter kept on his toes picking up the empty beer glasses scattered on the grounds. Between innings, children and adults swarmed Ruth to autograph everything from a baseball to a dinner menu. Players began to strip off their layers as the sun beat down. A shortstop for the Bachelors named Bill Behrens stripped down to a jumper and a pair of shorts with a crimson heart "where Bill rests when he sets," wrote Nancy Randolph in the *Daily News*. The Bachelors tied the game, 12–12, in the seventh and final inning. Ruth thought the game was over and was "loping off for a mug of beer." The married men yelled for him to return to the field. He was up. Ruth doubled in the winning run, then walked off to get his beer in the clubhouse while admiring the club's "magnificent mint juleps."[39]

The Braves played a doubleheader in Philadelphia on July 6 before a crowd of 8,000. Danny MacFayden won his fourth game in less than a month, and the Braves won the opener, 10–5. The nightcap was a different story. Bob Brown was lit up for 14 hits and 10 runs, launching his ERA to 10.45 as he fell to 0–3. Larry Benton's ERA continued upward as well as he allowed another four runs mopping up the 15–2 humiliation. On Sunday, the Phillies knocked around Huck Betts (0–6) in a 9–1 romp.

The Braves were 21–52 at the All-Star break, 29 games behind the first-place Giants and even 10 games behind the seventh-place Reds. Wally Berger, the lone Braves representative in the All-Star Game, started in center fielder for the NL. Fuchs took the train to Cleveland to meet with NL team owners, hoping for a miracle. Ironically, Babe Ruth was also on that train. He had no money problems at all; his trip was just for fun. Neither man had any idea where his career was going. Despite their proximity on the train, neither exchanged "a single harsh noun or mean look," according to John Lardner.[40]

Babe and Claire arrived at the train station on July 7, creating a stir of publicity. Reporters followed the Bambino around the depot. There was anticipation in the air of a record-breaking crowd in the monstrous Cleveland Stadium. The seldom used "standing room only" sign was being dusted off. Reds GM Larry MacPhail was seen promoting night baseball to anyone who would listen, and Fuchs was "taking bids in the public square." Joe E. Brown arrived, as did Hollywood's sassy star Mae West, the highest-paid woman in America and whose latest film, *Goin' to Town*, was released in April. "Street corners were baseball camps," wrote Roelif Loveland in the *Plain Dealer*.[41] No nightlife for Babe and Claire, though. They took it easy, drinking ice water at the hotel. He was exhausted from playing golf that day, and she was exhausted answering the phone and explaining what he was up to.

Three local Cleveland radio stations covered the game: WTAM, WGAR, and WHK, in additional to the three national networks: NBC, CBS, and the Mutual Broadcasting System. There were no exclusive rights in those days. If Ruth had time

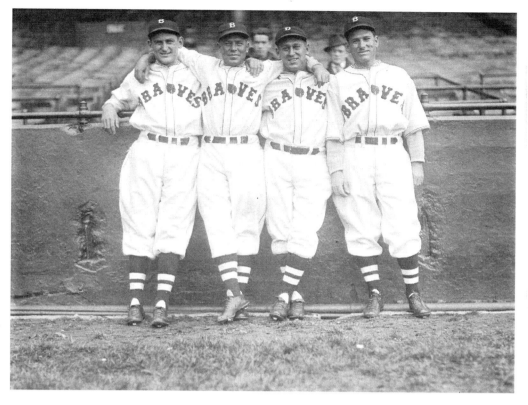

The 1935 Braves infield (from left): 1B Buck Jordan, 2B Les Mallon, SS Billy Urbanski, 3B Pinky Whitney (courtesy of the Boston Public Library, Leslie Jones Collection).

to grab a newspaper before nodding off, he may have read that "after years of rumors, false starts and renewed hopes, television has emerged from the laboratory and field experiments have begun in important centers of the world."[42] Television was on the horizon, but the first televised game was still four years away.

National League Meeting

"The Boston problems have been so great," Ford Frick said to the National League magnates on July 7, "that our finances have been seriously hampered." Like hosts whose guests never go home but still help themselves to the fridge, the NL treasury was drained from keeping the Braves afloat. The club's 1934 taxes, back rent on Braves Field, expenses from the previous special meeting, and even baseballs were expenses the NL had to cover. Total debt: $26,497.11.[43] "Within another three months our treasury is going to be depleted," Frick warned. "The Boston case must be settled or there is going to have to be an assessment among the other clubs in this League."[44]

The *Boston Post* reported that Fuchs' original investment in the Braves was only $49,000, and only $25,000 of that was in cash. The *Post* also claimed that he had drawn salary and benefits totaling $335,000 over those years. The NL held Braves stock as collateral for a $20,000 loan, but the biggest issue was the $200,000 note Fuchs had with the First National Bank of Boston.[45]

Fuchs reported that the Braves had a balance of only $8,500, with just $10,000 in reserve. Despite paying off $60,000 in debt through the ticket book campaign, the weather, Ruth, poor attendance, and the lousy pitching had the team on the ropes. "The question of whether I can dispose of the club is going to be settled within not longer than two weeks," Fuchs promised. "I think it would be great if I could terminate my 14 years' connection with baseball without any further embarrassment."[46]

Fuchs demanded a higher price for his holdings than Adams did for his. Fuchs needed to pay off his debts, while Adams was glad to take pennies on the dollar. What buyer would negotiate with Fuchs for $60 per share when Adams was offering $35 per share? Fuchs said Adams' discounted price had "handicapped me in disposing of the club so far." Fuchs couldn't afford taking pennies on the dollar, given his mounting debt. "The people I have now could give a price that would take care of the Stevens' interest, and they would probably give me a few dollars, so that I could walk out of there without at least owing all this money, with some chance of making settlement on that basis."[47] Fuchs believed he could have sold the club earlier if would-be purchasers didn't ask, "'Why should we pay you so much if we can wait until the first of August and get it?'"[48]

Friends were advising Fuchs to file for bankruptcy, but he was determined to pay back every dime. "Give me a chance to go to work and make it up, and that is what I am going to do."[49]

"Except for one thing, Judge," Frick said to Fuchs.

"And what is that?"

"Your price for the club is too high. You can't sell it for that price."

"That may be perfectly true," Fuchs agreed. "I am willing to sacrifice everything. If I could walk out of here without a dollar, I would walk out, but there are some pressing obligations which I don't think it would do the League any good where I may be sued. I am just asking, and I think I am entitled to this, gentlemen, for a square deal and an opportunity to sell this club without any further publication."[50]

Sam Breadon, owner of the Cardinals, saw no hope for Fuchs. "I will say that if nothing is done by the 1st of August," he forewarned, "the League President ought to take the club over, or sell it themselves, or put it in bankruptcy or whatever is necessary to clean the thing up."[51]

Adams' plan, in discounting the Fuchs shares he held, would enable him to walk away with only $129,000 from his original $200,000 investment. Fuchs would walk away with a mere $30,000, "which would mean," Fuchs explained, "I would have to send for them [creditors] and draw up a proposition for this money and divide it up among them." Fuchs also owed $20,000 to the NL, and 2,000 shares of unaccounted for stock given out for personal loans needed to be re-purchased.[52] The only reason anyone would purchase stock at Fuchs' asking price would be fear of being outbid. Outbid by whom?

"Someone is going to be bankrupt," Frick interjected.

> It is either going to be the Boston Baseball Club or it is going to be the National League, and, by the grace of God, it isn't going to be the National League. So far as we are concerned, if we have got to chop any necks, it has got to be that [Boston], and my suggestion is that you recommend that the League President, together with whomever he may choose to help him, go out and make the best deal they can get, the best proposition they can for the Boston Ball Club and put it up to Mr. Adams and Judge Fuchs, and say, "Here it is. That is the best we can do."[53]

The owners discussed whether they should wait until August 1 and work with Adams or try to get the best deal possible for Fuchs before then. "I don't want to be foreclosed in the few moments that I have left," Fuchs pleaded.[54] They decided to wait and act on August 1. "Either get their money or foreclose and throw it into bankruptcy and settle the whole thing," said Breadon.[55]

Fuchs had three weeks. He had authority to sell his stock and secure proxies from friends to sell on their behalf. Many friends purchased the stock at $80 per share, 20 points below par value, during the 1933 crisis, as a favor to the Judge. Adams was selling his holdings for $30–35 per share, "so anxious is he to unload and divorce himself from an investment he tired of two years ago," wrote Paul Shannon in *The Sporting News*. They were a tough sell. "The inroads of horses and dogs, internal squabbles and the realization that the Braves are the weakest outfit to represent the Hub in either circuit for more than two decades hasn't stimulated the interest of investors."[56]

Fame Hasn't Any Brains

The attendance at the All-Star Game was just under 70,000. The American League prevailed, 4–1. Berger went 0-for-2. Babe and Claire Ruth arrived 20 minutes before game time and made their way to their front-row seats behind the American League dugout. Photographers stopped what they were doing to capture the moment, and AL players immediately left the dugout to shake his hand while he smoked a black cigar in his brown sport coat. "He still was the Sultan of Swat," wrote Alvin Silverman.[57]

"Fame is a spotlight one minute and a bullseye the next," Ruth wrote, likely through a ghostwriter, in a guest editorial in the August issue of *American Magazine*. "The people who cheer loudest when you succeed are those who throw pop bottles the hardest when you fail. Loud cheers make heroes. Pop bottles make martyrs. Why can't people be sensible and take a man just for what he us? If we really understand a man, we do not worship him and we do not abuse him." Appropriate words for a man staring into an empty void after decades of applause. "I think it is better to be known by a few good friends—trusted and liked and respected by them in spite of all of one's weaknesses and shortcomings—than to be cheered on every continent by people who think you're great."[58]

Ruth continued as he wrestled with the big questions of existence.

> They used to cheer me because I could hit a baseball often and hard—nothing more. They picked me for fame just for that. They didn't know who built the stadium, who engineered the traffic, who invented baseball. I knew an old priest once. His hair was white, his face shone. I have written my name on thousands and thousands of baseballs in my life. The old priest wrote his name on just a few simple hearts. How I envy him.[59]

Ruth was just a month into his retirement, yet these existential questions nagged at him. Who was he? He lived for crowds, but they were no more. Ruth's signatures would be collector's items for all time, but the old priests, like Brother Matthias, left their signatures on troubled youth, like himself. "Beside that obscure priest, who was so good and so wise, I never got to first base." He concluded that "Fame hasn't any brains."[60]

The Braves visited Detroit for an exhibition game against the Tigers. This was their second exhibition game over the break, having defeated McKeesport (Pennsylvania), their minor league affiliate, on July 8.[61] The Braves lost to the AL champion Tigers, 8–7, in 11 innings before 35,000 fans at Navin Field.[62]

One of Judge Fuchs' strongest supporters was James Roosevelt (right), son of President Franklin D. Roosevelt (courtesy Boston Public Library, Leslie Jones Collection).

McKechnie spent the game in the stands chatting with Fuchs. There was plenty to discuss.[63]

15 in a Row

The Braves resumed regular play on July 10 in Chicago. The third-place Cubs were 40–32 and 9½ games behind the Giants. Wally Berger launched his 17th home run, and the Braves took an early 4–1 lead, but the Cubs chipped away against Fred Frankhouse (5–7), and Joe Coscarart "kicked the ball hither and thither" at second base. The Cubs won, 6–4.[64] Few in Boston noticed.

It was the grand opening of Suffolk Downs where "close to 35,000 persons poured into the track by ferry, subway, train and tunnel and wagered $425,546 on the eight-race card," reported the *Globe*. Nearly 7,000 vehicles passed through the one-year-old Sumner Tunnel under Boston Harbor. C.F. Adams was grinning ear-to-ear about his investment.[65] "Perhaps yesterday marked a clean break with Puritan tradition," quipped Richard O. Boyer in the *Boston Herald*, "since everyone had a good time."[66] Not everyone, of course. Representative Thomas E. Barry of East Boston complained of the traffic, demanding that the tunnel be expanded to four lanes.[67] The Callahan Tunnel would help relieve the congestion, 25 years later.

The Braves lost, 5–3, on Wednesday, then on Friday, July 12, they pounded the Wisconsin Rapids of the Wisconsin State League, 26–9 in an exhibition.[68] Back to the Cubs on Saturday, they lost a doubleheader by scores of 10–2 and 3–1. Danny MacFayden allowed seven runs in the opener. The series concluded on July 14 before 7,700 fans. The Cubs pulled off an 8–7 victory, their ninth straight win over the Braves and 13 of 15 overall. The Braves led, 7–5, into the bottom of the eighth inning, but the Cubs jumped on Ed Brandt (5–10) for three runs. The Braves lost their seventh straight.

The Braves moved on to St. Louis for a four-game series. The second-place Cardinals were on the heels of the Giants, just six games back, and were riding a 10-game winning streak. The Birds were perfect so far in July, while the Braves had only won once. Fred Frankhouse (5–8) didn't make it out of the third inning, allowing 11 hits and 10 runs in the opener, an easy 15th win for Dizzy Dean, 13–6.

On July 16, 41-year-old Jesse Haines dominated the Braves before 20,000 spectators at Sportsman's Park on Tuberculosis Day, an annual charity event. Ben Cantwell pitched superbly but lost his ninth in a row to fall to 1–12 as the Braves lost, 2–1. "I've heard and read a lot about teams that simply can't get a break," McKechnie said, "but I never knew how it felt to manage such a team until now."[69]

On Wednesday, Brandt shut out the Cardinals through seven innings. The game was tied, 1–1, in the ninth when Terry Moore hit a walk-off home run, their 13th straight win, Boston's 10th straight loss. In the finale, the Cardinals pounced all over MacFayden (5–7) for six runs and Bob Smith for seven more. The Cards won, 13–3, and with their 14th straight win were just four games back of the Giants. The Braves couldn't wait to jump on the 6 p.m. train to Pittsburgh.

The fourth-place Pirates (42–41) were reeling, 14 games behind, and losers of nine of their last 10 home games. The Braves were a welcome sight. A storm was brewing, and "the huge flagpoles holding Old Glory threatened to crack off from the strain of the wind," wrote Charles J. Doyle in the *Pittsburgh Sun-Telegraph*.[70] The game was played under heavy clouds of dust. The Braves took a 5–3 lead into the bottom of the ninth inning. Paul Waner doubled, and Arky Vaughan, the NL's leading hitter, homered to tie the game. Pep Young lofted a pop fly into the dust over the left field corner. The ball drifted foul, but a gust of wind pushed it fair, and Hal Lee over-ran it. The ball bounded away, and Young reached third. Tommy Thevenow singled, and the Braves and lost their 12th straight. After winning his first start of the year, Ben Cantwell had lost 13 straight decisions. "As the game ended the clouds opened and the heavens wept," wrote Ralph Clifford in the *Herald*, "whether at the fate of the Braves, or at the spectacle which had been witnessed, no one knows. Just dumb baseball, that's all."[71]

The doubleheader on July 20 was "a sorry showing for the Braves," Clifford wrote, as the Pirates won, 14–2 and 6–3, to run the Braves' winless streak to 14.[72] Berger's 18th home run was the highlight for the "hapless, not to mention helpless, Braves," wrote Volney Walsh in the *Pittsburgh Press*.[73] The series wrapped up on Sunday, July 21, with a 7–0 loss. Brandt (5–12) and the Braves lost their 15th straight game.

McKechnie moaned about his pitching staff going to pieces, and rightly so. But their batting over the losing streak was also a factor in taking this team from very bad to very very bad.

Team Batting Averages Before the Streak

BA	OBP	SLG	OPS	H PG	HR PG	RBI PG	BB PG	SO PG	LOB PG
.268	.321	.380	.701	9.3	0.6	4.0	2.5	2.9	7.0

Team Batting Averages During the Streak

BA	OBP	SLG	OPS	H PG	HR PG	RBI PG	BB PG	SO PG	LOB PG
.248	.281	.313	.595	8.6	0.3	2.7	1.7	2.7	6.9

Team Pitching Averages Before the Streak

ERA	ER PG	H PG	BB PG	SO PG	HR PG	2B PG	3B PG
4.81	4.7	10.8	2.7	2.6	0.6	1.6	0.5

Team Pitching Averages During the Streak

ERA	ER PG	H PG	BB PG	SO PG	HR PG	2B PG	3B PG
7.76	6.9	12.8	2.8	2.3	0.8	2.0	0.3

The Braves struggled to draw fans to Braves Field, but huge crowds streamed into Suffolk Downs as New England was caught in a racing craze (courtesy Boston Public Library, Leslie Jones Collection).

Few pitchers escaped the onslaught during the streak. The tough-luck Cantwell looked the best, with Smith not far behind. Some couldn't get anyone out.

Pitcher	ERA	BB	SO	BA	OBP	WHIP
Cantwell	4.35	2	0	.302	.333	1.50
Smith	4.15	5	8	.322	.358	1.58
Brandt	5.70	6	7	.366	.402	1.81
Betts	6.19	8	4	.296	.367	1.81
MacFayden	9.00	4	4	.382	.413	1.94
Benton	12.60	5	3	.364	.429	2.10
Frankhouse	14.14	8	6	.375	.438	2.50
Brown	11.25	4	2	.465	.511	3.00

Finally, a W

The Braves concluded their road trip with four games in Cincinnati, beginning on July 22, where only 542 Cincinnatians were inspired enough to show up.

McKechnie managed the game like the pennant was on the line to finally get the Braves a victory.

Cantwell again pitched well but fell behind, 2–1, through seven innings in a pitchers' duel with Don Brennan. With one on and two out in the top of the eighth, rookie catcher Ray Mueller singled, and McKechnie sent lefty Randy Moore up to pinch-hit for Cantwell. Reds manager Chuck Dressen countered with lefty Tony Freitas from the bullpen. McKechnie replaced Moore with switch-hitter Joe Mowry, who doubled in two runs, and the Braves led, 3–2. Bob Smith saved the Braves' rare victory, 4–2. Cantwell (2–13) finally was victorious as well, but there were no celebrations. The team quietly walked across the field to the clubhouse. This was not winning the lottery but paying overdue bills. Once they left, a downpour covered the field.[74]

Another pitiful crowd under 600 saw the Braves win their second straight on Tuesday. The Braves jumped to a 6–2 lead, but Betts didn't last the third inning. The game was 6–6 in the 12th inning when Wally Berger took Gene Schott to the cleaners, literally, when his 20th home run cleared the wall and the street, landing on the roof of a laundry. Smith saved the 7–6 victory.[75]

Wednesday's game was the fifth night game in Major League history, a sparkling affair which drew 23,000 fans. It was the largest night crowd so far in the new experiment, although the Negro Leagues and some minor league teams had been playing under lights for years. Temporary seats were placed in left field to accommodate the Crosley Field crowd. Over 200 soldiers attended, and a 38-piece band of the 10th Infantry from Fort Thomas, Kentucky performed a stirring pregame concert. Braves coach Hank Gowdy, who fought in the trenches in World War I, participated. Gowdy would serve his country again in World War II, the only major leaguer to serve in both wars.[76]

Tommy Thompson tripled in the top of the ninth inning and was the potential tying run with one out. Les Mallon's pop fly to right curled foul. It was deep enough to score Thompson, but Babe Herman smartly muffed the ball intentionally so Thompson couldn't advance. Mallon's next fly was not deep enough, and Hal Lee fouled out to end the Braves' winning streak, 5–4.

Thursday's game was rained out. The Braves stopped in Auburn, New York, for an exhibition against Toronto of the International League.[77] The Maple Leafs beat the lackluster Braves, 4–1.[78]

The crowd of 4,000 had originally bought their tickets anticipating Babe Ruth.

If they wanted to see him, they needed to go to a golf course.

The Babe Over Par

On July 26, Ruth was invited to play in the Westchester Country Club's annual golf tournament. A pouring rain accompanied the golfers, but it failed to dampen the enthusiasm of the 500 people who surrounded Ruth all day. "We're off," he announced as he sank a ten-foot putt for a birdie three on the first hole. "It's too bad they can't make this a doubleheader for tomorrow. The crowd would be bigger."[79] At the 14th hole, Ruth stopped at the refreshment stand and bought beers and cigars for everyone. He lit a fat cigar, teed off, and headed to the green. He missed a 12-foot putt and bogeyed the hole.

"Smoke got in my eyes," he said, shaking out the ashes. "Now that I'm used to it, watch me go." He reminded everyone of the "rollicking Babe of baseball days," wrote Kevin Jones in the *New York Daily News*.[80] He pulled off a miracle shot on the 15th hole, a par three. With his seven-iron, he lifted the ball up, and it landed with a splat in the mud. "Use your head," advised his partner, Dick Chapman, a legend in amateur golf. Ruth wanted to use his weight. He swung, ripping a hole in the turf several inches deep, and "blew the ball out of there to a foot and a half of the cup," wrote Jones.

"Just as I thought," Ruth smiled. "Weight will help once in a lifetime in golf— and this was the once!" He finished with an 81, nine over par, nine off the pace of the winner, William Tobin. Not bad for an amateur. He ranked 15th out of 150 competitors but missed qualifying for the National Amateur Tournament, held in Cleveland in August. Ruth thought he belonged. "If I can play like this in the rain," he barked, "and at that, a bit careless, I don't see why I shouldn't be able to qualify for the amateur." He finished one stroke better than Chapman, the previous year's winner. "If I could putt," Ruth said, "I'd be great. I'm an awful long, straight hitter. Don't get the idea that I can't putt damn good too when I'm hot, but the next time around I never remember what I did that made me sink 'em."[81]

Close friends thought Ruth was on the fast track to golf stardom. Ruth wasn't enthused, however. The little white ball he putted and the horsehide ball he clobbered were played on much different greens.

> I wouldn't call golf a better game than baseball, but I will say it's more of a science. In baseball all you have to do is swing at the ball as it comes toward you. If you hit it too soon, it goes one way, if you hit it too late it goes another. And if you hit it square it may be a homer. But—golf! In the first place, the ball isn't moving; it's sitting right there waiting for you. And, strangely enough, you have to hit it just exactly right or it goes way out of the lot. In baseball all you have to do is hit a target two or three hundred yards wide—somewhere between the foul lines. But in golf you've got to play over a 5,000-yard course, not a few hundred feet.

This begged a question.

"Are you still through with baseball?" He was asked.

"I certainly am. And while I've got nothing else to do, I'm going to keep right on with golf."

Ruth hoped the Amateur Invitational in Cleveland would come calling. He had already been to Cleveland that month as a mere spectator of his old game. Now he wanted to play his new game. But some were content with Ruth just batting balls for grand openings of playgrounds and playing golf for the fun of it.

"He's enjoying life for the first time I can remember," his daughter, Julia, said.[82] Ruth didn't have time to finish the tournament anyway. He had a new road to travel. There were hundreds of children among the 4,000 who turned out for the opening of the Interborough Parkway, a five-mile stretch of highway connecting Brooklyn and Queens to Grand Central Parkway. Funded by the New Deal works projects, the parkway would be named for Jackie Robinson over 60 years later.[83] The festivities included the grand opening of the 26-acre Alley Pond Park in Queens, which included baseball diamonds. Who else but George Herman Ruth should smash out that first ball?

Mayor La Guardia introduced Ruth as "the finest character in the sports world." Ruth told the boys there that they needed to apply themselves "like hell" to their favorite sport. The new park would mean little if they didn't exhibit hard work. The mayor threw a high fastball Ruth didn't like, which gave the crowd an easy chance to boo the mayor. His second pitch was lobbed over the plate, but Ruth only managed a weak popup to a young lad with a glove at second base. He disappointed hundreds of kids standing far off, hoping for a Ruth home run. The *New York Daily News* quipped that the mayor and Ruth were "two fattys," going through the motions of ballplayers.[84]

Hobbling Home

After dropping 16 of 19 games on the road, the Braves hobbled home to begin a series with the 36–50 Phillies on July 27. Curt Davis shut out the Braves, 5–0. Cantwell (2–14) went back to losing, and the 600 youngsters of the Knot Hole Gang in the left field bleachers began heckling their team. Adults were more professional, acting as if they were at a funeral. There were fewer than 1,500 fans there.[85]

On Sunday, July 28, the teams split a doubleheader before a crowd of 5,000. Si Johnson beat Bob Smith, 4–1, in the opener. In the nightcap, the Braves trailed, 10–7, in the bottom of the eighth inning. Three hits and three errors allowed the Braves to tie the game, 10–10. In the bottom of the ninth, Pinky Whitney reached on an error and wound up at third. Phils manager Jimmy Wilson walked the next two batters intentionally to load the bases. Al Spohrer grounded to Dolph Camilli at first, who forced Whitney at the plate. Catcher Al Todd threw back to first to attempt a double play, but his throw hit Spohrer in the back, bringing in the winning run, and the Braves were thankful for a team willing to throw a game away. Braves 11, Phillies 10.

Their next scheduled matchup on July 29 was rained out.

A Red-Hot Mamma

"Whatever became of all those fellows who were going to buy the Braves?" the *Globe* asked sarcastically.[86] News on potential buyers had died down, but one name appeared at the end of July. Miss Sophie Tucker. The Russian-born, brash, saucy, heavyset comedian, actress, singer and over-the-top personality called "the Last of the Red-Hot Mammas" was interested in owning the Boston Braves.

"And if I take over the club," she promised, "I'll go right after Babe Ruth and have him as my right-hand man in operating the Braves. The Babe and I have been friends for years—and he's too good a fellow to be getting kicked around the way he is. If Judge Fuchs makes me a fair offer, or if reasonable in his reply, I will go to Boston immediately and try to swing the deal as soon as possible."

How would the sassy celebrity run a baseball club? "I'd apply showmanship to baseball. I think every club in the majors could use a lot more showmanship. Say— I'd put over the Braves like I've put over all my acts—just like I'm putting over my new song, *Life Begins at Forty*. I'd put the Braves over in a big way." Fuchs wasn't amused. "The Braves are not for sale," he said. "There have been too many people trying to cash in on the publicity incident to the contemplated sale of the club, and please do not bother me again."[87]

Sophie Tucker would have brought a new type of entertainment to Braves Field. Paul Bowser brought another type.

A Championship at Braves Field

Bowser had been promoting wrestling events in Boston since the 1920s. He found success promoting Ed "Strangler" Lewis, Stanley Stasiak, "The Golden Greek," Jim Londos, Gus Sonnenberg, Ed Don George, and his latest star, Danno O'Mahoney. Bowser knew an Irish tough guy from Ireland would be a popular draw in Boston like John L. Sullivan was in the 19th century. O'Mahoney, with his unique Irish Whip maneuver, was booked to a 60-victory undefeated streak. "The young giant was given a rousing reception as he entered the ring," wrote James C. O'Leary of his first match in Boston in January, "to the accompaniment of Irish melodies, and an ovation as he left the mat."[88]

O'Mahoney defeated Londos on June 27 at Fenway Park before 25,000 fans and became the recognized champion of two wrestling governing bodies. Bowser saw money signs in booking O'Mahoney against his American Wrestling Association (AWA) champion, Ed Don George, at Braves Field on July 30. The victor would become the "undisputed champion."[89] The Boston sports scene was relatively dull, Jones wrote in the *Globe*, "and if it weren't for the lively news and feature concoctions which are emerging from the publicity mill of Paul Bowser, there'd be nothing on the sports pages except a lot of agate box scores and race charts."[90] Fuchs would see a championship at Braves Field after all, even if it was 'rasslin.

Braves Field was packed for the 8 p.m. show which drew 40,000 fans, snarling traffic for a half-mile. The crowd brought in $70,000 in gate receipts, the Braves taking a 10 percent cut. Judge Fuchs, son Robert, Bill McKechnie, and Governor Curley occupied from-row seats. Heavyweight boxing champion Jimmy Braddock, dubbed the "Cinderella Man," was the special guest referee, Bowser capitalizing on his recent title win.

O'Mahoney won the match in 90 minutes, with Braddock giving the 20-count to George after he was thrown from the ring. Braddock punched out George supporters who protested, and a riot brought in Boston police.[91] More chaos followed with "the worst traffic jam in the history of Braves Field," the *Herald* reported, as 20,000 automobiles choked the roadways until 1 a.m.[92]

Swan Song

Judge Fuchs would also soon be counted out at Braves Field on August 1. He spent his last day as president of the Braves trying to work out an 11th-hour deal. "I have made an offer to some prospective purchasers," he said, "who I hope will take over the team and pay to Vice-president C.F. Adams the money I owe him. I expected to hear from the interested parties today but have not."[93] Ford Frick expected Adams to take control as owner and sell the club as soon as possible.[94]

The Braves had a doubleheader on Wednesday, July 31, against the sixth-place Dodgers (41–52) before only 1,700 fans. MacFayden took another loss, 5–3, despite Berger's 21st home run. Frankhouse, subbing for Brandt, who had a lame arm, in the nightcap, pitched a 4–0 shutout for his sixth win.

Judge Fuchs left behind a team which went 5–23 in the final month of his ownership and stood at 25–69. The team batting declined from June's numbers as they were outscored, 201–102.

Braves Batting in June & July

Month	H	HR	R	BA	OBP	SLG
June (30 games)	299	16	133	.285	.326	.398
July (28 games)	260	11	102	.262	.304	.353

Top 5 Hitters in July by On-Base-Percentage (min. 30 at-bats)

Player	OBP	BA	AB	H	HR	BB
Hogan	.413	.357	42	15	0	4
Spohrer	.343	.303	33	10	0	2
Mallon	.342	.324	37	12	0	1
Berger	.333	.260	100	26	5	14
Coscarart	.323	.279	61	17	0	4

Braves Pitching in June & July

Month	H	ER	BB	SO	ERA	WHIP
June	329	129	66	90	4.23	1.438
July	345	179	71	.69	6.78	1.750

Braves Pitchers, Sorted by ERA

Pitcher	Rec	IP	H	ER	BB	SO	ERA	WHIP
Smith	1–3	38.2	50	19	7	15	4.42	1.474
Cantwell	2–4	28.1	29	15	5	5	4.76	1.200
Brandt	0–5	35.2	53	24	14	14	6.06	1.879
MacFayden	1–4	36.2	58	29	9	8	6.63	1.827
Betts	0–1	25.1	40	20	8	6	7.11	1.895
Brown	0–2	16	28	15	6	2	8.44	2.125
Benton	0–0	17.1	25	17	5	5	8.83	1.731
Frankhouse	1–4	39.2	62	42	17	14	9.53	1.992

National League Standings Thru July 31, 1935

Team	W	L	.PCT	GB
New York	60	33	.645	----
Chicago	62	36	.633	0.5
St. Louis	55	39	.585	5.5
Pittsburgh	54	44	.551	8.5
Cincinnati	42	53	.442	19.0
Brooklyn	41	52	.441	19.0
Philadelphia	40	53	.430	20.0
Boston	25	69	.266	35.5

"I have given up all hope of getting a buyer for my holdings in the Boston Baseball Club," Fuchs said after the Braves were swept in the doubleheader. "After midnight, Thursday, I will have sung my swan song in baseball."[95] The *Boston Herald* said the Judge's shortcomings were "due to over-generosity," but "he made a lot of friends, many of whom stuck to him even in adversity."[96] Fuchs was "a fan who tried hard to be an owner," Harold Kaese aptly put. "Fuchs also tried to be a manager, a financier, and a public-relations man. He was successful as a public-relations man."[97]

He left behind a public-relations nightmare.

11

Doesn't Anybody Want
to Buy This Team?
(August–September 1935)

"One would think that some role could be found for this colorful character even now when his competitive days are at an end,"—Charles Johnson of the *Minneapolis Star* on Babe Ruth

"His popularity knew neither race, creed, nor color."—*Amsterdam News* on Babe Ruth

"It is so serious that unless the club finds some immediate financial support, there is danger of the loss of its franchise and player assets." —Charles F. Adams

The Statue Comes Down

On Juneteenth, the day to commemorate the end of slavery in the United States, June 19, 2020, a statue came down in Washington, D.C., outside the abandoned RFK Stadium. The statue was removed by Events DC, which manages the city's sports and conventions. "This symbol of a person," their statement read, "who didn't believe all men and women were created equal and who actually worked against integration is counter to all that we as people, a city, and nation represent. We believe that injustice and inequity of all forms is reprehensible."[1] The statue honored George Preston Marshall.

Before moving the team to D.C. in 1937, Marshall's football team originated in Boston, first known as the Braves and then the Redskins. The franchise was the last to integrate in the NFL, and it only did in 1962 in response to pressure from the federal government. The conservative Marshall felt government should always stay out of his affairs. Secretary of the Interior Stewart Udall and Attorney General Robert F. Kennedy said Marshall's all-white team could not play in a federally funded stadium.

For years, activists called for the Marshall statue to be removed, but the racially charged George Floyd murder in 2020 hastened its removal and other monuments glorifying segregationists. In 2022, the team name of Redskins was finally replaced after decades of controversy.

In 1935, the brash young owner Marshall was close to purchasing the Boston Braves. Charles F. Adams would have gladly turned over the keys to Braves Field to him. It would have changed Boston sports history.

Fuchs Says "Goodbye"; Marshall Says "Hello."

C.F. Adams spent his first official day as club president on his scenic estate in Framingham. It was a picturesque environment where he could do some thinking. He wanted out of baseball but was willing to hold on to his Braves stock if someone else ran the club. Someone not named Judge Fuchs. The success of the Braves hinged on how much money Adams would or would not further invest.

Judge Fuchs gave his farewell wishes to the Braves around noon on August 1, thanking them for their loyalty. "I've sacrificed everything," the Judge said. "Now that I've been forced to surrender, I've got to start all over again. I've kept in touch with legal practice. I have friends in New York who wish me to take up my old work here. And I probably shall try to develop practice in both cities. The airplane, you know, makes that possible."[2]

Fuchs watched the game from the back of the grandstand, along with only 500 others.[3] He watched the Braves lose to the Dodgers, 4–2, and Ben Cantwell's record fall to 3–15. The Braves left for the Polo Grounds, but manager Bill McKechnie wasn't with them. Deacon Bill met with National League President Ford Frick, Adams, and Braves stockholders on August 2 at Adams' Boston office on Milk St. McKechnie assumed the role of general manager along with his managerial duties. Adams controlled the team, with assistance from the National League when needed. When the meeting concluded, George Preston Marshall called from Washington, D.C. He pitched his ideas to Adams on how to fix the Braves. Adams told Marshall to get to Boston ASAP.[4]

That night, Marshall released a statement. "I am naturally very enthusiastic over the outlook," he wrote of the Braves, "especially because of my past experience with the Boston Redskins."[5] "You know what I think of Boston as a sports town. I'm 'nutty' about it. I've been up there three years with pro football. I saw it grow from 3,000 crowds to crowds of 17,000 to 25,000. It is a sportsminded [*sic*] community. They know their sports."[6] It was the newest pursuit of Marshall, whom Jack Walsh of the *Washington Post* called someone "people admired or violently disagreed with" and who "seldom let his controversial opinion go unexpressed. He could be vain, uncompromising. At other times he could turn on the charm and captivate a stubborn adversary or audience."[7]

Marshall was born October 11, 1896, in Grafton, West Virginia, the son of Thomas Hildebrand Marshall and Blanche Preston Marshall. Thomas was editor of the short-lived *Grafton Standard* newspaper. The family wintered in Washington, D.C., and lived the rest of the year on a West Virginia farm. George milked cows, rode horses, and by age 14 organized a barnstorming football team which traveled the mountain hollers.[8] They moved year-round to D.C., and Thomas started the Palace Laundry on Ninth Street, the city's first steam laundromat. William Howard Taft was known to pop in and pick up his spacious trousers. George was involved with athletics, but he found the spectacle of crowds, entertainment, and music far more appealing. A born showman, he launched a stage career in 1914 but was a lousy actor. He made up for it, Walsh wrote, since he "considered it a wasted opportunity were he not the center of attention." A stage manager career ended when Marshall was drafted into the 63rd Machine Gun Company during World War I.[9]

The Spanish Flu ravaged the country in 1918 and claimed the life of his father. George returned to take over the fledgling Palace Laundry with little capital. He turned laundry into a spectacle. He created entertaining newspaper ads such as a blank white page: "this page was cleaned by Palace Laundry." His slogan "Long Live Linen!" and colorful blue and gold storefronts led to a thriving, million-dollar business of 50+ stores washing 50,000 shirts per week. They even had curbside pickup.[10]

In the mid–1920s, Marshall sponsored the Washington Palace Five professional basketball team. In 1932, he and partners purchased the Boston Braves professional football team, which played at Braves Field. Marshall took his football team, renamed the Redskins, to Fenway Park the following year for cheaper rent. The Braves lost money from the upkeep of the field. Marshall liked Fenway's intimacy, anyway.[11]

Marshall now turned his sights to baseball, and Adams was ready to deal.

Catch as Catchers Can

The first-place Giants, one game ahead of the Cubs, took a 4–1 win in the August 2 opener against the Braves. On Saturday, Danny MacFayden and the Giants' Roy Parmelee matched zeros through six innings. The Giants looked lackluster, and John Drebinger in the *New York Times* blamed it on "the spirit of depression" the Braves brought with them. The Braves jumped from the dugout to take the field, only to realize there were just two outs. "Odd but jolly fellows these Braves," quipped Drebinger.[12] The Giants won, 3–2.

They played a doubleheader on Sunday, August 4, before 19,000 fans, including Babe Ruth, sitting behind the Giants' dugout. "The existing Braves might as well have been sitting there with him," joked Rud Rennie in the *New York Tribune*. "They were just ornaments for a Giant field day." In the opener, Wally Berger hit home run #22, their only offense in a 9–2 loss. Fred Frankhouse (6–10) was 1–6 since June 16, with an ERA puffed from 2.91 to 5.21. Huck Betts was still winless as he dropped the nightcap, 3–1, to fall to 0–7 with a 5.59 ERA.

Moving on to Philadelphia, the Braves were trampled, 9–1, on Monday for their sixth straight loss and 75th of the season. Tommy Thompson's home run ruined the shutout by Orville Jorgens. Bob Brown walked seven. The Braves hoped Brown would rediscover his success from 1932, but with only one win in three years, they must have wondered who that pitcher really was back in 1932. Old Larry Benton was mauled yet again, allowing seven earned runs in relief.[13]

McKechnie made his first personnel move by releasing Shanty Hogan. The heavyset catcher violated team training regulations and, McKechnie said, "has passed his usefulness because of his slowing up. I like him personally, but he isn't the value to the club that he should be. He has permitted himself to put on weight through disregard of training rules. I have talked with him and pleaded with him to keep in shape, but he paid no attention to my suggestions."[14]

In spring training, writers joked that Hogan's weight made him a perfect stand-in for Ruth. At his death at age 61 in 1967, Hogan was labeled "the Babe Ruth of catchers."[15] The jolly catcher had learned baseball on the sandlots of Somerville, Massachusetts. He had played in the majors since 1925 with the Braves, the Giants, and then back to the Braves. Hogan was signed by Minneapolis of the American Association since "he ate himself back into the minor leagues," the Associated Press wrote.[16] Hogan retired at 33, but his jovial attitude gave him plenty of stories to tell as he worked for the City of Somerville.

On August 6, the 40-year-old Bob Smith threw one of the best games of his career, a perfect game through 7 1/3 innings, finishing with a three-hitter in the 4–0 win.[17] McKechnie called it "good tonic to the rest of the squad" as he celebrated his 48th birthday.[18]

The Marshall Plan

Meanwhile, Marshall, Redskins GM Dennis Shea, and coach Eddie Casey met Adams at Boston's Ritz-Carleton. Adams laid open the financial books. The club made a profit between $10,000–20,000 (accounts differ) through July 1, no doubt because of Ruth's presence.[19] They emerged from the meeting at 2 p.m. "We have worked out the deal to its minutest detail and have progressed very favorably," Adams said as he left to confer with First National Bank of Boston.[20] He could not sign on the dotted line until receiving consent from the bank, which held the $200,000 note.

A second meeting was held in Adams' office at 4:30 p.m. John Toulman of First National Bank of Boston, Robert Thach, vice-president and chief counsel for Pan American Airlines, and Adams' attorney, Robert Goodwin, were present. Goodwin founded the prestigious Goodwin & Proctor law firm in Boston which still bears his name. Two of his earliest cases included defending *Titanic* survivor Mary Newell in her $110,400 suit against White Star Line for their negligence and acting as bankruptcy referee for claims made against convicted con artist Charles Ponzi.[21]

Marshall's plan was not to acquire stock but to run the Braves as a management company, ensuring that stockholders would not lose the value of their holdings.

After five years, Marshall would have the option of purchasing Adams' shares for controlling interest. This new organization would protect the club from financial loss.[22] The deal was a win-win for Adams, who didn't have time to devote to the Braves. He had recently seen a crowd of 60,000 pack into Suffolk Downs and bet $638,927.[23] Adams and V.C. Bruce Wetmore would retain their 9,400 shares of the total 15,000 shares in the club, but Adams wouldn't have day-to-day duties. "If we can get a good, aggressive management with the Braves," Adams said, "I would be strongly inclined to leave my money in them as a minority stockholder. I think such a management can be obtained, in which case I'd just as soon 'play ball' as my get out, even if I could get out at my price."[24] If he didn't have to consult the bank, Adams would have sealed the deal immediately.[25] In the meantime, the O'Malleys were still interested.[26]

Marshall was optimistic as he boarded his train. "The next move is up to C.F. and the creditors of the Braves."[27] One of the key figures in Marshall's syndicate was Woolworth Donahue, the playboy socialite and heir to the Woolworth's department store fortune.[28]

Marshall had big plans for Braves Field. "We can't do any worse than the Braves have been doing, and if we don't improve, we can at least let the fans see us lose in more comfort." A new scoreboard, loudspeakers, bar and restaurant, night baseball, lounge seating with telephones, and a stock market ticker were some of his ideas to "pep up baseball." But "I want no part of Babe Ruth in Boston," he asserted.[29]

The Berger King

After a rainout, the Braves took the field in Brooklyn on Friday, August 9. Casey Stengel mixed up his Dodgers lineup with seven players out of position. "I'm shifting my men about so the other team won't think they're playing the Dodgers," he joked.[30] MacFayden kept the Braves in the game, trailing, 2–1, through seven innings. The Braves led, 5–2, going to the bottom of the ninth.

Tough-luck Ben Cantwell had two out with Lonny Frey on first. Jim Bucher singled to right. Sam Leslie lofted a high fly to left-center which Berger lost in the sun. Two runs scored on what should have been the final out. Tony Cuccinello hammered Cantwell's pitch into the left-field bleachers to give the Dodgers the shocking 6–5 win. The 2,000 youngsters admitted free swarmed Cuccinello while Cantwell hung his head and walked off, 3–16.[31]

Berger atoned for his gaffe on Saturday by slamming his 24th home run as the Braves grabbed an early 5–1 lead for Fred Frankhouse. The Dodgers tied the game in the sixth, 5–5. The winless Huck Betts came on in relief. Berger reached on a Cuccinello error and moved to second on a wild pitch. Catcher Al Lopez's attempted pickoff throw went into center field, and Berger scored on Joe Coscarart's single. The Braves prevailed, 6–5, and Betts (1–7) finally claimed a victory.

"We try to keep the ball high to him and inside so that he'll hit the ball with the handle of his bat," Stengel said about Berger.

"Yeah?" a reporter asked.

"Yeah, because if you keep the ball high, he'll only hit it into the lower stands. If you give him low balls he'll hit 'em into the upper tier."[32]

Berger dominated the August 11 doubleheader. He crushed a grand slam in the third inning to put the Braves ahead, 4–2. The Dodgers batted around in the fifth inning off Bob Smith and sprang ahead, 7–4. Berger tripled in the fifth and doubled in the seventh. In the ninth he doubled again, driving in a run. Too bad he couldn't pitch. The Braves lost, 7–5, and Smith fell to 6–12. In the nightcap, Berger missed his 26th home run when the ball struck the railing in left-center and bounded back in play. Poor Ben Cantwell allowed only five hits but suffered a 3–2 loss, making him 3–17.[33]

Berger's 25 home runs and 96 RBI led the National League, but the Braves (27–78) were now 40 games behind the first-place Giants (67–38). They returned to Boston.

O'Malley's Back Out

On August 14, the O'Malleys announced that they were no longer interested buyers of the team. "It will take a million dollars to take over the team," they stated, "and half of that sum will be for the payment of back debts." They must have been the only ones who didn't read the newspapers, since everyone in Boston seemed to know this.[34]

McKechnie made more household changes. His old teammate, Tommy Leach, became a scout. First baseman Elbie Fletcher was recalled from Wilkes-Barre of the New York–Pennsylvania League, where he batted .365 in 71 games. Fletcher was a graduate of nearby Milton High School and debuted with the Braves in 1934. The tall, slender, left-handed batter was a solid contact hitter and fielder. Fletcher would finish the season as the Braves' regular first baseman, replacing Buck Jordan, whose numbers (.266 average with only a .294 OBP) were about 30 points below his average the previous three years.[35]

Others were leaving. Ed Cunningham, Braves club secretary since 1926, resigned to go to work for Judge Fuchs. Business anager Fred Mitchell also resigned. Paul Curley, son of Gov. James Michael Curley, resigned as traveling secretary to begin law school. He wouldn't be there long. Paul's young life was a tragedy as "the demon rum always tripped him up," wrote Jack Beatty in his biography, *The Rascal King: The Life and Times of James Michael Curley (1874–1958)*.

Paul Curley had been charged in 1933 with leaving the scene of a hit-and-run accident while also having an expired license.[36] His drunkenness got in the way of his potential, embarrassing his prominent family. He would die in 1945 at age 32, but at home instead of in a gutter, where his father expected.[37] These positions were left vacant.

Puttering Around

Babe Ruth was out of baseball, "but he still has his golf and his hobby of collecting calories," one newspaper mocked.[38] No one was even asking where he was, wrote Edward J. Neil. "Nothing could be more calculated to bother the Bam than that. He's lived like a goldfish so long—complaining all the time that he had no privacy, yet loving the crowds, the hero-worship, the excitement just the same—that tramping lonely fairways with only a caddy for companionship must gripe deeply."[39] Ruth had dropped from the public eye faster than anyone. He needed to make a big splash.

Ruth showed up at the wharf off Zach's Bay at Jones Beach State Park on Long Island. The weekend of August 4 was the Water Circus, which drew 60,000 spectators looking for summer fun. Ruth hit fungoes into the bay and watched the mass of children leaping into the water. "With almost one accord," wrote Paul Gallico, "they hit the water, and the best race of the day was on, an unscheduled event, with every boy and girl on the premises splashing out as fast as he was able to retrieve the white baseballs now bobbing on the surface of the bay." Ruth got a kick out of the scene. "Look at 'em go!" he chuckled. He kept hitting, and youngsters kept swimming. They brought the wet balls to him to autograph, ignoring other races because "baseballs signed by the Babe were greater prizes to them than any gold or silver metals." Ruth gave a heartwarming speech. "He laughed and howled and slapped his thighs like any youngster there," Gallico wrote.[40] He was still a big kid, after all.

In the evening, Ruth smacked phosphorescent balls into the night sky.[41] It was good-natured fun, but it made Gallico pause, angry at the "dopes who are permitting George Herman Ruth to remain among the unemployed." How could they neglect their greatest attraction, their greatest showman, their greatest entertainer? Was there really "no one smart enough to figure out some way to connect this man with baseball again and cash in on the fact that he is a big, lovable showman that people want to see and be friendly with to the last day of his life?"[42]

Ruth golfed at the Westchester Country Club on Tuesday, August 6. He sped home in his roadster along Seaman Ave. in Upper Manhattan. Crossing at Cummings Street was 58-year-old Julia Strauss. Ruth swerved to avoid her, but his front tire struck Strauss. Ruth scooped her up and brought her to the hospital. The police reported that Ruth had the green light and was not responsible. Strauss suffered a concussion and bruised leg.[43]

Ruth had a lot of time on his hands. Some thought he would open a restaurant like Jack Dempsey did in New York City earlier that year. But it was just rumor. Billy Rose invited Ruth to be in his musical production of *Jumbo*, where the Bambino would have joined Jimmy Durante. "Ruth has no ambitions to start a stage career," his agent, Christy Walsh, affirmed. Ruth had received over 75 offers to appear in exhibitions and had several vaudeville offers. He rejected them all.[44] But he had golf.

On August 12, Ruth participated in a "Hole-in-One" contest at the Salisbury Country Club on Long Island. Ruth teamed with the enigmatic amateur, Tommy Goodwin, against the team of 1934 PGA champion Paul Runyan and rookie amateur Frank Strafaci. Ruth wore "a button-down collarless shirt that barely contains his ample belly," wrote Patrick Hand.[45] Goodwin and Ruth lost the match, which the Bambino blamed on the noisy planes at nearby Roosevelt Field. "How can a guy putt with all those grasshoppers!" Ruth yelled.[46]

On August 15, Ruth traveled to Cleveland for the True Temper Open Championship at Acacia Country Club. A hoard of photographers met him. "Honest, you guys will follow me to the grave!" Ruth said.[47] On the first day, Ruth shot an 85, well behind the 68 of leader Ted Luther, but he provided the entertainment after hooking one to the rough. "I should have brought a shovel," he joked.[48]

Homestand

The Braves returned to Boston. Hank Gowdy and several players boarded a train for an endless trip to Houlton, Maine, for an exhibition game near the Canadian Border. The Braves defeated a group of local all-stars, 6–2.[49]

Their 19-game homestand began on August 14 with a doubleheader sweep against the lowly seventh-place Reds. "Pinch myself and rub these eyes as they declare in Dixie," kidded Burt Whitman in the *Herald*, about the Braves' triumphs.[50] The Braves slapped 12 hits together, and Frankhouse pitched a dandy for his seventh victory in the 8–1 win. They continued the onslaught in the nightcap, 11–5. Buck Jordan went 5-for-10 in the doubleheader, and Pinky Whitney had seven RBI. Only 2,000 fans welcomed the Braves home. On Thursday, the Braves won their third straight, an 8–0 shutout by Bob Brown, his first win since July 1, 1934, and just his second since 1932. Berger hit home run #26, yet barely 1,000 people saw it.

The teams played another doubleheader on August 16, and Cantwell lost another tough one, 3–1, to fall 3–18. The Braves fell behind, 3–0, in the nightcap with Betts pitching a strong eight innings. In the ninth, Mowry, Urbanski, and Mallon doubled to make the score 3–2. Moore singled to score Mallon and tie the game. The Reds squeezed out a 4–3 win, but folks were paying more attention to the afternoon papers reporting that American's favorite humorist and cowboy philosopher, Will Rogers, had tragically died in a plane crash in Alaska. The Braves were 30–80 and 50 wins under .500.

Smith (8–12) closed out the series by pitching a complete-game victory, 6–1. Only 500 spectators saw Berger pass 100 RBI on the season and saw the Braves take their third win in five games against the Reds.

The World Champion Cardinals (66–42) came to Boston for a Sunday

Shortstop Rabbit Maranville was 43 and well past his prime in 1935, but he could still have a ball doing tricks to entertain youngsters (courtesy Boston Public Library, Leslie Jones Collection).

doubleheader, trailing the Giants by just two games. The largest crowd since the Fourth of July (12,000) came to Braves Field. Frankhouse did everything in the opener, driving in two runs and helping the Braves to a tight win over the champions, 2–1. In the nightcap, the Braves trailed 4–1 in the eighth inning. Mallon was at third and Urbanski at second. Pinch-hitter Joe Mowry lofted a sacrifice fly to score Mallon, and Berger singled in Urbanski. The Braves trailed, 4–3. Al Spohrer brought the large crowd to its feet when he slammed a game-tying home run in the bottom of the ninth. In the tenth, Betts walked three Cardinals and surrendered a grand slam to Leo Durocher. He was now 1–8 as the Cardinals prevailed, 9–4.

The Braves tweaked the schedule, creating a August 18 doubleheader so they could have Monday free for an exhibition game in Lewiston, Maine. The Cardinals were not thrilled. "I ain't missed an exhibition game this year and I don't aim to miss none," Dizzy Dean aptly said, "but how about a rule that don't permit teams to change the big league schedule so they can squeeze in an extra barnstorming trip?"[51] "This is making a joke out of a club that is fighting for the pennant," another player grumbled. "A day of rest would do a lot of the boys considerable good."[52]

About 6,000 Mainers were glad they weren't resting. They were part of the largest crowd ever reported at the Maine mill town, half of them children admitted free.

The Cardinals went to Maine with the Braves for the exhibition game, which they weren't thrilled about. Phil Collins of the Cardinals won the contest and Blanche and Benton, both Braves, pitched. The Cards won, 8–3. Rookie pitcher Al Blanche pitched five scoreless relief innings after Larry Benton was bombed for eight runs.

Benton, pitching professionally since 1920, was released and offered a scouting position for the team.[53] After Benton retired, he drove a bus in Cincinnati. He collapsed and died on a golf course in 1953 at age 55.[54]

Back in Boston, the Cardinals defeated Brown and the Braves, 6–5, on Tuesday, despite Berger's 27th home run. Dizzy Dean had an easy day in the finale as the Cardinals blasted Smith and MacFayden, 13–3.

The fourth-place Pirates (64–55) and star shortstop Arky Vaughan, batting .401, came to town. The Pirates won the August 23 opener, 7–5, with Cantwell losing his 19th game. Blanche made his major league debut, allowing two runs. Fewer than a thousand folks came out to see Saturday's pitching duel as Cy Blanton bested Frankhouse, 3–2. Sunday's doubleheader drew 8,000 fans who witnessed a Pirates sweep. Smith (8–14) lost the opener, 9–2. The nightcap was tied, 4–4, after eight innings. An error by Urbanski in the 11th gave Betts (1–9) another loss. The Braves had lost ten straight against Pittsburgh.

The Braves played an exhibition game on Monday, August 26, at Memorial Park in Rockland, Massachusetts, against Falmouth of the Cape Cod League. The game benefited the Rockland School Children's Milk Fund, which assisted needy families. Bob Brown may as well have been delivering milk at that point in his career as the Braves pitcher was hammered by the semipros for five runs in the first inning.[55] This was the last game for Hal Lee, the Braves' leading hitter with a .303 average. He fractured his thumb and had his arm in a cast the rest of the season.[56] The Mississippian would play one final season in 1936.

At the top of the National League, the Cardinals led the Giants by half a game, helped by two eight-game winning streaks and taking three out of five against the Giants. The Giants won five in a row to begin the month, four against the Braves, but played a subpar 9–14 in their next 23 games. The team attracting attention, however, was the Chicago Cubs, who began August just a half-game behind the Giants. The Cubs trailed St. Louis by just two games as they got off the train in Boston. The August 27 game was rained out, so they played a doubleheader on Wednesday.

Bill McKechnie wasn't with them. He "took a shirt, collar and toothbrush," said the *Herald*, "and hied himself west to look for young ballplayers." McKechnie looked over talent overseen by Branch Rickey in his Cardinals farm system. In 1935, before his connections to Jackie Robinson, Rickey was known as the mastermind of the minor leagues for developing talent for the Cardinals or as trade bait. The Braves needed young, low-cost players.[57]

Ben Cantwell saw luck on his side for a change. He surrendered just four hits and a run in throwing a complete-game victory over the Cubs, 2–1. Berger smashed his 28th home run deep to the back of the left-field bleachers, where "a little lad with a baseball cap but no glove in the top of the bleachers nonchalantly reached up and caught the big bertha smash," wrote Whitman.[58] Cantwell was 4–19, but his ERA in August was 3.50. Cantwell made nine appearances, five of them starts, from July 28 to August 28. His ERA was 3.42, opponents batted only .257 against him, and his WHIP was 1.23. On the Giants, Cubs, or Cardinals, Cantwell likely would have won 15–20 games.

Smith lost the nightcap, 5–2. The series wrapped up on August 29, the final East Coast game for the Cubs. Frankhouse (8–12) was lit up for five runs, and Bill Lee won his 15th game in the 8–2 Cubs victory. The Cubs remained two games behind the Cardinals.

On the 31st, the Braves lost to

"Deacon Bill" McKechnie is in the Baseball Hall of Fame as a manager, but the 1935 season seemed to never end. "I've heard and read a lot about teams that simply can't get a break," he said, "but I never knew how it felt to manage such a team until now" (courtesy Boston Public Library, Leslie Jones Collection).

the Dodgers, 5–2. MacFayden dropped to 5–11, and the Braves lost their 90th game. The month of August was over, and the Braves were 44 games out of first place. They went 8–21 in August, remarkably 2½ games better than they did in July. Mercifully, just 30 games remained.

The pitching improved during August:

Month	HA	ER	BB	SO	ERA	WHIP
June (30 games)	329	129	67	90	4.23	1.438
July (28 games)	345	179	71	69	6.78	1.750
August (29 games)	277	125	92	58	4.31	1.438

Cantwell and Betts sparkled despite the irrelevant won-lost records:

Pitcher	Rec	IP	HA	ER	BB	SO	ERA	WHIP
Cantwell	1–5	46.1	47	18	11	11	3.50	1.252
Betts	1–3	36	35	14	11	7	3.50	1.278
Blanche	0–0	5	4	2	4	1	3.60	1.600
Frankhouse	2–3	45.2	50	21	20	8	4.14	1.533
Brown	1–2	15	7	7	15	2	4.20	1.467
Smith	3–5	50	60	26	11	14	4.68	1.420

Pitcher	Rec	IP	HA	ER	BB	SO	ERA	WHIP
MacFayden	0–2	47.2	58	26	13	11	4.91	1.490
Brandt	0–0	3	4	2	3	2	6.00	2.333
Benton	0–1	8	12	9	4	1	10.13	2.000

The team batting in August was much like July:

Month	H	HR	RBI	BA	OBP	SLG
June (30 games)	299	16	128	.285	.326	.398
July (28 games)	260	11	98	.262	.304	.353
August (29 games)	261	13	100	.263	.314	.356

Top 5 Hitters in August by On-Base-Percentage (min. 30 at-bats)

Player	OBP	BA	AB	H	HR	BB
Jordan	.379	.345	55	19	1	3
Berger	.371	.310	113	35	7	9
Urbanski	.366	.291	117	34	2	14
Thompson	.363	.287	101	29	2	11
Lee	.333	.289	90	26	0	6

National League Standings Thru August 31, 1935

Team	W	L	.PCT	GB
St. Louis	77	46	.626	----
New York	76	47	.618	1.0
Chicago	77	51	.602	2.5
Pittsburgh	74	55	.574	6.0
Brooklyn	57	68	.456	21.0
Philadelphia	53	71	.427	24.5
Cincinnati	54	73	.425	25.0
Boston	33	90	.268	44.0

C.F. Adams wanted to call a meeting of all stockholders, but had no idea who they all were. Fuchs left no official list of who owned the 4,800-something minority shares, and Ed Cunningham resigned before providing the promised list. They promised to provide him the list. Tired of waiting, Adams sent out a plea to anyone who owned stock in the Braves to contact him. He received phone calls. "Each of them told me they had received a letter from Judge Fuchs requesting that they give him proxies to represent them at the coming meeting and vote their stock," Adams said. "Just what the idea is, is a mystery to me."[59] Adams still couldn't rid himself of Fuchs. "There are many blocks of stock outstanding of the ownership of which he is ignorant," the *Herald* reported, "and of which there is no record."[60] Fuchs didn't like the negative press he received. "I have been so busy that I did not get around to it, assuming there was no particular haste required," he explained.[61]

Police Squads

Babe Ruth began September by visiting Minneapolis, Minnesota, for an exhibition game between the Minneapolis and St. Paul Police. Ruth was an honorary member of the Minneapolis Police Benevolent Association and was playing "to give his old friends there a lift." Ruth and Claire arrived at the Milwaukee Road Depot on Saturday night, August 31, he wearing a brown suit and wide grin. Thousands anxiously awaited his arrival. The cheers went up as they exited the train. He patted several youngsters on the back with his typical "Hiya, son!" greeting. "I'm enjoying this rest plenty," he told reporters. "The golf game is not so hot." The police band played as fans paraded their hero to the Radisson Hotel, where he autographed baseballs until retiring to his room.[62]

Earlier that day in Minnesota, a crowd of 6,000 watched 17-year-old, 5'2" golf phenom, Minneapolis' own Patty Berg, lose the U.S. Women's Amateur Golf Championship to Glenna Collett Vare. "That little girl must be pretty good," Ruth remarked about the story. "She ought to be a champion pretty soon."[63] She would do just that. Berg would go on to dominate the amateur golf circuit before and after World War II. She, Babe Didrikson, and others formed the Ladies Professional Golf Association (LPGA) in 1950. Berg advanced the sport for all women golfers. She died in 2006 at the age of 88.[64]

Ruth put on a show in batting practice at Nicollet Park, knocking out a dozen balls. More than 22,000 tickets were sold, some fans seated on the field behind ropes. He posed for pictures and autographed "everything from scraps of paper to baseball gloves to cigaret (*sic*) cases," wrote Fred Hutchinson in the *Minneapolis Star*.[65]

Ruth played the whole game, splitting time equally between the two teams. He walked twice, hit a mile-high popup, doubled into the crowd, and struck out against local hero Pete Guzy, the Edison High School football coach. Ruth, blaming a sore arm, threw the ball away, allowing a run to score. He also fumbled a grounder which bounced off his chest. He snared it, dove, and tagged the base, to the delight of the crowd. Minneapolis defeated St. Paul, 10–4, and Ruth "proved himself a colorful performer and the massive crowd seemed to go home in a well-satisfied mood," wrote Hutchinson.[66]

Ruth was paid $1,200 for the appearance but turned down over 15 offers to appear at various baseball functions. He claimed that he had forfeited $100,000 with all the offers turned down since leaving the Braves. Charles Johnson in the *Minneapolis Star* wrote that it was "a mistake that baseball moguls should permit such a great box office attraction to slip into oblivion as fast as the Bambino has this summer.

One would think that some role could be found for this colorful character even now when his competitive days are at an end."[67] Babe and Claire caught an 11:30 p.m. train for Chicago, where more golf awaited.[68]

The Road to Nowhere

The Braves played the Dodgers one final time at Braves Field before their road trip. C.F. Adams allowed children ages 16 and under admitted free when accompanied by an adult, but only 2,500 people showed up.[69] The Dodgers scored seven runs off Cantwell, who lost his 20th game. Berger hit his 29th home run in the 8–4 loss. Both clubs hopped the 6 p.m. train for Brooklyn.[70] The Labor Day doubleheader was rained out, so the Braves moved on to St. Louis.

Before they left, Bill McKechnie phoned from Columbus, Ohio, to announce that he had found new pitching talent. None of them would ever throw a pitch for the Braves. The name of note was Johnny Vander Meer, who would find fame in Cincinnati. McKechnie was also looking for a catcher since Ray Mueller broke a finger, and Bill Lewis was recalled from Montreal.[71]

With four games each at St. Louis and Chicago, the Braves had a say in who would win the NL Pennant, or as Hank Gowdy said, "toss plenty of monkey wrenches into the machinery."[72] The Cardinals led the Giants by two games and the Cubs by 2½ going into play on September 4. Ed Brandt, who hadn't pitched in a month, was a monkey wrench to the Cardinals for seven innings. The Braves led, 3–2, and the scoreboard showed that both the Giants and Cubs had won. Berger hit home run #30, but the Cards awoke. Ripper Collins doubled in Frankie Frisch to tie the game. McKechnie brought in Cantwell, and the roof fell in. Spud Davis doubled to score Collins, and Leo Durocher singled to score Davis. St. Louis won, 6–3, dropping Brandt to 5–14. The loss was the Braves' 44th out of 54 road games. It didn't end there.

Thursday's game was over before it started in a comedy of errors. Terry Moore went 6-for-6 as the Cardinals rolled, 15–3. The Cardinals led the Cubs by 2½ games, the Giants by three.

On Friday, the Cardinals rallied from a 2–0 deficit to win, 6–4. Dizzy Dean, relieving, won his 24th game. Smith fell to 8–16, and the Braves lost their seventh in a row. Saturday was the finale, and Daffy Dean (17–11) got the win, 8–5, the Braves' 95th loss. Danny MacFayden was 0–7 since July 6 with a 6.21 ERA, with opponents batting .331.

Before leaving St. Louis, McKechnie stated that the Braves were on the path to financial recovery and were ready to make trades. W.H. James of the *St. Louis Globe-Democrat* quipped, "just in case we need another bat boy we may do some dickering with them."[73] Maybe someone wanted Rabbit Maranville. The 43-year-old announced that the stiffness in his leg had finally disappeared, and he was ready for another 10 years on the diamond.[74] "So far as money is concerned," McKechnie said, "we're all right. We have made enough to pay salaries and expenses, and whenever I need money all I have to do is see Mr. Adams and he will supply it. In fact, right now I know what we need for the team, and I have more money to seek it than I ever had before. The players were paid before we left on the road, and everybody is happy."[75] Paying the player salaries was a sign of good times.

He had no idea what was going on back in Boston.

Brother, Can You Spare a Buck Per Share?

Adams called a special meeting of the Eastern Racing Association on Friday morning, September 6. An additional $1.1 million was needed for the expanding enterprise. The last racing card of the season drew 70,000 fans, who wagered $720,000. Suffolk Downs brought in $10 million total in its 28-day inaugural season.[76] The stockholders agreed to raise the capital themselves, confident Suffolk Downs would pay for itself in six years. "It is apparent that the founding fathers have the greatest of confidence in their investment," said the *Boston Globe*.[77]

Later that day, Adams announced an update to the Braves' situation. He still didn't even know who all the Braves' stockholders were, but knew the team drew just 232,754 fans for 75 home games. His racing and baseball investments were on two different planets. Without immediate cash, the Braves could not finish the season. He shared the letter he had sent to the 150 known shareholders. It included:

> It is so serious that unless the club finds some immediate financial support, there is danger of the loss of its franchise and player assets. Briefly stated, the club now owes $200,000 on demand notes and approximately $50,000 of known current liabilities. The demand notes are held by one of the Boston banks and in order to support the credit of the club, I was obliged some time ago to assume a 50 per cent participation in the loan. The club has practically no liquid assets with which to meet these obligations. It is essential, therefore, that something be done promptly. I estimate that it will require about $15,000 in new cash to enable the club to complete the season's schedule. There are approximately 15,000 shares outstanding. It, therefore, seems to me that the quickest, fairest and most practical way of raising the cash necessary to complete the season would be to ask the stockholders to contribute at the rate of $1 per share.[78]

If the funds were not raised, the team would fall into the hands of the National League or a receivership. Adams' reorganization plan required $500,000 of new capital for the club to cover player contracts, equipment, and lease, with $225,000 of cash on hand to run the club. "If a substantial interest among the stockholders responds favorably, I am prepared to give my time and attention to accomplish what I believe is a desirable and realizable result, and to contribute a substantial amount to the new capital requirements of a reorganization."[79] Adams would guarantee at least $8,000 of the needed $15,000 and could legally turn the club over to Marshall, but did not believe it was fair to the minority stockholders, and the bank was not favorable.[80] He shared a ledger of the Braves' expenses since 1929:

Boston National League Baseball Company
Comparative Statement of Operating Expenses Covering Seasons 1929–1934.
Inclusive and Portion of 1935.

Expense	1929	1930	1931	1932	1933	1934	1935
Net Cost Spring Training After Receipts	$19,397	$9,133	$7,237	$9,811	$10,883	$9,874	$2,449
Team Expenses- Salaries, Traveling, Coaches,	$19,397	$9,133	$7,237	$9,811	$10,883	$9,874	$2,449
Scouts, etc.	$242,208	$239,985	$245,798	$240,970	$214,215	$235,604	-----
Park Expense Including Rental and Taxes	$82,461	$94,692	$102,374	$88,266	$77,739	$37,778	-----
Administration Expense— Salaries, etc.	$152,541	$129,585	$107,985	$92,823	$82,465	$74,502	-----
Loss on Minor League Operations	$34,000	$39,767	$0	$3,177	$14,666	$12,152	-----
Totals	$530,607	$513,162	$463,394	$435,047	$399,968	$389,910	-----

Source: Gerry Moore, "C.F. Adams Appeals to Braves' Shareholders," Boston Globe, September 7, 1935: 5.

"Whereas his coholders of stock in the pari-mutuel running track in East Boston have rallied to him 100 percent," wrote Hy Hurwitz in the *Globe*, "the baseball stockholders are not so keen in supplying the necessary funds." The Braves, he wrote, were a "pathetic flop."[81] Even the Boston Redskins' preseason intrasquad game at Malden High School attracted a crowd of 8,000, double a Braves game.[82]

One Losing Streak Ends; Another Begins

The Cubs rode a four-game winning streak and were just 2½ games behind the Cardinals as the Braves arrived, losers of eight consecutive games. The Sunday game was rained out, forcing a doubleheader on Monday, September 9. There were plenty of distractions that day, just from a quick glance at the *Chicago Tribune*. The British Government was attempting to gather support among countries in the League of Nations to prevent Italy dictator Benito Mussolini's impending invasion of Ethiopia. An Italian army of 200,000 now stood ready at the dictator's disposal. The invasion is considered one of the major events which steered the globe towards the Second World War.[83] In Germany, Nazis were planning celebrations with tanks, parades, and a Hitler speech. On September 10, Germany announced that all Jewish children would be barred from public schools in 1936. "Complete racial segregation of German pupils in all schools must be enforced," the statement read. "Racial segregation is necessary to create a Nazi community of classes on the foundation of German national ideals."[84] Soon it would be illegal in Germany for an Aryan and non–Aryan to marry.[85]

The biggest headline of the day was Louisiana senator and Democratic presidential candidate Huey Long dying from an assassin's bullet. Long's populist "Share the Wealth" plan appealed to large numbers of poor white Southerners. He provided roads and bridges while following a path to authoritarianism, becoming what many considered America's first dictator.[86] He would soon succumb to the fatal bullet, leaving us with questions of what he might have become. However, his partner, Gerald L.K. Smith. was a Nazi sympathizer who founded the America First Party.

The National League pennant race was a nice diversion. Tex Carleton defeated the Braves, 5–1. Brandt's loss took him to 5–15. The second game was a pitchers' duel between Larry French and Frankhouse. Frankhouse (8–14) was the tough-luck loser, 2–1. The Cardinals lost to the Phillies, so the Cubs were just a game behind. The Cubs had won six in a row; the Braves had lost ten straight games.

On September 10, Charlie Root shut out the Braves and Ben Cantwell (4–21), 4–0. The Cubs remained one game behind St. Louis. Wednesday's game was a blowout win for the Cubs, 15–3. MacFayden fell to 5–13. Losers of 12 straight, the Braves traveled to Cincinnati (60–79) to face the sixth-place Reds.

Back in Boston, 25,000 spectators poured into Fenway Park on Wednesday night to watch the rematch of Danno O'Mahoney and Ed Don George for the world wrestling title. O'Mahoney, the pride of Boston's Irish, retained his championship a little after midnight when his Irish Whip sent George tumbling to the mat. Governor Curley was at ringside, sitting next to his newly named Unemployment Compensation Commission Chairman: Judge Emil E. Fuchs. The position was a six-year term that paid Fuchs $6,500 a year for directing the state's Social Security office. The Social Security Act was signed into law on August 14.[87] Boston Mayor Frederick Mansfield went on Boston radio, calling Curley a "modern Nero" and claiming that his appointments were to those "in on the 'pay off.'"[88]

The Braves lost their 100th game and 13th straight in falling to the Reds, 4–2, on September 12. Bob Brown pitched well but fell to 1–6 before a pitiful crowd of 627 who couldn't care less. The same small crowd came out again on Friday the 13th. Brandt allowed just six hits but fell to 5–16 as the Braves lost, 1–0, to Whitey Hilcher.

The Braves' 14-game losing streak came to an end on September 14. Frankhouse (9–14) prevailed, 6–4. The Braves finished with Cincinnati in a doubleheader on Sunday which drew over 13,000. Reds manager Chuck Dressen was presented with a new Auburn Supercharged Sedan by the mayor in a pregame ceremony. Not bad for a sixth-place club. Dressen drove around the field and out through the right field exit, arriving back at home plate minutes later. He would eventually be driven out of town after failing to win in Cincinnati.[89]

Between games, ten players ran an 80-yard dash. Wally Berger finished third and won $10, the only Braves player to compete. The Reds led the National League that season with 72 stolen bases; the Braves were last with 20. Tommy Thompson and Reds rookie Les Scarsella ran a relay around the bases twice. They never said who won, but Rabbit Maranville got in on the act. He was playing back when those two were in diapers, but he walked the bases once in a faster time than they ran them twice. As a prize, he was awarded a cuspidor, "with his honor being the first to spit into it and the Rabbit a close second," reported the *Herald*.[90]

The Braves' season was like spitting in the wind, and the doubleheader was more of the same. Cantwell allowed just four hits but lost, 1–0, his 22nd of the year. Paul Derringer won his 19th. The Braves trailed, 6–1, in the nightcap, but rallied to tie the game. The Reds walked off to a 7–6 win as darkness descended. The sprinting Cubs were two games in front of the Cardinals after sweeping Brooklyn four straight. The fading Giants were 3½ games behind.

Marshall Out; Adams Remains In

C.F. Adams' $1 per share plan was successful. "Some of the bigger holders have signified their desire for a conference," he said. After refusing to contribute more capital for Fuchs, Adams offered to do the opposite for the stockholders. "I am prepared to give my time and attention to accomplishing what I believe is a desirable and realizable result and to contribute a substantial amount to the new capital requirements of a reorganization."[91]

Adams held a stockholder meeting on Tuesday, September 17, and all but confirmed that the Marshall plan was dead. Adams announced plans "to reorganize and properly refinance the club. A plan will be submitted to all stockholders early in October which will offer every stockholder, no matter how large or how small his interest may be, a participation in the plan of reorganization on a basis equally favorable."[92]

Adams set sail on the SS *Saint John* bound for vacation in New Brunswick. He would not return until the disastrous season was over. When he arrived at Saint John, a reporter asked about the reorganization plan. Adams replied that $250,000 had been pledged, and Bob Quinn, former Red Sox President and current general manager of the Dodgers, would be named both president and GM of the Braves. That was news to everyone, including Quinn. "I have not talked with Adams, or anyone connected with the Boston club," he clarified. Weston Adams, C.F.'s son, said, "everyone present agreed Bob Quinn would be the man for the presidency of the club if available. Of course, we are not certain Mr. Quinn would be interested."[93] C.F. would be miles from a telephone for the rest of the month at his hunting camp on the Miramichi River, deep in the New Brunswick woods.

Playing Out the String, Hanging by a Thread

The Braves weren't out of the woods yet. They faced the fourth-place Pirates (80–63) in Pittsburgh. Betts started the opener on September 16 and lasted just one-third of an inning, and the Pirates prevailed, 5–3. The first inning was also the culprit on Tuesday. Brandt surrendered five runs in the first and was pounded for 15 hits through six innings as the Pirates won again, 6–4, despite Berger's 32nd home run. Brandt was 5–17; the Braves were 34–105.

"It was the same old story today," the *Globe* said of the September 18 game.[94] Cy Blanton won his 18th game, 5–2, and Frankhouse took the loss (9–15). The Braves had one final game in the Steel City on Thursday. They took a 5–4 lead into the bottom of the eighth inning. Cantwell was on the mound, desperate for a win. The skies darkened and the Braves stalled, hoping for the game to be called with them ahead. "But the weatherman seemed in no hurry," wrote Edward F. Balinger in the *Post-Gazette*.[95] Cantwell got the first two out, but hits by Pep Young, Cookie Lavagetto, and Gus Suhr produced a run. Earl Grace was walked intentionally so Cantwell could face the pitcher, Waite Hoyt, who stung a single to score two more. The Pirates led, 7–5. The Braves mounted a comeback in the ninth inning. Jordan singled and scored on Thompson's double to make the score 7–6. Mallon grounded to first, but Hoyt dropped the throw covering the bag and everyone was safe. Elbie Fletcher lofted to short fly to left. Woody Jensen camped under it. Thompson took off and was thrown out at the plate to end the game. Cantwell was 4–23.

The Braves couldn't buy a win, while the Cubs couldn't lose. Their winning streak was 16 after a four-game sweep of the fading Giants. The Cubs led St. Louis by 2½ games. In the American League, Detroit clinched its second straight pennant and looked to avenge its World Series loss in 1934. The Braves were on to Philadelphia to play the seventh-place Phillies in back-to-back doubleheaders on Saturday and Sunday, September 21–22.

Curt Davis shut out the Braves 6–0 in the opener, ruining Tommy Thompson's 4-for-4 performance. MacFayden fell to 5–15 and had not won since July 6. His ERA over that time ballooned from 3.61 to 5.32. In the nightcap, Huck Betts threw a three-hit shutout in a 4–0 win. Johnnie Tyler smashed his first major league home run onto Broad Street, and Berger followed by smashing a ball off the brick wall at the top of the left field bleachers for his 33rd.[96] Art Doll made his major league debut at catcher.

A crowd of 7,000 came out for Sunday's doubleheader. The Braves fell behind, 4–0, in the opener, but rallied to tie the game in the fifth inning. Bob Smith was effective in relief from the fifth inning on, and the game was tied, 5–5, in the last of the ninth. George Watkins singled, and Jo-Jo Moore slammed one onto Broad Street for a walk-off home run. Ironically, Phillies rookie Hugh Mulcahy, one of the unluckiest pitchers in baseball history, got his first major league win. You didn't have to be lucky to beat the Braves.[97]

In the nightcap, Cantwell held a 3–2 lead in the bottom of the seventh inning. Watkins blasted another home run to help the Phillies win, 4–3. Cantwell was 4–24, and the Braves had lost their 110th game. They surpassed the 1928 Phillies for the most losses by a National League club in the 20th century, and the most since the inept 1899 Cleveland Spiders went 20–134. The Spiders' owner, Frank Robison, also owned the St. Louis Browns and moved his Cleveland stars to St. Louis, confident of more fan support. It left the Spiders with a tangled web to weave.[98] The Braves didn't have such an excuse.

The Braves traveled to the Polo Grounds to face the deflated Giants, now eight games behind the Cubs with 11 to play. "Alas, Poor Giants—They're Out!" cried the *New York Daily News*.[99] The Giants had spent 88 days in first place, the last time on August 24. The Braves had spent one day in first place, when Ruth helped them defeat the Giants on Opening Day, April 16. The Cubs had an 18-game winning streak and closed in on a pennant.

Fewer than 1,500 people bothered to come for the September 23 doubleheader. In an Opening Day rematch, Ed Brandt faced Carl Hubbell. Brandt won on Opening Day but was 4–17 with a 5.06 ERA since. Hubbell was 22–10 with a 3.15 ERA, his third straight 20+-win season. Hubbell bested Brandt in this opener, 3–2, making the Braves 0–10 at the Polo Grounds. They managed to salvage one victory in their final appearance in the nightcap, beating the Giants, 9–7. The unmotivated Giants pitchers allowed 12 hits and 10 walks. Frankhouse (10–15) got the win despite six earned runs and five walks.

Only 500 fans turned out to Ebbets Field as the Braves played a doubleheader with the Dodgers on September 24. Bob Brown lost, 5–3, to Johnny Babich and finished the season 1–8 with a 6.65 ERA. He pitched briefly in 1936, never finding his earlier success. After baseball, Brown worked as an iron worker. He died in 1990 at the age of 79.[100]

In the second game, the Braves rallied from a 5–2 deficit in the ninth inning to tie the game. The game went 11 innings, and Smith allowed the winning run as the Dodgers won, 6–5. Bobby Reis, a converted infielder, pitched all 11 innings for Brooklyn. The biggest applause was for Rabbit Maranville, who was also a hero in Brooklyn. Fans lined up to shake his hand after the game.[101] Boston newspapers barely devoted four paragraphs to coverage of the Braves, but there was a good reason. Everything happening in the world in 1935 was magnified on September 24 at Yankee Stadium.

The Fight

Joe Louis, the Detroit African American boxing hero, captured the hearts of the nation, whether black or white. Jackie Robinson would integrate baseball a decade later, but Louis broke the color barrier of American sports. Robinson and Louis shared much in common. Branch Rickey advised Robinson over a decade later not to fight back when racial slurs were hurled. Louis was carefully portrayed to show no aggression, stay mild-mannered, live squeaky clean, and not be seen in public with a white woman. The "Brown Bomber" portrayal was more acceptable to white audiences. "Although Joe Louis is colored," the ring announcer declared in the cigar smoke filled ring, "he is a great fighter."[102]

Louis was undefeated since beginning his professional career in 1934. He defeated former heavyweight champion Primo Carnera, touted by Benito Mussolini as the symbol of Fascist Italy. Louis' color represented the "little" Ethiopians the dictator would soon conquer. Louis now faced Max Baer, who had recently lost the championship belt to Jimmy Braddock, but expectations of a huge crowd and payday remained. "Rarely a day passed when the Detroit papers didn't mention Joe Louis," wrote Tom Stanton. "His string of victories, his ballooning national fame and his likable public demeanor made him a regular presence on newsprint."[103]

A crowd of 90,000 packed Yankee Stadium, bringing in nearly $1 million. Some people paid $125 for a ringside seat. Celebrities were prominent: former President Hoover, Ernest Hemingway, Edward G. Robinson, James Cagney, Tigers manager Mickey Cochrane, and of course, Babe Ruth, sporting a snazzy dark blue sport coat. "I like Maxie," he said. The *Illustrated Daily News* in Los Angeles reported that Ruth joined Baer and Jack Dempsey in the locker room before the fight.

"Boy, I feel great!" Baer boasted to the Bambino. "I'm going to show you tonight how I really can fight." He slapped his stomach. "Look at that! I'm in better shape than I've ever been in my life!" Then he broke a shoelace.

"What'll you do if you break one in the ring?" Ruth asked.

"I'll just sit down and make Joe wait awhile until I get a new one," he said with confidence.[104]

The 15-round fight lasted only four as Louis knocked out Baer. Louis would again represent America through his loss and comeback victory over Max Schmeling, who Adolf Hitler declared was the example of the superiority of the Aryan race. "White Americans—even while some of them were lynching black people in the south," Louis wrote years later, "were depending on me to K.O. a German. I knew I had to get Schmeling good. I had my own personal reasons, and the whole damned country was depending on me."[105]

Home for the Finale

The Braves were over 700 miles from Joe Louis, playing an exhibition game in Yarmouth, Nova Scotia, versus the Yarmouth Gateways, champions of the Maritimes Provinces. The game was sponsored by the Kiwanis Club to support the Sunshine Camp for underprivileged children and drew a crowd of 2,500. The Braves won, 21–2, prompting a headline: "Braves Find Team They Can Defeat." Halley

Horton of the Gateways said it best. "Everyone else had to pay $2.00 to see the Braves play and we watched them for free."[106]

The Braves returned to Boston for a doubleheader against the Giants, with one of the games a makeup from April 18. It was Shriner's Day at Braves Field, and any player with a hit would win a box of cigars. Buck Jordan had five hits and received five boxes, even though he didn't smoke. The Braves smoked Carl Hubbell for eight hits and six runs in two innings. Frankhouse (11–15) got the 6–4 victory.

It looked like the Braves would sweep the doubleheader, as Cantwell held a 4–2 lead in the seventh inning. But when the smoke cleared, he was trailing, 5–4, and the Giants went on to win, 8–5. Cantwell finished his season 4–25. Wally Berger slammed his 34th and final home run. Most of the 4,000 spectators were likely watching out-of-town scores. The Cubs beat the Cardinals for their 21st straight victory and celebrated the National League pennant.

This was the last major league appearance for Huck Betts, the Millsboro, Delaware, native. He had a terrible season, finishing 2–9 with a 5.47 ERA and 1.58 WHIP. His major league career was split between the Phillies (1920–1925) and Braves (1932–1935). In between, he toiled away in the minors, working his way back. He finished 61–68 in his 10 major-league seasons.

Betts returned to Millsboro and opened a theater. In 1977, he recalled his half-season with Babe Ruth. "Halfway through a game, Babe would always ask the trainer to bring him a glass of milk—probably with a little belt in it—to soothe the old belly. When Babe finally told us he was hanging it up—during a Decoration Day doubleheader in Philadelphia—one of our fellows yelled to the trainer, 'Hey Jimmy! You can get rid of the cow now!'"[107] Walter McKinley "Huck" Betts died in 1987 at the age of 90.

It was raining in Boston on Saturday, September 28, meaning Sunday's season finale would be yet another doubleheader, and one game would not be made up. No one complained about that. Daylight Savings Time ended, so Bostonians could get an extra hour of sleep before the season finale. "Because makers of timepieces advertise that it is harmful to the mechanism to push the hour hand back," the *Globe* warned, "clocks and watches should be halted for one hour and then started again."[108] If only the Braves could have stopped time on Opening Day.

Everyone was in a hurry to go home. The doubleheader began at 1:25 p.m. and finished at 4:15 p.m. The Giants won the first game, 5–3. Brandt took the loss, finishing 5–19 with an even 5.00 ERA. Al Blanche pitched six scoreless innings of relief to finish the game. He pitched 17⅓ innings in 1935 with a 1.56 ERA. He was invited back with the Braves in 1936 and threw another 16 innings before being optioned to Syracuse, ending his major league career. His post-baseball career was much sweeter as he worked for the Schrafft's candy and chocolate company in Cambridge, Massachusetts. Blanche died in 1997 at the age of 87.[109]

The final game of this awful season was played in 61 minutes and called after eight innings as a light mist fell and the Giants wanted to catch an early train.

MacFayden shut out the Giants, 3–0, finishing 6–15 with a 5.04 ERA. A crowd of 1,000 turned out for the finale, bringing the season attendance to 232,754. Only the Phillies (205,470) drew fewer fans in the National League, but both were still far better than the 80,922 who went to watch the American League's inept St. Louis Browns.

And so, there we have it: 38–115. The 1935 Braves remain among the very worst teams in baseball history. Along with the previously mentioned Spiders, three other 19th-century clubs are included among the ten worst clubs (by winning percentage) of all time. Others only view 1901 to current in the discussion of best/worst clubs. But the 1935 Braves are bad on either list. Here it is with the worst club at the top. The Tigers of modern times round out the list:

Team	W	L	W–L %
1899 Cleveland (NL)	20	134	.130
1890 Pittsburgh (NL)	23	113	.169
1897 St. Louis (NL)	29	102	.221
1916 Philadelphia (AL)	36	117	.235
1935 Braves (NL)	38	115	.248
1962 New York (NL)	40	120	.250
1904 Washington (AL)	38	113	.252
1919 Philadelphia (AL)	36	104	.257
1898 St. Louis (NL)	39	111	.260
2003 Detroit (AL)	43	119	.265

The Braves were the worst in nearly all major hitting and pitching categories:

Batting Stat	NL	Rank
BA	.263	8th
OBP	.311	8th
SLG	.362	8th
OPS	.673	8th
Tot Bases	1920	8th
Runs	575	8th
R/G	3.76	8th
Hits	1396	8th
RBI	544	8th
SB	20	8th
BB	353	8th

Pitching Stat	NL	Rank
ERA	4.93	8th
SHO	6	8th

Pitching Stat	NL	Rank
H	1645	7th
R	852	7th
ER	729	8th
R	852	7th
RA/G	5.57	7th
Hits	1645	7th
SO	355	8th
ERA+	77	8th
WHIP	1.541	7th
SO/W	0.88	8th
SO/9	2.4	8th
H/9	11.1	8th

Wally Berger's 34 home runs and 130 RBI led the National League, and he finished in the top ten of most offensive categories. Hal Lee led the team in batting at .303. The Braves led the NL in grounding into double plays, with Urbanski hitting into 16 of them (tied for third). On the pitching side, Cantwell (4–25), Brandt (5–19), Smith (8–18), Frankhouse (11–15), and MacFayden (6–15) were the league leaders in losses.

The Last Day

For five Braves players, September 29 was their final day in the major leagues.

Les Mallon

Mallon was the regular second baseman, appearing in 75 games there. He batted .274. A native Texan, he was purchased by Dallas of the Texas League at his request. He was part-owner of a bowling alley, and folks would also see him driving around in a milk truck in the off-season. "I had a business in Dallas that paid $18,000 and I only made $12,000 playing for the Braves," he recalled in 1988. "We didn't have any agents back then and we did our own dealing, so I had to make a choice between playing in Boston and losing my share of the partnership or leaving the team. So, I demanded to be traded to Dallas, where I could play ball and work in the business."[110]

Mallon retired in 1940. He joined the Navy during World War II and managed the Grand Prairie Naval Air Station team. After the war, he managed a wholesale wine and liquor distribution company. He told stories over the decades of living in the same hotel as Babe Ruth.[111] "I don't even look at *The Babe Ruth Story* [film] when it comes on because it's nothing like the man really was," he said. "He was one of the nicest men I ever met, although he was already a legend. After games, thousands of kids would be waiting outside the stadium for him. Sometimes, he'd stand there signing autographs until dark. I never saw him refuse anyone any time."[112]

He recalled a mild Ruth in 1935. "The stories about Ruth's eating and drinking binges just aren't true," he insisted. "He drank and he ate a lot, but I never saw him overindulge. He didn't keep in shape the way some of the other great ones did and he wasn't built like a ballplayer, but he was a powerful man and he had perfect coordination." In 1980, Mallon said, "Babe was a marvelous fellow. He was jovial, and he took defeat like a man. In my own opinion, I don't think he would have been a good manager, though. He was just too good a guy. He liked to live a fast life, and he would have had trouble adjusting to management."[113]

It was a different world then. "We had to travel by train, and the locker rooms didn't have lounge chairs, whirlpools, weight rooms or lobbies, but we didn't care," he said. "We were just happy to be there and playing ball."[114]

Leslie Clyde Mallon died in 1991 at the age of 85.

Joe Mowry

Mowry batted .265 in 81 games in 1935, playing all three outfield spots. The St. Louis native spent the next six years bouncing around the minors and then managed clubs in Winnipeg and Moline. After his playing days, he worked over 30 years for Mobile Oil as the safety director at a refinery. Mowry had fond memories in 1984 of the two legends on the team: Ruth and Maranville.

> My, he was fat and 40, and he couldn't field or run anymore. Not too smart, either, because they'd beat him regularly in fan-tan [card] games. He didn't hit like Ruth, either. But when he swung and missed, his bat still "swished" with a hum. And when he connected, about half were homers. He was still remarkable. In the clubhouse he knew who you were. But outside, heck, you just got a "Hi, kid." He got so many fan letters that they had to create a separate box for him in the clubhouse. My, he was something.[115]

Mowry was a Knot-Hole Gang kid in the bleachers in St. Louis when Rabbit Maranville helped the Cardinals win the 1928 pennant. He later roomed with his hero. "Rab was on the wagon," Mowry said, "but he was still funny. He could double talk anyone. He should have been in vaudeville. Quite a guy to be taking care of me."[116]

Joseph Aloysius Mowry died in 1994 at the age of 85.

Johnnie Tyler

It was surprising that Tyler, who batted .340 with two home runs in 47 at-bats in 13 games for the 1935 Braves, was not retained. His nine pinch-hits were second in the league despite so few at-bats. It wasn't enough to make him stick in the major leagues. After 16 major league games and 15 seasons in the minors, Tyler returned to his native Pennsylvania coal country and lived out his life as a short-order cook. He could always tell his customers he once pinch-ran for Babe Ruth. "The Braves had a very good outfield and some good prospects they paid from $30,000 to $40,000 for. I only cost the club $2,000, and that had a lot to do with everything."[117] John Anthony Tyler died in 1972 at the age of 65.

Rabbit Maranville

September 29 was Rabbit Maranville's final day after a 23-year, Hall of Fame career. He played in 2,670 games, and the modern statistic of Defensive WAR (which measures a player's value on defensive stats alone) ranks him seventh all-time, behind such legends as Ozzie Smith, Mark Belanger, Brooks Robinson, Cal Ripken, Jr., Joe Tinker, and Luis Aparicio. Rabbit Maranville was a joker, prankster, children's entertainer, and storyteller. He managed minor league clubs between 1936 and 1941.

There wasn't much to say about 1935, when he played in just 23 games and batted .149. There were, however, the many jokes and goofing around he did with Ruth. The first day Ruth joined the Braves at spring training, they didn't have a uniform for him, so he squeezed into Shanty Hogan's uniform and waddled out to the bench. Hank Gowdy came by with a dozen baseballs.

"What are those?" Ruth growled.

"Baseballs. We practice with them," the coach sarcastically snapped back. "Oh," said the relieved Babe. "I thought I had to autograph the damn things."

"Listen, Ruth," interjected Maranville. "Don't be worrying about autographing baseballs. On this club you start at the bottom like the rest of us and work your way up."

"I can still hear the Babe's laughter thundering from the kettle drum he was wearing under his belt in those happy days," Maranville recalled in 1948.[118]

Walter James Vincent "Rabbit" Maranville lived the rest of his life in Springfield, Massachusetts, and died in 1954 at the age of 62.

Al Spohrer

Born in Philadelphia, Spohrer played eight years in the major leagues, all but two games with the Braves. He played 92 games for the 1935 Braves, starting 74 of them behind the plate. He batted .242, and his 12 errors were third-most among NL catchers. Spohrer was best remembered for the boxing match he had with future Braves teammate Al Shires at the Boston Garden in 1930. The bout was far more profitable than his Braves salary that year. In 1936, Spohrer went into the building supply business rather than be sent to the minors. He worked for Judge Fuchs in the Unemployment Compensation Commission and later as a salesman for Miller Brewing Company.

He died in Plymouth, New Hampshire, in 1972 at the age of 69.[119]

The Bigot Who Almost Bought the Braves

The Red Sox also finished their season on September 29, coming in fourth (78–75), 16 games behind Detroit. Their season ended at Yankee Stadium, but Fenway Park was still in use. George Preston Marshall's Boston Redskins kicked off their football season against the Brooklyn football Dodgers. The Redskins won their opening game, 7–3, but finished 2–8–1. The Redskins improved to 7–5 in 1936 and met Green Bay in the NFL Championship Game. But the club attendance ranked seventh both years, and Marshall moved the championship game from Boston to the Polo Grounds. The Packers rolled, 21–6, and Marshall rolled his football team to Washington, D.C., where they remain to this day, without the old nickname. You wonder what might have happened had Marshall remained in Boston alongside Tom Yawkey. They were the last two major professional sports club owners to integrate their teams.

"His [Marshall's] political and economic views lean so far over to the right that they are practically horizontal," wrote Ed Linn in a feature on Marshall for *Sport* magazine in 1957. "He calls himself a conservative, and his opponents call him a 19th Century reactionary."[120]

Marshall's views can't be denied.

"There is no place in professional football for the Negro," he told Ric Roberts of the *Pittsburgh Courier* in the early 1940s, "because the white players would resent his presence and 'frame' him for terrible and, perhaps, fatal injuries." Marshall prevented the all-black Washington Lions football team from using Griffith Stadium, and he opposed black high school teams from using the stadium.[121]

The Boston National League club had been known by several unofficial nicknames since its beginning in 1871: Red Stockings, Red Caps, Beaneaters, Rustlers, Doves, or the more prominent Nationals (in contrast to the Boston Americans, who became the Red Sox). Nicknames were not the official marketing vehicle they are today and were often invented by sportswriters. In 1912, the team became known as the "Braves" after the Tammany Hall political society which owner James Gaffney belonged to. Tammany members were known as "Braves," and their logo was the familiar Native American.[122] Marshall took the name and image a further step, devoid of its political origins.

"I did exploit Indians in Boston," he admitted in 1957. "I'll admit that, and the same kind of exploitation has taken place with the Negro in baseball. It's wrong. Negroes play against us, so what's the difference?"[123] Shirley Povich of the *Washington Post* was Marshall's harshest critic. African American athletes, Povich wrote, "are incompatible with the décor Marshall has chosen for the Redskins, which is burgundy, gold, and Caucasian. For those Redskin fans who are not members of the White Citizens Council, it is too bad that too many good football players are ineligible for the Redskins from birth."[124] A picketer outside the 1957 NFL meetings in Philadelphia held a sign which read, "Hitler Banned Jews; Marshall Bans Negroes."[125]

When Corinne Griffith, star of the silent film era, accepted Marshall's proposal of marriage, he presented her a heartwarming engagement gift. "A Confederate Flag," she wrote, "one that had been in his family since the Civil War."[126] She helped write the lyrics to "Hail to the Redskins," which originally included the verses:

> *Scalp 'em, swamp 'em, we will, Take 'um big score.*
> *Read 'um, weep 'um, touchdown, We want heap more.*[127]

"The Redskins professional football team was founded in New England by a bigoted Southerner," wrote Thomas G. Smith in his book, *Showdown: JFK and the Integration of the Washington Redskins.* But the modern controversy over names and logos of Native Americans is beyond our scope here. This was 1935, Marshall (and other segregationists) were not yet viewed negatively in the public eye, and he was known more for laundry than sports. C.F. Adams had no qualms turning the Braves over to him, since Marshall was a business genius with capital to save the Braves. African American newspapers, such as the *Pittsburgh Courier,* would take issue with Marshall's views on race. What might have happened if Marshall had taken control of the Braves and dominated the Boston sports scene, sharing the city with Tom Yawkey, who Jackie Robinson said was "probably one of the most bigoted guys in organized baseball"?[128]

Tom Yawkey and George Preston Marshall were opposites in personality. Marshall was a flashy, outspoken showman mixing sports and entertainment, while Yawkey was the quiet, behind-the-scenes, hands-off traditionalist. Both held out on integrating their club. Marshall boasted of staying true to his Southern heritage, while Yawkey let day-to-day decisions of the Red Sox be handled by others.

Pinky Higgins, who managed the Red Sox from 1955 to 1962, said, "There'll be no niggers on this ball club as long as I have anything to do with it."[129] Joe Cronin and Eddie Collins, Yawkey's right-hand men in the front office, were cronies who maintained the status quo. The Red Sox staged a phony "tryout" of Negro League players, including Jackie Robinson. Cronin's excuse, given 11 years later, for not signing players of color, was that "we didn't have a farm team to send them to. We couldn't send them to Louisville." But the Red Sox also had a club in Scranton, Pennsylvania. Cronin said they were willing to sign a black player "who measures up to major league specifications."[130] That meant the players of color other teams had signed over the previous decade weren't good enough for the Red Sox. Scout Ted McGrew held a tryout for 500 players of color in 1955. Amazingly, none of them qualified either. The answer to why the Red Sox did not have a player of color, Al Hirshberg wrote, was that the Red Sox said, "We will when we find a good one."[131]

We'll never know what might have happened in Boston's social and sports history if Yawkey *and* Marshall stayed in the same city. We'll never know because the Braves were so far in debt the bank had a say in who could run the team.

Money talks, and Marshall's plan never happened.

At the Dyckman Oval

In glaring contrast to Marshall and Yawkey was Babe Ruth, who played an exhibition game at the Dyckman Oval at the end of September. "The 'Great Man' himself," the *New York Amsterdam News* hailed Ruth's arrival, "his popularity knew neither race, creed, nor color."[132] The Oval hosted many great Negro Leagues games since opening around 1915.[133] Ruth barnstormed there in 1920. Now, he brought a group of (somewhat) all-stars to face the New York Cubans.

A crowd of 12,000 packed the park, and others watched from nearby rooftops. Ruth put on a show in batting practice, launching over 30 balls out of the park. Ruth's team was "a bunch of guys named 'Jim' masquerading as all-stars," wrote Joe Bostic in the *New York Amsterdam News*. The Cubans had Luis E. Tiant, the crafty Cuban ace and father of the famed Red Sox pitcher of the 1970s. The Cubans had recently lost the Negro National League championship to the Pittsburgh Crawfords.

Tiant allowed a double to Ruth in the first inning but only five hits total in a 6–1 victory. A Ruth-less second game saw the Cubans clobber the all-stars, 15–4. "The game only served to further prove," wrote Bostic, "what has been known by us ebony scribes for these many years, viz: that so-called semi pro and minor league white ball tossers have absolutely no business in the same town with the top-flight Negro teams, to say nothing of in the same ball yard at the same time."[134]

Maybe Yawkey's Red Sox would have been good enough to beat them.

12

A Forfeited Franchise
(October–December 1935)

"Nope! I have no plans. Don't know what I am going to do next year—probably just play golf."—Babe Ruth

"This action taken should have been taken a few years back and it would have saved a lot of headaches."—Charles F. Adams

October: The Babe Still Waits

Bill McKechnie was on his way to Detroit for the World Series and the minor league draft. Deacon Bill was looking for bargain-basement deals and hoping fellow executives would help him out. "They should bolster the Boston team if they can do it without weakening themselves," he said. "A stronger team in Boston means that every club will profit financially."[1] National League President Ford C. Frick agreed and was optimistic. "I'm tickled to death about the whole situation," he said. "The League believes it can help the Braves negotiate a couple of deals that they otherwise couldn't put through."[2] The minor league draft brought no new players to the Braves, so McKechnie needed help elsewhere.

"Madness" was the word the *Detroit Free Press* used to describe the crowd at Game One of the World Series on October 2. Fans had waited all night for the gates to open. Wearing fur coats and drinking from thermoses reminded many of a football game at Ann Arbor. The crowd dashed for available bleacher seats. Two men who didn't need such a scramble for a seat were Henry Ford and his son, Edsel. Real madness was happening elsewhere. "A rumor that hostilities had begun in Africa ripped through the crowd," said the *Free Press* of Benito Mussolini's imminent invasion of Ethiopia.[3] But those worries were a world away.

The crowd stirred as "a bulky figure, head hunched deep into broad shoulders, as if trying to escape detection by the throng,"said the *Chicago Tribune* about Babe Ruth and wife Claire making their way to the box seats. His brown suit and white carnation blended with the "big, fat cigar in his face."[4] "I haven't any plans for the Babe," Claire said when asked of his plans. "We must be very careful. The Babe has been the idol of American youth for a long while, and I won't have him mixed up in anything that isn't just right."[5] Crowds mobbed him for autographs when the Series moved to Chicago. "I'm wearing the point off my pencil," he joked. He sneaked out in the 10th inning of Game Three. "I'll fool 'em," he said. But he was followed by 30 fans.[6]

The Tigers beat the Cubs, four games to two, to win the World Series.

Ruth played two exhibition games at Dexter Park in Queens, home of the semi-pro Brooklyn Bushwicks and site of many Negro League contests. On October 14, Ruth faced Dazzy Vance, who at 44 had played his last major league game after a 16-year career. An immense crowd of 16,500 turned out to see Ruth slam a home run over the right field wall in a 3–2 loss. Ruth was invited back on the 20th and singled in a 6–5 win. He gave a speech that he was quitting baseball.[7] "That was pathetic," wrote Marshall Smelser. "Baseball had quit him."[8]

Ruth pondered an offer to teach baseball in Great Britain. "I see no reason why it [baseball] can't be built up in other countries so that in the time of our children it would be an international as well as a national sport." Nothing came of the offer.[9] Ruth spoke at the Circus Saints and Sinners Club, a charity organization established by philanthropic businessmen in 1929 to care for retired circus performers in financial need. Ruth was decked out in a crown, robe, beard, and monstrous baseball bat. He swung and hit popcorn balls thrown from bearded players mimicking the House of David.[10]

November: Adams Wants Out

Charles F. Adams returned to Boston after a month away at his hunting lodge. A meeting of major stockholders included Adams, V.C. Bruce Wetmore, Major Francis P. Murphy, the wealthy New Hampshire shoe manufacturer and Republican gubernatorial candidate, and Harry Beckwith, owner of the Wentworth Hotel of Portsmouth, New Hampshire. Murphy rose in the newspaper headlines as the new owner of this syndicate. Gerry Moore in the *Globe* wrote, "Nobody else in sight is capable of rescuing the local National League baseball club from the swamp of desolation and poverty."[11] The Braves needed new organization and new financing.[12]

The meeting was held on November 6 and 7, and $175,000 was pledged of the needed $350,000. "Each of those present at our meeting agreed to take one share of new stock for five of the old," Adams said. "Such stock would be preferred stock with a par value of $100, and two shares of the common stock would be included in the transfer."[13] There were 12,000 shares in total. The other $175,000 needed to be raised before the National League meeting on November 26, or the NL would take over the club.[14] Five thousand shares of stock would be held in the treasury as a benefit for whoever became general manager.[15] Frick and Bob Quinn came to Boston on November 15 to meet with Adams and Murphy. Quinn, the Dodgers' GM, believed the club was worth $350,000.[16]

Baseball's minor league annual meetings, held November 21 and 22 in Dayton, Ohio, saw little trade activity. Teams with young talent held on to their assets for possible trades if Wally Berger became available. If the Braves ownership played it right, they could unload Berger's salary and acquire several prospects to be building blocks of a new dynasty.[17]

Adams and Murphy presented their individual reorganization plans to the NL club owners on November 26, with Adams representing the major shareholders and Murphy the minor shareholders. Neither could agree on a plan. The club was in debt $325,000, and anyone wanting the team needed to pay that off plus invest new working capital.[18] "Nobody desires to buy a lot of bills," Hy Hurwitz wrote in the *Boston Globe*. "If the league fails to receive bids more than $325,000, the present stockholders, majority and minority, may just as well tear up their shares as they will be worthless."[19]

"Running the club ourselves," Frick said, "is something which we do not look forward to with any great pleasure."[20] Another option was to allow Adams (with his horse racing ventures) to continue to run the club, but without approval from Judge Landis this was nearly impossible. Adams could invest more in the Braves but refused unless someone brought in new capital. "I wouldn't put in a nickel if I thought there was only $100,000 available," he said. "I wouldn't put any more money in this pot unless that pot is big enough to do the job for the club. It seems to me that—I may be wrong here—that we ought to have $300,000 more new capital."[21] The Braves owed the NL $38,000, $18,000 in back taxes, and $6,500 for bats and balls.

Murphy suggested the NL should generously cancel the debt and allow the Braves to start clean. The answer was a clear no. "To me this is all a joke," Murphy griped, saying that small debt was of greater importance to them than the $100,000 he and his partners were willing to invest. His associates sought to "help the community of Boston and the ball club. If they are willing to do this, certainly there is some obligation on your part." Powell Crosley, Jr., president of the Reds, said he once owed money to the NL "but I didn't come down and cry to the League to release us of any loan we made."[22]

"I am not crying," Murphy snapped back. "You probably have plenty of money; I haven't. I have put up a business proposition. Don't accuse me of crying. I have contributed already to the National League Club a good many thousands of dollars. That is gone, and I still want to come in and contribute more."[23] Adams countered with the option of amortizing the loan with the bank ($250,000 over five years), so the team could at least limp along.

Murphy presented a plan with included Harry Beckwith and S.A. Patterson, who worked with Murphy in the shoe business. The trio wanted a complete reorganization of the club officers and a new board of directors, which Adams opposed. Murphy pledged twice as much capital to run the club as the figure set by Quinn's appraisal. "The new interests would be entirely local as the outsiders have created a situation which is far from pleasant," wrote Hurwitz.[24]

Only Philip K. Wrigley of the Cubs believed Murphy's plan was viable. "Adams opposed this so flatly," wrote Paul H. Shannon in the *Boston Post*, "that Murphy left the meeting in a huff and disposed to let the other Boston stockholders paddle their own canoe."[25] Murphy fumed. "I wanted to clean house, and for the psychological effect introduce new blood and give the Braves' administration more color," he said. "But my suggestion was turned down, and though they gave it out that I left before the conference ended in order to keep an appointment, I tell you frankly that I walked out on them. I am all done now as far as the Braves are concerned."[26]

The National League held a separate directors meeting, and seven club owners unanimously voted for expulsion of the Braves from the National League. The National League took possession of the team. "Under the provisions of the Constitution," Frick declared, "the franchise and players of the Boston Base Ball Company now revert to the National League."[27] Frick publicly called the action a "friendly forfeiture."[28] The league statement read:

> At a meeting of the National League today by vote of the presidents of the individual clubs unanimously carried, Boston not voting, the National League repossessed the franchise and players' contracts of the Boston National League Baseball Company under authority provided by section 9 of the National League constitution. This action was taken because of the failure of the Boston National League Baseball Company to fulfill its contractual obligations over an extended period. As a result of this action, the National League is now in position to receive proposals for the acquisition of the Boston franchise and players' contracts and will consider all proposals submitted in writing.[29]

Those proposals needed to be submitted by December 10.

The 1906 Phillies were the only other club in baseball history to be "forfeited." The Phillies ownership faced lawsuits stemming from the tragic collapse of the Baker Bowl bleachers in 1903 which killed 12 people.[30]

"This action taken should have been taken a few years back and it would have saved a lot of headaches," Adams said. Adams could pay the $325,000 debt himself and run the club, but he wasn't about to. "If the league doesn't make me a proposition, I'll just have to take my medicine." Adams paid player salaries out of his own pocket at the end of the season. "I made a mistake getting into baseball several years ago and I don't intend making any more mistakes," he affirmed. Sportswriters grew bored waiting for some word as they remained outside the NL office.

One of them changed the sign on the door to read, "The National League of 7 professional baseball clubs."[31] Frick wasn't amused.

"There is no question of Boston losing its National League club," he said. "We will be prepared to run it ourselves, after securing the proper executives, etc. We will do nothing in a hurry. Mr. Adams sees a plan for the club's salvation. He has been working hard along such a line for many weeks, and I feel confident that by Dec. 10 things will be satisfactorily adjusted."[32]

Baltimore insurance man Harry Goldman sent a telegram to Frick stating that he was interested in buying the Braves and moving them there. Goldman had been involved in Baltimore baseball since the beginning of the American League with the 1901–1902 Orioles, who were relocated to New York and became the Yankees. Goldman was also involved in Baltimore's Federal League Terrapins in 1914–1915. In the spring of 1935, Goldman unsuccessfully attempted to purchase and move the Phillies to Baltimore. "Baltimore is ripe for big-league baseball," he stated. "I don't think there is the slightest doubt about it, and that Baltimore will raise sufficient money to bring the major leagues to this city if such a thing becomes possible."[33] Frick never considered a move to Baltimore a possibility.

Frick had three options. First was to wait and see if the current stockholders could save the club by providing extra capital. The second was to find a suitable purchaser by December 10. If those options failed, the third was for the National League to run the club indefinitely.[34] Adams was determined that all Braves stockholders would receive 100 cents on the dollar. He was antsy over Thanksgiving and released a statement on November 30, which said in part:

> It has become embarrassing, if not unfair, that I should further withhold from the press and Boston baseball fans a definite statement concerning the present "mysterious" situation which involves the Boston Braves and the club's future, its stockholders, and its creditors. Such a statement from me might also well serve a constructive purpose. The situation is briefly as follows:
>
> Because of the National League's attitude and that of Judge Landis in the recent case of dog racing vs Organized Baseball, and since I have been reliably informed that interests formerly connected with the club have recently written Judge Landis calling to his attention and emphasizing my personal interest in the Eastern Racing Association, Inc. [Suffolk Downs], which racing connection, by the way, I personally forecast in a conference with Judge Landis in New York at the time of his ruling in the Fuchs complication, it has seemed a fair position for me to take and to avoid underserved embarrassment to the National League that I first give "right of way" to the Murphy interests in a plan of reorganization, accepting a minority position in ownership and operation of the Boston Braves or entirely retire if it might be possible for the Murphy stockholder group to finance the club's future without my participation.
>
> However, in any event, before I have agreed to step aside—at least willingly—was contingent upon any new interests that might secure the club being financially able and willing to pay enough for the club that its present creditors might receive "one hundred cents on the dollar," as I intend if I am forced to finally accept the burden, and, with it a majority interest in the Boston club and a consequent responsibility and care for the club's future.
>
> I also made it clear to the directors of the National League, I hope, that I would not invest further in the Boston club, either as a minority or a majority interest, unless Robert (Bob) Quinn would accept the general management of the Braves and Bill McKechnie offered the opportunity to remain in his present official capacity until there seemed ample justification for any change in the club's executive personnel.

If, by disposing of this property at less than its fair value but with a definite assurance that the club will be able to pay its present creditors in full, I can accept the loss of my personal investment in the Braves with equanimity, but beyond this, I cannot gracefully accede as I feel it an obligation to protect every creditor of the club as well as its future credit standing and that of Organized Baseball whether in Boston or elsewhere.[35]

December: Quinn Takes Charge

As Braves fans glanced at the front pages of Saturday morning papers on December 7, they learned that Bob Quinn was going to buy the Braves. Quinn and Adams were on their way to Chicago for the annual baseball ownership meeting. Adams sent a letter to the old stockholders that a deal was in the works, and Quinn "will be pleased to have associated with him the equity owners of the old club in such amounts as they may wish to subscribe to the same terms that he himself and others subscribe for cash. In this way it is expected that those who wish to remain associated with a Boston National League club will have an opportunity to do so."[36] Adams would own no holdings in the team, in deference to Commissioner Landis and his hatred of all things gambling.

"If somebody bid a million dollars for the Braves and was acceptable for the National League, it would be grand," Adams said unrealistically. "That would give the stockholders something for themselves. I do not want the ball club and I never did want it. Yet, I am convinced that under proper management—and that does not mean any slashing economy in the matter of player salaries—the club should make money."[37]

The Quinn deal was completed in Chicago on December 10. "Mr. Quinn, in his proposal," Frick announced, "agrees to assume all the present balance sheet obligations of the defunct Boston Company and to provide sufficient additional working capital to put the club back on its feet." Quinn's was the only legitimate bid, with $75,000 as new capital from the bank and other investors, and the total purchase price being $400,000.[38] Quinn was given 10 years to pay Adams $325,000.[39] Adams lost $250,000 on the team.[40]

Quinn, often called "Honest Bob," was grateful for the opportunity. "I appreciate more than I can express the vote of confidence given me by each and every member of the National League and pledge myself to try in every way possible to help put the Boston Braves on a sound basis. The Bunker Hill Monument and Old State House on Beacon Hill will certainly be a most welcome sight and will give me a real thrill."[41]

Gerry Moore of the *Globe* called December 10, 1935, "the greatest day in the history of Boston baseball," but it had nothing to do with the Braves.[42] Quinn's greatest obstacle was still Tom Yawkey and his "magic pocketbook." While Quinn was signing papers, the opulent Yawkey was making trades.[43] Yawkey, who had already signed future Hall of Famer Bobby Doerr from the minors for $75,000, now dished out $150,000 for Jimmie Foxx and Johnny Marcum. He would later acquire Doc Cramer and Eric McNair from the Athletics for $175,000. "All are agreed that Yawkey now holds the position of the greatest spender in the history of baseball," wrote Moore. Yawkey had spent $3.5 million since 1932.[44] Quinn's purchase was overshadowed by Yawkey's trades.

The Braves survived the near collapse of 1935 when Bob Quinn (left) became president of the club, and he kept it solvent through the mid–1940s. His son John became the Braves' farm director and later succeeded his father as GM. Under John, the Braves won the 1948 NL pennant and later the World Series after the club relocated to Milwaukee (courtesy Boston Public Library, Leslie Jones Collection).

Wheeling and Dealing

Quinn took little time transforming the Braves, trading Ed Brandt and "Handy" Randy Moore to Brooklyn for four players: second baseman Tony Cuccinello, catcher Al Lopez, and pitchers Ray Benge and Bobby Reis. Two of them, Cuccinello and Lopez, helped an improved 1936 club.

Brandt went 94–119 for the Braves over eight seasons with a solid 3.86 ERA. Had he played for a better team, we may remember him as one of the best left-handers of his era. Brandt retired after the 1939 season. He returned to his native Spokane, Washington, and ran a hunting lodge and dude ranch before serving in the Army in World War II. He later ran a tavern. He and his fiancé were involved in a minor traffic accident in 1944. Brandt was in the road, talking to the driver of the other car, when an approaching vehicle struck and killed him at the age of 39.[45] He was the first member of the 1935 Braves to pass away.

Moore played only 42 games with Brooklyn in 1936 after breaking his leg and played even fewer games in 1937. He retired after 10 seasons, then returned to Texas and became a profitable rancher, oil investor, and bank executive. Casey Stengel invested in Moore's oil venture and became far wealthier than he ever did managing.[46]

Moore was a fishing buddy of Babe Ruth. "Babe's favorite post-game drink was simple," Moore recalled in 1979. "He'd fill a big glass with crushed ice and then fill it in again with Seagram's Seven. One day he had a waitress put seven of them on my bill. I thought I'd get even so I hid about a dozen of his big cigars under my mattress. He figured I did it, and I was so afraid he was going to kill me before I could get 'em back to him." The jokes aside, Moore had fond memories of Ruth, calling him "my all-time favorite baseball player. He was the greatest. He had more power than anybody I ever saw."[47]

Randy Moore died in 1992 at the age of 85.

Old Acquaintance Not Forgot

Quinn raised $200,000 in new capital and purchased 1,500 shares of Class A ($97 per share) and 4,500 shares of Class B stock ($1 per share). Quinn encouraged old stockholders to contribute $99,000 in total shares.[48]

On December 31, stockholders held a fiery meeting at the Copley-Plaza Hotel to officially dissolve the Boston National League Baseball Company. A total of 12,278 shares were represented out of the 15,000 total shares. There were 11,074 affirmative votes to authorize the sale or disposition of all assets of the company for liquidation and dissolution. There were 1,404 shares held by members who voted against this move at the three-hour meeting. Samuel Silverman, attorney for Major Murphy, objected to the sale and made a case for Murphy's reorganization plan. There would be no wishes for a happy new year at the end of the meeting.

Silverman had a check for $100,000 from Murphy and associates, who were prepared to buy the club for $250,000. Silverman stated that Murphy's plan was to retain Quinn under a better plan than Adams had, and there was no conflict with horse racing. Adams assured them he was not involved in the reorganization. Quinn arrived and affirmed Adams' plan. One member threatened to take Quinn on "at any time or place." Quinn was furious and exited the meeting, saying it was Adams' plan or nobody's.[49]

Some felt the old stockholders were getting a raw deal. Judge Fuchs, still a stockholder, was present and claimed he had lost $700,000 in the club, and said he felt morally responsible to those who bought stock from him. Fuchs believed these stockholders should have an extension until July to purchase new stock, "in the spirit of fair play."[50] Fuchs refused to cast the votes for the 1,000 proxies he had received. Adams denied the extension request. February 25 remained the deadline.[51]

"Thus," wrote James C. O'Leary in the *Globe*, "the Boston National League Baseball Company bows itself into retirement."[52] The Boston National League Baseball Company, the corporate entity of the Braves franchise, was incorporated in 1906. The previous entity, the Boston Baseball Association, was incorporated in 1871 when professional baseball was organized.[53]

Quinn sought a new identity, and a new Boston baseball organization was founded in early 1936. The 38–115 season was the end of an era, and Quinn looked ahead to better days for the franchise. "Bob Quinn," wrote Al Hirshberg, "one of the finest gentlemen the game has ever produced, was also one of the unluckiest. Everything he touched after 1922 turned to ashes, and most of what he touched in connection with big league baseball was in Boston."[54] Quinn had in mind a new name for the team, so the Braves, temporarily at least, faded into history.

Is that So....

Babe Ruth feared he was also fading from history. He had disappeared from the public eye and depended on golf for visibility. He was returning from golfing when he was involved in a hit-and-run accident near Rego Park in Queens in mid–November. He thought the damage was not more than a bump and sped home. The owner of the car, Max Katz of Queens, took down Ruth's license plate number and contacted the police, who set up a trap at the Queensboro Bridge.

Patrolman Abe Coleman was waiting with a rifle, expecting possible trouble from the driver of a Convertible Coupe. "Thrusting the rifle through the window," reported the *New York Tribune*, "he ordered the bulky driver to get out. Babe Ruth, looking menacing in cocoa-colored golf cap, suit, topcoat and shoes, climbed to the street and demanded to know what was going on." They went to the police station, and soon a crowd gathered upon hearing the Bambino had been arrested.

Katz didn't recognize him and gave Ruth a tongue-lashing while he chomped on a cigar. The two argued about how damaged Katz's car was and how much it would cost. They exchanged addresses, and someone told Katz Ruth was a famous ballplayer.

"Is that so?" he remarked.[55]

Little had changed by Christmas Eve, when Ruth was hanging his stocking by the mantlepiece of his New York apartment. "Nope! I'm not considering good offers right now," he said. The Bambino had played the role of baseball's Santa Claus, but now he depended on a club gifting him with a managerial position he had on his

Christmas list. "Nope! I have no plans. Don't know what I am going to do next year—probably just play golf." There were rumors of him teaching baseball in England or Japan, but Ruth had little interest. Did he want to stay in the game? "Sure would, rather than anything I know of," he said. "Baseball's been my life. But right now, I don't see how I'm going to do it."[56]

For both the Braves and Babe Ruth, 1935 ended as it began, with uncertainty.

13

Long Live the Boston Braves

"The club went to pieces, and as the seasons passed, the pieces kept getting smaller."—Harold Kaese

The Bees Buzzed: 1936–1941

Bob Quinn and other directors of the Boston Braves met at the law offices of Goodwin, Procter & Hoar on State Street in Boston on January 3, 1936. The Boston National League Baseball Company became Boston National Sports, Inc. The new corporation was to include not only baseball but also boxing, wrestling, football, polo, and other athletic and entertainment ventures.[1] Quinn also rebranded the Braves, asking fans to choose a replacement to the nickname they had since 1912.

"I never liked the nickname of the Braves," he declared. "Why should the Boston National League team carry a nickname which had its origin in the fact that a Tammany politician bought control of the team 22 or 23 years ago?" That was James Gaffney, the New York City businessman with strong ties to Tammany Hall, the center of New York's Democratic Party. Gaffney called the team "Braves," the nickname Tammany members were given, and adopted their Indian Head logo. "I'd like to have done the same thing to the nickname of the Dodgers in Brooklyn," Quinn said, "but never got around to it."[2]

Fans submitted their entries. Sportswriters also suggested nicknames: Beans, Terriers, Bags, Pilgrims, Puritans, Professors, Blues, or Nationals.[3] On January 30, Quinn met with the writers to choose the new nickname out of the 1,327 entries, which included Blue Birds, Beacons, Colonials, Bulldogs, Bulls, Braddocks, Codders, Garters, G-Men, Hubs, Lions, Tanks, Teddy Bears, Mark Twains, Rose Maries and Finasts, after Charles F. Adams' grocery chain. Thirteen of those votes were for Bees, the winning entry. Albert J. Rockwood, a sheet metal worker and father of nine from East Weymouth, Massachusetts, was the winner and recipient of season tickets. "If your club develops the bee characteristics," he wrote in his entry, "you should have honey this fall."[4] Uniforms were transformed from red and white to yellow and blue. Braves Field became National League Park with expectations that fans would call it the "Bee Hive."

Quinn continued to dismantle the disastrous 1935 team. Fred Frankhouse was traded to Brooklyn, where he would stay for two years before concluding his career back with the Bees in 1939. He retired to his native Port Royal, Pennsylvania, and ran a tree nursery. He could tell customers of that day in Pittsburgh when Babe Ruth hit three home runs. "That's the longest ball I ever saw hit," Frankhouse said of the third home run. "It was still rising when it left the park. What a man."[5] Frederick Meloy Frankhouse died in 1989 at the age of 85.

Pinky Whitney was traded to the Phillies. He would spend four seasons there and retire. He ran a bowling alley and become a brewing company salesman. He ran into Ruth in a hotel lobby on his honeymoon in Dallas and was invited to his suite to chat about the old days. "He was a grand, grand man," Whitney said.[6] Arthur Carter "Pinky" Whitney died in 1987 at the age of 82.

Joe Coscarart was traded away in July and never played in the majors again. "Coffee Joe" was not as notable as his brother Pete, but had stories to tell about Ruth for the rest of his life. "Even opposing players used to come out to batting practice to watch his swing," he said. "There'll only be one Ruth. Just to see him swing was a thrill. As Babe came around the bases (after that third home run in Pittsburgh) he said, 'The old guy can still hit 'em once in a while' and laughed. He's tops as far as I'm concerned."[7] Joseph Marvin Coscarart died in 1993 at the age of 83.

Bill McKechnie took "a patched-up team of nondescript athletes," in Al Hirshberg's description, and guided them to a much improved 71–83 record in 1936. The new additions of catcher Al Lopez and second baseman Tony Cuccinello paid dividends with improved pitching and fielding. Buck Jordan batted .323, and Wally Berger hit 25 home runs. Lopez helped Danny MacFayden win 17 games with a 2.87 ERA. Attendance rose to 340,585 fans who cheered on their sixth-place team. They were at least out of the gutter.[8]

After the 1936 season concluded, Tommy Thompson was traded to San Diego of the Pacific Coast League. He returned to the major leagues in 1938–1939 as a reserve outfielder for the White Sox and Browns, then was a player-manager in the minor leagues through 1953. One of his prized possessions was an autographed ball from Babe Ruth. Rupert Lockart "Tommy" Thompson died in 1971 at the age of 61.[9]

Also departing was backup catcher Bill "Buddy" Lewis, who played and managed in the minors until the mid–1940s. Lewis became a scout for the Cardinals for the next two decades of his 50+ years in the game and is credited with discovering Tim McCarver. William Henry Lewis died in 1977 at the age of 73.[10]

Ben Cantwell, a 25-game loser in 1935, and outfielder Hal Lee, their top hitter, were sent to the New York Giants for cash. "Somebody had to lose them," Cantwell recalled in 1960 of his 25 losses. "I just had the misfortune to be good enough to be a regular pitcher. And any regular pitcher for the 1935 Braves was bound to lose. I'll tell you how bad the Braves were in 1935. After my record of 4–25 that season, they didn't cut my salary a penny."[11] Cantwell finished in 1937 with the Giants and Dodgers. He later worked in shipbuilding before becoming a baseball instructor. Benjamin Caldwell Cantwell died in 1962 at the age of 60.[12]

Hal "Sheriff" Lee, the Braves' only regular to bat over .300 in 1935, never returned to the major leagues. He played and managed in the minors for eight seasons, then became a welding foreman in a shipyard. He replaced Ruth in his final game. Harold Burnham Lee died in 1989 at the age of 84.[13]

The 1937 Bees led the NL in ERA (3.22) and WHIP (1.262) and achieved a winning record of 79–73. The team batting average (.247) was the NL's worst, showing even more of McKechnie's managerial genius. Quinn continued to revamp. Billy Urbanski, Boston's regular shortstop from 1932 to 1936, was traded to the Giants. He played in the minors for three seasons and retired, opening a café. William Michael Urbanski died in 1973 at the age of 70.

Buck Jordan was dealt to Cincinnati. A solid contact hitter (.299 career) with a steady glove at first base, Jordan finished his 10-year career with the Phillies in 1938. Jordan struck out just once in every 27.34 at-bats, ranking him 35th all-time. Jordan had a lasting memory of Ruth. "He was the greatest thing that ever happened in baseball," he recalled in 1989. "I don't care how good you were, you were always in awe of Babe. And here I was, a guy from Cooleemee, North Carolina, on the same team. It was really something being with him. His knees were taped, and he had aches and pains. But Babe could drink and eat pretty good." Ruth once said of Jordan, "If I could swing the bat like you, I'd hit .500."[14] Baxter Byerly "Buck" Jordan died in 1993 at the age of 86.

Wally Berger, still 10th all-time in Braves home runs through 2021, was shipped off to the Giants at the June 15 trading deadline. Berger hit 12 home runs for the Giants and experienced the World Series as the Giants lost to the Yankees. Berger retired in 1939. He coached baseball for the Naval Air Training Station in San Diego during World War II, then worked for Northrop Corporation. Over 50 years later, he remembered Babe Ruth. "He was gone, his legs were gone, when he came to us, but in his day he used to hit even the balls he was fooled on so high that it was like catching a meteor. He found nothing difficult about hitting a pitched ball."[15] Walter Anton Berger died in 1988 at the age of 83.

Forty-two-year-old Bob Smith retired after the 1937 season. Smith went 83–120 over 11 seasons for Boston with a 4.06 ERA. He coached in the minor leagues in the 1940s and later ran a gas station in Atlanta.[16] Robert Eldridge Smith died in 1987 at the age of 92.

Bill McKechnie was *The Sporting News* Manager of the Year for 1937. "The honor, usually, is bestowed on the leader of a pennant winner," wrote Edward G. Brands, "but in putting the Bees as high as he did, Wilkinsburg Bill showed rare managerial skill and acumen that stamped him as a genius in handling men, especially pitchers. Always kindly and patient with his players, he makes them believe in him, opening the way for the youngster and easing the path for the veteran. McKechnie combines the spirit of a youngster and the canniness of a Scot."[17] What was his secret?

"Bill McKechnie can do more with less than any other manager in the majors," Fred Lieb wrote in *The Sporting News*.[18] McKechnie could find players through bargain-basement deals, focusing on control pitchers and defense to keep the Bees respectable. But his time in Boston had come to an end. McKechnie left to resurrect last-place Cincinnati. "There were actually tears in McKechnie's eyes when he was asked to speak," wrote Gerry Moore in the *Boston Globe* as McKechnie announced his decision.[19] In 1938, McKechnie guided the Reds to an improved fourth-place finish (82–68). The 1939–1940 Reds led the NL in ERA through his strategy. They won the 1939 NL pennant, losing to the Yankees in the World Series. In 1940, they beat the Tigers in the World Series. Unlike in Boston, McKechnie was able to rebuild a team all the way to the top.

Casey Stengel replaced McKechnie, but the Bees finished fifth, sixth, and seventh from 1938 to 1940. By 1940, no members of the 1935 club remained. The 1940 Red Sox were a power-hitting club featuring Ted Williams, Bobby Doerr, Joe Cronin, Jimmie Foxx, and Dom DiMaggio. They finished fourth (82–72) and drew 716,234 to Fenway Park. The Bees (65–87) drew only 241,616.

In December 1940, Charles F. Adams finally had a potential buyer for the Braves: coal magnate Albert Powell, who had owned stock in the team during the Fuchs years. Adams was willing to take a loss to be rid of the club. The deal fell through, however. But Quinn was building his own syndicate, which included Casey Stengel, who invested $50,000, and his friend, Max Meyer, who put in $40,000. Quinn and his son John invested, as did Lou Perini, Joe Maney, and Guido Rugo. There were so many investors, in fact, the joke was that there were more owners than newspaper writers at the bar. Quinn remained club president, and John became farm director.[20]

"The money is in the bank for Mr. Adams," Bob Quinn said, at long last. Commissioner Kenesaw Mountain Landis had renewed pressure on Adams to relinquish his assets due to his involvement in Suffolk Downs. "I found myself in an impossible situation with the ball club," Adams said. "I had to get out and I figured it was the best thing to give Bob [Quinn] the very best deal possible, which I did. It's OK with me if Bob is satisfied. His whole life is baseball, and I must admit that it has been an incident in mine."[21]

Adams' long baseball venture officially came to an end. He had already transferred ownership of the Boston Bruins to his son, Weston, in 1936. Adams and his business partner, V.C. Bruce Wetmore, sold their Suffolk Downs shares for $4 million in 1945. "Thus, the colorful career of the man who brought professional hockey to Boston," wrote Eddie Welch in the *Boston Globe*, "salvaged the Boston Braves at a time when the outlook was dark, and who incidentally took over the baseball situation as a matter of civic pride, and who was the directing genius of Suffolk Downs, comes to an end in Boston's sports world."[22]

Charles Francis "C.F." Adams died in 1947 at the age of 70. He was posthumously inducted into the Hockey Hall of Fame.

"The syndicate that bought Adams out in 1941 was too big," wrote Hirshberg.

"Quinn ran the ball club to the best of his ability, but he had to check with too many people before he could make a deal or spend any money."[23] Little changed for Quinn in 1941, financially or on the field, where the club again finished seventh (62–92). Well, one thing changed.

"I am heartily in favor of the change back to Braves," Quinn announced of the team nickname, "and I hope it will encourage our players to perform the way the famous Braves of 1914 did." But there was no "miracle" in these "new" Braves yet.[24]

Rebirth and Demise: 1942–1952

Pearl Harbor drew the U.S. into World War II, and baseball was depleted of its stars. The 1942–1943 Braves finished seventh and sixth. On January 21, 1944, Quinn called a press conference. Lou Perini, Guido Rugo, and Joe Maney, three wealthy contractors who had been team stockholders since 1941, were buying out the other stockholders. Called the "Three Little Steam Shovels," the trio pumped money into the franchise and retained Quinn for the 1944 season.[25] Stengel was out. He, like McKechnie, would end up in the Hall of Fame as a manager who made a stop with the Braves.

Bob Coleman managed the Braves to a sixth-place finish in 1944, and the next February Bob Quinn resigned as general manager at the age of 75. John Quinn replaced his father, and Bob replaced him as farm director for one season. The Braves finished the 1945 season 67–85, again in sixth place. Bob Quinn retired at the end of the season. He had stabilized the Braves following Fuchs' departure and kept the team afloat for a decade.[26]

The post-war years saw a boom in baseball attendance everywhere. The Red Sox's attendance grew from 603,794 in 1945 to 1.4 million in 1946, and the Braves' attendance grew from 374,178 to 969,673. Perini installed lights at Braves Field, but the Red Sox were still Boston's team, winning the pennant (their first since Babe Ruth) and losing a heartbreaking World Series to the Cardinals. The Braves rebounded to finish fourth (81–72), then improved to third place in 1947 (86–68), hitting a new attendance record of over 1.2 million.

The 1948 season had a tremendous amount of interest in Boston. Perini installed a new electric scoreboard at Braves Field. In May, several Braves players gathered for a radio program held at Children's Hospital in Boston to visit a young cancer patient nicknamed "Jimmy." The program raised money for children's cancer research. The Jimmy Fund was born, and its influence continues to the present day. WBZ became Boston's first television station on June 9, 1948, and within a week televised the first baseball game in Boston at Braves Field. The unthinkable happened that season as both Boston teams seemed destined to play each other in the World Series. The Braves drew 1.4 million, the Red Sox 1.5 million.[27]

The Braves won the 1948 National League pennant with a team built by the

Quinns, either through John leading the farm system or Bob wheeling and dealing. The team included: Earl Torgeson, Eddie Stanky, Alvin Dark, Bob Elliott, Tommy Holmes, Warren Spahn, and Johnny Sain. The Red Sox and Cleveland tied for the AL pennant, and Cleveland won the one-game playoff. A Boston-Boston World Series never happened. Braves Field hosted Game One of the World Series, Braves against Cleveland, on October 5.

It seemed that 1935 and 1948 were connected as people gathered for the Series. Bob Quinn, who had never seen the Braves finish higher than fifth, shook hands with his son, John, who had a pennant winner. Lou Perini shook hands with Judge Fuchs, who had never seen such success. Bill McKechnie was also there as a member of the Cleveland coaching staff, telling stories whenever prompted.[28] Cleveland won the Series, four games to two. It seemed a new day had dawned in Braves history. Perini, unsuccessful in exploring plans for a new stadium in suburban Boston, purchased Braves Field outright, which had been leased from the Gaffney Estate.

No one realized that the end of the Boston Braves was near. "No sooner had a pennant been won," wrote Harold Kaese, "than the club went to pieces, and as the seasons passed, the pieces kept getting smaller." Kaese referred to the 1948 pennant as "the last convulsive effort of a dying giant, the last flaming eruption of a volcano before it becomes a clinker."[29] The Red Sox continued to have strong attendances topping one million customers per season, while the Braves steadily dropped. They drew barely over one million in 1949 and dropped to 944,391 in 1950, both fourth-place finishes. The Braves had the 1950 Rookie of the Year, speedster Sam "The Jet" Jethroe, the first black player in Boston. Yawkey would finally integrate the Red Sox nine years later, the last team to do so.

The Braves also brought back two players still around from the 1935 team.

High school senior Elbie Fletcher won a contest to play with the Braves in spring training 1934.

He returned in 1935 and met Babe Ruth. "We were all awed by his presence," Fletcher remembered. "He still had that marvelous swing, and what a follow-through, just beautiful, like a great golfer. But he was forty years old. He couldn't run, he could hardly bend down for a ball, and of course he couldn't hit the way he used to. It was sad to watch those great skills fading away. And to see it happening to Babe Ruth, to see Babe Ruth struggling on a ball field, well, then you realize we're all mortal and nothing lasts forever."[30] Fletcher was the Braves' regular first baseman in 1937–1938, then was sent to Pittsburgh, where he remained through 1947. He returned to the Braves in 1949, retired, and became Parks Commissioner in his hometown of Milton, Massachusetts.[31] Elburt Preston Fletcher died in 1994 at the age of 77.

Ray Mueller was a rookie catcher on the 1935 Braves, and he remembered Ruth's three home runs in Pittsburgh. "I can remember Babe standing at the batting cage that day at Forbes Field," Mueller remembered in 1957, "waiting his turn at practice when the bell rang for the end of the drill. Guy Bush stood nearby yelling 'Let him

Elbie Fletcher was the Bees' regular first baseman in 1937–1938 and also returned to the club in 1949 (courtesy Boston Public Library, Leslie Jones Collection).

hit. I'd like to see one go over the roof.' When Babe hit one over the right-field roof, Bush was doing the pitching. He saw it, all right."[32] Mueller earned the nickname "Iron Man" by catching all 155 games for the 1944 Reds and having a streak of 233 consecutive games behind the plate. Mueller, the last member of the 1935 club to be active, ended his 14-year career with the Braves in 1951. He was still

Infielder Joe Coscarart with the Bees in 1936 (courtesy Boston Public Library, Leslie Jones Collection).

Ray Mueller (right) was a rookie for the 1935 Braves. He returned in 1951 to finish his career. Vern Bickford was one of his pitchers (courtesy Boston Public Library, Leslie Jones Collection).

active in the game in the 1970s as a scout for the Phillies.[33] Ray Coleman Mueller died in 1994 at the age of 82.

The fourth-place Braves saw attendance drop dramatically in half in 1951 to 487,475, while the Red Sox drew 1.3 million. Broadcasting was a major factor. Yawkey hired Curt Gowdy to broadcast Red Sox games home and away. "It didn't take long," wrote Charlie Bevis, "to determine the preference among the Braves-leaning general baseball fans who followed both teams. Given the choice between (a) attending a Braves home game, listening to the game on radio, or watching it on television and (b) listening to a Red Sox road game on radio, most of the dual-supporting fans picked option (b) to tune into the radio. This was devastating to the Braves, as the voice of Gowdy doing Red Sox road games on the radio siphoned off general baseball fans."[34]

The Braves suffered an awful 1952 season in which they drew just 281,278 while the Red Sox drew 1.1 million. Perini lost half a million dollars on the seventh-place club. Some saw the writing on the wall. "One of these days," wrote Kaese, "the Braves may go on the road and never come back."[35]

"I'm not going to be stubborn about this thing," Perini said at the end of the 1952 season. "I don't intend to spend 10 years here when people don't want to see

Catcher Bill Lewis (left), with Al Lopez and the Bees in 1936 (courtesy Boston Public Library, Leslie Jones Collection).

the Braves. This season has been a nightmare." Many cities were itching for a major league club, including Milwaukee, where Perini owned the Braves' Triple-A affiliate. "They [Milwaukee] have a stadium now that can be enlarged to seat 80,000," he said. "The Braves can't stand in the way of Milwaukee becoming a major league city."[36]

Perini had already decided to move the team to Milwaukee. In late November, he and his brothers bought out all remaining Braves stockholders.[37] The Braves left for spring training in 1953 and never returned to the city they had called home since 1871. It was a successful move, business-wise, for the Massachusetts-born Perini. The Milwaukee Braves led the NL in attendance through the end of the decade and never had a losing season until after moving to Atlanta in 1966. They won the World Series in 1957 and the NL pennant in 1958. If the Braves had remained in Boston just one more season, Hank Aaron would have been a Boston product. It doesn't take much to dream about Aaron breaking Babe Ruth's home run record with the same Boston Braves Ruth had finished his career with nearly 40 years before. But it wasn't to be. Still, the Atlanta Braves won the 2021 World Series as they celebrated the 150th anniversary of the franchise.

"I have absolutely no criticism of Lou Perini for moving the team," Judge Fuchs said in 1958. "There is nothing more tragic than to be playing to almost empty seats in a ballpark that holds almost 45,000 people. He is a practical and good businessman, something that I lay no claim to."[38]

14

Living for the Kids

"It didn't take a student of human nature or a mind reader to know that deep down inside he was a big, lonely man waiting for the day when he could break loose from the memories for the glories of today."—Paul Mickelson, on Babe Ruth

"I've always been for the youth of America, and I will be till the day I die."—Babe Ruth

"It is the story of a man who is much greater nearing the trail's end of glory than he ever was when hitting his 714 home runs and giving a vast nation the greatest thrills that sport has ever know."—Grantland Rice

"I wanted to stay in baseball more than I ever wanted anything in my life," Babe Ruth told ghostwriter Bob Considine. "I felt completely lost at first. I thought I'd wake up and find it was a bad dream, and when it became apparent that it wasn't a dream, I felt certain that the phone would ring, and it would be the Yankees or some other big-league team in search of me—telling me it was all a mistake.

"But the phone didn't ring."[1]

Babe Ruth thought attending ball games would snap him out of his post-playing depression, but it made him worse. He remembered who he used to be. He wanted to be on the field and didn't know where else to go. He went to St. Petersburgh and was cheered just sitting in the stands. "I'd stand up in my box and wave," he said. "The people were kind and would cheer, and I'd sit down—wishing I could get out there and really give them something to cheer about." Golf was his only savior. "Without it," he said, "I would have gone nuts."[2]

He celebrated his 42nd birthday (thinking he was 43) at his apartment in 1937. He continued to celebrate the incorrect birth date of February 7, 1894, originally given him, instead of the correct date his sister discovered: February 6, 1895.[3] His exact age didn't matter, but whether he felt alive at all. Paul Mickelson of the Associated Press observed Ruth's demeanor.

"He was jovial, but it didn't take a student of human nature or a mind reader to know that deep down inside he was a big, lonely man waiting for the day when he could break loose from the memories for the glories of today." Claire brought out his cake with a single rose that a fan sent him. "Babe gets about 300 letters every day, even now, from fans around the country" she said.[4]

Ruth stared at the cake. "I can't tell you whether I'm just beginning to live," he said somberly. "If it's okay with everyone, I'd just as soon be 21 again."[5]

"I know no words for his despondency," Claire wrote. "He kept himself busy with his hunting and fishing and golf. Whenever he entered the house there was always the same unspoken question plastered all over his big, tanned face. 'Any phone calls?'"

"Oh, how I hated baseball and everything in it in those days," she said.[6]

Ruth attended the annual baseball writers' dinner that month. "I gave the best years of my life, 22 of them, to the big leagues," he said, "but just when it seemed to me I was at the top, why, I was dumped out. Baseball's my game. I don't know what I would do without golf now, but my life has always been devoted to baseball. I would be willing to give the next 25 years to the game, even if it killed me."[7]

The Phone Finally Rang: 1938

When Ruth came back one night from a fishing trip, Claire told him there *had* been a phone call, from Larry MacPhail, Dodgers GM. Ruth was overcome with

Ruth returned to Braves Field in 1938 as the Dodgers' first base coach (courtesy Boston Public Library, Leslie Jones Collection).

anxiety. "What's he want? What's his telephone number? Where is he? How'd the Dodgers do today?" Ruth visited MacPhail and returned with glee. Ruth was wanted to coach first base and put on a show during batting practice to draw fans. "I'll be the manager next year!" Ruth bellowed.

"It had been years since I had seen my husband so happy," wrote Claire. "Many years."[8]

The job was merely a public relations gimmick, but Ruth was desperate, settling for a $15,000 contract instead of the $25,000 he requested. Ruth assumed the job would lead to becoming manager the following year, just as he had thought in 1935. Ruth had hope and purpose. Leo Durocher didn't care.

"Leo the Lip," Dodgers shortstop, was Ruth's teammate on the Yankees in the late 1920s, and the two never got along. Their hostility continued into 1938. Durocher blamed Ruth for messing up signs at first base, and the two had an altercation in the clubhouse. Word of the incident came out during the World Series. Ruth hoped to replace Burleigh Grimes as manager, but he was never even considered. The job went to Durocher.

"Babe was crushed," Claire wrote. "He had done everything they asked of him, and it hadn't been enough. He sat in the kitchen, head in hands, crying once again. He was out of baseball. And this time he hadn't even had the privilege of quitting. He was fired."[9]

Ruth lost more than a job, he also lost the community and sense of belonging he longed for.

"He couldn't get enough of people," Ruth's granddaughter, Donna Analovitch, said decades later, "but I don't know if he was ever attached to anything other than his fans and the game. And I don't think he had to have it because he was an egomaniac. I think he had to have it … for that sense of family." She thought Ruth spent his life as if he were looking into the windows of other people's lives. "He really related to his fans on a level of his pals or his mom or his pop. You have all these people, but you can't be close to any of them. They're not yours; they're not your people. You get to enjoy them and then they go home to their family, their parents, siblings, wives. And there he is alone again."[10]

The game had rejected him again, and he felt ostracized from his community. Hunting, fishing, and golfing at least distracted him from his emptiness. "Although only in his early forties," his daughter Dorothy recalled, "he was a forgotten man, relegated to listening to games on the radio. At home, he often managed from his armchair, calling the plays, and making the substitutions before they happened. There should have been a job for him somewhere in baseball, but baseball's attitude was, out of sight, out of mind."[11]

Ruth no longer felt useful. "Ruth was a kind of ornament, a living shrine, a walking reliquary of baseball records," Marshall Smelser wrote. "He found it very hard being a Grand Old Man in his early forties."[12]

"My Old Game Does Not Appear to Want Me": 1939–1945

Ruth still hoped for a managerial job in 1939, but mortality overshadowed everything. His old boss, Colonel Jacob Ruppert, died in January. The two had a rocky relationship over the years, but Ruth's deathbed visit brought the home run king to uncontrollable tears as he ran from the room. "It was the only time in his life he called me 'Babe' to my face," Ruth said.[13]

On the Fourth of July, Ruth attended Lou Gehrig's farewell at Yankee Stadium after learning of his terminal disease. Ruth and Gehrig hadn't spoken in several years. Ruth, in his white linen suit, teared up when speaking of the old days. Gehrig gave his famous "luckiest man" speech, Ruth came over and put his arm around him, and the two smiled. "Damn it," said Ruth later. "I wanted to laugh and cheer him up. I wound up crying like a baby."[14]

Ruth attended the first Hall of Fame induction ceremony in 1939, stealing the show "from the moment he stepped from the train and spread his infectious grin over the crowd," wrote Robert C. McCormick of the Associated Press. He autographed anything fans would bring him, while Ty Cobb walked around unnoticed. "It was like the old days," Ruth said. "My arm got terribly tired writing so many autographs. I didn't know there were so many people who didn't have my signature."

"Gee," gasped a 10-year-old boy, "ain't the Babe wonderful?"[15]

Ruth, boxer Tony Galento, and the comedy duo of Abbott & Costello dressed in Santa Claus costumes to hand out food to the needy at Jimmy Kelly's Montmartre in Greenwich Village just before Christmas.[16] Ruth's weight neared 270, perfect for playing Santa, but he suffered a mild heart attack while golfing that year. He contracted a cold while hunting in Canada and was in bed for a week.[17] Ruth made headlines in 1941 for playing against Cobb in charity golf tournaments.[18] Then came Pearl Harbor. An infuriated Ruth threw all his Japanese souvenirs out his apartment window on Riverside Drive. "To say he was upset would be putting it mildly," his daughter Julia recalled over 70 years later.[19]

Gehrig died in 1941, and Ruth signed on to play himself in *The Pride of the Yankees* film about Gehrig's life starring Gary Cooper. Ruth lost nearly 50 pounds in binge dieting to look like the Ruth of old. The strain was too much. He collapsed in January 1942 and was taken to the hospital. He was pronounced fit and made the trip to Hollywood for the filming. In April, he was again rushed to the hospital, suffering from pneumonia, with the *Los Angeles Times* reporting Ruth was "fighting for life."[20] He recovered, finished filming, and was back in New York by the end of April.

Ruth stayed busy during World War II doing events for the Red Cross, promoting war bonds, and golfing. All proceeds from a Yankees-Senators doubleheader at Yankee Stadium on August 23, 1942, went to the war effort. A special feature between games was a hitting exhibition with Ruth batting against Walter Johnson. It was Ruth's first time at the plate in the stadium built for him since he left in 1934.[21] There was "deafening applause" from the near-70,000 on hand, James P. Dawson wrote in the *New York Times*, as the two legends took the field. Ruth fretted that he couldn't hit any more but hit he did … into the third deck. It landed foul but Ruth trotted the bases anyway. He doffed his cap, "in that old familiar salute to the cheering throng, his moon-like face spread in a grin."[22] Claire said the huge crowd sensed "how very, very much Babe Ruth had wanted to do just what he had done."[23] "I'm sure glad Ruth busted one," the ever-humble Johnson said of the moment.[24] Everyone needed it.

The event raised $80,000, but Ruth's joy was fleeting. "There was a kind of sadness in both of us," Ruth said. "It's hard to be on the outside of something you love. Just looking in doesn't help."[25] Even with the game stripped of talent during World War II, no club owner was willing to invest in the attraction Ruth could provide. Crowds still loved him wherever he went. "I felt that the public was as bewildered over my absence from baseball as I was," he said.[26] Ruth bowled for charity and spoke at movie theaters about war bonds. "I think we should get behind those men and women who are striving to make a living for us over there," he said. "We should stick behind them and buy war bonds and stamps."[27]

Ruth returned to Boston on July 12, 1943, for Boston Mayor Maurice J. Tobin's annual field day to benefit underprivileged children and wounded soldiers. Ruth visited the Braves Field press box "chewing on a big, black cigar and extending his mammoth paw to one and all alike," wrote Fred Barry in the *Boston Globe*.[28] Ruth managed Ted Williams and other military personnel, including Dom DiMaggio, against the Braves in an exhibition game at Fenway Park. Rabbit Maranville and other old-timers showed up. The highlight was a pregame hitting contest between the chubby Ruth and the stringbean Williams. Williams slammed three home runs to right field in the contest, one of them landing 15 rows behind the bullpen. Ruth took comfort in the thousands of children, too young to have seen him play, cheering him on. Ruth desperately wanted to hit home runs for them. He swung mightily but never got in a groove. He fouled a ball off his foot and gimped off to a tremendous ovation. Ruth inserted himself as a pinch-hitter in the game, popping out to second. "Fat and forty-eightish," the Associated Press wrote, "but still fabulous."[29] Ruth's all-stars defeated the Braves, 9–8.

At the end of July, Ruth managed a "Yanklands" mixed team of Yankees and Cleveland players against the Navy pre-flight school "Cloudbusters" from North Carolina, which included Williams, Johnny Sain, and Johnny Pesky. The charity event at Yankee Stadium was a fundraiser for the Red Cross. The managerial role was "one brief moment of glory in the role he sought so eagerly before becoming baseball's forgotten man," wrote Oscar Fraley in the *Brooklyn Citizen*.[30] Ruth drew cheers like days of old "from the minute he stuck his graying head out of the dugout and doffed his cap" wrote Harold C. Burr in the *Brooklyn Daily Eagle*.[31] A crowd of 27,281 watched the contest and donated $30,000. Ruth put himself up to pinch-hit "while the flashlight bulbs of the cameramen exploded like flares all around his massive form," Burr wrote. Ruth walked when he "gets his belly out of the way of an outside pitch" mused the *Daily News*. A single sent Ruth huffing and puffing to second, limping on a bad ankle. He had enough. His club was defeated, 11–5, and it was his last appearance in a game.[32]

At the end of August, a charity event drew 40,000 to the Polo Grounds. Soldiers from Camp Cumberland, including Hank Greenberg and Enos Slaughter, played the "War Bond Team" loaded with major leaguers. Stars of stage and screen included Ethel Merman, Jimmy Cagney, and Milton Berle, and several bands, including Cab Calloway's, performed. But they were overshadowed by a group of old-time ballplayers. "There were still 35,000 lumps in 35,000 throats around the village today," wrote the Associated Press, "all because a dozen old men walked out on a ball field." They took their familiar places on the field. George Sisler, Eddie Collins, Honus Wagner, Frankie Frisch, Tris Speaker, Duffy Lewis, Red Murray, Roger Bresnahan, manager Connie Mack, umpire Bill Klem, Walter Johnson, and of course, Ruth. He faced Johnson again, hitting weak pop flies the old-timers struggled to corral. Then he smashed a Johnson pitch into the right field seats. "That was the icing on the cake," the Associated Press wrote.[33]

Over 300 wounded soldiers and sailors were there as invited guests. Ruth signed collars on sailors and the cast on a wounded soldier's leg. The four-hour program concluded as 75 automobiles arrived to transport them home. They had witnessed Babe Ruth's last home run in a major league ballpark.

Another birthday rolled around in 1944, and Ruth was seen lounging in his pajamas. "He's a gentleman of unwanted leisure," wrote Whitney Martin of Ruth, who looked like "he had been invited to a pot-luck supper and swallowed the pot." He was still restless as a caged bear and had no ambition to talk about it. The phone rang.

"I'm not in," Babe said.

"It's so-and-so," Claire told him, her ear to the phone. "They want to wish you a happy birthday."

Babe lumbered across the room to take the call. He returned. "Better order more cheese for tonight. I suppose 40 or 50 will show up for the party."[34]

Babe and Claire wanted a quiet celebration, but around 60 guests soon arrived at his Riverside Drive apartment. Babe cut the cake, but as he sliced, he clumsily knocked it onto the floor and it landed with a plop, frosting side down. Servants retrieved it, but whether guests were served any of the fallen sweet is unknown. This truly took the cake. This birthday held less promise than his 1936 one. He still had no place in the game and no direction for his life. Japanese soldiers had adopted an audible war cry: "To hell with Babe Ruth."[35] Ruth wanted to entertain the troops as a measure of revenge, but doctors warned that his legs couldn't handle it. He had recently had cartilage removed from his right knee and somehow thought he could return to the game as a pinch-hitter.[36] Claire would have none of that.

Ruth refereed a couple of pro wrestling matches in April of 1945. "I've been out of baseball for 11 years now," he said, "and since my old game does not seem to want me anywhere, I haven't had much chance to keep in touch with the crowds. I like being with people and enjoying them and I'll have an opportunity to see them as a wrestling referee." The gigs weren't for the money. "He does need the excitement, the crowds, the interviews, the feeling of belonging to the public again," wrote Jerry Nason in the *Globe*. "He needs those things because he is those things."[37]

In 1946, Ruth was still hopeful for a job with the Yankees, who were now run by Larry MacPhail. Ruth contacted him, offering to manage Newark, but MacPhail delayed in responding.[38] The request was denied, and MacPhail irreverently suggested that Ruth could try organizing sandlot games around Manhattan.[39]

"Babe walked into the kitchen, numb," Claire wrote. "It was the same old kitchen where he had sat before on a chair, head in hands, and wept in fury and frustration. He wept once again."[40]

Ruth's dream of managing was over. Soon, he was fighting for his life.

Babe's First and Last Love: 1946–1948

Ruth experienced a sharp pain over his left eye which he attributed to sinuses. It didn't ease up, and in November 1946 he was in French Hospital. He was soon unable to raise his left eyelid, swallow, or speak. He was operated on January 5, 1947. Surgeons tied off an artery in his neck to try and relieve the pain. Ruth had a rare cancer, nasopharyngeal, in the air passages behind his nose and mouth, and a mass had formed at the base of his skull. The operation couldn't remove all the tumor. He lost 80 pounds, lost his voice, and his hair fell out in clumps due to the radiation. "I couldn't believe it, at first," Ruth said. "Lying in that little room I often felt so alone that the tears would run helplessly down my cheeks. But then Claire began bringing in some letters." There were 30,000 of them, many of them written in pencil.[41] The simple words of cheer from children gave him motivation to go on. Ruth remained hospitalized for weeks. Commissioner Happy Chandler came to visit him. "Babe, you are Mr. Baseball," he said. "I'm going to say a little prayer for you." They both wept.[42]

Ruth celebrated his 52nd birthday in the hospital, cheered by "Pal," his large brown boxer who kept him company in bed.[43] He was released from the hospital on February 15, helped to the car while a crowd of 100 cheered.[44] A month later, he was rejuvenated and golfing in Queens. He also spent a couple of weeks back in Florida, golfing and catching a 50-pound sailfish in Miami Beach.[45]

There was a cure, of sorts, for Ruth, who had felt rejected since 1935 by the game he loved. Ford Motor Company offered him a job as a consultant to promote the American Legion Junior Baseball Program. Ruth finally had purpose. He could travel the country, meeting and inspiring young ballplayers who reminded him of his younger self. He could take long treks to visit those who meant the most to him— kids. Ruth said he wanted to:

Help the kids of America by spending the rest of my life teaching them baseball. They call me a "consultant," but I'm going to work as hard on this program as my health will permit. It's a great responsibility. I love kids. They're the cause of my getting as far as I did. Naturally, they couldn't swing that bat for me, but their encouragement put me up so high. I'm getting pretty old, and I want to keep doing the right thing by them. I've always been for the youth of America, and I will be till the day I die.[46]

Children were always close to Ruth's heart, from the very beginning. "He loved kids and kids loved him," wrote Richard C. Crepeau. "He was in fact a kid himself: the child-man playing a children's game and getting paid enormous sums of money. He frolicked like a child and defied the rules of the baseball establishment like a perpetual adolescent."[47]

Ruth returned to Yankee Stadium on April 27, declared "Babe Ruth Day" in all major league ballparks. Speeches were made honoring him before 58,000 fans and a worldwide audience. One was from youngster Larry Cutler, chosen to speak on behalf of the American Legion youth ballplayers, the masses of children who inspired Ruth to keep going.

I guess there are thousands of 13-year-old fellows like myself in this country who have heard about Babe Ruth ever since the first time they learned there was such a game as baseball. It's a great honor to be here. Just to be able to tell Babe Ruth how proud we are to have him back in baseball. Back where he belongs. To know that Babe Ruth is going to be with us kids, well, that's the biggest and best thing that could happen in baseball. From all of us kids, Babe, it's swell to have you back.[48]

The frail Ruth, victim of radiation treatments which had taken his hair, spoke in a short, raspy speech.

You know how bad my voice sounds. Well, it feels just as bad. You know, this baseball game of ours comes up from the youth. That means the boys. And after you're a boy and grow up to know how to play ball, then you come to the boys you see representing themselves today in your national pastime. The only real game—I think—in the world, baseball. As a rule, some people think if you give them a football, or a baseball, or something like that—naturally they're athletes right away. You can't do that with baseball. You've got to start from way down, at the bottom, when you're six or seven years of age. You can't wait until you're fifteen or sixteen. You gotta let it grow up with you. And if you're successful, and you try hard enough, you're bound to come out on top—just like these boys have come out on top now.

Ruth thanked the crowd.

He was an "older, grayer, no longer the robust Babe," Louis Effrat wrote in the *New York Times*. Some feared he would be too choked up to get through his words, but those who surrounded him were the most choked up. "He trudged slowly back to the dugout," Claire remembered, "his eyes filling with tears as he listened to the roaring salute which fans fired back at him. And this time Babe did not cry alone—not by many, many thousands did he cry alone."[49] It was a sacred moment.

Ruth's first stop on his tour was Syracuse in early June. He was exhausted from the flight yet was glad to see some youngsters who sneaked past security for autographs. He was "fatherly in his attitude towards the youngsters," wrote Ed Reddy in the *Post-Standard*, "and his flashing smile evidenced a break in the strain for himself as he relaxed."[50]

His pain worsened later that month. Ruth was given one of the first clinical trials of both chemotherapy and radiation, with daily injections of Teropterin. Fifty years later, Lawrence K. Altman, M.D., reported in the *New York Times* that "knowledge gained from his [Ruth's] case helped shape the combination therapy that is now standard for his disease."[51] The treatments likely extended Ruth's life for another year. He gained 20 pounds, and the mass in his neck disappeared. The *Wall Street Journal* prematurely announced that a cure for cancer was near.[52]

Ruth flew to Detroit for the American Legion Junior All-Star Game at Briggs Stadium, which attracted over 13,000 fans on June 22. Ruth whispered a few words of encouragement to the youth, but the bigger noise came from ovations for him. The day before, his open car was mobbed by autograph seekers when he arrived to watch some golf.[53] The trip was too much for him, and he ended up back in Mt. Sinai Hospital in New York for the rest of June. "I even get tired taking a walk around my living room," he dejectedly said.[54] He attended the Dodgers-Giants game on July 2 and saw rookie Jackie Robinson, who broke baseball's color barrier in April. He remained unnoticed until Shorty Laurice's "Sym-phony" band played "For He's a Jolly Good Fellow," and the crowd rose to their feet.[55]

Ruth visited children in Dallas. "After we reach a certain age," he said, "when we figure we are no good to ourselves—well, we can turn around and help somebody else, like the kids of America."[56] The flight on July 8 wore him down. "The eyes that once picked out home run pitches," wrote Felix R. McNight in the *Dallas Morning News*, "are deep pools. The bull shoulders that rocketed 714 home runs out of major league parks are bent and sloped. The massive frame is slender and stooped and the hair is grey. The voice is raspy and the slight coughs frequent. But the heart? Bigger than ever." Ruth greeted five-year-old Carlton Crittenden in the hotel lobby and put his hand around the boy's arm. "Gee fellow!" Ruth bellowed. "That muscle is just like the size of the handle on my old bat!"[57] He arrived to cheers at the ballpark in a Ford-provided, lemon-colored convertible.[58]

Ruth was mobbed in Houston on July 10. He teared up talking about his career. He wished "I could do it all over again."[59] He returned home for a couple of weeks before heading to Montgomery, Alabama, on July 24. "I wish I could talk to you more than a few minutes," he said, "but my trip from New York today has been long and tiresome." Patrolmen cleared a path for Babe and Claire, who clambered into a convertible following his speech. A youngster sneaked through the crowd and found his way to the Bambino. He stuck his hand out to the Babe, who smiled and clasped the boy's hand. "He shook the Babe's hand," wrote Max Moseley of the *Montgomery Advertiser*, "and a huge grin was spread across the kid's face."[60] Ruth attended an American Legion game at Shibe Park in Philadelphia at the end of July. He was greeted by a teary-eyed Connie Mack and an ovation from the crowd of 10,000, mostly youngsters.[61] The excursion was again too much for him, and he returned to the hospital for a blood transfusion, forcing him to miss a game in Paterson, New Jersey, and a planned visit to a paralyzed girl.[62] He sent her an autographed picture, and she sent him jewelry she made for him. Against the wishes of his doctors, Ruth kept his promise to visit Cincinnati and Indianapolis, where large crowds applauded him.[63]

As time went on, Ruth's became more reflective on his life's journey, perhaps sensing that his time was short. "During those long nights in the 11 months that I was battling for my life," he wheezed at a luncheon in Chicago on August 15, "I kept telling myself I've lived my life. I told myself, too, to pass that life on to the kids I love." He sat down and wept. The room was deathly quiet while guests wiped away tears.[64]

Ruth watched an American Legion game at Comiskey Park and stayed for a few days in the Windy City, then flew off to Montana. He made a brief 45-minute stop at the airport in Minneapolis to change planes, but that was enough time for a press conference. When he finished, a little kid appeared in front of him, asking for an autograph. "Babe obliged and broke into his biggest grin of the morning," the *Minneapolis Star* said. "There's no one who can pat a kid on the head quite like Babe Ruth."[65]

Ruth wore a 10-gallon hat when he arrived in Billings, Montana, on August 19. He took a stagecoach ride to downtown and was exhausted, so he rested before the evening banquet. He had time to reflect again on the past year and spoke a few words. "Lying in the hospital gives a fellow a chance to think," he said. "I said to myself, 'What can I do with the rest of my life?' The answer was, help the kids. And that's what I'm trying to do." He closed with a voice barely beyond a whisper. "I've lived my life. Now I'm living a new life—and that's for you kids."[66]

Ken Davenport was a 19-year-old who worked as a sales manager at the Mercury car dealership in Billings owned by Hall-of-Famer Mickey Cochrane, who had been given the dealership by Henry Ford himself. Davenport chauffeured Ruth to Cobb Field in a black Mercury Convertible. Ruth had a box of autographed baseballs with him to hand out to the Legion players. Davenport believed one of those players sold their ball years later for $104,000. He regrets not asking for one.[67] "These boys are preparing to take my place and the places in organized baseball of yesterday's stars," Ruth told the crowd.[68]

Ruth spoke honestly at a stopover in Spokane, Washington. "Before I got sick," he said, "I sort of hankered for a manager's job with a good club somewhere. But now, since I'm slowed up a little, I'm going to spend my time teaching the American kids the value of baseball. I used to be ambitious for a managerial post somewhere. But I'm not anymore. I'm happy [doing] just what I'm doing."[69]

Ruth arrived in San Francisco on August 22 and held a press conference. He was "gaunt and drawn," Prescott Sullivan of the *San Francisco Examiner* observed, "and there wasn't much meat on that broad face of his. He coughed repeatedly behind a big, boney hand, and his voice was hoarse and whispered." But his eyes sparkled when asked about working with kids. "It's a wonderful job," he beamed. "More than that, it is the answer to a prayer." Ruth had done some thinking in the hospital.

"Then it came to me. If I ever get well, I'd devote the rest of my life to kids. And I did get well … well enough, anyway, to leave that hospital … and then, as if in answer to my prayer, the Ford Company created for me the very opportunity I wanted … the opportunity to be with kids. How do I like my job? It's a wonderful job. A wonderful job!"[70]

An emotional, raucous crowd of 12,000 greeted Ruth at Seals Stadium, escorted by the Marine Corps Color Guard. "The big guy loved every minute of it," wrote Bob Brachman in the *San Francisco Examiner*. "From the time he arrived in a trim, low cut Lincoln Continental until he reluctantly departed in the seventh inning of the second game, the Sultan of Swat literally bathed in the 'tonic' that his doctors say only kids can give him." Ruth turned to Claire and asked, "Isn't this wonderful?" Six-year-old "Babe" Francis presented a scroll to Ruth on behalf of the Boys Clubs of San Francisco. His uniform was too big, and his hat kept sliding off. Ruth picked it up, put it back on the youngster's head, and gave a bear-like pat.[71] "I was lying in my hospital bed thinking about the future," he said to the crowd. "I decided one thing right there and then. I can live for the kids."[72]

Ruth flew to Los Angeles for the Junior American Legion's "Little World Series." Braven Dyer in the *Los Angeles Times* wrote, "the Ford Motor Co. deserves an assist for keeping the Babe alive. Nobody in organized baseball had anything for Ruth to do, apparently, but whoever thought of tying him in with the kids deserves a medal."[73] A Legion Post team from Cincinnati won the championship, and Ruth handed them the plaque.[74] His western tour was over.

Ruth made a final return to Boston on September 12, attending the Red Sox–Indians game at Fenway Park. The Lincoln convertible brought him onto the field while "spectators rose spontaneously and clapped thunderously," wrote Will Cloney of the *Boston Herald*. "But it was the kind of clapping you hear at the final curtain of a great play, not the kind you associate with a baseball park." The small crowd sensed the finality of the moment. "God love you, Babe!" yelled a lady in the stands, drawing a grin from Ruth.[75] Ted Williams came out of the dugout, and old and new sluggers chatted. The mostly empty park which once thundered with Ruth's mighty clouts now reverberated with his deep, raspy coughs.

Ruth awarded scholarships that night to Boston University for six New England American Legion ballplayers. "Babe has always been my idol," said Williams, also on hand. Ruth grimaced in pain throughout the evening, and Red Sox manager Joe Cronin helped him through his coughing spells "that racked his body and reduced his once resonant voice to a husky whisper, for which he apologized," wrote Cloney.[76] "My time is—well, I'm getting old, and I'm almost at the end," Ruth said.

Despite his declining health, Ruth played Santa Claus in December for a group of 50 children who were polio victims.[77] The Ruths traveled to Miami Beach on February 4, 1948, accompanied by a physician and nurse. A crowd of 150 were there to greet them. His trip south was "not so good," he said. "I feel pretty rugged. I'm going to try and get some sun on this old ear of mine."[78]

15

The Trail's End of Glory

Ruth at least looked better than he had the year before. His hair came back, and he put weight back on. He celebrated two birthdays: his actual birthday of February 6 in which he turned 53, and his mistaken date of February 7. "I'm full of aches and pains," he said on his sun porch. "My arms hurt, and I can't stretch them out. My neck hurts and I'm hopeful the sun will do the job." The milkman came to the door. "May I shake your hand?" he asked. "I want to go back to the plant and tell the boys I shook the hand of the greatest ballplayer who ever lived." Ruth smiled.[1]

Ruth attended some spring training games, and photographers caught a conversation with Ted Williams in St. Petersburg. The haggard, frail Ruth was sitting behind the screen at home plate talking with the eager, attentive Williams.[2]

Ruth faced the reality of not living to see his 54th year. There was a push to get his life story in print and on screen while he was still alive. Ruth sporadically collaborated with journalist Bob Considine on his autobiography, *The Babe Ruth Story*. Considine was Ruth's ghostwriter, but because Ruth was ill and unfocused, Considine had to hire his own ghostwriter, sportswriter Fred Lieb, who had covered Ruth's career. "The Babe Ruth book is under Considine's name," said Lieb, "but I gave him most of his information. I dictated that book for about a week prior to the 1947 World Series. I told everything I knew or could recall about the Babe. Well, everything that could be printed, anyway."[3]

The book was made into a feature film starring William Bendix. *The Babe Ruth Story* will always be considered one of the worst sports films ever made. While Lieb could add credibility to the book, not so with the film. "Ruth emerged, in the person of William Bendix, as a caricature of a caricature," wrote Jane Leavy.[4] Even in 1948, Bosley Crowther of the *New Your Times* wrote, "it is hard to accept the presentation of a great, mawkish, noble-spirited buffoon which William Bendix gives in this picture as a reasonable facsimile of the Babe."[5] Years later, Claire called it a "masterpiece in mush."

Babe and Claire met Bendix in Los Angeles in May of 1948. The "technical advising" Ruth was supposed to do was really publicity for a horrible film mostly completed. "We had three or four appointments to watch location shooting," Claire said, "but by some macabre coincidence we always got to the location just as shooting stopped." Ruth showed Bendix his famous swing, but it "was a mystery he never conquered." Seeing Ruth's decline, the film's producers pushed to get it finished

ASAP. "Apparently it's tougher to exploit a dead man's picture than a live one's," Claire wrote.[6]

Ruth's contract with Ford was renewed for another year. They returned home and in June, Babe donated a signed manuscript of the *Babe Ruth Story* to Yale University, with baseball captain George Herbert Walker Bush receiving it at the pitcher's mound.[7]

It was damp and cold on Sunday, June 13, 1948, not a good day to be out if you were dying. Babe Ruth finally had the opportunity to manage the New York Yankees … for one game. It was the 25th anniversary of Yankee Stadium, and the surviving members of that 1923 team were invited back. Ruth finally received that call from the Yankees, but he was too weak to enjoy it. "The Yankees," wrote Claire, "who at times didn't even seem aware that Babe had a telephone in his home, were clever enough to find his unlisted number and invite him to participate." Ruth's #3 would be permanently retired. "Babe's emotions were far purer than mine," Claire said about Babe's joy in attending.[8]

A crowd of 50,000 packed Yankee Stadium. Inside, Ruth arrived with someone supporting each arm. Photographers, as if standing in the Holy of Holies, just stood in awe. They gave Ruth time to get ready, savoring each moment, knowing they would not come again. The Yankees' clubhouse had moved to the first-base side since Ruth's day, but the old lockers remained, including Ruth's #3, which stood as if it were a historical landmark. It was a shrine. Pictures were taken of him in his uniform for the final time. A man pushed a small boy through the crowd to get a look. "There he is," he whispered to the boy. "That's Babe Ruth." The boy was too young and confused to appreciate the moment. But the father was satisfied. His son had met Babe Ruth.

Ruth made his way to the Cleveland dugout, draped in his topcoat for warmth. Cleveland first baseman Eddie Robinson saw Ruth teetering. He grabbed Bob Feller's bat for Ruth to use as a cane. "It's got good balance," Ruth said. W.C. Heinz, in his legendary reflection on the moment for the *New York Sun*, wrote that as soon as Mel Allen began to introduce Ruth, the Cleveland players took a step back, "and when they did Babe looked up to see a wall of two dozen photographers focused on him. He stood up and the topcoat fell off his shoulders."[9]

"He stood there, so very thin and bent," Claire wrote. "He had a bat in his hand. Now the bat was no longer a weapon of destruction. It was a thinly disguised support for his trembling body. They cheered and cheered. And he took off his hat and his head hung low … the familiar cheers that he must have known he was hearing for the last time."[10] He entered, as Heinz so eloquently described, to "the cauldron of sound he must know better than any other man."[11]

"He was the man whose prowess, personality and reputation built the Yankee Stadium," said the *New York Times*, "the man who revolutionized the national pastime with his mighty home runs, the man whom everyone loved—then and now." Misty-eyed fans watched him enter the field and receive a hug from Ed Barrow, the man who converted Ruth from a pitcher to an outfielder but also kept him from managing in his later years. Ruth spoke to the crowd and the radio and television audiences, mediums not in existence when his career started. "Ladies and gentlemen, I just want to say one thing," he said. "I am proud I hit the first home run here. It is great to see the men from twenty-five years ago back here today and it makes me feel proud to be with them."[12]

"We just stood and watched," said Yogi Berra, remembering the moment decades later. Ruth swung the bat for photographers one final time.[13]

Ruth's 1923 Yankees defeated the mishmash team of other Yankees old-timers, 2–0, in a two-inning game. But Ruth wasn't feeling well and had left early. He never did manage a Yankees game, even for two innings. What strength he had left was devoted to the kids.

Ruth flew to St. Louis for a youth baseball clinic on June 19 at Sportsman's Park attended by 12,000. Yankees and Browns players performed baseball drills, but kids weren't in the mood for lessons. They wanted to know, "Where is the Babe?" They perked up when they saw a police motorcycle escort a shiny Lincoln convertible into the stadium, with Ruth riding in the front seat.

They rushed to the railings. Ruth stepped to the microphone and encouraged the kids to play hard and honest. "I hope one of these kids grows up to take my place as the leading home run hitter," he said.

Dizzy Dean stood nearby with tears in his eyes. In 1935, Dean was the brash, young pitcher who faced the fading Ruth before the Florida crowds. Dean was now retired and broadcasting on radio and television. Ruth finished and walked to the youngsters crowding for autographs. "It's a funny thing," said Ruth's attending nurse, Frank Dulaney. "Whenever Mr. Ruth is doing something for baseball and the youngsters, he never seems to tire."[14] "It's no secret that baseball and children are the Babe's first and last love," Dulaney added as Ruth posed with kids for photographs.[15]

Grantland Rice wrote that the last months of Babe Ruth's life were his finest. He faced "suffering beyond all comprehension," he wrote, but Ruth's story was "much greater nearing the trail's end of glory than he ever was hitting 714 home runs and giving a vast nation the greatest thrills that sport has ever known."[16] It would have been easier for Ruth to decline appearances in favor of rest, but that wasn't who Ruth was. "No one can keep him from visiting a sick kid or a broken or blind human being," Rice wrote. "He seems to feel they belong to him—and he belongs to them."

Ruth was staring death in the face but, as Rice added, "his only thought has been that he will travel the few remaining miles for the betterment of the kids, the cripples, the heart-weary and the underprivileged, those who might need help and inspiration, as he once needed such help so badly.

"He sits in the twilight of the gods."[17]

Ruth flew to Iowa. One of the reporters waiting for him at the Sioux City Airport was Bill Bryson, Jr. Ruth's voice was too weak for the planned press conference, but reporters were invited to his hotel suite, where Ruth flopped into an easy chair.

"Just a few minutes now, please, fellows," said one of the Ford representatives. "He tires easily, you know." Bryson observed the "tired old man" who still retained his "lust for life." Ruth enjoyed answering questions about home run records, but his eyes sparkled when he spoke about American Legion youth ballplayers. "There aren't enough lighted parks for these kids," he said. "They play in the sunlight, then go into organized ball and have to play practically all the time at night."[18]

The next day Ruth was in Spencer, Iowa, speaking to 4,000 youngsters who waited out a six-hour rain delay for his barely audible speech. "It's wonderful to see these young chaps wearing these junior League uniforms," he wheezed. "There had to be someone to take my place, and these youngsters are the ones to do it."[19] He flew to Minneapolis and had a layover in Sioux Falls, South Dakota. Two boys awaited Ruth's plane and had the time of their lives chatting with him at the airport.[20]

In Minneapolis, Ruth was scheduled to talk to reporters at the Radisson Hotel, but it was decided it would be easier on him to have just one person interview him. Reporters decided a child should do it, so Babe would feel most comfortable. Johnny Ross, an 11-year-old blind boy who was frequently at area sporting events with his father, was selected. Ross had been vision-impaired all his life and totally blind since the age of seven when, after a horrific accident in a backyard football game when thorn bushes punctured his eyes.

> Ross: How are you, Babe?
> Ruth: I don't feel so good. I have a very bad throat and my head aches.
> Ross: Did you quit baseball for injury or old age?
> Ruth started to laugh until it gave way to a cough, and he had to turn away. He patted
>   Johnny on the back.
> Ruth: I'm afraid it was old age that put me out of there.
> Ross: Who'll win the National League Pennant?
> Ruth: That's a tough race, but I think it will be the Cardinals.
> Ross: Who's your favorite ball team?
> Ruth: I think I'll have to stick with the Yanks. They'll win the American League Pennant.
> Ross: Who'll take it all?
> Ruth: The Yankees.
> Ross: I know they say the time you called your homer was your biggest thrill, but was it?
> Ruth: Johnny, I think the time that I pitched 29 consecutive innings without giving up a
>   run. (Ruth turned away to clear his throat.)
> Ross: Would you sooner pitch or play in the outfield?
> Ruth: I'd like to be in there every day. That's how much I like to play. I think that tells you,
>   Johnny.
> Ross: How'd you have liked to hit your own pitching?
> Ruth: I guess I wouldn't.
> Ross: How'd it seem to go into the department store and buy your life history?
> Ruth: I didn't have to. They were kind enough to send me a copy.
> Johnny paused as he tried to find another question.
> Ross: What is that word I want?
> Ruth: I think both of us are out of words, Johnny.

The interview was done. "Tears started to well up in my eyes," Ross recalled. "He [Ruth] patted my shoulder and said in an obviously painful voice, 'Goodbye,

Johnny, and I hope to see you again someday.' I had actually met Babe Ruth, and he made me feel like I was really his friend. And I instinctively knew I would never see him again."[21]

Ruth retired for the night and flew back to New York the following day, June 23. "He had pitched another inning for the future of the game he loves so much," wrote Joe Hendrickson in the *Minneapolis Star Tribune*. "He and Johnny."[22]

It is believed to be the last interview Ruth ever gave.

Ruth went straight to the hospital when he returned. Reporters knew of Ruth's declining health but nevertheless wrote headlines of Ruth "getting

Babe Ruth's last interview was with 11-year-old blind boy Johnny Ross, who would later be known as "The Father of Beepball" (Minnesota Historical Society).

along fine," "doing well," and "improving." They knew he was reading those columns. Ruth may have taken joy in reading that *The Babe Ruth Story* hit the *New York Times* Bestseller List among notable nonfiction works: *Peace of Mind* by Joshua Liebman, *Sexual Behavior in the Human Male* by Alfred Kinsey, *How to Stop Worrying and Start Living* by Dale Carnegie, *The Gathering Storm* by Winston Churchill, and a *Guide to Confident Living* by Norman Vincent Peale.[23]

Ruth had one more rally left in him. He was going home.

Baltimore was hosting an interfaith charity game on July 13, organized by the B'nai B'rith, Knights of Columbus, and the Boumi Temple of the Shrine. The International League's Baltimore Orioles and Jersey City Giants would play at Baltimore Stadium. Ruth was slated to present prizes to recognized youth, including a boy at St. Mary's Industrial School, where his legend began. Ruth turned down an invitation to the Major League All-Star Game in St. Louis, happening the same day. Kids were more important.[24]

Rain cancelled all the festivities, but Ruth still spent three final hours in his hometown. On the steps of the plane, he was greeted by his only living sibling, his sister, Mamie Moberly. He looked out to see a 21-car caravan waiting for him. A father and son approached on the steps. "Could you sign this for the boy?" Sig Seidenman's father asked. Ruth smiled and signed the ball, one of the last he autographed. More kids rushed him as he walked down the stairs. The procession was led by police motorcycles and blaring sirens. It was if a king were making a grand entrance. Ruth rode in the first car and saw the streets of his youth lined with people standing in the rain just to get a glimpse and wave. "That's him!" "There goes the Babe!" people shouted. A young mother ran to the window of a house on Fayette Street, holding out her baby and pointing. "Crowds of gawking people," wrote Walter Taylor in the *Baltimore Sun,* "from those who saw him debark at the airport to those who were in the lobby of the Lord Baltimore Hotel when he arrived, made way with deference as for a king. They whispered silently."[25]

The frail Ruth entered and posed for pictures, but was unable to hold a press conference. He met Rodger Pippen, Baltimore sportswriter who was on the field that day in Fayetteville, North Carolina, in 1914 when Ruth hit his first professional home run.[26] Ruth's stay was brief but meaningful. Many believe his last visit to Yankee Stadium was the grand finale of his life, but perhaps his final visit to the city where he was born, neglected, given up, and nurtured was a more fitting culmination.

Ruth was unable to attend a charity game at Braves Field on July 24 to benefit his new charity, The Babe Ruth Foundation for needy children. He received a call from Boston, however, and heard from Ted Williams and others. "You've done more for baseball and the kids of this country than any other man," the Splendid Splinter told him.[27] Bill McKechnie, Cleveland coach and Ruth's old manager, also gave greetings.

Bill McKechnie would finish his long career in the game as a coach with the Red Sox in 1952–1953. Deacon Bill died in 1965 at the age of 79.

Ruth's last public appearance was at the Astor Theater on July 26 to see the premier of *The Babe Ruth Story*. Ruth may not have even attended had not Mayor William O'Dwyer arrived in his room the day before with photographers, newsreels, and reporters crowding the hospital corridor. The scene reeked of a political photo-op as Ruth struggled out of bed and into a rocking chair.

He handed the mayor an invitation to the film. O'Dwyer declared the day "Babe Ruth Day," "as one of honor to a beloved American." Ruth was brought to tears, and photographers asked for photos. "Out to the terrace shuffled the Babe, accompanied by the mayor," the *Times* said. Mobility was a big challenge at this point, and Ruth spent a lot of energy promoting a film filled with "sloppy sentiment" and "debasement of human qualities in the muck of the cliché," Bosley Crowther wrote.[28]

Dorothy remembered her father being pulled from his deathbed to see the film, leaving such a bad taste in her mouth that she never saw the film for 40 years. Babe "had no idea where he was because of the amount of drugs that were in his system," she wrote. "It was one of the cruelest scenes that I have ever witnessed in my life."[29] Ruth's gallant fight in meeting kids with his last breaths far eclipsed the shallow make-believe portrayal by Bendix.

"Ruth walked slowly into the theater," reported the *Times*, "supported by both arms, perspiring heavily, and seemingly too ill and too tired to do anything but smile warmly and painfully at the avid spectators."[30] He didn't stay very long, if he even knew what he was watching. Considering the poor representation of the true Babe Ruth in the film, he may have been better off watching *Abbott and Costello Meet Frankenstein*, playing at another theater.[31]

A more meaningful moment came in one of the hot August days when the end was imminent. Joe Dugan, his old teammate, came and sat by his side. "I'm gone, Joe. I'm gone," he whispered.

Babe Ruth was gone on August 16. His body was available for public viewing at Yankee Stadium on August 17 and 18, with 75,000–200,000 fans passing by to say their final goodbyes. On August 19, 75,000 stood outside in the rain as the funeral proceeded inside St. Patrick's Cathedral. "The greatest figure the world of sport has ever known has passed from the field," wrote Grantland Rice. "There has been only one Babe Ruth—one Bambino, who caught and held the love and admiration of countless millions around the world." Of special note, Rice mentioned the kids. "Ruth's appeal to the kids of this nation was something beyond belief. He loved them and the kids knew it. There was nothing phony about his act."[32]

Ruth's relationship with Major League Baseball ended in emptiness. He could not fathom life outside of it, and at the time the only way to stay in it was, for him, a managerial role. He was the greatest attraction the game had ever seen, and children have never flocked to a retired player the way they did to Ruth. He still held out hope for a decade until cancer gave the final word. "The newspapers said Babe Ruth died in Memorial Hospital, at 8:01 p.m., August 16, 1948," wrote Tom Meany. "That isn't so. Babe Ruth died in the club house at Braves Field about 5:30 p.m., June 2, 1935. I know, because I was there and all the other newspapermen who were there knew it, too."[33]

Such sentiments encapsulate Ruth's desire to manage, and nothing else would do. Oscar Fraley described the refusal of Major League Baseball to provide Ruth a chance at a managerial position "a millstone around his neck as the years marched past. It was a constant complaint, as he golfed and bowled after turning his back on the game he loved."[34] If Ruth had lived two or three more decades, what might he have become? A managerial career somewhere? A voice on the *Game of the Week*? "If Babe Ruth had lived into his sixties," Marshall Smelser theorized, "he would have mellowed into the phase of a man's life when he puts aside many of this world's commitments. Consciously or unconsciously, old people usually adjust their demands to what is possible, in order to get peace of mind. Ruth never reached that age. Ruth was an unwanted man and didn't live to be old enough not to care."[35]

Yet, Ruth *did* find peace of mind in his last months. We learn about Babe Ruth the person because of his distance from professional baseball's politics and control. Ford Motor Company rejuvenated him and placed him where he always needed to be, with the kids. Ruth made up for lost years by seeing as many American Legion youth ballplayers he could in the time he had left. Ruth couldn't find fulfillment by seeking a manager position. The system told him he didn't belong, that there was no place for him. But beyond the power and the politics, he found a place to belong. It was with a bunch of kids who had no fame, no fortune, but only dreams. As Rice wrote, "He seems to feel they belong to him—and he belongs to them."[36]

"The Babe must know, somehow," Fraley wrote two years after Ruth's death, "that he's still the manager for an awful lot of kids. And you know that the Babe isn't bitter anymore."[37]

Beep Ball

Johnny Ross was one those kids. Five years after the blind boy interviewed the ailing Ruth, Ross won the Minnesota state high school wrestling championship for Marshall High School. Ross also played football, golfed, and skied. Ross and his dog, "Major," participated in water shows and operated an aquaplane. He graduated from the University of Minnesota Journalism School in 1960, where he earned a letter in wrestling. In 1965 he received a teaching degree from Mankato State College. He taught English classes and coached wrestling at the Comfrey school district, assisted by "Ringo," his German Shepherd. In 1975, Ross founded a monthly Braille sports publication called *Feeling Sports,* which ran for 17 years through his nonprofit organization: Braille Sports Foundation. He was convinced, wrote James Parsons in the *Minneapolis Tribune*, "that far too many blind people withdraw from life, and he decided one way to do something about that is to publish a sports magazine in Braille and on vinyl records for the blind." Subscriptions for the magazine grew after his appearance on NBC's *Today Show*.[38]

"My mother and father never babied me," Ross said. "I grew up thinking I wasn't handicapped. About the only thing I can't do that you can do is drive a car."[39]

In 1975 Ross organized the first Beep Ball competition in Minnesota, a baseball game for the blind re-invented by Ross. The ball and bases beeped, and the batter needed to reach a base before a fielder found the ball. The Braille Sports Foundation team took on a club of blindfolded Minnesota athletes.[40]

Today, the National Beep Baseball Association fields teams across the country and hosts an annual world series. John Ross is called "The Father of Beep Baseball" according to its website.[41] The frail, dying Babe Ruth played a part in establishing baseball for the blind through his interview with little Johnny Ross.

The Judge and His Legacy

Judge Fuchs remained active as a Boston baseball fan right to the end of his life. Fuchs survived bankruptcy in 1938 and followed through on his promise to pay back all his friends who loaned him money. The Judge and his son Robert were law partners until 1948. In 1958, Judge Fuchs celebrated his 80th birthday party, attended by 300 people who no doubt had once attended a party the Judge had thrown. Fuchs loved tossing "fabulous banquets on the slightest excuse," wrote Austen Lake, and he "loved baseball and people, forgetting that it cost large sums of fresh cash to support both." Fuchs was remembered for his charity and charm, which "won much applause but did not help the Braves box office."[42]

On a cold, raw day on September 28, 1960, Ted Williams took his last at-bat at Fenway Park. His home run put the final touch on his legendary career. Judge Fuchs was there to congratulate him in the Red Sox clubhouse. The following summer, the Judge was still a regular at Fenway, climbing his way up into the press box "although his legs were tender," wrote the *Globe's* Hy Hurwitz. "The Boston baseball writers who knew him when, will never forget his many kindnesses."[43]

Babe Ruth realized fulfillment in his last days, despite not seeing the managerial job he craved. Major League Baseball had no place for him, but he was able to spend time with those who recognized him for who he was: children. Fuchs' legacy is judged in a similar manner. He was not a successful owner or businessman,

In 1955, a crane demolished the left field bleachers of what was once Braves Field to make room for the new athletic field for Boston University (courtesy Boston Public Library, Leslie Jones Collection).

but he left behind a legacy in the people he touched. "I had a grand time while it lasted," Fuchs said. "But I learned that happiness doesn't balance the baseball ledgers. It takes about a million dollars' worth of public sentiment to do that." Ladies' Days, the Knot-Hole Gang, Sunday baseball, and broadcasting are among his lasting accomplishments.

"I lost over $1,000,000 in my venture in major league baseball in Boston," Fuchs said in his later years, "but I have no regrets. I made many friends, and the people of Boston and New England were very kind to me."[44] Fuchs also gave back to the game by establishing the Judge Emil Fuchs Memorial Award, given to those recognized for long and meritorious service to the game. The award is presented every year by the Boston baseball writers.

"His career was not a bright one," said *The Sporting News*. "There is this, though, to be said. With his own resources, he kept alive a franchise that would have collapsed. He kept it in Boston, where the Braves lasted for almost two more decades before the franchise was moved to Milwaukee. For these efforts, baseball should be grateful to Emil Fuchs, though futile and unrewarding was his role."[45]

Judge Emil Edwin Fuchs died December 5, 1961, at the age of 83.

Ruth spent the last months of his life traveling the country to encourage youth ballplayers, as he did here in St. Louis just months before his passing. "I've always been for the youth of America," he said, "and I will be till the day I die" (AP/Shutterstock).

A crane appeared at the Boston University athletic field on December 7, 1959. The University announced remodeling plans which called for the demolition of all but a few remaining relics of what was once known as Braves Field. BU purchased the property, later called Nickerson Field, from Lou Perini when the Braves left town. Austen Lake of the *Boston American* took time to give a tribute in his article, "Goodbye to Old Friend."[46]

"It has crumbled slowly toward ruin," he wrote of the stadium, "until now it is little more than a tombstone in memory's cemetery." The hallowed grounds, devoid of life, still contained images of days gone by. "Bricks, mortar, paint, concrete and architectural blueprints can't erase the traditions of 39 years. In imagination I see the Babe standing in the murky shadows; his pendant stomach, flamingo legs, and pumpkin features, as he rumbles, 'I hate to quit, but...'"

Lake remembered the "pipe rail box where Judge Emil Fuchs suffered and quaked for ten summers, burning cigars into a hot coal and white ash as he tried to quiet the uproar in his soul." He remembered Bill McKechnie pacing the third base coach's box. This was the place where Fuchs and Ruth had a final journey together in the game. It ended in disaster, and both walked away from the game dejected and empty. But their legacies were so much more, and they live on. The building where Ruth and Fuchs talked business, and the right-field pavilion where Boston fans watched that fatal season, still stands. Few structures remain that can make that claim.

"Here lies the site where a piece of Boston's heart lies buried. Farewell, old friend," wrote Lake. "The place still reeks with the odor of the Braves."[47]

It always will.

Chapter Notes

Preface

1. Roger Kahn, "The Real Babe Ruth," *Esquire* 52, no. 2 (August 1959): 27.
2. Grantland Rice, "Rice Calls Ruth Greater Than Ever, Forgetting Own Pain to Cheer Others," *Boston Globe*, March 24, 1948, 18.
3. Grantland Rice, "McKechnie Takes Blame, Ruth Again Flays Fuchs," *Boston Globe*, June 4, 1935, 22.
4. Rice, "Rice Calls Ruth Greater Than Ever."

Introduction

1. Charles C. Alexander, *Breaking the Slump: Baseball in the Depression Era* (New York: Columbia University Press, 2002), 79.
2. Alexander, 80; David George Surdam, *Wins, Losses, and Empty Seats: How Baseball Outlasted the Great Depression* (Lincoln: University of Nebraska Press, 2011), 317.

Chapter 1

1. Paul H. Shannon, "Vast Fan Army Acclaims Ruth," *Boston Post*, August 13, 1934, 1.
2. *Ibid.,* 14.
3. *Ibid.*
4. "New Subway Entrance in Use," *Boston Globe*, July 27, 1914, 8; "New Boylston St Subway," *Boston Globe*, July 23, 1914, 1; "Gov SQ Now Officially Known as Kenmore," *Boston Globe*, January 1, 1932, 5; Derek Strahan, "Kenmore Subway Incline, Boston," lostnewengland.com/2015/10/kenmore-subway-incline-boston/, retrieved January 5, 2019; Charlie Bevis, *Red Sox vs. Braves in Boston: The Battle for Fans' Hearts, 1901–1952* (Jefferson, NC: McFarland, 2017), 81; Glenn Stout, *Fenway 1912: The Birth of a Ballpark, a Championship Season, and Fenway's Remarkable First Year* (Boston: Houghton Mifflin, 2011), 73–74.
5. "Agrees on Salem Aid," *Boston Globe*, July 11, 1914. 1.
6. R.E. McMillin, "Lannin Purchases Three of Orioles," *Boston Journal*, July 10, 1914, 8.
7. C. Starr Matthews, "Two Oriole Stars Sold to Cincinnati," *Baltimore Sun*, July 8, 1914, 5.
8. McMillin, "Lannin Purchases Three of Orioles."

9. Leigh Montville, *The Big Bam: The Life and Times of Babe Ruth* (New York: Anchor Books, 2006), 9.
10. Jane Leavy, *The Big Fella: Babe Ruth and the World He Created* (New York: HarperCollins, 2018), 35–39.
11. *Ibid.*, 39.
12. *Ibid.*, 39–41.
13. *Ibid.*, 39–44.
14. *Ibid.*, 4.
15. *Ibid.*, 1, 5.
16. Babe Ruth as told to Bob Considine, *The Babe Ruth Story* (New York: Penguin, 1992), 1–2.
17. Leavy, 42.
18. *Ibid.*, 55; Ruth as told to Considine, 2.
19. Leavy, 155, 49–52.
20. *Ibid.*, 99.
21. Brian Martin, *The Man Who Made Babe Ruth: Brother Matthias of St. Mary's School* (Jefferson, NC: McFarland, 2020), 2.
22. Harry T. Brundidge, "Ruth Wants to Forget 'Bad Boy' Days as He Keeps Right on Swatting Home Runs After 16 Years in Game," *The Sporting News*, January 8, 1931, 7.
23. Ruth as told to Considine, 2.
24. *Baltimore-News Post* story from 1947 quoted in Leavy, 11.
25. Leavy, 94.
26. *A Classified and Descriptive Directory to the Charitable and Beneficent Societies and Institutions of the City of Baltimore* (Baltimore: Hamilton & Co., 1885), 18.
27. Harry Rothgerber, "Introduction" in *Young Babe Ruth: His Early Life and Baseball Career, from the Memoirs of a Xaverian Brother* by Brother C.F.X. Gilbert (Jefferson, NC: McFarland, 1999), 5.
28. S.J. Woolf, "Babe Ruth Yields to Time, the Umpire," *New York Times Magazine*, September 2, 1934, 4.
29. Robert W. Creamer, *Babe: The Legend Comes to Life* (New York: Penguin, 1986), 39.
30. Brother John Joseph Sterne, a student at St. Mary's after the time of Ruth, recalled these memories for the forward in Brother Gilbert's memoir, *Young Babe Ruth: His Early Life and Baseball Career, from the Memoirs of a Xaverian Brother* (Jefferson, NC: McFarland, 1999), ix–x.
31. Leavy, 147.

32. Marshall Smelser, *The Life That Ruth Built: A Biography* (Lincoln: University of Nebraska Press, 1975), 17.

33. Leavy, 95.

34. Martin, 26.

35. Leavy, 150.

36. Ruth as told to Considine, 3–4.

37. Mrs. Babe Ruth (Claire), with Bill Slocum, *The Babe and I* (Englewood Cliffs, NJ: Prentice-Hall, 1959), 44.

38. Leavy, 153.

39. Creamer, 52.

40. Smelser, 36.

41. "Dunn Now Trying to Bolster Club," *Baltimore Sun*, February 15, 1914, 15.

42. "Home by Ruth Feature of Game," Baltimore Sun, March 8, 1914, 13.

43. Jesse A. Linthicum, "Ruth Scores Shutout," *Baltimore Sun*, April 23, 1914, 11.

44. C. Starr Matthews, "The Rise of Babe Ruth," *Baltimore Sun*, July 10, 1914, 5.

45. "Red Sox Pay $30,000 for Three Minor Stars," *Boston Herald*, July 10, 1914, 4.

46. T.H. Murnane, "Ruth Leads Red Sox to Victory," *Boston Globe*, July 12, 1914, 11.

47. Paul H. Shannon, "Naps Tie Twice but Red Sox Win," *Boston Sunday Post*, July 12, 1914, 12.

48. Leavy, xxv–xxvi.

49. *Ibid.*, 59.

50. Douglas Brinkley, *American Heritage History of the United States* (New York: Viking, 1998), 247.

51. Leavy, 104.

52. Marshall Smelser, 549; Joe Williams, "Christy Walsh, the Man Behind Mr. Babe Ruth. About These Literary Athletes," *New York World-Telegram*, July 29, 1927.

53. Thomas Barthel, *Babe Ruth and the Creation of the Celebrity Athlete* (Jefferson, NC: McFarland, 2018), 92; Leavy, 103.

54. Leavy, 111.

55. *Ibid.*, 221–222.

56. Jules Tygiel, *Past Time: Baseball as History* (New York: Oxford University Press, 2000), 83–84.

57. Leavy, 412.

58. Montville, 237.

59. Smelser, 149.

60. *Ibid.*, 468.

61. Leigh Montville, *The Big Bam: The Life and Times of Babe Ruth* (New York: Random House, 2006), 316.

62. Associated Press, "Babe Admits He Discussed Sox Deal; but Says He Is Not Ready to Quit Yet," *Boston Herald*, May 29, 1932.

63. Montville, 323–324; "Sid Keener's Column," *St. Louis Star & Times*, November 2, 1933, 19; Charles P. Ward, "Bambino First Choice Among Detroit's Fans," *Detroit Free Press*, September 25, 1933, 13.

64. John Drebinger, "Ruth, 235, Begins Indoor Training; Hints He Will Become a Manager," *New York Times*, January 4, 1934, 25; Ruppert ran a brewery on Fifth Avenue in New York City.

65. Babe Ruth, "How It Feels to Be a Has-Been," in *How It Feels to Be a Has-Been by Babe Ruth and Other Essays from Baseball Greats in Their Own Words,"* Liberty Library Corporation, 2012.

66. Associated Press, "Ruth Plans to Quit at End of Season," *New York Times*, August 11, 1934.

67. Bill Slocum, "Babe Ruth, Through as a Regular, to Seek Job as Pinch-Hitting Manager," *St. Louis Post-Dispatch*, August 11, 1934, 9.

68. Associated Press, "Ruth to Retire After Season," *Baltimore Sun*, August 11, 1934: 10.

69. John Drebinger, "48,000 See Yanks and Red Sox Split," *New York Times*, August 13, 1934.

70. Hy Hurwitz, "Fans Storm Fenway Park in Tribute to Babe Ruth," *Boston Globe*, August 13, 1934: 1, 7.

71. Burt Whitman, "Babe Ruth Wet-Eyed as 46,766 Boston Fans Say Farewell," *Boston Herald*, August 13, 1934, 1.

72. Hurwitz, "Fans Storm Fenway Park."

73. Woolf, "Babe Ruth Yields to Time."

74. "Ruth Makes Last Bow as Regular While Senators Top Yankees, 5–3," *New York Times*, October 1, 1934.

75. Associated Press, "Ruth, Seeking Managerial Post, Insists Playing Career Is Over," *New York Times*, October 9, 1934, 23.

76. *New York Daily News*, October 26, 1934, 66.

77. William Peet, "Big Leaguers Beat Hawaiian Stars, 8 to 1," *Honolulu Advertiser*, October 26, 1934, 12.

78. Red McQueen, "Ruth May Manage Mackmen," *Honolulu Advertiser*, October 26, 1934, 13.

79. Loui Leong Hop, "Slugging Twins Steal Baseball Show," *Honolulu Star Bulletin*, October 26, 1934, 11; "Babe's Status in Yanks Starts 'Hot Stove' Talk, "*Boston Globe*, October 26, 1934, 26; Don Watson, "Japanese Pro Team Coming," *Honolulu Star-Bulletin*, October 26, 1934, 11.

80. Associated Press, "Ruth Definitely Out as Senators' Pilot; Harris Confers with Griffith About Post," *New York Times*, October 28, 1934, S11; William Peet, "Sport Flashes," *Honolulu Advertiser*, October 26, 1934, 12; One interesting non-event involved Tillinghast L'Hommedieu Huston, the one-time part-owner of the Yankees responsible for purchasing Ruth in 1919. Having sold his shares in the club to Ruppert in 1923, Huston had been out of the game for over a decade. He now was giving thought to purchasing the Brooklyn Dodgers, and if he did, he affirmed that Ruth was his first choice as manager. It was far-fetched, however, as the club was not for sale. "Ex-Yankee Head May Buy Dodgers," *Boston Herald*, October 31, 1934, 25.

81. John Drebinger, "Ruppert Willing to Release Ruth," *New York Times*, October 27, 1935, 10.

82. G.W. Daley, "Ruth Slated in Baseball Circles to Succeed Mack in Philadelphia," *New York Times*, October 26, 1934, 29; Ruppert Willing to Release Ruth."

83. Associated Press, "Managerial Alignment

for 1935 Leaves Ruth's Future Speculative," *New York Times*, November 1, 1934, 27.

84. "35,000 Offer to Ruth," *New York Times*, November 2, 1934, 31.

85. "Babe Lands as 100,000 Japs Cheer," *New York Daily News*, November 3, 1934, 31; Robert K. Fitts. *Banzai Babe Ruth: Baseball, Espionage and Assassination During the 1934 Tour of Japan* (Lincoln: University of Nebraska Press, 2012), 93.

86. "Babe Fails to Get Home Run in Game," *Boston Globe*, November 5, 1934, 8; The All-Stars easily dismantled the Tokyo All-Stars, 17–1.

87. Fitts, 275.

88. George Kenney, "Ruppert Buys $75,000 'Babe' for Fall Debut," *New York Daily News*, November 22, 1934, 66.

89. Recounted by Tom Meany, "Babe Ruth," *Milwaukee Journal Sentinel*, September 20, 1948, 46.

90. Associated Press, "Hear Management Is Ready for Ruth," *New York Times*, December 12, 1934.

91. Jimmy Powers, "Circus Seeks Babe with $75,000 Bait," *New York Daily News*, January 18, 1935, 64.

92. John Lardner, "What About It?" *Boston Globe*, November 17, 1934, 10.

93. "McKechnie, Not Ruth, to Manage Braves," *Boston Herald*, October 27, 1934, 10.

94. Smelser, 489.

Chapter 2

1. "Man Beats Lady Godiva by Nudist March in Back Bay," *Boston Globe*, April 17, 1935, 9; "The Weather," *Boston Herald*, April 17, 1935, 3.

2. James C. O'Leary, "Governors of Five States Attend Game," *Boston Globe*, April 17, 1935, 29.

3. "Ticket Pledges Exceed $28,000," *Boston Globe*, February 1, 1935, 23.

4. Gerry Moore, "Expect 40,000 to See Braves," *Boston Globe*, April 16, 1935, 21.

5. O'Leary, "Governors of Five States."

6. Harold Kaese. The Boston Braves 1871–1953 (Boston: Northeastern University Press, 1954), 193.

7. Carolyn Fuchs, interview with the author, March 25, 2019, April 2, 2019.

8. Kaese, 192.

9. Poznan Project, poznan-project.psnc.pl/#prettyPhoto, retrieved March 8, 2020.

10. Ancestry.com provided the ship and census information. Castlegarden.org confirmed the information.

11. *Superior Court of the City of New York, Herman Fuchs, Plaintiff, Against Thomas E. Koerner, Defendant, Appellant* (New York: C.G. Burgoyne 'Quick' Printing House, 1885), 1–28. Retrieved September 3, 2021. books.google.com/books?id=Vgu9wWraAkC&newbks=1&newbks_redir=0&dq=%22Herman%20Fuchs%2C%20Plaintiff%22&pg=RA40-PP3#v=onepage&q=%22Herman%20Fuchs,%20Plaintiff%22&f=false.

12. "Hermann Fuchs," *New York Times*, June 22,

1917, 12; Immigration year is according to the 1910 census.

13. Established in 1886, University Settlement was "a physical, psychological and spiritual haven where people of all ages, from all countries and every walk of life could seek advice, assistance, education or a simple respite from the harsh realities of everyday life," according to the University Settlement website. Date accessed: July 5, 2018. universitysettlement.org/us/about/history/

14. *Official Gazette of the United States Patent Office* Vol. 16 (Washington: Government Printing Office, 1880), 98. books.google.com/books?id=q7alth3j840C&newbks=1&newbks_redir=0&dq=Official%20Gazette%20of%20the%20United%20States%20Patent%20Office%20Vol.%2016.&pg=PA98#v=onepage&q=pinckney&f=false; *The Pharmacist* Vol. 8. (Chicago: College of Pharmacy, 1875), 296.

15. Harold Seymour, *Baseball: The Early Years* (New York: Oxford University Press, 1989), 7; John Thorn, *Baseball in the Garden of Eden: The Secret History of the Early Game* (New York: Simon & Schuster, 2011), 46; Edward Wong, "Baseball's Disputed Origin Is Traced Back, Back, Back," *New York Times*, July 8, 2001, 1; Harold C. Burr, "Judge Fuchs Might Have Made Big League Player Except for Wild Pitch," *Brooklyn Daily Eagle*, May 28, 1929, 30.

16. Dan Daniel, "Daniel's Dope," *New York World-Telegram*, August 2, 1935.

17. *Ibid.*

18. Stanley Nadel, *Little Germany: Ethnicity, Religion, and Class in New York City, 1845–80* (Urbana: University of Illinois Press, 1990), 1.

19. *Ibid.*, 14.

20. *Ibid.*, 32.

21. *Ibid.*, 32, 38, Appendix B.

22. *Ibid.*, 37.

23. Percy Hutchison, "An East Side Oasis Holds Its Jubilee," *New York Times*, November 29, 1936, SM12.

24. Tyler Anbinder, *City of Dreams: The 400-Year Epic History of Immigrant New York* (Boston: Mariner Books, 2016), 356.

25. *Ibid.*, 358.

26. New York (State). Legislature. Assembly. Tenement House Committee. *Report of the Tenement House Committee as Authorized by Chapter 479 of the Laws of 1894.* Albany: J.B. Lyon, state printer, 1895: 11.

27. *Report of the Tenement House Committee as Authorized by Chapter 479 of the Laws of 1894*: 12–13.

28. *Ibid.*, 25.

29. "Coit, Stanton," *Social Welfare History Project*, VCU Libraries, retrieved September 4, 2021. socialwelfare.library.vcu.edu/people/coit-stanton/

30. "Appeal for Funds," *New York Times*, October 29, 1896, 4.

31. "University Settlement," *New York Times*, January 29, 1899, 12.

32. No records seem to exist of the New Jersey

State League, which lasted from May–June of 1897. Other than some exhibition games listed, no championship games were played. Other sources say Fuchs played on a Morristown team, but no such team is listed in newspaper accounts of the league, which list Elizabeth, Trenton, Millville, Bridgeton, Asbury Park, and Atlantic City. *New York Sun*, April 13, 1897, 4.

33. "Social Reform Club Debate" *New York Times*, March 2, 1898, 7; "Wants Sunday Baseball," *New York Herald*, February 28, 1898, 11.

34. Robert S. Fuchs and Wayne Soini, *Judge Fuchs and the Boston Braves, 1923–1935* (Jefferson, NC: McFarland, 1998), 3.

35. Jeffrey A. Kroessler, "Baseball and the Blue Laws," *Long Island* 5, no. 2 (Spring, 1993): 172–174; "Women Ball Players at Maspeth," *Brooklyn Daily Eagle*, September 8, 1890, 1.

36. "Situations Wanted-Male," *The World*, October 13, 1894, 7.

37. Luther Harris, "Eighth Street History," Village Alliance, https://greenwichvillage.nyc/eighth-street-history, retrieved July 25.

38. 1908–09 New York City directory.

39. "Survey of the Food World," *The American Food Journal* 8, no. 8 (August 1913): 372.

40. "News Notes of the Trade," *Simmons Spice Mill* XL, no. 8 (August 1917): 924.

41. "Lawyers as Deputies," *New York Tribune*, September 13, 1905, 2; "Vice in New York City," *Indianapolis Journal*, January 10, 1901, 4.

42. "Capt. Herlihy's Trial," *New York Times*, January 10, 1901, 2.

43. "Vice in New York City."

44. "Crusader Was Only Curious," *Morning Telegraph*, January 10, 1901, 2; Letter by Fuchs' son, Robert S. Fuchs, addressed to the Baseball Hall of Fame, dated July 24, 1962; "Capt. Herlihy's Trial," *New York Times*, January 10, 1901, 2; "Supt. M'Cullagh's Charge," *New York Times*, February 6, 1902, 16; "Mathot Looks Up a Case," *New York Times*, August 11, 1906, 9; "Curran Succeeds Deuel," *New York Times*, May 4, 1917, 12.

45. "Curran Made a Magistrate," *New York Sun*, May 4, 1917, 8.

46. Irma and Paul Milstein Division of United States History, Local History and Genealogy, The New York Public Library. (1912). *New York City directory* Retrieved from http://digitalcollections.nypl.org/items/1d0e74d0-7d15-0134-4d88-00505686a51c; The 1920–21 directory lists his address as 312 W. 99th, near Riverside Drive.

47. *Ibid.*

48. Cited in David Pietrusza's *Rothstein: The Life, Times and Murder of the Criminal Genius Who Fixed the 1919 World Series* (New York: Basic Books, 2011), 140–145; "Man Accused of Shooting Two Detectives Is Freed," *New York Tribune*, July 25, 1919, 18.

49. Robert S. Fuchs and Wayne Soini. *Judge Fuchs and the Boston Braves* (Jefferson, NC: McFarland, 1998), 11.

50. "Whitman Case Goes to Highest Court," *Ithaca Journal*, December 6, 1918, 1.

51. "Kauff Released on Bail," *New York Tribune*, February 21, 1920, 8; David Jones, "Benny Kauff," SABR BioProject. Date accessed, June 30, 2018. sabr.org/bioproj/person/4a224847; "Swann Summons M'Graw in Investigation to Learn Cause of Injury to Slavin'," *Evening World*, August 10, 1920, 1; Bill Lamb, "New York Giants Ownership History," SABR Team Ownership Histories Project. Retrieved June 30, 2018. sabr.org/research/new-york-giants-team-ownership-history.

52. Harold Kaese, 190.

53. *Ibid.*

54. *Ibid.*, 181; Although never proven, the rumor was that Grant had received $100,000 from Giants owner Charles A. Stoneham to purchase the Braves. Grant was close with Stoneham, both having offices on Wall Street and private boxes next to each other at the Polo Grounds. This was one instance among many at the time in which there was an intimate familiarity between the upper managements of the Braves and Giants. Trades between the two teams did little to squash those conspiracy theories, since they always seemed to heavily favor the Giants.

55. G.W. Grant Buys Braves," *New York Times*, January 31, 1919, 12; Gus Rooney, "Boston Fans Sorry at Passing of Grant," *The Sporting News*, March 1, 1923, 1.

56. Fuchs and Soini, 21.

57. *Ibid.*, 24.

58. Some reports had $350,000, while the Associated Press reported that McDonough stated $500,000 ("Sale of Boston Team Involves Over $500,000," *Springfield Republican*, February 22, 1923, 10). No official figure was given, but Grant said he "got his price to the last penny of his demands," *Hartford Courant*, February 21, 1923, 12; McDonough's name is sometimes spelled with an "a," but his divorce proceedings in the 1933 *New York Supreme Court* minutes do not. tinyurl.com/y85gx9qj

59. "A Messenger Boy's Rise to Wealth," *Hartford Courant*, September 5, 1926, 43.

60. Burton Whitman, "Powell Biggest Gun of Braves," *Boston Herald*, November 28, 1923.

61. Fuchs and Soini, 24.

62. Burton Whitman, "Christy Mathewson Is President of Braves; Grant Sells Out Club," *Boston Herald*, February 21, 1923, 11.

63. "Fuchs Prominent Member of Bar," *Boston Herald*, February 21, 1923, 11.

64. "Marcus Loew Shows Matty the Dotted Line," *Boston Herald*, May 1, 1923, 23; "Will Utilize Braves Field Summer Nights," *Boston Herald*, June 3, 1923, 15.

65. "Electric Layout for Show Is Vast. Lighting Loew Entertainment at Braves Field Big Task," *Boston Herald*, July 15, 1923, 45; "Stars of Stage and Screen Appear. Opening Night at Braves Field Draws Great Crowd," *Boston Herald*, June 26, 1923, 6; "Braves Field Exhibition Company Gets Charter," *Springfield Republican*, June 2, 1923, 2.

66. "Women Have a Chance to See Braves Free Today," *Boston Globe*, July 20, 1923, 10.

67. James C. O'Leary, "Dave Bancroft Coming to Braves as Manager," *Boston Globe*, November 13, 1923, 1.

68. "WBZ Will Put Major League Game on Air Today, New Departure," *Springfield Republican*, April 14, 1925, 1.

69. Wayne Soini, interview with the author.

70. "Worcester Club Sold to Braves," *Boston Herald*, May 20, 1925, 20; "'Casey' Stengel Becomes President-Manager of Worcester Baseball Club," *Boston Herald*, May 21, 1925, 19. Donald B. Bagg, "Games in Hartford on Half-a-Dozen Sundays," *Boston Herald*, June 9, 1925, 12.

71. Michael Hartley. *Christy Mathewson: A Biography* (Jefferson, NC: McFarland Press, 2004), 168.

72. "Judge Fuchs Is Elected President of Braves to Fill Mathewson Vacancy," *Boston Herald*, October 22, 1925, 13.

73. "Live Tips and Topics," *Boston Globe*, September 3, 1926, 21.

74. "Judge Fuchs Buys Out Powell's One-Third Interest in Braves," *Boston Herald*, September 1, 1926, 10.

75. Fuchs and Soini, 58. The story in Robert Fuchs' memory was the cash totaled $250,000, not the actual $200,000 many sources, including Fuchs himself, verify; "Buying Interests of Adams, Wetmore," *Boston Globe*, July 20, 1933, 10.

76. "Buying Interests of Adams, Wetmore," *Boston Globe*, July 20, 1933, 10.

77. "C.H. Farnsworth Buried in Cambridge," *Boston Globe*, February 13, 1933, 15; "Bruce Wetmore Dies; Noted Hub Sportsman," *Boston Globe*, April 12, 1953, 1; James C. O'Leary, "Boston Men Buy Share in Braves," *Boston Globe*, May 16, 1927: 1.

78. Burt Whitman, "C.F. Adams, Owner of Boston Hockey Team Buys Shares in Braves," *Boston Herald,* May 16, 1927, 12.

79. "Special Meeting of the National League of Professional Base Ball Clubs," January 18, 1935. Provided by the Baseball Hall of Fame, BA_MSS_55_Box 7_ folder 15: 63.

80. Burt Whitman, "C.F. Adams, Owner of Boston Hockey Team, Buys Shares in Braves," *Boston Herald*, May 16, 1927, 1; "Weather Again Holds Up Start of Paris Flight," *Boston Herald*, May 16, 1927, 1.

81. Burt Whitman, "Braves Get Hornsby from Giants in Trade for Hogan and Welsh," *Boston Herald*, January 11, 1928, 1.

82. Burt Whitman, "Slattery Will Manage Braves," *Boston Herald*, November 3, 1927, 1, 17.

83. W.E. Mullins, "$40,600 a Year for Hornsby; Signs Three-Year Contract," *Boston Herald*, March 2, 1928, 1.

84. Kaese, 190; Burt Whitman, "Hornsby New Manager of Braves. Jack Slattery Resigns from Tribal Berth," *Boston Herald*, May 24, 1928, 1.

85. Ray Miller, "A Biography of Braves Field," in *Braves Field: Memorable Moments at Boston's Lost Diamond*. Ed. Bill Nowlin and Bob Brady.

(Phoenix: Society for American Baseball Research, 2015), 6; See also Kaese, 205 and Philip J. Lowry, *Green Cathedrals: The Ultimate Celebration of Major League and Negro League Ballparks* (New York: Walker & Co., 2006), 32; Burt Whitman, "Johnny Cooney Will Begin His Comeback Campaign at the Braves Camp After New Year," *Boston Herald*, December 22, 1927, 15.

86. "Bob Dunbar" column, *Boston Herald* April 23, 1928, 9.

87. Burt Whitman, "Braves to Put High Wire Net on New Bleachers; Unwise to Move Stands This Year," *Boston Herald*, April 29, 1928, 23; "Braves to Erect 30-foot Canvas Screen on Top of New Bleachers," *Boston Herald*, June 14, 1928, 15; "New Arrangement at Wigwam Should Be OK," *Boston Globe*, July 3, 1928, 11.

88. Berton A. Boxerman and Benita W. Boxerman, *Jews and Baseball: Vol. 1, Entering the Mainstream, 1871–1948* (Jefferson, NC: McFarland, 2006), 119.

89. "Sunday Pro Sports Approved by the State," *Boston Globe*, November 8, 1928, 21.

90. The law stated, "No tradesman, artificer, labourer or other person whatsoever, shall, upon the land or water, do or exercise any labour, business or work of their ordinary callings, nor use any game, sport, play or recreation on the Lord's Day." *Acts and Resolves, Public and Private, of the Province of the Massachusetts Bay, Vol. I.* (Boston: Wright & Porter, 1869), 58.

91. Charlie Bevis, *Red Sox vs. Braves in Boston: The Battle for Fans' Hearts, 1901–1952* (Jefferson, NC: McFarland, 2017), 101.

92. Bevis, 107; "Sunday Sports Vote Ban Asked," *Boston Globe*, June 9, 1926, 1; "Sunday Sports Law not to Appear on Ballot," *Boston Globe*, September 18, 1926, 1; Bevis, *Red Sox vs. Braves*, 111.

93. The new North Station saw 80,000 travelers a day. "Hot Talk Banded on Sunday Sports," *Boston Globe*, February 1, 1928, 1; "Red Sox and Braves May Play in Boston Sundays," *Boston Globe*, March 4, 1928, B56; "New North Station Proves Adequate," *Boston Globe*, August 21, 1928, 8; "Throng Opens Boston Garden," *Boston Globe*, November 18, 1928, 1; "Defeat of Bruins Didn't Prevent Success of Hockey Opening at New Boston Garden," *Boston Globe*, November 21, 1928, 24; "Hot Talk Bandied," 4.

94. "Fuchs Declares Lynch Asked 13 $5000 Bribes," *Boston Globe*, January 3, 1929, 1; Bevis, *Red Sox vs. Braves*, 116.

95. "Parts of 'Sports' Testimony 'Look Bad' to Atty Gen Warner," *Boston Globe*, January 5, 1929, 1, 3.

96. Kaese, 207.

97. Fuchs and Soini, 62.

98. Burt Whitman, "Hornsby Sold to Cubs for 5 Men and Cash," *Boston Herald*, November 8, 1928, 1.

99. Kaese, 209.

100. James C. O'Leary, "Evers Declines to Be Tribal Pilot," *Boston Globe*, June 1, 1929, 7; "Fuchs

Undecided as to Managing Team," *Boston Globe*, June 13, 1929, 1.

101. David F. Egan, "Rumor Says Fuchs to Quit as Manager," *Boston Globe*, June 13, 1929, 28.

102. Burt Whitman, "McKechnie Signs Four-Year Contract to Manage Braves, Fuchs Announces at Chicago," *Boston Herald*, October 8, 1929, 31.

103. James C. O'Leary, "Red Sox' Big Eighth Defeats Braves, 6–3," *Boston Globe*, June 30, 1932, 22.

104. See Bill Nowlin, "The Beards Versus the Braves," in *Braves Field: Memorable Moments at Boston's Lost Diamond*. (Phoenix: SABR, 2015), 124–126.

105. *Study of monopoly power: hearings before the Subcommittee on Study of Monopoly Power of the Committee on the Judiciary, House of Representatives, Eighty-second Congress, first session* (Washington: U.S. G.P.O., 1951): 1600.

106. James C. O'Leary, "Braves and Red Sox Announce 'Ladies' Day' Will Be Held at Both Parks on Saturday," *Boston Globe*, January 7, 1933, 10; James C. O'Leary, "Boston National League Club to Have 5200 Bleacher Seats at Lowest Admission Price," *Boston Globe*, January 25, 1933, 21.

107. James C. O'Leary, "Few Braves Balk at Salary Cuts," *Boston Globe*, February 15, 1933, 9.

108. Bill Nowlin. *Tom Yawkey: Patriarch of the Boston Red Sox* (Lincoln: University of Nebraska Press, 2018), 23–38.

109. Nowlin, 16; "Fenway Park to Be Improved at Once," *Boston Globe*, September 19, 1933, 21.

110. W.A. Whitcomb, "Today's Inquest," *Boston Globe*, December 16, 1933, 8.

111. See Dave Roos, "How Joseph Kennedy Made His Fortune (Hint: It Wasn't Bootlegging)," History Stories. October 28, 2019. Retrieved December 24, 2019. history.com/news/joseph-kennedy-wealth-alcohol-prohibition; Kennedy had the reputation of being a bootlegger. Historians debate this claim, but for our purposes Joseph seems to be referred to here; "Executive Meeting of the National League of Professional Base Ball Clubs, Held at the Commodore Hotel, New York, June 20, 1933, 2:00 p.m." Minutes made available by the Baseball Hall of Fame.

112. *New York Times*, June 21, 1933, 1.

113. "Judge Fuchs Denies Sale of Braves Stock," *Boston Globe*, October 5, 1932, 20; Joe Gooter, "Boston Braves Sold to New York Hub Magnate by Fuchs," *The News* (Paterson, NJ), October 12, 1932, 1.

114. "'All Bunk!' Says Adams of Braves Control Deal," *Boston Herald*, October 13, 1932. 18.

115. Al Hirshberg, *The Braves: The Pick and the Shovel* (Boston: Waverly House, 1948), 64.

116. "Executive Meeting of the National League of Professional Base Ball Clubs, Held at the Commodore Hotel, New York, June 20, 1933, 2:00 PM." BA_MSS_55_Box 7_Folder7-Executive MTG. Provided by the Bartlett Giamatti Research Center, Cooperstown New York. *Executive Meeting 6/20/1933*: 77.

117. *Ibid.*: 78–79.

118. Special Meeting 1/18/1935: 63–64.

119. "$500,000 in 1933," Saving.org. Retrieved December 30, 2019. saving.org/inflation/custom/500000-in-1933-3605.

120. Executive Meeting 6/20/1933: 91–92.

121. *Ibid.*, 111.

122. *Ibid.*, 90.

123. *Ibid.*, 84–85.

124. Also included in his inner circle were Massachusetts Governor Joseph B. Ely; Samuel Longley Bickford, founder of the Bickford's restaurant chain; Chauncey Williams of Sears-Roebuck; and former Massachusetts Governor Frank G. Allen. Charles W. Hurd, "Roosevelt Greeted Royally by Canada at Campobello Island," *New York Times*, June 30, 1933, 1; James Roosevelts Take New Cottage," *Boston Globe*, June 16, 1933, 3; Dennis Hevesi, "James Roosevelt, Ex-Congressman and a President's Son, Dies at 83," *New York Times*, August 14, 1991, D19; Executive Meeting 6/20/1933: 90.

125. Executive Meeting 6/20/1933, 104; *Boston Globe*, December 15, 1933, 38.

126. *Ibid.*, 105.

127. *Ibid.*, 86.

128. *Ibid.*, 112–113.

129. *Ibid.*, 118; "Son of Roosevelt Seeks to Buy Braves," *St. Louis Star and Times*, July 7, 1933, 15.

130. James C. O'Leary, "Roosevelt Aids Fuchs in New Deal on Braves," *Boston Globe*, July 8, 1933, 1; "Report Fuchs to Hold Braves," *Boston Globe*, July 19, 1933, 1.

131. "Buying Interests of Adams, Wetmore," *Boston Globe*, July 20, 1933, 10; "Tribal Control to Judge Fuchs," *Boston Globe*, July 21, 1933, 20; "Fuchs, in First Payment of $100,000, Moves to Regain Control of Braves," *Boston Herald*, July 20, 1933, 20.

132. Special Meeting 1/18/1935: 64.

133. Victor O. Jones, "Boston's Biggest Crowd Sees Braves Lose Two," *Boston Globe*, September 2, 1933, 1.

134. "Judge Praises Players for Efforts," *Boston Globe*, September 4, 1933, 19.

135. Kaese, 225.

136. Burt Whitman, "Fuchs Confident League Will Approve His Carrying Out of Its Assignments," *Boston Herald*, February 3, 1935: 31; *Study of monopoly power: hearings before the Subcommittee on Study of Monopoly Power of the Committee on the Judiciary, House of Representatives, Eighty-second Congress, first session* (Washington: U.S. G.P.O., 1951): 1599–1600.

137. T.D. Thornton, *Not by a Long Shot: A Season at a Hard-Luck Horse Track* (New York: Public Affairs, 2007), 31.

138. Charlie Bevis, *Red Sox Vs. Braves in Boston: The Battle for Fans' Hearts, 1901–1952* (Jefferson, NC: McFarland, 2017), 150.

Chapter 3

1. W.A. Whitcomb, "Today's Inquest," *Boston Globe*, September 5, 1933, 19.

2. "Would Legalize Pari-Mutuel Pool Betting," *Portsmouth Herald*, January 25, 1933, 4; Associated Press, "Race Track Bill Becomes a Law," *Portsmouth Herald*, April 3, 1933, 1; James C. O'Leary, "'Pinkey' Whitney Packs Game Away," *Boston Globe*, June 22, 1933, 22; "Pari-mutuel," *Encyclopedia Britannica*. November 26, 2010. Retrieved May 24, 2020. britannica.com/topic/pari-mutuel

3. John Barry, "Vaughan Filly Wins Rockingham Feature," *Boston Globe*, September 5, 1933, 10.

4. "Rockingham Park Opening Proves Decided Success," *Portsmouth Herald*, June 22, 1933, 1.

5. John Barry, "Star Is Winner in Steeplechase," *Boston Globe*, September 7, 1933, 23.

6. "Would Make Bets on Dog Races Legal," *Boston Globe*, January 12, 1934, 8; "House Approves Race Betting Bill," *Boston Globe*, June 1, 1934, 1; "Massachusetts Counties Will Vote Tuesday on Race Betting," *Boston Globe*, November 3, 1934, 13; "Pari-Mutuel Betting on Horse Races Wins," *Boston Globe*, November 7, 1934, 21.

7. "Fuchs Plans Dog Racing at Wigwam; Will Not Interfere with Baseball," *Boston Herald*, November 17, 1934, 11.

8. James C. O'Leary, "Braves Directors to Apply for License to Race Dogs," *Boston Globe*, November 17, 1934, 5.

9. Bill Corum, "Landis Intends Quit If Dog-Racing Gets Foothold in Boston," *Lincoln Star*, December 1, 1934, 8; "Fuchs Surprised at Landis Report," *Boston Globe*, December 1, 1934, 11.

10. John Barry, "Summoned to Racing Hearing," *Boston Globe*, December 5, 1934, 6; "Fuchs Attacks Rumor He's Out as Braves Head," *Boston Herald*, December 18, 1934, 1; Richard O. Boyer, "18 Summonsed by Council in Race Hearing," *Boston Herald*, December 5, 1934, 7; "Combine Will Race Horses in E. Boston," *Boston Globe*, January 10, 1935, 22.

11. "Fuchs and Garden Dog Race Rivals," *Boston Globe*, December 7, 1934, 19; "Fuchs to Seek League Permit," *Boston Herald*, December 8, 1934, 9.

12. Victor O. Jones, "Frick Opposes Fuchs' Action. Would Bar Dog Racing in Baseball Parks," *Boston Globe*, December 8, 1934, 1.

13. "Braves President Plans to Conduct Dog-Racing Track," *Christian Science Monitor*, December 8, 1934, 8; "National League Won't Allow Braves to Use Park for Ball Games and Dog Racing," Associated Press story printed in the *Hartford Courant*, December 8, 1934, 13.

14. John Drebinger, "Major Problems Confront Baseball Magnates at Conventions Opening Today," *New York Times*, December 11, 1934, 30.

15. Victor O. Jones, "What About It?" *Boston Globe*, December 10, 1934, 16.

16. Burt Whitman, "Red Sox Certain to Make Trades," *Boston Herald*, December 9, 1934, 34.

17. Albert W. Keane, "Calling 'Em Right," *Hartford Courant*, December 12, 1934, 15.

18. Dan Busby, "Kenesaw Mountain Landis," SABR BioProject. Retrieved May 24, 2020. sabr.org/node/33871

19. Charles A. Barton, "Sportographs," *Star Tribune*, December 12, 1934, 13.

20. Bill Cunningham, "Calls Racing Craze Blight," *Boston Post*, November 4, 1934, 16.

21. Bill Cunningham, "'Tote' Board Will Cut Dog Racket," *Boston Post*, January 23, 1935, 18.

22. Steven A. Riess, "When Chicago Went to the Dogs: Al Capone and Greyhound Racing in the Windy City, 1927–1933," *Journal of the Illinois State Historical Society* 112, no. 3 (Fall 2019): 270.

23. Riess, 273.

24. *Ibid.*, 279–280.

25. "Charges Taunton Track Under International," *Boston Globe*, October 13, 1936, 18; "O'Hare, Track Chief, Shot to Death by Gang at Chicago," *Boston Globe*, November 9, 1939, 1; Alejandro Cancino, "70 Years Later, Slaying Will Get Another Look," *Chicago Tribune*, January 13, 2010.

26. Cunningham, "'Tote' Board Will Cut Dog Racket," *Boston Post*, January 23, 1935.

27. David George Surdam, *Wins, Losses, & Empty Seats: How Baseball Outlasted the Great Depression* (Lincoln: University of Nebraska Press, 2011), 8, 10.

28. Surdam, 318; Team financial records were reported to Congress in 1951, giving us a general picture of which teams were barely scraping by at this time.

29. Associated Press, "Major League Magnates Do Plenty of Talking but Fail to Accomplish Anything," *Hartford Courant*, December 12, 1934, 15.

30. Dialogue from the meeting is taken from "Annual Meeting of the National League of Professional Baseball Clubs, Held at the Waldorf Astoria Hotel, New York, NY, December 12, 1934; 1:20 PM" (167–174). Provided by the A. Bartlett Giamatti Research Center, Cooperstown, NY. BA_MSS_55_Box7.

31. "No Major Changes in 1935," *Boston Globe*, December 13, 1934, 26.

32. Dialogue from this meeting is taken from "Annual Meeting of the Board of Directors of the American League of Professional Base Ball Clubs Held at the Hotel Commodore, New York, N.Y., December 11, 1934," pages 45–51. Provided by the Baseball Hall of Fame.

33. John Lardner, "Lardner Searches Hotel Lobby, but Fails to Find Ruth's Future Job," *Dayton Daily News*, December 13, 1934, 24.

34. James C. Isaminger, "Ruth May Help Direct Macks," *Philadelphia Inquirer*, December 13, 1934, 17; Associated Press, "Babe Ruth Sought by Boston Braves," *Oakland Tribune*, December 13, 1934, 1; Associated Press, "Whatever They Do's

O.K.—Babe," *New York Daily News*, December 13, 1934, 68; International News Service, "Babe Ruth Says: 'I Should Worry!'" *News-Messenger* (Fremont, Ohio), December 14, 1934, 11; Daniel R. Levitt, "Jacob Ruppert," SABR BioProject. Retrieved May 28, 2020. sabr.org/bioproj/person/b96b262d

35. James C. O'Leary, "Adams Denies Seeking Ruth," *Boston Globe*, December 14, 1934, 31.

36. Melville E. Webb, Jr., "The Old Stone League," *Boston Globe*, December 15, 1934, 8.

37. Associated Press, "Adams Amazed Over the Furor of Babe Ruth," *Burlington Free Press*, December 15, 1934, 13.

38. Henry McLeMore, "Sports Parade," *Courier-Post* (Camden, NJ). December 17, 1934, 20.

39. Edmund F. Wehrle, *Breaking Babe Ruth: Baseball's Campaign Against Its Biggest Star.* (Columbia: University of Missouri Press, 2018), 117, 210–211.

40. Edward J. Neil, "What to Do with Babe Ruth Is a Question," *Burlington Free Press*, December 21, 1934, 21.

41. "Taking Care of Babe Ruth," *Dayton Herald*, December 15, 1934, 4.

42. Alan Gould, "Doubt Shrouds Future of Baseball's Idol," *Central New Jersey Home News* (New Brunswick, NJ), December 26, 1934, 11.

43. Westbrook Pegler, "The Save-Babe-Ruth Campaign Keeps the Magnates Puzzled," *Kansas City Times*, December 27, 1934, 10.

44. James Jermail, "The Inquiring Photographer," *New York Daily News*, December 23, 1934, 27.

45. Associated Press, "Ruppert to Slash Ruth's $80,000 Salary; Declares Day of Big Contracts Is Past," *New York Times*, December 5, 1931, 22.

46. James P. Dawson, "Ruth and Ruppert Agree on $52,000," *New York Times*, March 23, 1933, 21.

47. John Kieran, "Mr. Ruth, the Manager," *New York Times*, October 22, 1933, S2.

48. Michael Haupert, "MLB's Annual Salary Leaders Since 1874," Society for American Baseball Research. Retrieved June 4, 2020. sabr.org/research/mlbs-annual-salary-leaders-1874-2012.

49. Jane Leavy, *The Big Fella: Babe Ruth and the World He Created* (New York: Harper Collins, 2018), 410.

50. *Boston Globe*, June 6, 1934, 21.

51. Leavy, 410–411.

52. Wehrle, 225–226.

Chapter 4

1. Sam B. Warner, Jr., *Streetcar Suburbs: The Process of Growth in Boston 1870–1900.* (New York: Atheneum, 1962), 14, 41–42, 53.

2. "Jamaicaway Real Estate," *Boston Globe*, August 5, 1932, 27.

3. Lawrence W. Kennedy, *Planning the City Upon a Hill: Boston Since 1630* (Amherst: University of Massachusetts Press, 1992), 129.

4. *Ibid.*, 142.

5. *Ibid.,* 143; Michael J. Ryan, "Where Did Curley Get the Cash?" *Boston Globe*, April 17, 1988, 91.

6. Charles H. Trout, *Boston, the Great Depression and the New Deal* (New York: Oxford University Press, 1977), 38–39.

7. *Ibid.*, 40.

8. James C. O'Leary, "Judge Fuchs Praises Young Road Secretary," *Boston* Globe, December 11, 1933, 19; Jack Beatty, *The Rascal King: The Life and Times of James Michael Curley (1874–1958)* (Reading, MA, 1992), 429, 459–460; "James G. Curley, Son of Congressman, Dies," *Boston Globe*, October 15, 1945, 1.

9. Associated Press, "Braves Line Up 25 Games," *Spokesman-Review* (Spokane, WA), January 1, 1935, 11.

10. "Combine Will Race Horses in E. Boston," *Boston Globe*, January 10, 1935, 22.

11. "Seeks Braves Field License," *Boston Globe*, January 12, 1935, 3; Arthur Siegel, "Boston Kennel Club Files Application for Racing License at Braves Field; Buys Lease from Baseball Interests," *Boston Herald*, January 13, 1935, 38.

12. Burt Whitman, "Warriors Sell Old Homestead," *Boston Herald*, January 13, 1935, 38; Associated Press, "Permission Needed," *Boston Herald*, January 13, 1935, 38.

13. "Permission Needed."

14. Siegel, "Boston Kennel Club"; Roscoe McGowen, "Dog Racing Asked for Braves Field," *New York Times*, January 13, 1935, S1.

15. "Braves Lose Field," 13; Paul H. Shannon, "Fuchs Was Notified," *Boston Post*, January 15, 1935, 19; Jack Malaney, "Collins Says No Such Arrangements Have Been Made as New Group Seeks Wigwam Dog License," *Boston Post*, January 13, 1935, 15; Associated Press, "Braves Lose Field, Sox Will Not Rent Fenway," *Springfield Republican*, January 15, 1935, 1.

16. James C. O'Leary, "Homeless Braves Are Awaiting the Decision," *Boston Globe*, January 17, 1935, 18; "Baltimore's Mayor Is Strong for Major Ball," *Boston Globe*, January 17, 1935, 18; Burt Whitman, "N.L. President Calls Meeting of Club Owners," *Boston Herald*, January 15, 1935, 19.

17. Burt Whitman, "N.L. President Calls Meeting of Club Owners," *Boston Herald*, January 15, 1935, 19.

18. Paul H. Shannon, "Magnates Take Up Tribal Fate," *Boston Post*, January 18, 1935, 24.

19. Associated Press, "Braves' Fate Up to League Clubs," *Boston Post*, January 15, 1935, 19; Associated Press, "C.F. Adams Refuses to Carry Braves' Burden," *Springfield Republican*, January 17, 1935, 20.

20. "Braves Lose Field," 13.

21. James C. O'Leary, "Braves' Fate Up to League," *Boston Globe*, January 15, 1935, 20.

22. Bill Cunningham, "Fuchs Should Quit Baseball," *Boston Post*, January 18, 1935, 24.

23. *New York Times*, January 19, 1935, 8.

24. John Kieran, "Sports of the Times," January 21, 1935, 7.

25. "Special Meeting of the National League of Professional Baseball Clubs, Held at the Offices of the National League, RCA Building, New York City, January 18, 1935: 10 a.m.,"3–4. Provided by the A. Bartlett Giamatti Research Center at the National Baseball Hall of Fame, Cooperstown, New York. Hereafter referred to as "Special Meeting 1/18/1935."

26. Tommy Holmes, "League Meeting Can't Show Fuchs Baseball Profit," *Brooklyn Daily Eagle*, January 18, 1935, 24.

27. Davis J. Walsh, "National Leaguers Will Decide Boston's Fate," *Evening News* (Wilkes-Barre, PA), January 18, 1935, 15; Bill McCullough, "Owner Lost Favor with His Public," *Brooklyn Times Union*, January 18, 1935, 1A.

28. Special Meeting 1/18/1935: 6.

29. *Ibid.*,11–12.

30. John Drebinger, "National League Reaffirms Ban on Dog Racing; Braves to Stay in Own Park," *New York Times*, January 19, 1935, 16.

31. Special Meeting 1/18/1935: 41–42.

32. *Ibid.*,44–46, 50.

33. *Ibid.*, 50–56.

34. *Ibid.*, 68, 71.

35. *Ibid.*, 39, 62–67.

36. Paul H. Shannon, "Fuchs Lucky to Be Tribal Head," *Boston Post*, January 20, 1935, 15.

37. George Kenney, "Hot Air Blast by N.L. Fails to Help Braves," *New York Daily News*, January 20, 1935, 36C.

38. Special Meeting 1/18/1935, 82.

39. Bill Cunningham, "Contradiction Clouds Entire Tribal Mixup," *Boston Post*, January 20, 1935, 15.

40. *Ibid.*

41. "Governor Among 'Certain Parties' to Be Consulted," *Springfield Republican*, January 20, 1935, 5B.

42. "League Takes Long Lease of Braves Field," *Boston Herald*, January 29, 1935, 16.

43. Bill Cunningham, "Fuchs Ready to Quit," *Boston Post*, January 30, 1935, 18.

44. *Ibid.*

45. James C. O'Leary, "Braves Profits Went for Players," *Boston Globe*, February 3, 1935, A22; Burt Whitman, "Fuchs Confident League Will Approve His Carrying Out of Its Assignments," *Boston Herald*, February 3, 1935, 32.

46. James C. O'Leary, "National League to Save Boston Braves," *Boston Globe*, January 30, 1935, 16.

47. James C. O'Leary, "Braves' Committee Will Meet Tonight," *Boston Globe*, January 31, 1935, 21.

48. "Ticket Pledges Exceed $28,000," *Boston Globe*, February 1, 1935, 23.

49. "Reconvened Annual and Schedule Meeting, Feb. 5, 1935" BA_MSS_55_Box7_Folder16: 60. Hereafter referred to as "Meeting 2/5/1935."

50. *Ibid.*, 80.

51. *Ibid.*, 97.

52. "Attendance in NYP Shows Gain," *Evening News* (Harrisburg, PA), November 17, 1934, 9;

Ed Van Dyke, "Baseball Club Action Deferred Another Week," *Star-Gazette* (Elmira, NY), February 1, 1935, 17; "Joe Cambria Intends to Take Over Club," *Harrisburg Telegraph*, February 7, 1935, 19; Meeting 2/5/1935, 77.

53. "McKeesport Club Will Be Farm of Braves," *Pittsburgh-Post Gazette*, February 15, 1935, 19.

54. Meeting 2/5/1935: 108–109.

55. *Ibid.*, 110–112.

56. *Ibid.*, 113.

57. *Ibid.*, 119.

58. *Ibid.*, 119.

59. *Ibid.*, 124–125.

60. Meeting 2/5/1935: 128.

61. Glenn Stout and Richard A. Johnson, *Red Sox Century: The Definitive History of Baseball's Most Storied Franchise* (Boston: Houghton Mifflin, 2005), 160–161, 172.

62. Paul H. Shannon, "Braves to Play Ball in Boston," *Boston Post*, January 19, 1935, 11.

63. Bill Cunningham, "Bob Quinn Ideal Man for Adams," *Boston Post*, January 26, 1935: 13.

64. Meeting 2/5/1935: 130–132.

65. *Ibid.*, 146.

66. *Ibid.*, 152–153.

67. *Ibid.*, 153.

68. Associated Press, "Fuchs Remains Braves' Head," *Boston Globe*, February 6, 1935, 20.

69. "Ruth Insists He Won't Play as Yank, Seeks Manager Job," *Times Union*, January 16, 1935.

70. Richard G. Massock, "Place Mail in the Unclaimed Letter Bureau," *Honolulu Star-Bulletin*, February 2, 1935, 10.

71. Associated Press, "Ruth Is Anxious to Get Back Home," *Boston Globe*, January 19, 1935, 5.

72. Walter Gilhooly, "In the Realm of Sport," *Ottawa Journal*, January 19, 1935, 29.

Chapter 5

1. Associated Press, "Babe Ruth Tries Cricket, but Balks at $40 a Week Top Wage," *Harrisburg Telegraph*, February 9, 1935, 1.

2. Associated Press, "Ruth's Terrific Blows Break Cricket Bat; Crowd in London Is Thrilled by His Skill," *New York Times*, February 10, 1935, S1.

3. "'Mr.' Babe Ruth Looks at England," *The Guardian* (London, England), February 13, 1935, 3.

4. Jack Cuddy, "Ruth Worried Over 1935 Job, to Hurry Home," *Times Union* (Brooklyn, NY), February 8, 1935, 1A.

5. *Ibid.*

6. "Incomes of Families and Single Persons, 1935–36," in *Monthly Labor Review* 47, no.4 (October 1938): 729.

7. "Ruth Will Put $100,000 in Trust," *Brooklyn Citizen*, March 9, 1930, 13.

8. Brad Snyder, *A Well-Paid Slave: Curt Flood's Fight for Free Agency in Professional Sports* (New York: Viking, 2006), 104.

9. David Walker, "Babe Ruth, £25,000 Slave, Is Snooping Around," *Daily Mirror*, February 8, 1935, 2.

10. Clifford Webb, "Meet Babe Ruth—Baseball's Best Paid Ball Player," *Daily Herald* (London), February 8, 1935, 19.

11. David Walker, "Babe Ruth, £25,000 Slave, Is Snooping Around," *Daily Mirror*, February 8, 1935, 2.

12. "Ocean Travelers," *New York Times*, February 20, 1935, 24.

13. Rud Rennie, "Babe Ruth Returns, Expressing Desire to Remain in Baseball, but Not as Bench Warmer," *New York Tribune*, February 21, 1935, 23.

14. Harold Parrott, "'I'll Never Be a Benchwarmer—Ruth," *Brooklyn Daily Eagle*, February 21, 1935, 12.

15. James P. Dawson, "Return from World Tour Finds Babe Ruth Hopeful of Remaining in Baseball," *New York Times*, February 21, 1935, 25.

16. "Return from World Tour"; "May Change Mind Hints Babe at Pier," *Times Union*, February 20, 1935, 1.

17. "May Change Mind."

18. Rennie, "Babe Ruth Returns," 14.

19. "Braves Would Like Ruth, but Not as Club Manager," *Springfield Republican*, February 22, 1935, 26.

20. James P. Dawson, "Snow Balks Ruth in Golf Workout," *New York Times*, February 23, 1935, 21.

21. Robert W. Creamer, *Babe: The Legend Comes to Life* (New York: Penguin Books, 1974), 386–388.

22. "Babe Ruth Returns"; Ruth is shown in an Associated Press photo leaving on that hunting trip on Sunday, February 24; "Wire Photo-Ruth Still Here," *Cleveland Plain Dealer*, February 25, 1935, 16.

23. Babe Ruth and Bob Considine, *The Babe Ruth Story* (New York: Signet, 1992), 208.

24. Rud Rennie, "Future of 'Poor' Ruth Causes Worry to All Sports Followers Except Babe, Assured of $15,000 Yearly for Life," *New York Tribune*, January 27, 1935, B5.

25. James C. O'Leary, "Braves Lose First Game to Yankees," *Boston Globe*, March 9, 1930, A22.

26. Marshall Smelser, *The Life That Ruth Built: A Biography* (Lincoln: University of Nebraska Press, 1975), 493.

27. Smelser, 496.

28. Associated Press, "Babe Ruth, Paul Dean Head List of Unsigned Athletes of Rank," *Lincoln Star Journal*, February 26, 1935, 8; "800 Quit Sidewalks to Learn Farming," *Brooklyn Times Union*, April 14, 1935, 2; Ellen Barry, "A Shelter Far from the Streets," *Los Angeles Times*, January 9, 2007.

29. James P. Dawson, "15-Year Career as Yankee Star Terminated by Ruth to Enlist with Braves," *New York Times*, February 27, 1935, 23.

30. Babe Ruth as told to Bob Considine, 209.

31. Harold Parrott, "Cost to Acquire Babe Exactly $47.50," *Brooklyn Daily Eagle*, February 27, 1935, 20.

32. Babe Ruth as told to Bob Considine, 209.

33. Robert S. Fuchs and Wayne Soini, *Judge*

Fuchs and the Boston Braves (Jefferson, NC: McFarland, 1998), 104.

34. *Ibid.*, 105.

35. *Ibid.*, 106–107.

36. Smelser, 493.

37. Hy Hurwitz, "Assistant Manager," *Boston Globe*, February 26, 1935, 4.

38. Dawson, "15-Year Career as Yankee Star Terminated."

39. According to Surdam, 1931, 1933 and 1934 were financial net losses for the Braves. David George Surdam, *Wins, Losses & Empty Seats* (Lincoln: University of Nebraska Press, 2011), 318.

40. Fuchs letter to Ruth 2/26/35. Babe Ruth Central. baberuthcentral.com/babesimpact/memborabilia-collection/ruth-agreements/ Retrieved November 19, 2020.

41. George Dixon, "Braves Sign Ruth for 3 Years; To Be Assistant Manager," *New York Daily News*, February 27, 1935, 50.

42. Dawson, "15-Year Career as Yankee Star Terminated."

43. Jack Barnwell, "Babe Will Come Here Today to Sign Contract," *Boston Post*, February 28, 1935, 15.

44. "Braves Sign Ruth for 3 Years," 50.

45. Jack Barnwell, "Babe to Pilot Braves Team for 3 Years," *Boston Post*, February 27, 1935, 16.

46. John Kieran, "Sports of the Times," *Boston Herald*, February 27, 1935, 17.

47. "Babe Ruth Joins Braves as Player and Magnate; Will Assist McKechnie," *Brooklyn Times Union*, February 26, 1935, 3A.

48. "Braves Sign Ruth for 3 Years," 52.

49. James C. O'Leary, "Babe Is Coming to Braves for Three Years as Player and Official," *Boston Globe*, February 27, 1935, 1.

50. Hy Hurwitz, "Ruth's Diamond Career Stands Without Parallel," *Boston Globe*, February 27, 1935, 19.

51. Grantland Rice, "Back to Boston, Where He Started," *Boston Globe*, February 27, 1935, 20.

52. Burt Whitman, "Will Be Player, Asst. Manager, 2D Vice-Pres," *Boston Herald*, February 27, 1935.

53. *New York Times*, February 28, 1935, 23.

54. Pat Robinson, "Claims Ruth Deal Face-Saving Move," *Worcester Evening Gazette*, February 27, 1935, 12.

55. "Babe Ruth Comes Back," *Boston Herald*, February 27, 1935, 15.

56. Bill Cunningham, "Shed No Tears for Poor Babe," *Boston Post*, February 23, 1935, 12.

57. "Babe Is Coming to Braves for Three Years," 19; Arthur Sampson, "Judge Fuchs, Back in Boston, Plans Dinner for Bambino Tomorrow Night; Says Ruth Is Easy Man to Deal With," *Boston Herald*, February 27, 1935: 16.

58. George Dixon, "Ruth Will Lead Tribe This Year," *New York Daily News*, February 28, 1935, 50.

59. Burt Whitman, "Babe Expects to Pilot Braves in 1936 If Assured McKechnie Will Not Suffer; Situation Resembles Hornsby's Reign," *Boston Herald*, February 28, 1935, 16.

60. James C. O'Leary, "Ruth to Lead Braves in 1936," *Boston Globe*, February 28, 1935, 20.

61. "Babe to Pilot Braves Team for 3 Years," *Boston Post*, February 27, 1935, 16.

62. "Ruth Says Job His in 1936 in N.Y. Interview," *Boston Herald*, February 28, 1935, 16.

63. Burt Whitman, "Boston Hails Babe Ruth as Hero," *Boston Herald*, March 1, 1935, 40.

64. Robert S. Fuchs and Wayne Soini, *Judge Fuchs and the Boston Braves* (Jefferson, NC: McFarland, 1998), 108.

65. James C. O'Leary, "Thousands Here Welcome Ruth," *Boston Globe*, March 1, 1935, 1.

66. Jack Barnwell, "Hub Roars Great Welcome to Babe," *Boston Post*, Mach 1, 1935, 1.

67. "Hub Roars Great Welcome," 24.

68. "Boston Hails Babe Ruth as Hero," 40.

69. "Hub Roars Great Welcome to Babe," 24.

70. "Babe Walks from Train to Hotel," *Boston Post*, March 1, 1935, 24.

71. "Boston Hails Babe Ruth as Hero," 40.

72. "Hub Roars Great Welcome to Babe," 24.

73. *Ibid.*

74. *Ibid.*

75. "Boston Hails Babe Ruth as Hero," 40.

76. "Thousands Here Welcome Ruth," 27.

77. *Ibid.*

78. *Ibid.*

79. Ray Finnegan, "Babe Is Patient as Cameras Flash," *Boston Globe*, March 1, 1935, 23.

80. "Boston Hails Babe Ruth as Hero," 40.

81. "McKechnie to Represent Him, C.F. Adams Insists," *Boston Globe*, March 1, 1935, 27.

82. "Boston Hails Babe Ruth as Hero," 40.

83. Associated Press, "Adams Speaks Out," *Springfield Republican*, March 1, 1935, 19.

84. "Boston Hails Babe Ruth as Hero," 40.

85. Grace Davidson, "Mrs. Ruth Stepped on in Rush to Greet Babe," *Boston Post*, March 1, 1935, 24.

86. Smelser, 419.

87. Creamer, 341.

88. Edmund F. Wehrle, *Breaking Babe Ruth: Baseball's Campaign Against Its Biggest Star* (Columbia: University of Missouri Press, 2018), 214.

89. Davidson, "Mrs. Ruth."

90. "'Take Me Two Days to Recuperate,' 'See You in April,' Says Ruths, Leaving," *Boston Herald*, March 1, 1935: 40.

Chapter 6

1. "Babe Ruth Comes Back," *Boston Herald*, February 27, 2935: 12.

2. Louis Effrat, "Confident of Playing 100 Games, Ruth Starts for Training Camp of Braves," *New York Times*, March 4, 1935: 22.

3. Allan Gould, "Babe Ruth Heads South with The Boston Braves," *The Morning Call* (Paterson, New Jersey), March 4, 1935: 19.

4. Gould, "Babe Ruth Heads South with The Boston Braves,"

5. Paul H. Shannon, "Hail Babe at Braves Camp," *Boston Post*, March 5, 1935: 1.

6. "Acclaimed by a Tumultuous Throng, Braves' New Acquisition Battles Crowd Fifteen Minutes in Station—Assures McKechnie of Loyal Aid—Starts Work Today," *New York Times*, March 5, 1935: 25.

7. Alan Gould, "Bambino Given Big Welcome at St. Petersburg," *Tampa Bay Tribune*, March 5, 1935: 11.

8. Pete Norton, "Babe Is Nearly Mobbed by Big Crowd of Fans," *Tampa Bay Times*, March 5, 1935: 1

9. "Al Lang Dies; Was Florida's 'Mr. Baseball,'" *Tampa Bay Times*, February 28, 1960: 1; "St. Petersburg Invites You," *Boston Globe*, January 8, 1922: 20.

10. Gerry Moore, "Ruth Gets Fine Welcome," *Boston Globe*, March 5, 1935: 21.

11. Anthony Harkins, "From 'Sweet Mamas' to 'Bodacious' Hillbillies: Billy DeBeck's Impact on American Culture," *Studies in American Humor* (New Series 3, No 14, 2006): 55, 61.

12. Moore, "Ruth Gets Fine Welcome."

13. *Ibid.*

14. Alan Gould, "Huge Gallery Watches Babe at Waterfront," *Tampa Bay Times*, March 6, 1935.

15. "Bob Dunbar," *Boston Herald*, February 27, 1935, 17.

16. John Drohan, "Babe Clears Fence on Third Swing in First Workout with Tribal Squad; Gets Royal Welcome from All Hands," *Boston Herald*, March 6, 1935, 31.

17. Dick Leyden, "Rabbit Maranville," SABR BioProject. Retrieved December 5, 2020. sabr.org/bioproj/person/rabbit-maranville/

18. Bill James, *The New Bill James Historical Baseball Abstract* (New York: Free Press, 2001), 597.

19. *Ibid.*, 617.

20. Gerry Moore, "Maranville Limps, but Shows Pep in Practice," *Boston Globe*, March 5, 1935, 21.

21. Drohan, "Babe Clears Fence," 31.

22. Paul H. Shannon, "Babe Slams Two Over the Fence," *Boston Post*, March 6, 1935, 16.

23. Drohan, "Babe Clears Fence," 31.

24. "Bambino Shoots an 82 in Initial Round on Links," *Tampa Bay Times*, March 6, 1935, 13.

25. Gerry Moore, "Shanty Hogan Out of Game for Some Days," *Boston Globe*, March 7, 1935, 20.

26. Harold Kaese, "'Babe Ruth of Catchers,' Shanty Hogan, Dead at 61," *Boston Globe*, April 8, 1967, 20.

27. John Drohan, "Hogan Receives Slight Concussion from 'Beaning' by Bobby Brown," *Boston Herald*, March 7, 1935, 28.

28. John Drohan, "Yannigans Blank Braves Regulars, 2–0, After Babe Works with Them in Drill; Joe Coscarart Clouts Long Home Run," *Boston Herald*, March 8, 1935, 36; "F.M.A. Names Ruth Cadet Commandant," *Tampa Bay Times*, March 9, 1935, 12.

29. Drohan, "Yannigans Blank Braves Regulars, 2–0"; Bob LeMoine, "Joe Coscarart," SABR Bio

Project. Retrieved December 7, 2020. sabr.org/ bioproj/person/joe-coscarart/.

30. Burt Whitman, "Babe Answers Question— 'Where'd You Play Ruth?'" *Boston Herald*, April 5, 1919, 16.

31. Mac Parker, "Rotes Lead March to Shake Sunday's Hand," *Boston Herald*, April 5, 1919, 1; "Scores Respond to Invitations After Sermons," *Tampa Times*, April 5, 1919, 1, 19.

32. John Drohan, "Ruth to Play for Six Innings," *Boston Herald*, March 9, 1935, 8.

33. Alan Gould, "Babe's Single Scores Initial Run of the Contest," Associated Press article printed in the *St. Petersburg Times*, March 10, 1935, 2–1.

34. Red Newton, "Babe Ruth Singles Here in National League Debut," *Tampa Tribune*, March 10, 1935, 2–2.

35. *Ibid.*

36. "Writers Send Out 30,000 Words About Babe Ruth in Tampa," *Tampa Tribune*, March 10, 1935, 1.

37. Babe Ruth, "Babe Says Legs Right in Shape," *Boston Post*, March 17, 1935, 27.

38. Associated Press, "Why Doesn't Babe Stay in A.L., Dizzy Dean Wants to Know," *St. Louis Post-Dispatch*, February 27, 1935, 2B.

39. Red Newton, "Dizzy Dean Apologizes to Babe Ruth at Game Here," *Tampa Tribune*, March 11, 1935, 1.

40. Paul H. Shannon, "Babe Laughs at Injured Arm Tale," *Boston Post*, March 13, 1935, 18.

41. Gerry Moore, "Babe Nurses His Lame Arm," *Boston Globe*, March 13, 1935, 17.

42. Gerry Moore, "Babe Ruth Is Resting Elbow for Yankee Game," *Boston Globe*, March 15, 1935, 24.

43. Babe Ruth, "Dislikes to Quit Playing Ranks," *Boston Post*, March 14, 1935, 18; John Drohan, "Rabbit Displays 'Run-Down' Art," *Boston Herald*, March 13, 1935, 19.

44. John Drohan, "Tribal Varsity Gains 11–1 Balm," *Boston Herald*, March 14, 1935, 26.

45. Gerry Moore, "Babe Ruth Plays First Game with Braves Today," *Boston Globe*, March 16, 1935, 5.

46. John Drohan, "Babe Warms Up by Nudging Two," *Boston Herald*, March 16, 1935, 6.

47. Associated Press, "Germany Scraps Treaty, Will Raise Big Army," *Boston Globe*, March 16, 1935, 1–2; "Lessons Learned: Hitler's Rearmament of Germany," Council on Foreign Relations. Retrieved December 13, 2020. cfr.org/explainer-video/lessons-learned-hitlers-rearmament-germany

48. Pete Norton, "Jordan's Blow in Ninth Frame Decides Battle," *St. Petersburg Times*, March 17, 1935, 2–1; Gerry Moore, "Braves Beat Yanks on Hit by Jordan," *Boston Globe*, March 17, 1935, A26.

49. Paul H. Shannon, "Babe Hits Single as Tribe Win, 3–2," *Boston Post*, March 17, 1935, 27.

50. Ruth, "Babe Says Legs Right in Shape," *Boston Post,* March 27, 1935, 27.

51. Alan Gould, "Babe Draws Record Crowd Across Bay," *Tampa Tribune*, March 17, 1935, 17.

52. Shannon, "Babe Hits Single as Tribe Win, 3–2."

53. Bill Cunningham, "Babe's Name Has Plenty of Magic," *Boston Post*, March 18, 1935, 16.

54. Gerry Moore, "Braves Beat Yankees for the Second Time," *Boston Globe*, March 18, 193, 9.

55. John Drohan, "Braves Swing Shillelaghs to Defeat Yanks for Second Time in Row, 9–4," *Boston Herald*, March 18, 1935, 6.

56. "House of David," Atlas Obscura. Retrieved December 16, 2020. atlasobscura.com/ places/house-of-david; Bill Nowlin, "August 1, 1932: The Beards vs the Braves: House of David Visits Boston," SABR Games Project. Retrieved December 16, 2020. sabr.org/gamesproj/game/ august-1–1932-the-beards-versus-the-braves-house-of-david-visits-boston.

57. John Drohan, "Braves Rout Alleged House of David, 17–6, for Third Grapefruit Win in Row," *Boston Herald*, March 19, 1935, 18.

58. Gerry Moore, "Tribe Trims House of David Team, 17–6," *Boston Globe*, March 19, 1935, 21.

59. Burt Whitman, "Yankees Win First Game of the Year by Beating Braves, 4–1, Behind Gomez," *Boston Herald*, March 20, 1935, 27.

60. "Babe Ruth Denies Heart Is Ailing," *Boston Herald*, March 20, 1935, 27.

61. "News of Training Camps," *Brooklyn Daily Eagle*, March 20, 1935, 26.

62. Antonio Ford, "Harlem Race Riot of 1935," in *Encyclopedia of Race and Crime*; ed. Helen Taylor Greene and Shaun L. Gabbidon (2009: SAGE Publications), 333–336.

63. Gerry Moore, "Gene Moore Robs Babe Ruth of Homer," *Boston Globe*, March 21, 1935, 19.

64. *Ibid.*

65. Rick Rousos, "Historic Henley Field Is a Trip Back in Time for Players," *The Ledger* (Lakeland, Florida), April 4, 2002, 1.

66. Associated Press, "Ruth Has Drawn 20,000 at Gate for Braves; 150,000 Total Seen," *New York Times*, March 22, 1935, 29.

67. Gerry Moore, "Detroit Gets Two in Ninth to Win 5 to 4," *Boston Globe*, March 22, 1935, 26; Red Newton, "Crowd of 364 Turns Out for New Yorkers," *Tampa Tribune*, March 21, 1935, 13.

68. Stuart Cameron, "Ruppertmen Glad to See Babe Leave," *Brooklyn Times Union*, March 22, 1935, 13.

69. Burt Whitman, "Babe Attracts Another Record Crowd but Mates Get Short End of 5–4 Count When Detroit Stages Two-Run Ninth," *Boston Herald*, March 22, 1935, 46.

70. Harold Kaese, *The Boston Braves 1871–1953* (Boston: Northeastern University Press, 1954), 215; Jack Zerby, "Wally Berger," SABR BioProject. Retrieved December 20, 2020. sabr.org/bioproj/ person/wally-berger/.

71. James C. O'Leary, "Babe Ruth Out of Yanks' Game," *Boston Globe*, March 24, 1935, 26.

72. Burt Whitman, "Berger Homers as Braves

Bow to Saucy Yanks," *Boston Herald*, March 24, 1935, 26.

73. Burt Whitman, "Babe Triples, but Tribe Drops Sixth in Row, 7–3, as Brown, Smith Contribute Ten Walks, Eight Hits to Yankee Cause," *Boston Herald*, March 25, 1935, 15.

74. Grantland Rice, "'Never Happier,' Ruth Tells Rice," *Boston Globe*, March 26, 1935, 19.

75. *Ibid.*

76. Pete Norton, "Sport Outlook," *St. Petersburg Times*, March 26, 1935, 2–1.

77. John Drohan, "Red Sox Make It Two Up on Tribe, 7–2, Finding Frankhouse, Betts for 15 Hits, Cronin, Ferrell Get Three for Four," *Boston Herald*, March 26, 1935, 21.

78. Bill Cunningham, "Babe Draws Big Crowds in South," *Boston Post*, March 26, 1935, 15.

79. Associated Press, "Ruth Wasn't Speeding, Just Hurrying for Boat," *Boston Globe*, March 27, 1935, 24; "Babe Ruth Gets Ticket for Speeding," *Tampa Tribune*, March 27, 1935, 1; "Indignant Ruth Gets Ticket on Speeding Charge," *Bradenton Herald*, March 26, 1935, 1; James C. O'Leary, "McKechnie Denies Braves-Cards Deal," *Boston Globe*, March 26, 1935, 21; Vin Mannix, "Winters Brothers Remember Piney Point's Ferry Service of Long Ago," *Bradenton Herald*, August 12, 2011, D1.

80. James C. O'Leary, "Babe on First as Braves Beat Yanks," *Boston Globe*, March 27, 1935, 22.

81. Nancy Snell Griffith, "Flint Rhem," SABR BioProject. Retrieved December 25, 2020. sabr.org/bioproj/person/flint-rhem/.

82. Ronnie Gallagher, "Jordan Used Baseball to Escape Cooleemee's Mills," *Davie County Enterprise Record* (NC), September 28, 1989: 1B; Paul H. Shannon, "Buck Jordan His Quit the Braves," *Boston Post*, March 28, 1935, 15.

83. "Babe Writes Fuchs He Is Trying Harder Than Ever," *Boston Globe*, March 29, 1935, 32.

84. Burt Whitman, "Yankees Quell Braves, 7 to 3," *Boston Herald*, March 31, 1935, 25; James C. O'Leary, "Braves Are Held to but Four Hits," *Boston Globe*, March 30, 1935, 5.

85. Whitman, "Yankees Quell Braves," 26.

86. James C. O'Leary, "Rabbit Confident of Comeback," *Boston Globe*, March 25, 1935, 9.

87. James C. O'Leary, "Yankees Get Four in First, Win 7–3," *Boston Globe*, April 1, 1935, 9.

88. Burt Whitman, "C.F. Adams, Owner of Boston Hockey Team, Buys Shares in Braves," *Boston Herald*, May 16, 1927, 1.

89. Hy Hurwitz, "Suffolk Downs to Get License," *Boston Globe*, March 28, 1935, 23.

Chapter 7

1. Babe Ruth and Bob Considine, *The Babe Ruth Story* (New York, Penguin, 1992), 210.

2. Babe Ruth as told to Bob Considine, 211.

3. Burt Whitman, "Braves Busy on Day of Rest," *Boston Herald*, April 2, 1935, 16.

4. James C. O'Leary, "Braves Given Day of Complete Rest," *Boston Globe*, April 2, 1935, 20.

5. Burt Whitman, "Mangum, 'Mere Relief Man,' Pitches Brilliant Baseball to Shut Out Cardinals, 1–0," *Boston Herald*, June 28, 1933, 26; Mike Lackey, "Leo Mangum," SABR BioProject. Retrieved December 28, 2020. sabr.org/bioproj/person/leo-mangum/.

6. James C. O'Leary, "Yankees Rally in Ninth to Win, 7–5," *Boston Globe*, April 3, 1935, 22.

7. Burt Whitman, "Babe Ruth Clouts First N.L. Homer as Braves Swamp Teachers Team, 15–1, in Extra Stop Over at Savannah, Ga.," *Boston Herald*, April 5, 1935, 21.

8. "Boston Braves Beat Teachers," *The George-Anne* (South Georgia Teachers' College), April 8, 1935, 3.

9. James C. O'Leary, "Ruth Connects for First 1935 Homer," *Boston Globe*, April 5, 1935, 30.

10. "Live Tips and Topics by the 'Sportsman,'" *Boston Globe*, April 5, 1935, 30.

11. "Storm Wreckage Strewn Over City and the East," *Baltimore Sun*, March 3, 1914, 1.

12. "Dozen Orioles Leave," *Baltimore Sun*, March 3, 1914, 9; Robert W. Creamer, *Babe: The Legend Comes to Life* (New York: Penguin, 1986), 56–59.

13. "Young Birds Work Out," *Baltimore Sun*, March 4, 1914, 9.

14. "Homer by Ruth Feature of Game," *Baltimore Sun*, March 8, 1914, 13.

15. Creamer, 61.

16. *Ibid.*, 65–67.

17. Paul H. Shannon, "Whole County Out to Welcome Babe," *Boston Post*, April 6, 1935, 12.

18. *Ibid.*

19. Burt Whitman, "Fayetteville's 5000 Risk Life and Limb at Babe's Return to Old Spring Camp," *Boston Herald*, April 6, 1935, 8.

20. James C. O'Leary, "Babe Ruth Visits Town of His Rookie Days," *Boston Globe*, April 6, 1935, 6; Anthony J. McKevlin, "100 Baseballs Not Enough for Game and 7,000 Fans," *News and Observer* (Raleigh, NC), April 6, 1935, 6; Scott Mason, "Former N.C. State Pitcher Struck Out Babe Ruth," WRAL-TV Travel Video. June 3, 2010. Retrieved December 30, 2020. wral.com/lifestyles/travel/video/7719790/; "Olney R. 'Lefty' Freeman," Obituary. Legacy.com. Retrieved December 30, 2020. legacy.com/obituaries/name/olney-freeman-obituary?pid=159728897.

21. Burt Whitman, "Rabbit to Play Second Today," *Boston Herald*, April 7, 1935, 31–32.

22. "Babe Sees Giants Against Yankees in World Series," *Boston Herald*, April 7, 1935, 32.

23. W.N. Cox, "Breaks of the Game," *Virginian-Pilot*, April 7, 1935, 5:2.

24. Grantland Rice, "Sportlight," *Boston Globe*, April 12, 1935, 28.

25. "Babe Ruth–Jordan Marsh Club for Boys Open to Every Youngster in New England," *Boston Globe*, March 31, 1935, A24.

26. "Brooklyn Man Sues Braves for $96,000 Share in Club" *Brooklyn Times-Union*, March 29, 1935, 1; "Seeks $96,000 from Braves," *Boston*

Globe, March 29, 1935, 29; "Judge Fuchs Is Sued for $96,600 Braves Assets," *Boston Herald*, March 29, 1935, 1–2.

27. Associated Press, "Emil Fuchs Scores Double Victory Winning Court Case and Stalling Bankers," *Hartford Courant*, April 6, 1935, 12.

28. Louis Effrat, "Ruth Drives Two as the Braves Win," *New York Times*, April 8, 1935, 25.

29. Burt Whitman, "Ruth Hits Two Homers Before 10,000, as Braves Rally to Top Newark, 10–8; Second Drive Lands 500 Feet Away," *Boston Herald*, April 8, 1935, 14.

30. James C. O'Leary, "Jordan in the Fold as Braves Return," *Boston Globe*, April 10, 1935, 20.

31. "Braves Have Workout in the Harvard Cage," *Boston Globe*, April 11, 1935, 26; James C. O'Leary, "Red Sox and Braves All Set for Series," *Boston Globe*, April 12, 1935, 28.

32. Burt Whitman, "Braves, Red Sox to Try Again Today; Grove Will Start If Weather Is Mild; Cronin Works Regulars in Briggs Cage," *Boston Herald*, April 13, 1935, 4.

33. "Anti-War Strike Almost Fizzle," *Boston Globe*, April 13, 1935, 13.

34. John Fenton, "Braves, Sox, Both in Traveling Uniforms, Given Warm Welcome by Chilled Crowd," *Boston Herald*, April 15, 1935, 14.

35. "Thousands Receive Palms at Services," *Boston Globe*, April 15, 1935, 1.

36. Kat Eschner, "This 1000-Mile Long Storm Showed the Horror of Life in the Dust Bowl," *Smithsonian*, April 14, 2017. Retrieved January 10, 2021. smithsonianmag.com/smart-news/1000-mile-long-storm-showed-horror-life-dust-bowl-180962847/.

37. Gerry Moore, "Braves Beat Red Sox, 3–2, Coming from Behind," *Boston Globe*, April 15, 1935, 1, 9.

38. Burt Whitman, "Babe in Role of Pied Piper of Baseball to 12,000-Odd as Braves Score Three in Ninth to Beat Good Purple Nine, 5–2," *Boston Herald*, April 16, 1935, 18.

39. James C. O'Leary, "Braves Beat Holy Cross in Ninth, 5–2," *Boston Globe*, April 16, 1935, 20.

40. Paul H. Shannon, "Braves Face Giants Today," *Boston Post*, April 16, 1935, 18.

41. "'Inspirational Genius,' Says Wright of Ruth," *Boston Herald*, April 17, 1935, 28.

42. C. Paul Rogers III, "Ed Brandt," SABR BioProject. Retrieved January 18, 2021. sabr.org/bioproj/person/ed-brandt/.

43. "Senate Meets Early So as to See Braves Game," *Boston Globe*, April 15, 1935, 19.

44. Arthur Siegel, "'That's One for the Old Lady,' Says Babe; Rescues Vice-Presidents from Oblivion," *Boston Herald*, April 17, 1935, 28.

45. Victor O. Jones, "Quotation on World Series Now a Dime," *Boston Globe*, April 17, 1935, 28.

46. James P. Dawson, "Ruth's Home Run Defeats Giants in Boston by 4–2," *New York Times*, April 17, 1935, 29.

47. Gerry Moore, "Ruth's Homer Wins for the Braves," *Boston Globe*, April 17, 1935, 28.

48. Bill Cunningham, "Babe Certainly Made It His Day," *Boston Post*, April 17, 1935, 20.

49. Burt Whitman, "Babe Has Hand in Every Run Against Giants," *Boston Herald*, April 17, 1935, 1.

50. Siegel, "'That's One for the Old Lady.'"

51. Moore, "Ruth's Homer Wins for the Braves," 1.

52. Dawson, "Ruth's Home Run Defeats Giants."

53. Hy Hurwitz, "Ruth Gets Home to Delight Fans," *Boston Globe*, April 17, 1935, 28.

54. James C. O'Leary, "Governors of Five States Attend Game," *Boston Globe*, April 17, 1935, 29.

55. Robert S. Fuchs and Wayne Soini, *Judge Fuchs and the Boston Braves* (Jefferson, NC: McFarland, 1998), 109.

56. Paul Gallico, "'Second-Hand Ruth' Is as Good as New, Gallico Finds in Boston," *Washington Post*, April 17, 1935, 20.

57. Gerry Moore, "Babe Ruth Feels Fine as the Dodgers Threaten," *Boston Globe*, April 19, 1935, 27.

58. "Crowds Cheer Riders of 1775," *Boston Globe*, April 20, 1935, 1.

59. Tommy Holmes, "Stengel Realizes Ruth Is Still Powerful at Plate," *Brooklyn Daily Eagle*, April 19, 1935, 20.

60. Bob LeMoine, "Johnnie Tyler," SABR BioProject. Retrieved January 23, 2021. sabr.org/bioproj/person/johnnie-tyler/.

61. Tom Long, "Boston Marathon Man Johnny Kelley Dies at 97," *Boston Globe*, October 8, 2004, 1.

62. "Amelia Off," *Boston Globe*, April 20, 1935, 1; Associated Press, "Death to Pacifists Decreed by Hitler as a War Measure," *Brooklyn Daily Eagle*, April 19, 1935, 1.

63. National Bureau of Economic Research, Unemployment Rate for United States [M0892AUSM156SNBR], retrieved from FRED, Federal Reserve Bank of St. Louis; https://fred.stlouisfed.org/series/M0892AUSM156SNBR, January 23, 2021.

64. Robert S. McElvaine, *The Great Depression: America, 1929–1941* (New York: Times Books, 1984), 256–257; *Jackson Daily News* quotation also taken from McElvaine.

65. Hy Hurwitz, "Babe No Pushover, Says Casey Stengel," *Boston Globe*, April 20, 1935, 9.

66. "Babe Hailed by 2500 Youngsters in Jordan's Club Debut at Arena," *Boston Herald*, April 21, 1935, 34.

67. "2000 Youngsters Mob Babe Ruth," *Boston Globe*, April 20, 1935, 5.

68. Robert S. Fuchs and Wayne Soini, *Judge Fuchs and the Boston Braves* (Jefferson, NC: McFarland, 1998), 113.

69. Gregory H. Wolf, "Ben Cantwell," SABR BioProject. Retrieved January 24, 2021. sabr.org/bioproj/person/ben-cantwell/.

70. "Braves Knot Hole Gang to Yell for Tribe Today," *Boston Globe*, June 21, 1924, 9; James C. O'Leary, "Giants Outhit but Trim Braves Again,"

Boston Globe, June 22, 1924, 20; Charlie Bevis, *Red Sox Vs. Braves in Boston: The Battle for Fans' Hearts, 1901–1952* (Jefferson, NC: McFarland, 2017), 106. Gerry Moore, "Cantwell Wins in Duel with Mungo," *Boston Globe*, April 21, 1935, A26.

71. "Beauty Marks Easter Parade," *Boston Globe*, April 22, 1935, 1.

72. Gerry Moore, "Babe's Second Home Run a Bright Spot," *Boston Globe*, April 22, 1935, 9.

73. Con Heffernan, "Ruth Hits Pair of Doubles," *Albany Times-Union*, April 23, 1935, 20; Arthur Siegel, "Ruth, Rabbit Star at Albany," *Boston Herald*, April 23, 1935, 18.

74. Bill Cunningham, "Will New York Welcome Babe?" *Boston Post*, April 23, 1935, 17.

75. Arthur Siegel, "Babe Ruth Returns to New York Today Alien in Uniform, Park and League," *Boston Herald*, April 23, 1935, 18.

76. Victor O. Jones, "Braves Lose to Giants by 6–5," *Boston Globe*, April 24, 1935, 1.

77. Bill Cunningham, "50,000 Greet Babe Royally," *Boston Post*, April 24, 1935, 21.

78. "Braves Lose to Giants by 6–5," 20; Arthur Siegel, "Ruth Hailed by 47,000 in New York as Braves Bow to Giants, 6–5, in 11th," *Boston Herald*, April 24, 1935, 1.

79. Siegel, "Ruth Hailed by 47,000."

80. James P. Dawson, "47,009 See Giants Top Braves in 11th," *New York Times*, April 24, 1935, 26.

81. Bill Cunningham, "Babe Swings but Doesn't Connect," *Boston Post*, April 25, 1935, 18.

82. Victor O. Jones, "Babe Ruth Fans, Up as a Pinch Hitter," *Boston Globe*, April 25, 1935, 22.

83. Victor O. Jones, "Ruthless Braves Drop Their Third Straight," *Boston Globe*, April 26, 1935, 30.

84. Victor O. Jones, "What About It?" *Boston Globe*, April 27, 1935, 8.

85. "Braves Stage Belated Rally but Lose 5–4," *Boston Globe*, April 27, 1935, 5.

86. "Ed Hughes' Column," *Brooklyn Daily Eagle*, April 27, 1935, 6.

87. Tommy Holmes, "Brandt, of Braves, Hurls Stengelmen Out of First Place," *Brooklyn Daily Eagle*, April 28, 1935, 1D.

88. Arthur Siegel, "Ruth Returns to Left Field as Tribe Wins," *Boston Herald*, April 28, 1935, 26.

89. Bill McCullough, "Braves, with Ruth Playing, Score over Flock by 4 to 2," *Brooklyn Times Union*, April 28, 1935, 1A.

90. "Babe Retried at First on an Apparent Hit," *Boston Globe*, April 29, 1935, 17.

91. Arthur Siegel, "Braves Beat Brooklyn Again, 5–3, Behind Bobby Smith's Great Hurling; Hogan Has Perfect Day Before 28,000," *Boston Herald*, April 29, 1935, 6.

92. Tommy Holmes, "Brandt, Smith Hurl Heady Games to Nip Dodger Win Streak," *Brooklyn Daily Eagle*, April 29, 1935, 10.

93. James C. O'Leary, "Braves Beat Phils, 7–5, Wilson Injured," *Boston Globe*, April 30, 1935, 20; Stan Baumgartner, "Haslin Attacks Pill, but Phillies Suffer 8th Straight Upset" *Philadelphia*

Inquirer, April 30, 1935, 17; Stan Baumgartner, "Hit by Fast Pitch, Phils Boss, Wilson, in Critical Shape," *Philadelphia Inquirer*, April 30, 1935, 1, 19.

94. Based on statistics published in the *Cincinnati Enquirer*, May 5, 1935, 38, and at Retrosheet.org.

95. Bill Cunningham, "Buried the Babe Much Too Soon," *Boston Post*, April 22, 1935, 17.

96. Bill Cunningham, "Insists Babe to Become Manager," *Boston Post*, April 26, 1935, 23.

Chapter 8

1. James C. O'Leary, "Braves Have Six Double Bills on the Schedule," *Boston Globe*, May 4, 1935, 7; Bill Cunningham had recently written that New York writers had insider information about Ruth becoming the Braves' manager. "Insists Babe to Become Manager," *Boston Post*, April 26, 1935, 23.

2. Burt Whitman, "Cards' Dizzy Shuts Out Braves, 7–0, Hits Homer, Quells Babe to Steal Show in Initial Duel of Rivals Before 30,000," *Boston Herald*, May 6, 1935, 14.

3. Bill King, "Ruth to Take Reigns Aug. 1 If He Fails as Player," *St. Louis Globe-Democrat*, May 7, 1935, 1B.

4. "Ruth May Pilot Tribe by Aug. 1," *Boston Herald*, May 7, 1935, 18.

5. Associated Press, "Fuchs Says He'll Pay Off Debts," *Hartford Courant*, May 9, 1935, 17; "McCarran Says Roosevelt Is Too Strong to Be Defeated," *Boston Globe*, May 5, 1935, A35.

6. "Deny Dissension in Braves' Ranks," *Boston Globe*, May 8, 1935, 22.

7. Ibid.

8. Janet Jones, "Babe Ruth Never Sees Those Begging Letters," *Boston Globe*, May 12, 1935, C5.

9. Burt Whitman, "Braves Drop Opener to Cubs, 5 to 1, Despite Presence of Rabbit and Babe; Homer by Berger Prevents Shutout," *Boston Herald*, May 10, 1935, 38.

10. "Heralds First Class Exceeds 5000 as Babe, Wally, Lon Teach Baseball," *Boston Herald*, May 12, 1935, 36.

11. Burt Whitman," Below Par Pitching, Ragged Fielding Topples Braves on Delayed Ladies' Day as Free-Swinging Cubs Romp, 14–7," *Boston Herald*, May 12, 1935, 36.

12. Gerry Moore, "Braves Drop Sixth in the Last Seven," *Boston Globe*, May 13, 1935, 9.

13. Robert Creamer, *Babe: The Legend Comes to Life* (New York: Penguin, 1986), 394.

14. Moore, "Braves Drop Sixth in the Last Seven."

15. George Kirksey, "Babe Ruth Is on the Verge of Hanging Up His Uniform," *Paterson Morning Call*, May 14, 1935, 23.

16. Mrs. Babe Ruth with Bill Slocum, *The Babe and I* (New York: Avon Books, 1959), 103.

17. Jack Ryder, "Si's Good Hurling Enables Reds to Crack Losing Streak," *Cincinnati Enquirer*, May 14, 1935, 13.

18. Burt Whitman, "Jim Bottomley's Eighth

Inning Double Is Balance of Power Between Cantwell, Johnson as Reds Beat Braves, 3–1," *Boston Herald*, May 14, 1935, 16.

19. Matthew Clifford, "Si Johnson," SABR BioProject. Retrieved February 21, 2021. sabr.org/bioproj/person/si-johnson/.

20. James C. O'Leary, "Braves Drop First One to the Reds," *Boston Globe*, May 14, 1935, 21.

21. Victor O. Jones, "What About It?" *Boston Globe*, May 14, 1935, 22 (evening edition).

22. *Ibid.*

23. *Ibid.*

24. Kirksey, "Babe Ruth Is on the Verge; "Babe Declared to Have Said He's Through; Pitchers Believe His Batting Eye Is Gone," *Cincinnati Enquirer*, May 14, 1935, 13; Jack Ryder, "Average Is .171," *Cincinnati Enquirer*, May 14, 1935, 13.

25. Melville E. Webb, "Fuchs Warns the Braves," *Boston Globe*, May 14, 1935, 24 (evening edition).

26. Burt Whitman, "Fuchs Gives Braves Squad Fight Talk; Threatens Major Changes Unless Team Shows Marked Improvement on Road," *Boston Herald*, May 15, 1935, 14.

27. "Braves Anger Some Fans by Postponement," *Springfield Republican*, May 15, 1935, 20.

28. Victor O. Jones, "What About It?" *Boston Globe*, May 15, 1935, 23; Eddie Welch, "Rockingham Ready to Open Wednesday," *Boston Globe*, May 12, 1935, A30; Ad for the "Rockingham Racer" in the *Boston Globe*, May 14, 1935, 24.

29. *Boston Globe*, May 15, 1935, 22.

30. Whitman, "Fuchs Gives Braves Squad Fight Talk."

31. Hy Hurwitz, "Crowd of 25,000 Wagers $325,310 at Rockingham Opening Day Races," *Boston Globe*, May 16, 1935, 1, 23.

32. Bill Corum, "Babe Ruth, Very Tired and Disappointed, Considering Leaving the Boston Team," *Scranton Times-Tribune*, May 16, 1935, 23.

33. *Ibid.*

34. *Ibid.*

35. Bill Corum, "Baseball Monarch Ready to Abdicate," *Evening Gazette* (Worcester, MA), May 16, 1935, 12.

36. Associated Press, "Fuchs Sorry If Ruth Means to Quit Game," *Fitchburg Sentinel*, May 16, 1935, 1.

37. Tim Bryant, "One Hundred Site Not Always a Parking Lot," *St. Louis Post-Dispatch*, December 9, 2016. Retrieved February 22, 2021. stltoday.com/business/columns/building-blocks/one-hundred-site-not-always-a-parking-lot/article_e5aa99ca-1a67-5f76-9047-4bf0f7fdec7a.html.

38. Ralph Clifford, "Nothing to It," *Boston Herald*, May 17, 1935, 32.

39. "Babe to Play as Long as Fans Want Him To," *Boston Globe*, May 17, 1935, 40.

40. Burt Whitman, "Babe Ruth Spikes Retirement Rumor, but N.Y. Story May Have Had Basis in Periodical Mood of Braves Star," *Boston Herald*, May 17, 1935, 32.

41. Bill Cunningham, "Bam Bit Out of Tune on Facts," *Boston Post*, May 17, 1935, 23.

42. W.J. McGoogan, "Babe Ruth Needs Sunshine and the Tonic of a Few Home Runs, Manager McKechnie Suggests," *St. Louis Post-Dispatch*, May 19, 1935, 16.

43. "Boycott Unjust, Says Wife of Leo Durocher," *St. Louis Star and Times*, May 18, 1935, 7; "3 Unions Picket Cards' Park, Air Their Grievances," *St. Louis Star and Times*, May 18, 1935, 7; "Strikers Complain to Landis About Cardinal Ball Player," *St. Louis Post-Dispatch*, April 14, 1935, 3A; "Central Trades Votes to Boycott Cardinals," *St. Louis Post-Dispatch*, April 29, 1935, 1; "Durocher Drops Charge Against Garment Striker," *St. Louis Star and Times*, May 24, 1935, 30; "Strike Called at Garment Plant, 9 Pickets Arrested," *St. Louis Star and Times*, February 6, 1935, 4.

44. "Fred Frankhouse Scatters Seven Hits as Braves Pound Four Card Hurlers and Open Western Trip with 7–1 Win," *Boston Herald*, May 18, 1935, 6.

45. "Walker Beats Braves for His Fourth Victory," *Boston Globe*, May 19, 1935, B26; Ralph Clifford, "Cards Triumph Behind Walker," *Boston Herald*, May 19, 1935, 28.

46. *St. Louis Globe-Democrat*, May 19, 1935.

47. Ray J. Gillespie, "Dizzy Dean and Ruth Provide Thrills as Cards Trim Braves, 7–3," *St. Louis Star-Times*, May 20, 1935, 17.

48. *Ibid.*

49. Dizzy Dean, "Dizzy Promises to Let babe Hit a Homer," *Boston Globe*, May 20, 1935, 1.

50. *Chicago Tribune*, May 20, 1935, 18.

51. Herbert Simons, "Cubs See a Ruth Who Hits Only .155," *Daily Times*, May 20, 1935, 28.

52. Marvin McCarthy, "Nope-Not So," *Daily Times*, May 20, 1935, 28.

53. Gregory H. Wolf, "Bill Lee ('Big Bill')," SABR BioProject. Retrieved February 28, 2021. sabr.org/bioproj/person/bill-lee-big-bill/.

54. Ralph Clifford, "Bill Lee Shuts Braves in N.L. Cellar, Yielding Six Hits as Cubs Win, 5–0," *Boston Herald*, May 21, 1935, 26.

55. Ralph Clifford, "Babe Homers, Makes Two Great Catches as Braves, Frankhouse Stop Cubs, 4–1," *Boston Herald*, May 22, 1935, 26.

56. Philip J. Lowry, *Green Cathedrals: The Ultimate Celebration of Major League and Negro League Ballparks* (New York: Walker, 2006), 185–187; Lawrence S. Ritter, *Lost Ballparks: A Celebration of Baseball's Legendary Fields* (New York: Viking, 1992), 63–65; "The Schenley Hotel and Apartments." The Brookline Connection: A Look Back at Our Community. Retrieved March 6, 2021. brooklineconnection.com/history/Facts/Schenley.html; Curt Smith, "Forbes Field," SABR BioProject. Retrieved April 15, 2021. sabr.org/bioproj/park/forbes-field-pittsburgh/.

57. "It's Warm Weather That Babe Ruth Wants," *Pittsburgh Press*, May 23, 1935, 27.

58. Charles J. Doyle, "Ruth, Here, Spikes Rumors He Plans to Quit Playing," *Pittsburgh Sun-Telegram*, May 23, 1935, 25.

59. Harvey J. Boyle, "Mirrors of Sport," *Pittsburgh Post-Gazette*, May 24, 1935, 18.

60. Gene Collier, "712...713...714. 50 Years Ago, Ruth Climaxed Career Here," *Pittsburgh Press*, May 26, 1985, D3.

61. William A. White, "Mighty Babe Fails in Four Attempts to Make Home Run," *Pittsburgh Post*, July 8, 1921, 8.

62. Chester L. Smith, "The Village Smithy," *Pittsburgh Press*, May 24, 1935, 39.

63. Boyle, "Mirror of Sport."

64. Edward F. Balinger, "Swift Holds Ruth Hitless as Bucs Win," *Pittsburgh Post-Gazette*, May 24, 1935. 18.

65. Boyle, "Mirror of Sport."

66. "Pirates Shell Three Braves Hurlers to Capture Series Opener, 7–1; P. Waner Robs Ruth; Berger Homers," *Boston Herald*, May 24, 1935. 46.

67. Charles J. Doyle, "Ruth's Speech High Spot of Rab's Fete," *Pittsburgh Sun-Telegraph*, May 24, 1935, 36; Associated Press, "Maranville Tribute by Ruth Stirs Fans at Pittsburgh Dinner," *Boston Globe*, May 24, 1935, 31; "Judge Egan Dies After Heart Attack," *Pittsburgh Press*, October 30, 1952, 1, 8; "Hush Comes Over Diners as Ruth Cries Praising Rabbit," *Pittsburgh Post-Gazette*, May 24, 1935, 19.

68. Creamer, 396.

69. Chester L. Smith, "The Village Smithy," *Pittsburgh Press*, May 25, 1935, 7.

70. "Thompson Hits Homer with the Bases Full," *Boston Globe*, May 25, 1935, 7; Charles J. Doyle, "Sun-Telegraph Newsies See Babe Ruth," *Pittsburgh Sun-Telegraph*, May 25, 1935, 9.

71. Jack Ryder, "Big Paul," *Cincinnati Enquirer*, May 25, 1935, 1.

72. Charles J. Doyle, "Perfect Day for Babe," *Pittsburgh Sun-Telegraph*, May 26, 1935, 2–1; Charles J. Doyle, "Sun-Telegraph Newsies See Babe Ruth," *Pittsburgh Sun-Telegraph*, May 25, 1935, 9.

73. Rick Shrum, "Parting Shots," *Pittsburgh Post-Gazette*, May 10, 2006, F-3; Brian O'Neil, "Our Bridges at Pittsburgh Greatness," *Pittsburgh Post-Gazette*, December 11, 2005, A-2.

74. Al Abrams, "Sidelights on Sports," *Pittsburgh Post-Gazette*, May 27, 1935, 16.

75. John Bibb, "Saturday Ayem," *The Tennessean*, May 26, 1973, 17.

76. Thomas Wolf, *The Called Shot: Babe Ruth, the Chicago Cubs, and the Unforgettable Major League Baseball Season of 1932* (Lincoln: University of Nebraska Press, 2020), 255.

77. Richard Vidmer, "Yankee Home Runs Crush Cubs, 7 to 5, Ruth and Gehrig Smashing Two Apiece in Third Straight World Series Victory," *New York Herald Tribune*, October 2, 1932, B1; Wolf, 261.

78. "Babe Ruth Gets Three Home Runs," *Boston Globe*, May 26, 1935, B1.

79. Doyle, "Perfect Day for Babe."

80. Volney Walsh, "There's Plenty of Life in the Old Boy Yet; Drives in Six Boston Runs," *Pittsburgh Press*, May 26, 1935, 15.

81. Robert Shaw, "Babe's 714th a Monumental Blast," *Cleveland Plain Dealer*, May 25, 1974, 6-C.

82. *Ibid.*

83. John Bibb, "Saturday Ayem," *The Tennessean*, May 26, 1973, 17.

84. Al Abrams, "Sidelights on Sports," *Pittsburgh Post-Gazette*, May 27, 1935, 16.

85. Jane Leavy, *The Big Fella: Babe Ruth and the World He Created* (New York: HarperCollins, 2018), 416–417; Christina Caron, "Phil Coyne, Pirates Usher Since the Great Depression, Retires at 99," *New York Times*, April 10, 2018; Jason Mackey, "'So Much More Than an Usher': Remembering the Great Phil Coyne," *Pittsburgh Post-Gazette*, April 9, 2021.

86. Associated Press, "End of an Era Up Close and Personal," *Augusta Chronicle*, May 24, 1995, 2C.

87. Collier, "712...713...71."

88. Tom Shieber, "A Mighty Blast into History," National Baseball Hall of Fame. Retrieved March 12, 2021. baseballhall.org/discover-more/stories/short-stops/a-mighty-blast-into-history; "Babe Ruth's Connection to Panther Hollow," Panther Hollow. Retrieved March 13, 2021. pantherhollow.us/babe-ruth.php; "Ruth's Home Run Goes 600 Feet," *Pittsburgh Post-Gazette*, May 27, 1935, 15.

89. Shrum.

90. Robert Dvorchak, "From a Rag to Riches," *Pittsburgh Post-Gazette*, July 9, 2008, D1, D6; Robert Dvorchak, "HR Ball Sells for $172,500," *Pittsburgh Post-Gazette*, July 18, 2008, D5.

91. Mrs. Babe Ruth with Bill Slocum, 104.

92. Creamer, 397–398.

93. Babe Ruth and Bob Considine, *The Babe Ruth Story* (New York, Penguin, 1992), 212.

94. Jack Ryder, "Redlegs Win, 6–3; Babe Fans Three Times," *Cincinnati Enquirer*, May 27, 1935, 1.

95. Ralph Clifford, "Braves Drop Fifth in Row, 9–5, as Reds Pound Three Hurlers for 14 Safeties," *Boston Herald*, May 28, 1935, 30.

96. Jack Ryder, "Lowly Braves Victims as Reds Chalk up Sixth in Row," *Cincinnati Enquirer*, May 29, 1935, 11.

97. "Reds Take Six in Row as Braves Drop Sixth," *Boston Globe*, May 29, 1935, 22.

98. "Berger's Homer Counts 4 Runs," *Boston Globe*, May 30, 1935, 19.

99. Stan Baumgartner, "Braves Beat Phils, 8–6; A's Bow, 10–9," *Philadelphia Inquirer*, May 30, 1935, 11, 13.

100. John M. McCullough, "City Pays Tribute to Its War Dead; Peace Is Keynote," *Philadelphia Inquirer*, May 31, 1935, 1.

101. John McDonough, "Remembering Last Reunion of Civil War Veterans." National Public Radio. Retrieved March 24, 2021. npr.org/templates/story/story.php?storyId=106259780.

102. Ed Nichols, "Shore Sports," *Daily Times* (Salisbury, MD), May 2, 1952, 12.

103. Stan Baumgartner, "Walters Makes It Double Win After Rally Lands First," *Philadelphia Inquirer*, May 31, 1935, 15.

104. Ralph Clifford, "Braves Drop Two to Phils, 11–6, 9–3; Seven-Run Eighth Decides First Tilt; Berger, Moore Homer, Walters Wins," *Boston Herald*, May 31, 1935, 16; Babe Ruth as told to Bob Considine, *The Babe Ruth Story* (New York: Penguin, 1992), 212.

105. Victor O. Jones, "What About It?" *Boston Globe*, June 1, 1935, 10.

106. Paul H. Shannon, "Big Shakeup in Tribe at Hand," *Boston Post*, June 2, 1935, 15, 17.

107. "The Queen of the Seven Seas," *Popular Mechanics* 63, no.6 (June, 1935): 826–827; Luke Crafton, "The Normandie—A Legend Undiminished. *Antiques Roadshow*, April 12, 2004. Retrieved April 10, 2021. pbs.org/wgbh/roadshow/stories/articles/2004/4/12/normandie-legend-undiminished; "Social Events on Ship," *New York Times*, June 4, 1935, 2; "200,000 Line Shore for First Glimpse," *New York Times*, June 4, 1935, 2.

Chapter 9

1. Burt Whitman, "Terry Recalls 1934 Meltdown," *Boston Herald*, June 2, 1935, 20.

2. Robert Creamer, *Babe: The Legend Comes to Life* (New York: Penguin, 1986), 399.

3. Gerry Moore, "Ruth Is Released by Braves," *Boston Globe*, June 3, 1935, 8.

4. James C. O'Leary, "Braves Hand Giants Their First Shutout," *Boston Globe*, June 3, 1935, 9.

5. "Fuchs Will Sell Equity in Braves If Team, Stockholders, Do Not Suffer," *Boston Herald*, June 3, 1935, 14.

6. *Ibid.*; The name of Lewis Wentz, the millionaire oil baron and philanthropist often interested in buying the Pirates or Cardinals, appeared in rumors. International News Service, "Wentz to Buy Braves, Rumor," *Pittsburgh Sun-Telegraph*, June 3, 1935, 29.

7. "Amelia Earhart Tests Parachute Tower Erected in Ocean County," *Asbury Park Evening Press*, June 3, 1935, 1.

8. Tom Meany, "Why Babe Ruth Quit Baseball Here in '35," *Boston Globe*, August 19, 1948, 14.

9. Burt Whitman, "Fuchs Releases Ruth After Row," *Boston Herald*, June 3, 1935, 14.

10. Paul H. Shannon, "Babe Ruth Is Fired from the Braves," *Boston Post*, June 3, 1935, 15.

11. Whitman, "Fuchs Releases Ruth After Row," 14.

12. *Ibid.*; Richard Vidmer, "Babe Ruth Quits Braves as He and Fuchs Split," *New York Tribune*, June 3, 1935, 18.

13. Vidmer, "Babe Ruth Quits," 1.

14. *Ibid.*, 18.

15. Shannon, "Babe Ruth Is Fired from the Braves," 15.

16. Whitman, "Fuchs Releases Ruth," 14.

17. Shannon, "Babe Ruth Is Fired from the Braves," 15.

18. Paul Gallico, "The Exciting Truth," *New York Daily News*, June 4, 1935, 46.

19. George Dixon, "Ruth's Retirement Charged to Fuchs," *New York Daily News*, June 9, 1935, 33.

20. Shannon, "Babe Ruth Is Fired from the Braves," 15; Moore, "Ruth Is Released by Braves," 8.

21. Vidmer, "Babe Ruth Quits," 18.

22. Moore, "Ruth Is Released by Braves," 8.

23. *Ibid.*

24. Whitman, "Fuchs Releases Ruth," 14.

25. "Babe Ruth 'Quits' Braves and Is Dropped by Club," *New York Times*, June 3, 1935, 23.

26. Shannon, "Babe Ruth Is Fired from the Braves," 15.

27. "Babe Ruth 'Quits' Braves," 23.

28. Whitman, "Fuchs Releases Ruth," 1.

29. Vidmer, "Babe Ruth Quits," 18.

30. Quoted in Robert S. Fuchs and Wayne Soini, *Judge Fuchs and the Boston Braves* (Jefferson, NC: McFarland, 1998), 117.

31. International News Service, "Ruth Says He Will Stay in Baseball," *Evening Gazette* (Worcester, MA), June 3, 1935, 16.

32. "Myles Standish Hall," Boston Preservation Alliance. Retrieved April 29, 2021. boston preservation.org/advocacy-project/myles-stand ish-hall.

33. Hy Hurwitz, "Ruth Leaves for New York," *Boston Globe* (evening edition), June 3, 1935, 1.

34. *Ibid.*, 8.

35. "Ruth Says He Will Stay in Baseball,"

36. Hurwitz, "Ruth Leaves for New York," 1.

37. *Ibid.*

38. Paul H. Shannon, "Wanted Babe to Be 'Fired,'" *Boston Post*, June 4, 1935, 1.

39. Jennifer Gould and C.J. Sullivan, "You Can Own Babe Ruth's Two-Bedroom UWS Apartment for $1.6 Million," *New York Post*, August 31, 2015.

40. Associated Press, "Babe Won't Believe It," *Boston Post*, June 4, 1935, 16.

41. "Says McKechnie Put in the Middle," *Boston Post*, June 5, 1935, 16.

42. Victor O. Jones, "What About It?" *Boston Globe*, June 4, 1935, 22.

43. Bill Cunningham, "Fuchs Next to Walk the Plank," *Boston Post*, June 5, 1935, 17.

44. "Boston Scribes Pin Blame on Fuchs in Ruth Case," *Brooklyn Times-Union*, June 5, 1935, 1A.

45. Burt Whitman, "McKechnie Says Ruth Fired Because He Undermined Braves," *Boston Herald*, June 4, 1935, 16; James P. Dawson, "Ruth Is Undecided on Future Plans," *New York Times*, June 4, 1935, 27.

46. Babe Ruth, "Babe Ruth Likes Idea of Vacation," *Boston Post*, June 9, 1935, 17.

47. Whitman, "McKechnie Says Ruth Fired."

48. *Ibid.*

49. Bill Cunningham, "Ruth Case Has Several Angles," *Boston Post*, June 3, 1935, 15.

50. Bill Cunningham, "Real Story of Ruth Vs. Braves," *Boston Post*, June 4, 1935, 17.

51. Gallico, "The Exciting Truth," *New York Daily News*, June 4, 1935, 46.

52. Dizzy Dean, "Dizzy Dean Says," *Boston Globe*, June 4, 1935, 23.

53. "Braves Defeat Pentucket, 9–4," *Boston Herald*, June 4, 1935, 16; Bob LeMoine, "Al Blanche," SABR BioProject. Retrieved April 28, 2021. sabr.org/bioproj/person/al-blanche/.

54. Grantland Rice, "McKechnie Takes Blame, Ruth Again Flays Fuchs," *Boston Globe*, June 4, 1935, 22.

55. *Ibid.*

56. "Topics of the Times," *New York Times*, June 4, 1935, 22.

57. John Kieran, "Sports of the Times," *New York Times*, June 4, 1935, 29.

58. George Dixon, "Job-Hunting Babe Gets No! From Owners," *New York Daily News*, June 4, 1935, 46–47.

59. "The Babe Idle and Free," *Kansas City Times*, June 5, 1935, 13.

60. "Bambino Sought by House of David," *Detroit Free Press*, June 5, 1935, 13.

61. "Babe Ruth Sought as Manager for Ball Clubs Here," *The Californian* (Salinas, CA), June 5, 1935, 1.

62. "Dangles $10,000 Before Babe Ruth," *News-Palladium* (Benton Harbor, MI), June 7, 1935, 13; "Farmers Offering Job to Babe Ruth," *Brooklyn Times Union*, June 7, 1935, 3A; "Ruth Given Offer to Drive Midget Car," *Albany Times-Union*, June 7, 1935, 21; "Want Ruth as Umpire," *Brooklyn Times-Union*, June 9, 1935, 2A; Pat Robinson, "Babe Ruth Has Many Offers for Baseball," *Evening News* (Wilkes-Barre, PA), June 10, 1935, 13.

63. "Babe Ruth Gets Offer to Manage Palatka Club in North Florida," *Boston Globe*, June 5, 1935, 23; "Sportsman's" column, *Boston Globe*, June 6, 1935, 24.

64. Westbrook Pegler, "Fair Enough," *Green Bay Press Gazette*, June 7, 1935, 17.

65. H.I. Phillips, "The Once Over," *Boston Globe*, June 7, 1935, 20.

66. Cunningham, "Fuchs Next to Walk Plank," *Boston Post*, June 5, 1935, 17.

67. Bill Cunningham, "Sample Letters Readers Write," *Boston Post*, June 6, 1935, 17.

68. Victor O. Jones, "What About It?" *Boston Globe*, June 5, 1935, 22.

69. James C. O'Leary, "Fuchs Denies 'Double-Cross," *Boston Globe*, June 5, 1935, 23; "Getting the Works," *New York Daily News*, June 5, 1935.

70. James C. O'Leary, "Frankhouse and Brandt to Pitch," *Boston Globe*, June 12, 1935, 22.

71. Bill McCullough, "Braves Will Keep Berger and Brandt," *Brooklyn Times-Union*, June 5, 1935, 1A.

72. Burt Whitman, "Dodgers' Mungo Blanks Braves, 3–0, but Berger's Booming Homer Wedge to Tribal Spree and 10–2 Win in Finale," *Boston Herald*, June 6, 1935, 30.

73. Louis Effrat, "Giants Fight Uphill Battle to Triumph Over Braves at the Polo Grounds," *New York Times*, June 10, 1935, 21; George Dixon, "Ruth in Stands as Giants Beat Old Mates, 5–4," *New York Daily News*, June 10, 1935, 38.

74. Dixon, "Ruth in Stands as Giants Beat Old Mates, 5–4," *New York Daily News*, June 10, 1935, 38.

75. "Braves Charity Game at Randolph Called Off," *Boston Globe*, June 10, 1935, 1.

76. Gerry Moore, "Braves Lose Two to the Cards," *Boston Globe*, June 13, 1935, 25.

77. Bill Nowlin, "Danny MacFayden," SABR BioProject. Retrieved May 23, 2021. sabr.org/bioproj/person/danny-macfayden/.

78. Gerry Moore, "Danny MacFayden Outpitches 'Daffy,'" *Boston Globe*, June 14, 1935, 28.

79. Gerry Moore, "Braves Just Miss Taking Two Games," *Boston Globe*, June 15, 1935, 7.

80. Burt Whitman, "Berger and Whitney Homer in Opener but Reds Win, 7–6; Tribe Earns Second, 7–4, Despite Three Cincy Circuit Belts," *Boston Herald*, June 17, 1935, 6; Gerry Moore, "Braves Chase That Cincinnati Jinx," *Boston Globe*, June 17, 1935, 7.

81. "Bunker Hill Day Parade of 12,000 Viewed by 250,000," *Boston Globe*, June 18, 1935, 1.

82. "Braves Lose Milk Fund Game, 6 to 3," *Boston Globe*, June 19, 1935, 22; "Quincy, Weymouth Players Help in Beating Braves," *Quincy Patriot Ledger*, June 19, 1935, 8; Fred Hanson, "Big-League Baseball Came to Randolph 71 Years Ago," *Quincy Patriot Ledger*, July 27, 2007. Retrieved May 16, 2021. patriotledger.com/article/20070727/NEWS/307279768.

83. James C. O'Leary, "Bob Smith Proves Master of the Cubs," *Boston Globe*, June 20, 1935, 23.

84. Burt Whitman, "Smith Hurls Braves to Fourth in Row, Beating Cubs in Opening Game, 2–1; Chicagoans Capture Nightcap, 3–0," *Boston Herald*, June 20, 1935, 18.

85. Eddie Welch, "Crowd of 19,375 Braves Weather to Attend Narragansett's First Day and Wagers $357,311," *Boston Globe*, June 20, 1935, 20; "Clattering Hoofs," *York Dispatch*, June 24, 1935, 12.

86. *2012 Holy Cross Baseball Yearbook*, 50.

87. "Braves Win at Malden by 11 to 2," *Boston Globe*, June 22, 1935, 6.

88. Gerry Moore, "Ed Moriarty's Hits Cheer Braves' Crowd," *Boston Globe*, June 23, 1935, 27.

89. Burt Whitman, "Ex H.C. Captain Gets Five Hits in Cubs Games," *Boston Herald*, June 23, 1935, 25.

90. "30,000 Autos Cross Bridges," *Boston Globe*, June 24, 1935, 1.

91. James C. O'Leary, "Pirates Win from Tribe in Portland," *Boston Globe*, June 25, 1935, 18; "2200 Knights Visit Portland," *Boston Globe*, June 25, 1935, 11.

92. Associated Press, "Paid Attendance 57,000, Gate $340,000," *Boston Globe*, June 26, 1935, 19.

93. Stephen V. Rice, "George Magerkurth," SABR BioProject. Retrieved June 2, 2021. sabr.org/bioproj/person/george-magerkurth/.

94. Gerry Moore, "Braves Drop Two to the Pirate Band," *Boston Globe*, June 27, 1935, 23.

95. Gerry Moore, "Moriarty Quits Boston Braves," *Boston Globe*, June 27, 1935, 23.

96. *Ibid.*, 1.

97. *Ibid.*, 23; Burt Whitman, "Ed Moriarty of Braves Quits Baseball to Enter Priesthood," *Boston Herald*, June 27, 1935, 1.

98. James C. O'Leary, "30,000 See Danno Pin Londos," *Boston Globe*, June 28, 1935, 1.

99. Gerry Moore, "Camilli's Home Run Beats Braves 4–2," *Boston Globe*, June 29, 1935, 6.

100. Gerry Moore, "Brandt Coasts to His Fifth Victory," *Boston Globe*, July 1, 1935, 7; Burt Whitman, "Braves Take Opener from Phils, 9–3, On Brandt's Pitching, Lee's Hitting, Then Wilt Before 23-Hit Deluge, 15–5," *Boston Herald*, July 1, 1935, 12.

101. Bill Cunningham, "Braves Bargain to Business Men," *Boston Post*, June 13, 1935, 16.

102. "Marshall Not Buying Braves," *Boston Globe*, June 12, 1935, 1; Dave Brady, "Football's George P. Marshall, Founder of Redskins, Dies at 72," *Washington Post*, August 10, 1969: 1; Associated Press, "Redskins Owner Marshall Dies," *Boston Globe*, August 10, 1969, 71; "George Preston Marshall Dies; Owned Redskins Football Team," *New York Times*, August 10, 1969, 77.

103. "Murphy Out for Control of Braves," *Nashua Telegraph*, June 14, 1935, 1; Associated Press, "Queen City Gets New Shoe Factory Unit," *Nashua Telegraph*, June 13, 1935, 6.

104. Gerry Moore, "Babe May Manage If O'Malley's Buy Braves," *Boston Globe*, June 26, 1935, 22.

105. "Retired Textile Head Succumbs in Sanford Home," *Bangor Daily News*, September 9, 1947, 1; Colin Sargent, "Inventing the Campbells," *Portland Monthly Magazine* July-August, 1997; "Braves Will Be Sold This Week," *Boston Post*, June 24, 1935, 17.

106. "Dean of City's Ad Men 80 Years Old Today," *Boston Globe*, May 11, 1947, 32.

107. "Charles J. O'Malley," *Boston Globe*, October 10, 1955, 24; "World Trip Lecture by Charles J. O'Malley," *Boston Globe*, January 11, 1938, 12; "Charles J. O'Malley Has 87th Birthday," *Boston Globe*, May 12, 1954, 4.

108. Gerry Moore, "Babe May Manage," "O'Malley Due to See Frick," *Boston Herald*, June 26, 1935, 20; "Associated Press, "Boston Interests Confer on Braves," *Worcester Evening Gazette*, June 27, 1935, 20.

109. "Mrs. Babe Ruth Denies Reports," *Springfield Republican*, June 26, 1935, 12.

110. United Press International, "Joe E. Brown Dies; Famous Comedian," *Hartford Courant*, July 7, 1973, 4.

111. International News Service, "Joey Brown Will Discuss Buying of Braves from Fuchs," *Quincy Patriot Ledger*, June 24, 1935, 1.

112. John Lardner, "Brown Shopping for the Braves," *Boston Globe*, June 26, 1935, 22.

113. "Late News Flashes," *Quincy Patriot Ledger*, June 22, 1935, 1; International News Service, "Reports Advance Three Owners for Boston Braves," *Denver Post*, June 22, 1935, 14.

114. Hy Hurwitz, "Marshall May Bid for Tribe," *Boston Globe*, June 25, 1935, 18; "Judge Fuchs in Mystery Parley," *Boston Globe*, June 24, 1935, 1.

115. Eddie Breitz, "What's Become of Babe Ruth? Scribe Discovers Answer," *Elmira Star-Gazette*, June 20, 1935, 23.

116. "Ruth Makes First Visit Since Yankee Release," *New York Herald Tribune*, July 1, 1935, 17.

117. Hy Hurwitz, "'No Immediate Sale of Braves,'" *Boston Globe*, June 25, 1935, 1.

Chapter 10

1. The "Sportsman" column, *Boston Globe*, July 10, 1935, 21.

2. "Two of the Same Name," *Boston Globe*, October 31, 1935, 19.

3. "Oscar D. Adams Dies from Shock," *Springfield Republican*, September 14, 1925, 1; *Springfield Republican*, March 15, 1906, 10.

4. "Employees Give Cup to Connor," *Boston Journal*, February 26, 1915, 5; "Progressive Grocer's Method," *Boston Globe*, December 10, 1901, 2.

5. *Boston Globe*, November 6, 1925, 7; *Boston Globe*, April 6, 1920, 11; "I Am Not Mistaken," *Boston Globe*, March 2, 1923, 18.

6. "Employee Ownership Within Five Years Is Predicted," *Boston Globe*, May 15, 1924, 6.

7. Bradford G. Blodget, "A Brief History of the Bellows Falls Co-Operative Creamery, Inc," Retrieved June 20, 2021. https://static1.squarespace.com/static/53a3b0e7e4b0356e962ad8f4/t/5e58ffc46e31e45f81252ab6/15828909554.65/Bellows+Falls+Creamery.pdf; Fred B. Barton, "More Business Where It 'Isn't," *Business* 5, no.6 (March, 1924): 10.

8. Barton, 10.

9. "Three Chain Grocery Stores to Be Merged," *Boston Globe*, November 16, 1925, 1; "Merger Agreement by Chain Store Firms," *Boston Globe*, November 20, 1925, 1; "First National Stores," *New York Times*, April 8, 1926, 38; "1,675 Stores in Merger," *New York Times*, November 26, 1935, 35; "First National Stores," April 8, 1926, 38.

10. Associated Press, "Dorr Company, Meat Firm, Merges with Grocery Chain," *Fitchburg Sentinel*, February 2, 1926, 4.

11. Fred B. Barton, "How the First National Stores, Inc., Is Cutting Its Overhead," *Chain Store Age* 2, no. 8 (August, 1926): 14.

12. "First National Stores' Birthday," *Boston Globe*, April 30, 1935, 30.

13. "First National Takeover," *Hartford Courant*, February 23, 1978, 81; "Adams, Founder of First National Stores, Dies at 70," *Burlington Free Press*, October 3, 1947, 1; James Andrew Ross, "Hockey Capital: Commerce, Culture, and the National Hockey League, 1917–1967. Thesis. University of Western Ontario, 2008. Retrieved July 7, 2018; "Charles F. Adams: Historical Pioneer." Vermont Sports Hall of Fame.

vermontsportshall.com/2013adams.html retrieved November 15, 2015; Bob Doherty, "The Somerville Times Historical Fact of the Week—January 22," *Somerville Times*, January 22, 2014. Accessed July 7, 2018. thesomervilletimes.com/archives/46039; Stanley Woodward, "That Adams Touch Has Firmly Shaped Boston Pro Sports," *Boston Globe*, March 24, 1944, 19.

14. "New Hockey Club Forming," *Boston Globe*, December 14, 1912, 7.

15. "New Arena, St. Botolph St, to Be Thrown Open to Public Saturday," *Boston Globe*, December 29, 1920, 7; "New Arena for Indoor Athletics," *Boston Globe*, June 8, 1920, 17; "Transform Arena for Athletics," *Boston Globe*, February 5, 1921, 1; "Vermont Boy Fan Becomes 'Pop' of Professional Hockey in U.S.," *Rutland Herald*, March 19, 1927, 11; Stephen Hardy, "Log Before Orr: Placing Hockey in Boston, 1897–1929," in *The Rock, The Curse and the Hub: A Random History of Boston Sports*," ed. Randy Roberts (Cambridge, MA: Harvard University Press, 2005), 256.

16. J. Andrew Ross, *Joining the Clubs: The Business of the National Hockey League to 1945* (Syracuse: Syracuse University Press, 2015), 102–103; Hardy, 265.

17. Ross, 114; Dick Dew, "Saga of Adams' Story of the Bruins," *Boston Herald*, January 7, 1973, 75; "Charles Adams," Hockey Hall of Fame. Retrieved December 27, 2019. hhof.com/LegendsOfHockey/jsp/LegendsMember.jsp?mem=B196001&type=Builder&page=bio&list=ByName.

18. Ross, 134; "Charles Adams," Hockey Hall of Fame. Retrieved June 13, 2021. hhof.com/LegendsOfHockey/jsp/LegendsMember.jsp?mem=b196001&type=Builder&page=bio&list=.

19. Victor O. Jones, "He Bought a Whole League to Bring Hockey to Boston," *Boston Globe*, February 15, 1967, 11.

20. "Charles F. Adams," *Boston Globe*, October 3, 1947, 36; "Sport Arena Will Be Ready by Nov. 1," *Boston Globe*, November 29, 1927, 21.

21. Victor O. Jones, "He Bought a Whole League to Bring Hockey to Boston," *Boston Globe*, February 15, 1967, 11.

22. "Charles F. Adams, Boston Sportsman," *New York Times*, October 3, 1947, 25; "Bryan Accepts Suffolk Post." *Boston Globe*, May 9, 1935, 25.

23. "Suffolk Downs Last Word in Race Tracks," *Boston Globe*, July 9, 1935, 20.

24. C. Joseph Harvey, "Modern Magic Has Transformed Dumping Ground into Suffolk Downs, One of Country's Finest Race Tracks," *Boston Globe*, July 6, 1935, 3.

25. "C.F. Adams, Owner Of," 12.

26. Ralph Clifford, "Braves Ready for Road Trip," *Boston Herald*, July 2, 1935, 26.

27. *Ibid.*

28. "Tangles Remain in Braves Deal," *Boston Herald*, July 2, 1935, 26.

29. "Ed Moriarty Passes Exams," *Boston Globe*, July 2, 1935, 1.

30. Lou Niss, "Anyway, Brooklyn Scribes Are in Baseball League," *Brooklyn Times-Union*, July 2, 1935, 1A.

31. "Ray Benge Returns to Shut Out the Braves," *Boston Globe*, July 3, 1935, 22.

32. Burt Whitman, "Definite Price Set on Braves During Frick, Fuchs, Adams, O'Malley Confabs; Indications Point to Early Sale of Tribe," *Boston Herald,* July 4, 1935, 17.

33. Gerry Moore, "Frick Confers on Sale of Braves," *Boston Globe*, July 4, 1935, 19.

34. Joe E. Brown and Ralph Hancock, *Laughter Is a Wonderful Thing* (Chicago: Papamoa Press, 2019), 227; Associated Press, "Jockey Club Grants Miss Hirsch License," *Boston Globe*, April 3, 1935, 22; Natalie Voss, "A Look Back at Mary Hirsch, Who Opened the Door for Female Trainers at Derby," Paulick Report. Retrieved June 23, 2021. paulickreport.com/news/triple-crown/a-look-back-at-mary-hirsch-who-opened-the-door-for-female-trainers-at-derby/; Eddie Welch, "Crowd Wrecks Mutuel Record," *Boston Globe*, July 4, 1935, 7; Hy Hurwitz, "Miss Hirsch Doing the Work She Likes … Training Horses," *Boston Globe*, May 18, 1935, 11; Eddie Welch, "Jockeys Stevenson and Howell Turn in Triples—John Werring Takes Fourth and Pays $42.80," *Boston Globe*, July 4, 1935, 20.

35. Paul Shannon, "Braves Buyers Still Strangers to Fuchs," *The Sporting News*, July 4, 1935, 1.

36. Associated Press, "Ford Frick Told Braves' Sale Price Is Half Million Dollars," *Hartford Courant*, July 4, 1935, 13.

37. Bill Cunningham, "Adams Has 65 P.C. of Braves Stock," *Boston Post*, July 4, 1935, 19.

38. Gerry Moore, "Schumacher Wins 10th Game in a Row," *Boston Globe*, July 5, 1935, 11.

39. Nancy Randolph, "Benedicts & Babe 1 Up on Bachelors," *New York Daily News*, July 5, 1935, 8.

40. John Lardner, "What About It?" *Boston Globe*, July 13, 1935, 10.

41. John Lardner, "From the Press Box," *Evening Post* (Charleston, SC), July 8, 1935, 7; *Cleveland Plain Dealer*, July 8, 1935, 1; Roelif Loveland, "Fans Flood City to See All-Stars," *Cleveland Plain Dealer*, July 7, 1935, 1.

42. David Sarnoff, "Radio Opens Its Eyes," *Cleveland Plain Dealer*, July 7, 1935 (Magazine section), 2; Loveland, 18.

43. NL Owners Meeting July 7, 1935, BA_MSS_55_Box 7_Folder 17-2, provided by the A. Bartlett Giamatti Research Center, Cooperstown, New York: 58–59; Hereafter listed as NL Owners Meeting July 7, 1935.

44. *Ibid.,* 59.

45. "Braves May Be Bought as Bargain," *Boston Post*, June 30, 1935, 15.

46. NL Owners Meeting July 7, 1935, 60–63.

47. *Ibid.,* 65.

48. *Ibid.,* 66.

49. *Ibid.,* 68.

50. *Ibid.,* 69–70.

51. *Ibid.*, 70.

52. *Ibid.*, 71–73.

53. *Ibid.*, 77.

54. *Ibid.*, 85.

55. *Ibid.*, 88–89.

56. Paul Shannon, "Braves to Be Sold to Local Syndicate," *The Sporting News*, July 11, 1935, 3.

57. Alvin Silverman, "Babe's Still King in All-Star Ring," *Cleveland Plain Dealer*, July 9, 1935, 16.

58. Babe Ruth, "Fame," *American Magazine* 120 (August 1935): 11. Reprinted in *Woodland Daily Democrat*, July 17, 1935: 8.

59. *Ibid.*

60. *Ibid.*

61. "Braves Defeat M'Keesport, 3–1," *Pittsburgh Post-Gazette*, July 9, 1935, 20.

62. Tod Rockwell, "Owen Smacks Double in 11th to Beat Braves," *Boston Globe*, July 10, 1935, 15; Melville Webb, Jr., "Notes of the Old Game," *Boston Globe*, July 11, 1935, 20.

63. "Detroit Edges Braves, 8–7," *Boston Herald*, July 10, 1935, 18.

64. "Berger Homer Not Enough as Cubs Beat Braves, 6–4," *Boston Globe*, July 11, 1935, 23.

65. "Outpouring of Turf Devotees at Suffolk Downs Inaugural," *Boston Herald*, July 11, 1935, 27.

66. Richard O. Boyer, "35,000 Wager $425,546 at Opening of Suffolk Downs," *Boston Herald*, July 11, 1935: 1.

67. "35,000 Throng Suffolk Downs," *Boston Globe*, July 11, 1935, 1; "Sumner Tunnel Has Biggest Day," *Boston Globe*, July 11, 1935, 1, 10.

68. "Braves Easy Winners," *Green Bay Press-Gazette*, July 13, 1935, 13.

69. Ray J. Gillespie, "Haines' 198th Cardinal Triumph Runs Birds' Streak to 12 in a Row," *St. Louis Star & Times*, July 17, 1935, 16.

70. Charles J. Doyle, "Pirates Win First Clash of the Series," *Pittsburgh Sun-Telegram*, July 20, 1935, 9.

71. Ralph Clifford, "Buccs Rally to Score Three in Ninth Off Cantwell for Tribe's 12th Loss, 6–5," *Boston Herald*, July 20, 1935, 8.

72. Ralph Clifford, "Buccs Win Two from Braves," *Boston Herald*, July 21, 1935, 23.

73. Volney Walsh, "Mace Brown Stars as Bucs Win Pair," *Pittsburgh Press*, July 21, 1935, 15.

74. Jack Ryder, "Braves, Too," *Cincinnati Enquirer,* July 23, 1935, 11.

75. Ralph Clifford, "Braves Turn Back Reds in 12th, 7–6, on Berger's Second Homer of the Game," *Boston Herald*, July 24, 1935, 17.

76. Jack Ryder, "Redlegs Tally Over Braves, 5 to 4," *Cincinnati Enquirer,* July 25, 1935, 1; Carol McMains and Frank Ceresi, "Hank Gowdy," SABR BioProject. Retrieved July 3, 2021. sabr.org/bioproj/person/hank-gowdy; "Braves Beaten in Night Game," *Boston Globe*, July 25, 1935, 23; "Derringer to Be in Box in Final Boston Battle," *Cincinnati Enquirer*, July 25, 1935, 12.

77. "War-Torn Braves Start for Tepee," *Boston Herald*, July 26, 1935, 27.

78. "Nekola of Toronto Turns Back Tribe," *Boston Globe*, July 27, 1935, 6.

79. Associated Press, "Golf to Claim Home Run King," *Daily Messenger* (Canandaigua, NY), July 26, 1935, 7.

80. Kevin Jones, "Ruth Whacks 81, Qualifies in Met Golf," *New York Daily News*, July 26, 1935, 48.

81. John Lardner, "Ruth Wants to Qualify in Amateur," *Hartford Courant*, July 27, 1935, 9.

82. Lou Wedemar, "Ruth Looking Forward to Amateur Golf Title," *Morning Post* (Camden, NJ), July 27, 1935, 19.

83. "Jackie Robinson Parkway," NYC Parks. Retrieved July 4, 2021. nycgovparks.org/parks/Q083/history.

84. "Ruth Fails to Knock Home Run at Alley Pond Park Opening," *Brooklyn Times Union*, July 27, 1935, 9; Robert F. Grannis, "Opening of Interborough Parkway's First Link Advances Highway System," *Brooklyn Daily Eagle*, July 27, 1935, 3; "Throw It, Mayor, Then Duck!" *New York Daily News*, July 27, 1935, 29.

85. Burt Whitman, "Davis's Curves Fool Tribe, 5–0," *Boston Herald*, July 28, 1935, 34.

86. "Sportsman" column, *Boston Globe*, July 20, 1935, 10.

87. Jack Cuddy, "'Red Hot Mamma' Bids for Braves; Would Use Babe Ruth," *Nevada State Journal*, July 19, 1935, 6.

88. James C. O'Leary, "At Least 14,000 Fans See Irish Champion Outrough Omaha Wrestler to Win First American Match," *Boston Globe*, January 5, 1935, 9.

89. Tim Hornbaker, "Paul Bowser Biography," Legacy of Wrestling. Retrieved July 6, 2021. legacyofwrestling.com/Bowser.html; Hy Hurwitz, "Londos, Licked, Thinks Danno Too Strong for Ed George," *Boston Globe*, June 28, 1935, 25.

90. Victor O. Jones, "What About It?" *Boston Globe*, July 27, 1935, 8.

91. Burt Whitman, "40,000 See O'Mahony Beat George—Match Ends in Brawl," *Boston Herald*, July 31, 1935, 29.

92. "20,000 Cars in Worst Traffic Tieup for Two Hours After Wrestling Bout," *Boston Herald*, July 31, 1935, 1.

93. Melville Webb, Jr., "Fuchs Fails to Hear from Prospective Purchasers Today," *Boston Globe*, July 31, 1935, 19.

94. Associated Press, "Fuchs' Stock Going to Adams, Says Frick," *Boston Globe*, July 31, 1935, 19.

95. Bill McCullough, "Fuchs Unable to Find Buyer for Holdings," *Brooklyn Times-Union*, August 1, 1935, 9.

96. Bob Dunbar column, *Boston Herald*, August 1, 1935, 25.

97. Harold Kaese, *The Boston Braves 1871–1953* (Boston: Northeastern University Press, 2004), 192.

Chapter 11

1. Liz Clarke and Rick Maese, "Segregationist George Preston Marshall's Monument Removed

from RFK Grounds," *Washington Post*, June 19, 2020.

2. "Fuchs' Career with Braves Closes in Note of Sadness," *Washington Post*, August 3, 1935, 15.

3. Gerry Moore, "Frick to Meet Braves Owners," *Boston Globe*, August 2, 1935, 20.

4. Gerry Moore, "Marshall's 'Five-Year Plan' Appears Salvation of Braves," *Boston Globe*, August 7, 1935, 20.

5. Gerry Moore, "George Marshall Bids for Braves," *Boston Globe*, August 3, 1935, 5.

6. Burt Whitman, "Owner of Boston Pro Football Team Negotiates for Control of Braves," *Boston Herald*, August 3, 1935, 1.

7. Jack Walsh, "Marshall Made the Redskins a Way of Life," *Washington Post*, August 10, 1969, 46.

8. Thomas Sugrue, "Soapsuds and Showmanship," *The American Magazine* 124, no.6 (December 1937), 132.

9. Walsh, Sugrue, 132–134.

10. Sugrue, 133; Walsh.

11. NL Owners Meeting July 7, 1935, BA_MSS_55_Box 7_Folder 17–2, provided by the A. Bartlett Giamatti Research Center, Cooperstown, New York: 88; "Redskins Football Team to Shift to Fenway Park," *Boston Globe*, July 21, 1933, 23.

12. John Drebinger, "Giants Top Braves on Late Drive, 3–2; Keep 2-Game Lead," *New York Times*, August 4, 1935, S1.

13. Phil Snaps," *Philadelphia Inquirer*, August 6, 1935, 15; Ralph Clifford, "Jorgens Holds Braves to Three Hits, Brown Wild as Hawk So Phils Win, 9–1," *Boston Herald*, August 6, 1935, 14.

14. Ralph Clifford, "M'Kechnie Airs Hogan Release," *Boston Herald*, August 6, 1935, 14.

15. Harold Kaese, "'Babe Ruth of Catchers,' Shanty Hogan, Dead at 61," *Boston Globe*, April 8, 1967, 20.

16. Associated Press, "Frank Hogan, Catcher, 61, Dies; Batted .339 with Giants in 1930," *New York Times*, April 8, 1967, 31.

17. Ralph Clifford, "Smith Hurls No-Hit, No-Reach Ball for Seven Innings and Braves Beat Phils, 4–0, While Berger Busts No. 23," *Boston Herald*, August 7, 1935, 22.

18. "Braves Are Idle, Move to Brooklyn," *Boston Globe*, August 8, 1935, 22.

19. "Corporation to Run Braves," *Boston Herald*, August 7, 1935, 22; Associated Press, "Adams Accepts Marshall's Terms on New Corporation for Braves," *New York Times*, August 7, 1935, 24; "On Tour of Inspection at Wigwam," *Boston Globe*, August 7, 1935, 8.

20. Gerry Moore, "Marshall's Bid for Braves Favorable," *Boston Globe*, August 6, 1935, 1.

21. "100 Years. Goodwin Proctor," Retrieved July 14, 2021. goodwinlaw.com/-/media/files/our-firm/centennial_book.pdf.

22. Gerry Moore, "Marshall Group Near Control," *Boston Globe*, August 7, 1935, 1; "Corporation to Run Braves," 22.

23. Victor O. Jones, "Crowd of 60,000 Sees Suffolk Downs Races," *Boston Globe*, August 4, 1935, B1; Burt Whitman, "Marshall Here Early This Week to Talk Over Control of Braves," *Boston Herald*, August 4, 1935, 26.

24. Moore, "Marshall's Bid for Braves Favorable," 1.

25. Moore, "Marshall Group Near Control," 8.

26. "O'Malley's Confer with C.F. Adams," *Boston Globe*, August 9, 1935, 19.

27. Moore, "Marshall Group Near Control," 8.

28. Gerry Moore, "Marshall's Bid," 14.

29. Associated Press, "Flashy Uniforms, Night Baseball, Planned for Braves by Marshall," *New York Times*, August 8, 1935, 20.

30. Bill McCullough, "Dodgers Win with 7 Out of Position," *Brooklyn Times-Union*, August 10, 1935, 1A.

31. Lee Scott, "First Major League Victory Thrills Ex-Outfielder Bobby Reis," *Brooklyn Citizen*, August 10, 1935, 6. Roscoe McGowen, "Cuccinello Stars in Dodger Victory," *New York Times*, August 10, 1935, 8.

32. Tommy Holmes, "Berger Is Hitsmith Par Excellence," *Brooklyn Daily Eagle*, August 12, 1935, 6.

33. "Berger's Homer Is Good for Four Runs," *Boston Globe*, August 12, 1935, 6.

34. Hy Hurwitz, "O'Malley's Not to Buy Braves," *Boston Globe*, August 14, 1935, 24.

35. *Ibid.*

36. "Paul Curley in Hit-and-Run Case," *Boston Globe*, April 1, 1933, 1.

37. Bill Nowlin, "Fred Mitchell," SABR BioProject. Retrieved July 21, 2021. sabr.org/bioproj/person/fred-mitchell/; Jack Beatty, *The Rascal King: The Life and Times of James Michael Curley (1874–1958)* (Reading, MA: Addison-Wesley, 1992), 429, 460; "Braves Officials Give Resignations," *Boston Herald*, August 16, 1935, 16.

38. "Park Baseball Leads Hinge on Sunday Games," *Minneapolis Star*, August 3, 1935, 10.

39. Edward J. Neil, "Fans Not Asking About Babe Ruth," *News and Observer* (Raleigh, NC), August 4, 1935, 7.

40. George Dixon, "Knight Sets New U.S. Mark, Eckert Leads Decathlon," *New York Daily News*, August 4, 1935, 76; Paul Gallico, "Babe Ruth and the Dopes," *St. Louis Star & Times*, August 6, 1935, 18.

41. Gallico, "Babe Ruth and the Dopes."

42. *Ibid.*

43. "Ruth's Auto on Home Run Hurts Woman," *New York Daily News*, August 7, 1935, 2; "Ruth Runs Down Woman," *New York Times*, August 7, 1935, 21.

44. "Ruth a Restaurateur?" *Knoxville News-Sentinel*, August 1, 1935, 9; "Babe Ruth Is Due to Reject Indoor Circus Offer," *Washington Post*, August 9, 1935, 19.

45. Patrick Hand, "Remembering Offbeat Amateur Tommy Goodwin," *Global Golf Post*, February 16, 2021. Retrieved August 14, 2021. globalgolfpost.com/more/remembering-

offbeat-amateur-tommy-goodwin/; "Babe Ruth to Try for Ace in Hole-in-One Meet," *New York Daily News*, August 11, 1935, 99.

46. "Joe Williams Says," *Pittsburgh Press*, August 13, 1935, 20.

47. "Babe Ruth a Magnet as Play in True Temper Open Starts Today," *Cleveland Plain Dealer*, August 16, 1935, 17.

48. Associated Press, "Gallery," *Cincinnati Enquirer*, August 17, 1935, 14; Associated Press, "Luther Gets 68 but Everybody Follows Babe Ruth at Acacia," *Akron Beacon Journal*, August 17, 1935, 15; John Dietrich, "Luther Rips Par Again, Leads Picard by Stroke in Open," *Cleveland Plain Dealer*, August 18, 1935, 3B.

49. Braves Defeat Aroostook, 6–2," *Boston Herald*, August 14, 1935, 25.

50. Burt Whitman, "Braves Blast 27 Hits, Play Faultlessly to Set Back Cincinnati Twice, 8–1, 11–5; Whitney Drives in Total of Seven Runs," *Boston Herald*, August 15, 1935, 27.

51. Dizzy Dean, "Extra Exhibitions Should Be Barred," *Boston Globe*, August 20, 1935, 21.

52. Sid C. Keener, "Medwick Hits 17th Homer with Man on as Cards Trim Braves, 6–5," *St. Louis Star & Times*, August 20, 1935, 16.

53. "Cards Win, 8–3, at Lewiston," *Boston Herald*, August 20, 1935, 19; "Cards-Braves Play Here Before 5,000," *Lewiston Evening Journal*, August 20, 1935; Bob LeMoine, "Al Blanche," SABR BioProject. Retrieved July 25, 2021. sabr.org/bioproj/person/al-blanche/.

54. "Larry Benton Is Stricken on Golf Course; Death Ends Career of Former Reds' Pitcher," *Cincinnati Enquirer*, April 4, 1953, 1.

55. "Braves Set Back by Falmouth, 8–6," *Boston Herald*, August 27, 1935, 15.

56. "Hal Lee Out of Game for Balance of Season," *Boston Globe*, September 11, 1935, 19.

57. Bob Dunbar column, *Boston Herald*, August 29, 1935, 22.

58. Burt Whitman, "Cantwell Wins Over Cubs, 2–1, in First Game," *Boston Herald*, August 29, 1935, 23.

59. James C. O'Leary, "Adams Asks for Minority List," *Boston Globe*, August 29, 1935, 9.

60. Bob Dunbar column, *Boston Herald*, August 27, 1935, 13.

61. O'Leary, "Adams Asks for Minority List," 9; Melville E. Webb, Jr., "Cards Go West 2½ in Lead," *Boston Globe*, August 29, 1935, 22.

62. Bob Beebe, "Ruth, Still Crowd Magnet, Arrives," *Minneapolis Tribune*, September 1, 1935, 2.

63. Fred Hutchinson, "Ruth Passes Up $100,000 in Exhibition Money to Get 'Good Rest,'" *Minneapolis Star*, September 2, 1935, 17.

64. Louis Greene, "Glenna Wins U.S. Golf Title," *Minneapolis Tribune*, September 1, 1935, 1; Michael Carlson, "Patty Berg," *The Guardian*, September 12, 2006. Retrieved August 15, 2021. theguardian.com/news/2006/sep/12/guardianobituaries.gender.

65. Hutchinson, "Ruth Passes Up."

66. *Ibid.*

67. Charles Johnson, "The Lowdown on Sports," *Minneapolis Star*, September 3, 1935, 16.

68. Associated Press, "Babe Ruth Plays in Police Game in Minneapolis," *Chicago Tribune*, September 2, 1935, 21; Associated Press, "National League Honors Babe Ruth," *Post-Star*, September 5, 1935, 8.

69. "Children Free at Braves-Dodgers Game Tomorrow," *Boston Globe*, August 31, 1935, 10.

70. Burt Whitman, "Berger's 29th Homer Only Happy Angle to Dodgers' Seven-Run Second, 8–4," *Boston Herald*, September 2, 1935, 18.

71. "M'Kechnie Buys Nashville Hurler," *Boston Herald*, September 1, 1935, 24; "McKechnie Gets Three New Men for Braves," *Boston Globe*, September 1, 1935, 5.

72. "Tribe, Dodgers Are Rained Out," *Boston Herald*, September 3, 1935, 12.

73. W.H. James, "Reflections from the Sidelines," *St. Louis Globe-Democrat*, September 6, 1935, 10.

74. "Moore Equals Batting Record," *Boston Globe*, September 6, 1935, 31.

75. W.J. McGoogan, "Braves are in Good Financial Condition and Ready to Make Trades, Bill McKechnie Says," *St. Louis Post-Dispatch*, September 5, 1935, 2B.

76. Victor O. Jones, "Huge Mob Jams Suffolk Downs," *Boston Globe*, August 11, 1935, 1.

77. "Downs Track Stock Bought by Officials," *Boston Globe*, September 7, 1935, 4; "Tuckerman on Racing in Ireland," *Boston Globe*, September 10, 1935, 11.

78. Burt Whitman, "Adams Seeking Aid for Braves," *Boston Herald*, September 7, 1935, 13.

79. *Ibid.*

80. Gerry Moore, "C.F. Adams Appeals to Braves' Shareholders," *Boston Globe*, September 7, 1935, 5.

81. Hy Hurwitz, "What About It?" *Boston Globe*, September 7, 1935, 8.

82. "Pinckert Team Wins Pro Game," *Boston Globe*, September 9, 1935, 7.

83. Edmund Taylor, "British Line Up League to Halt War in Africa," *Chicago Tribune*, September 9, 1935, 1; Associated Press, "Italy Calls 50,000 More," *Boston Globe*, September 6, 1935, 10.

84. Associated Press, "330,000 to Mark Military Rebirth at Nazi Meeting," *Chicago Tribune*, September 9, 1935, 3; "N.Y. Court Frees Five Arrested in Riot on Bremen," *Chicago Tribune*, September 7, 1935, 5; "New York Judge Arouses Wrath in Bremen Case," *Chicago Tribune*, September 8, 1935, 1; "Jewish Youth Barred from Nazi Schools," *Chicago Tribune*, September 11, 1935, 1.

85. Associated Press, "Hitler Cracks Down on Jews," *Boston Globe*, September 16, 1935, 1.

86. Associated Press, "Senator Huey Long Is Shot," *Chicago Tribune*, September 9, 1935, 1; Annika Neklason, "When Demagogic Populism

Swings Left," *The Atlantic*, March 3, 2019. Retrieved August 3, 2021. theatlantic.com/politics/archive/2019/03/huey-long-was-donald-trumps-left-wing-counterpart/583933/.

87. "Curley Appoints Judge Fuchs," *Boston Globe*, September 11, 1935, 1; "Belasco Full Moon Part of Show at Fenway Park," *Boston Globe*, September 12, 1935, 25; Victor O. Jones, "O'Mahoney Retains Mat Championship," *Boston Globe*, September 12, 1935, 1.

88. "Mayor Says Curley Would Be Dictator," *Boston Globe*, September 18, 1935, 1.

89. "Cuspidor," *Cincinnati Enquirer*, September 16, 1935, 12.

90. "Reds Twice Topple Tribe, 1–0, 7–6; Cantwell Loses Four-Hitter in Opener," *Boston Herald*, September 16, 1935, 14.

91. "Reorganization of Braves Near," *Boston Herald*, September 15, 1935, 36; "Shareholders in Braves Respond," *Boston Globe*, September 15, 1935, 26.

92. "Adams to Remain Active in Braves," *Boston Globe*, September 18, 1935, 22; "Braves Assured Reorganization," *Boston Herald*, September 18, 1935, 22.

93. "Braves' Owners Favor Bob Quinn," *Boston Globe*, September 19, 1935, 25; "Quinn Surprised to Hear of Job," *Brooklyn Times-Union*, September 19, 1935, 11; "To Reorganize Braves," *Montreal Gazette*, September 19, 1935, 12.

94. "Blanton Turns in His 18th Win," *Boston Globe*, September 19, 1935, 24.

95. Edward F. Balinger, "Spectacular Finish Wins for Pirates," *Pittsburgh Post-Gazette*, September 20, 1935, 18.

96. "Betts Pitches Three-Hit Ball," *Boston Herald*, September 22, 1935, 32.

97. C. Paul Rogers III, "Hugh Mulcahy," SABR BioProject. Retrieved August 9, 2021, sabr.org/bioproj/person/hugh-mulcahy/.

98. "Braves Break N.L. Loss Mark," *Boston Herald*, September 23, 1935, 16.

99. *New York Daily News*, September 23, 1935, 40.

100. "Deaths," *Boston Globe*, August 4, 1990, 24.

101. "Babich and Reis Beat the Braves," *Boston Globe*, September 25, 1935, 23.

102. Tom Stanton, "Excerpt: Joe Louis Got Married, The KO'd Max Baer in Front of Babe Ruth," *Detroit Free Press*, August 4, 2017. Retrieved August 10, 2021. freep.com/story/sports/2017/08/04/joe-louis-terror-in-the-city-of-champions/538882001/

103. Stanton.

104. "Max Tells Babe—I'll Show You How to Fight!" *Illustrated Daily News*, September 25, 1935, 14.

105. David Margolick, "Max Schmeling, Heavyweight Champion Caught in the Middle of Nazi Politics, Is Dead at 99," *New York Times*, February 5, 2005, A15; James P. Dawson, "Louis Stops Baer in 4th at Stadium as 95,000 Look On," *New York Times*, September 25, 1935, 1; "Our

Story: Joe Louis," National Museum of African American History & Culture. Retrieved August 11, 2021. nmaahc.si.edu/blog-post/joe-louis; "Joe Louis' Biggest Fights," *Sports Illustrated*, May 13, 2014. Retrieved August 11, 2021. si.com/boxing/2014/05/13/joe-louis-biggest-fights#gid=ci0255c50310012781&pid=june-25-1935-won-by-tko-over-primo-carnera.

106. "Braves Hammer Yarmouth, 20–2," *Boston Herald*, September 27, 1935, 46; "Braves Find Team They Can Defeat," *Windsor Star*, September 27, 1935, 27; The souvenir program and article are digitized at the Nova Museum. Retrieved August 16, 2021. novamuse.ca/index.php/Detail/objects/77320; novamuse.ca/index.php/Detail/objects/120347.

107. Al Cartwright, "Pitcher Huck Betts Is Still Plenty Sharp at 80," *News-Journal* (Wilmington, DE), August 17, 1977, 33.

108. "Daylight Saving Ends Tomorrow," *Boston Globe*, September 28, 1935, L 1.

109. Bob LeMoine, "Al Blanche," SABR BioProject. Retrieved August 16, 2021. sabr.org/bioproj/person/al-blanche/.

110. Steve Paschal, "A Boyhood Dream Come True," *Hood County News*, October 22, 1988, 13.

111. "Leslie Clyde 'Les' Mallon, Professional Baseball Player," *Fort-Worth Star Telegram*, April 19, 1991, 37; Hal Eustace, "The Sports Spade," *Brownsville Herald*, November 10, 1936, 18.

112. Paschal, "A Boyhood Dream Come True."

113. Pete Kendall, "In '35, Braves Had Ruth but Pitching Was Missing," *Dallas Morning News*, August 3, 1980, 3.

114. Paschal, "A Boyhood Dream Come True."

115. Bob Broeg, "Mowry: Playing It Smart Without Making It Big," *St. Louis Post-Dispatch*, July 2, 1984, 3C.

116. Harold Tuthill, "Joe Jr. Follows Mowry Tradition on the Diamond," *St. Louis Post-Dispatch*, May 24, 1959, 28.

117. John M. Butler, "Sportscope," *Scranton-Times*, June 24, 1954, 30.

118. Harold Kaese, "Griffith Told Cronin: 'Pass Ruth for Gehrig, but Never Vice-Versa!" *Boston Globe*, August 17, 1948, 9.

119. "Alfred Spohrer, Braves Catcher," *Boston Globe*, July 19, 1972, 30; Jerry Nason, "Al Spohrer Caught Everything Thrown at Him," *Boston Globe*, July 20, 1972, 29; Bob Ruzzo, "Boston's Boxing Braves," Boston Baseball History. Retrieved August 6, 2021. bostonbaseballhistory.com/bostons-boxing-braves/.

120. Ed Linn, "Big Noise in Washington," in *Sport* 24, no. 5 (November 1957): 87.

121. Ric Roberts, "Redskins' Owner Ties-Up Stadium," *Pittsburgh Courier*, September 23, 1944, 12.

122. T.H. Murnane, "Ward Wants His Team to Be Called the 'Boston Braves,'" *Boston Globe*, December 21, 1911, 7.

123. Linn, 90.

124. Shirley Povich, "This Morning," *Washington Post*, December 1, 1959, C1.

125. "Dozen Pickets Demand Redskins Pick Negro," *Evening Star* (Washington, D.C.), January 31, 1957, 56.

126. Quoted from Griffith's book, *Antiques I Have Known*. Cited in "The Man Who Gave the Redskins Their Name," *Pro Football Daily*, August 24, 2014. Retrieved August 18, 2021. profootballdaly.com/the-man-who-gave-the-redskins-their-name; Thomas G. Smith, *Showdown: JFK and the Integration of the Washington Redskins* (Boston: Beacon Press, 2011), 19.

127. Richard Leiby, "Bury My Heart at RFK," *Washington Post*, November 6, 1994, F1.

128. Quoted in Bill Nowlin, *Tom Yawkey: Patriarch of the Boston Red Sox* (Lincoln: University of Nebraska Press, 2018), 424.

129. Al Hirshberg, *What's the Matter with the Red Sox?* (New York: Dodd, Mead, 1973), 143.

130. Bob Holbrook, "Red Sox Eager to Sign Negro Players," *Boston Globe*, July 15, 1956, 58.

131. Hirshberg, 142.

132. "Bambino Coming with All-Stars," *New York Amsterdam News*, September 28, 1935, 13.

133. Lewis E. Dial, "The Sport Dial," *New York Age*, August 24, 1935, 8.

134. Joe Bostic, "Latins Hand Babe Ruth and His Team Lacing," *New York Amsterdam News*, October 5, 1935, 12.

Chapter 12

1. International News Service, "McKechnie Dreams of Stronger Braves," *Lansing State Journal*, October 1, 1935, 12; "Max Bishop Is Given Unconditional Release," *Boston Globe*, October 1, 1935, 23; Associated Press, "Draft Minor League Stars; A's Get Prizes," *Herald-Press* (St. Joseph, MI), October 2, 1935, 7.

2. Gerry Moore, "Yawkey Resigns as Santa Claus," *Boston Globe*, October 2, 1935, 22.

3. "Joy Epidemic Among 50,000 at Navin Field," *Detroit Free Press*, October 3, 1935, 1.

4. Associated Press, "Detroit Crowd Has to Like It; Only Boos Once," *Chicago Tribune*, October 3, 1935, 24.

5. Associated Press, "Babe Ruth Eats Anything Now; Wife Approves," *Chicago Tribune*, October 1, 1935, 26.

6. John Lardner, "Babe Ruth Is a Busy Man," *Boston Globe*, October 5, 1935, 8.

7. "Babe Slaps Daz for Homer but Mates Lose, 3–2," *New York Daily News*, October 14, 1935, 44; "Ruth, in Finale, Gets One Single," *New York Daily News*, October 21, 1935, 43.

8. Marshall Smelser, *The Life That Ruth Built* (Lincoln: University of Nebraska Press, 1975), 510.

9. "Babe Ruth Is Still Undecided," *Morning Call* (Paterson, NJ), November 1, 1935, 26; Associated Press, "Ruppert Anxious to Get Infielder," *New York Times*, October 23, 1935, 25; "Associated Press, "Ruth May Boom Baseball Abroad," *Boston Globe*, October 31, 1935, 23.

10. *New York Daily News*, October 31, 1935, 64.

11. Gerry Moore, "What About It?" *Boston Globe*, November 7, 1935, 25.

12. James C. O'Leary, "To Decide Fate of the Braves," *Boston Globe*, November 6, 1935, 24; James C. O'Leary, "Stockholders Try to Keep the Braves," *Boston Globe*, November 7, 1935, 21; James C. O'Leary, "Boston Braves to Be Reorganized," *Boston Globe*, November 2, 1935, 6; "Murphy Denies Rumor of Purchase of the Club," *Boston Globe*, November 2, 1925, 6.

13. Paul H. Shannon, "To Unravel the Braves' Problems," *Boston Post*, November 8, 1935, 24.

14. "Raising Braves New Capital," *Boston Globe*, November 8, 1935, 33.

15. Burt Whitman, "Half of $350,000 Needed for Braves Subscribed, Rest Likely by No. 15, Says Adams; Plan Partner-Manager," *Boston Herald*, November 8, 1935, 45.

16. Burt Whitman, "Adams, Murphy Braves' Agents," *Boston Herald*, November 16, 1935, 16.

17. Associated Press, "A's Get Cash for Players," *Boston Globe*, November 22, 1935, 29.

18. Hy Hurwitz, "Braves' Sale Unlikely," *Boston Globe*, November 27, 1935, 24 (evening edition).

19. Hy Hurwitz, "National League Takes Over Braves," *Boston Globe*, November 27, 1935, 21 (morning edition).

20. *Ibid.*

21. "Special Meeting of the National League of Professional Base Ball Clubs," Baseball Hall of Fame. BA_MSS_55_Box7_Folder 18-1, 6.

22. *Ibid.*, 30.

23. *Ibid.*, 30.

24. Hurwitz, "National League Takes Over Braves," 21; Al Hirshberg, *The Braves: The Pick and The Shovel* (Boston: Waverly House, 1948), 118–119.

25. Paul H. Shannon, "Braves Taken Over by League," *Boston Post*, November 27, 1935, 19.

26. *Ibid.*

27. "Special Meeting of the National League of Professional Base Ball Clubs," 44.

28. Burt Whitman, "Braves Forfeit Franchise, Players to League; Stockholders Lose Out," *Boston Herald*, November 27, 1935, 1.

29. Hurwitz, "National League Takes Over Braves," 21.

30. Robert D. Warrington, "Baseball's Deadliest Disaster: 'Black Saturday' in Philadelphia." Retrieved November 14, 2021. sabr.org/journal/article/baseballs-deadliest-disaster-black-saturday-in-philadelphia/.

31. Hurwitz, "Braves' Sale Unlikely," 24.

32. Shannon, "Braves Taken Over by League," 19.

33. "Mayor Backs Baltimorean's Big League Bid," *Baltimore Sun*, November 27, 1935, 22; "Harry Goldman, 84, Baseball Figure Here Since '90s, Dies," *Baltimore Sun*, December 26, 1941, 38.

34. John Drebinger, "Prospective Purchase Seen Expedited by Forfeit of Franchise—Stockholders' Reorganization and Operation by Circuit Also

Considered—Frick Confers with Adams," *New York Times*, November 28, 1935, 43.

35. James C. O'Leary, "Adams Is Willing to Step Aside," *Boston Globe*, December 1, 1935, 40.

36. Melville E. Webb, Jr., "Bob Quinn with C.F. Adams' Help, to Buy the Braves," *Boston Globe*, December 7, 1935, 8.

37. Burt Whitman, "Quinn to Bid for Braves with Adams's Backing," *Boston Herald*, December 7, 1935, 14.

38. Burt Whitman, "Red Sox Get Foxx, Marcum in Big Deal," *Boston Herald*, December 11, 1935, 34.

39. Associated Press, "Bob Quinn Has Taken Over Braves," *Boston Globe*, December 11, 1935, 20.

40. James C. O'Leary, "Calls Meeting of Old Stockholders," *Boston Globe*, December 21, 1935, 4.

41. Gerry Moore, "Bob Quinn Gets Braves," *Boston Globe*, December 10, 1935, 22.

42. Gerry Moore, "Jimmy Foxx and Marcum Bought by Red Sox for $250,000," *Boston Globe*, December 10, 1935, 22.

43. Gerry Moore, "Foxx, Marcum Join Red Sox," *Boston Globe*, December 11, 1935, 1.

44. Moore, "Jimmy Foxx and Marcum Bought by Red Sox,"; Associated Press, "Estimated Yawkey Has Spent $3,5000,000," *New York Times*, December 11, 1935, 30; Gerry Moore, "Mr. Yawkey Buys a Million Dollar Ball Club," *Boston Globe*, December 22, 1935, B3.

45. "Crash Fatal to 'Lefty' Brandt," *Spokesman-Review* (Spokane, WA), November 3, 1944, 23.

46. Ed Leach, "'Missing' Roan Finds Its Way Home Just in Time," *Longview News-Journal*, April 18, 1979, 4-A; Marty Appel, *Casey Stengel: Baseball's Greatest Character* (New York: Knopf Doubleday, 2018), 118.

47. Ed Leach, "Randy Moore Tells of Babe's Favorite Libation," *Longview News-Journal*, June 1, 1979, 4.

48. O'Leary, "Calls Meeting of Old Stockholders"; Associated Press, "Braves Have New Capital of $200,000," *St. Louis Globe-Democrat*, December 21, 1935, 7; Burt Whitman, "Stockholders in Braves Old Deal Given Chance to Share in New Regime," *Boston Herald*, December 21, 1935, 7.

49. Melville E. Webb, Jr., "Old Braves Co Is Dissolved," *Boston Globe*, December 21, 1935, 4.

50. Burt Whitman, "Dissolution of Old Braves Sees Quinn Quit Meeting in Anger, Turn Down $250,000 Offer by Murphy Syndicate," *Boston Herald*, January 1, 1936, 29.

51. James C. O'Leary, "By Vote of the Stockholders the Boston National League Baseball Company Is Dissolved," *Boston Globe*, January 1, 1936, 36.

52. *Ibid.*

53. "Boston Nationals Now in New Hands," *Boston Herald*, November 29, 1906, 11; "The Boston Club—Annual Meeting—Election of Officers," *Boston Journal*, December 8, 1871, 1."

54. Al Hirshberg, *The Braves: The Pick and the Shovel* (Boston: Waverly House, 1948), 69–70.

55. "Ruth Bunts Car. Rifle Stops Him Running It Out," *New York Herald Tribune*, November 15, 1935, 3.

56. United Press, "Babe Ruth Hangs Up Stocking and Hopes for Baseball Job," *Washington Post*, December 25, 1935, 14.

Chapter 13

1. "Charter Granted Boston National Sports, Inc," Boston Globe, January 18, 1936, 4.

2. Burt Whitman, "Bob Quinn Rids Boston of Baseball Indian," *Boston Herald*, January 4, 1936, 8.

3. Victor O. Jones, "What About It?" *Boston Globe*, January 6, 1936, 20.

4. Burt Whitman, "Braves Renamed Bees as Writers Concur with Father of Nine in Choice," *Boston Herald*, January 30, 1936, 1, 36; James C. O'Leary, "'Braves' Drop Old Nickname," *Boston Globe*, January 4, 1936, 1, 5.

5. Bob Drum, "Frankhouse Never Forgets Murderous 1928 Yankees," *Pittsburgh Press*, July 11, 1947, 24.

6. Charlie Vincent, "Whitney Was One of Game's Top Curveball Hitters," *San Antonio Express*, March 14, 1965, 89.

7. Scooter Chapman, "Coffee Joe Says Babe Ruth Was the Greatest," *Daily News* (Port Angeles, WA), July 11, 1974, 10.

8. Al Hirschberg, *The Braves, the Pick and the Shovel* (Boston: Waverly House, 1948), 79.

9. "Tommy Thompson," *Auburn Journal*, May 27, 1971, A-12; "Thompson Home from San Diego Induction into Pad Hall of Fame," *Auburn Journal*, August 3, 1967, A-7.

10. "Ex-Baseballer Buddy Lewis Dies," *The Tennessean*, October 26, 1977, 31.

11. Charles Love column, *Commercial Appeal*, August 27, 1960, 14.

12. Gregory H. Wolf, "Ben Cantwell," SABR BioProject. Retrieved December 11, 2021. sabr.org/bioproj/person/ben-cantwell/.

13. "Hal 'Sheriff' Lee," *The Sporting News*, September 25, 1989, 50.

14. "The Babe: 'The Greatest Man to Ever Play Baseball,'" *Davie County Enterprise Record*, September 28, 1989, 3B.

15. Jim Murray, "He Got More Hits Than Recognition," *Los Angeles Times*, July 24, 1988, 3-4; Jack Zerby, "Wally Berger," SABR BioProject. Retrieved December 12, 2021. sabr.org/bioproj/person/wally-berger/.

16. Warren Corbett, "Bob Smith," SABR BioProject. Retrieved December 12, 2021. sabr.org/bioproj/person/bob-smith-3/.

17. Edward G. Brands, "Barrow, McKechnie, Allen, LaMotte, Flowers and Keller Win '37 Accolade," *The Sporting News*, December 30, 1937, 1–2.

18. Frederick G. Lieb, "McKechnie Stretches Hits by Picking Spots for Pitchers," *The Sporting News*, September 23, 1937, 23.

19. Gerry Moore, "Bill McKechnie Signs to Manage Reds Two Years," *Boston Globe*, October 10, 1937, A1.

20. Hirshberg, 76; Associated Press, "Stengel Syndicate May Enable Quinn to Purchase Bees," *Boston Globe*, February 8, 1941, 1; Melville Webb, "Seems No Hitch in Sale of Bees," *Boston Globe*, December 10, 1940, 23; Melville Webb, "New Englanders Hold Bees Now," *Boston Globe*, April 21, 1941, 10.

21. Burt Whitman, "Syndicate Buys Bees," *Boston Herald*, April 21, 1941, 13.

22. Eddie Welch, "Adams Played Big Role in Three Major Sports," *Boston Globe*, March 6, 1945, 26; "Boston Bruins in New Hands," *Boston Globe*, October 10, 1936, 10; Associated Press, "C.F. Adams Dies; Sportsman, Food Chain Magnate," *Berkshire Eagle*, October 2, 1947, 2.

23. Hirshberg, 115–116.

24. "Bees No More, It's the Braves," *Boston Globe*, April 30, 1941, 20.

25. Melville E. Webb, "3 Boston Men Buy Controlling Stock in the Braves," *Boston Globe*, January 22, 1944, 1.

26. Melville Webb, "Quinn Quits as Braves Chief; Son Named General Manager," *Boston Globe*, February 15, 1945, 1.

27. Charlie Bevis, *Red Sox vs. Braves in Boston: The Battle for Fans' Hearts, 1901–1952* (Jefferson, NC: McFarland, 2017), 188–189.

28. *Boston Globe*, October 6, 1948, 24; "What Dad Didn't Do Son John Quinn Did," *Boston Traveler*, October 6, 1948, 32.

29. Harold Kaese, *The Boston Braves 1871–1953* (Boston: Northeastern University Press, 2004), 277–278.

30. Donald Honig, *Baseball When the Grass Was Real: Baseball from the Twenties to the Forties Told by the Men Who Played It* (New York: Coward, McCann & Geoghegan, 1975), 70.

31. Warren Corbett, "Elbie Fletcher," SABR BioProject. Retrieved December 18, 2021. sabr.org/bioproj/person/elbie-fletcher/.

32. Les Biederman, "Scoreboard," *Pittsburgh Press*, June 16, 1957, 71.

33. "Baseball Veteran Ray Mueller Dies," *The Patriot-News*, July 1, 1994.

34. Bevis, 212.

35. Harold Kaese, "How Long Will Braves Stand Financial Beating?" *Boston Globe*, June 26, 1952, 11.

36. Bob Holbrook, "Perini Sticks with Boston Despite 'Greatest Loss in Baseball History,'" *Boston Globe*, September 22, 1952, 8; Bevis, 216.

37. Roger Birtwell, "Perini Contracting Firm to Acquire Braves Stock," *Boston Globe*, November 27, 1952, 1.

38. Cullen Cain, "Giants, Braves Had to Move," *Miami News*, July 12, 1958, 13.

Chapter 14

1. Babe Ruth and Bob Considine, *The Babe Ruth Story* (New York: Signet, 1992), 215.

2. *Ibid.*, 215–216.

3. Paul Mickelson, "'Majors or Nothing from Now On,' Says Babe Ruth," *St. Louis Globe-Democrat*, February 7, 1937, 8E.

4. *Ibid.*

5. *Ibid.*

6. Mrs. Babe Ruth and Bill Slocum, *The Babe and I* (New York: Avon Books, 1959), 105.

7. Associated Press, "New Movement to Restore Babe Ruth to Baseball Spot," *Boston Globe*, February 8, 1937, 17.

8. Mrs. Babe Ruth and Bill Slocum, 106.

9. *Ibid.*, 108.

10. Jane Leavy, *The Big Fella: Babe Ruth and the World He Created* (New York: Harper Collins, 2018), 428.

11. Dorothy Ruth Pirone, *My Dad, The Babe: Growing Up with an American Hero* (Boston: Quinlan Press, 1988), 171–172.

12. Marshall Smelser, *The Life That Ruth Built.* (Lincoln: University of Nebraska Press, 1975), 528.

13. *Ibid.*, 524.

14. Smelser, 524.

15. Robert C. McCormick, "Babe Ruth Still Steals the Show from Under Noses of Other of Baseball's Immortals," *Kingsport Times*, June 13, 1939, 2.

16. "Galento, Babe Ruth Play Santa to Needy," *New York Times*, December 23, 1939, 13.

17. Creamer, 415; "Ruth Denies He's Dead," *New York Times*, September 18, 1940, 33; "Ruth's Condition Better," *New York Times*, November 30, 1940, 13.

18. "Ruth Sued Over Auto Crash," *New York Times*, January 15, 1941, 12; Associated Press, "Cobb Downs Ruth, Wins Golf Series," *New York Times*, July 30, 1941, 22.

19. Peter Kerasotis, "Home, at the Other House That Ruth Built," *New York Times*, March 11, 2014, B12.

20. "Babe Ruth Ill and Fighting for Life Here," *Los Angeles Times*, April 9, 1942, 1.

21. Mrs. Babe Ruth and Bill Slocum, 109–110.

22. James P. Dawson, "Ruth, Johnson, Turn Back Clock; Fans See What Made Them Click," *New York Times*, August 24, 1942, 19; Babe Ruth as told to Bob Considine, 221.

23. Mrs. Babe Ruth and Bill Slocum, 111.

24. George E. Coleman, "Sir Walter 'Glad Babe Busted One," *Brooklyn Daily Eagle*, August 24, 1942, 9.

25. Babe Ruth as told to Bob Considine, 221.

26. *Ibid.*

27. "Ruth Has a Birthday," *New York Times*, February 8, 1943, 22.

28. Fred Barry, "Babe Ruth Say's Cardinals Are 'In,'" *Boston Globe*, July 12, 1943, 6.

29. Associated Press, "Ruth Pilots Service Stars to Victory Over Braves," *New York Daily News*, July 13, 1943, 44.

30. Oscar Fraley, "Babe Ruth to Get His Thrill as a Manager," *Brooklyn Citizen*, July 28, 1943, 6.

31. Harold C. Burr, "Babe Ruth Cheers 27,281, Red Cross," *Brooklyn Daily Eagle*, July 29, 1943, 13.

32. James P. Dawson, "27,281 See Cloudbusters Top Babe Ruth's Team After Yanks Lose to Indians," *New York Times*, July 29, 1943, 14; "Cadets Upset Ruth's Debut," *New York Daily News*, July 29, 1943, 40.

33. John Drebinger, "40,000 War Bond Buyers Thrill Buyers to Baseball Spectacle and Variety Program," *New York Times*, August 27, 1943, 11; Associated Press, "Baseball's Immortals Help Sell $800,000,000 in War Bond Show," *St. Louis Post-Dispatch*, August 27, 1943, 22.

34. Associated Press, "Bambino Still Can Cut the Cake, Clicking Before Slip from Table: Celebrating Fiftieth Birthday, Ruth Deplores Overseas Trip Ban—Return to Baseball His Hope in Search for More Privacy," *New York Times*, February 8, 1944, 18; "Ruth Reaches 50, Seeks War Action," *Daily News*, February 8, 1944, 16C.

35. "Japan and Babe Ruth," *New York Times*, March 4, 1944, 12.

36. "Ruth to Lose Cartilage in Ailing Knee and Then May Try to Pinch Hit Again," *New York Times*, June 10, 1944, 18.

37. Jerry Nason, "Applause of Mat Fans Music to Ruth, but Oh, to Be Back in Baseball!" *Boston Globe*, April 3, 1945, 23; Clif Keane, "Casey Wins Szabo as Ruth Works," *Boston Globe*, April 5, 1945, 8.

38. "Ruth Turned Down as Newark's Pilot," *New York Times*, June 2, 1946, S3.

39. Mrs. Babe Ruth and Bill Slocum, 111–113.

40. *Ibid.*, 113.

41. Babe Ruth as told to Bob Considine, 234; Eleanor Cummins, "No One Told Babe Ruth He Had Cancer, but His Death Changed The Way We Fight It," *Popular Science*, February 6, 2018. Retrieved December 26, 2021. popsci.com/babe-ruth-cancer-treatment/; Smelser, 532–533.

42. "Chandler Calls on Ruth, Both Break into Tears," *New York Times*, February 4, 1947, 27.

43. "Many Felicitate Babe Ruth at 53," *New York Times*, February 8, 1947, 14.

44. "Babe Ruth Weeps as He Goes Home," *New York Times*, February 16, 1947, 50.

45. "Babe Ruth Catches Sailfish Off Miami," *New York Times*, April 12, 1947, 13.

46. Hy Turkin, "Ruth Signed by Legion to Aid Young Players," *New York Daily News*, April 8, 1947, 49; "Ruth Golfs at Bayside," *New York Times*, March 22, 1947, 17; Joseph M. Sheehan, "Ford Co. Signs Ruth to Life Post as Consultant in Legion Baseball," *New York Times*, April 8, 1947, 37.

47. Richard C. Crepeau, *Baseball: American's Diamond Mind, 1919–1941* (Lincoln: University of Nebraska Press), 82.

48. Max Goodman, "Exclusive Video, Timeless Stories from Babe Ruth Day in 1947 Brought to Life with New York Sports Tours Virtual Experience," *Sports Illustrated*, June 24, 2020. Retrieved January 24, 2022. si.com/mlb/yankees/mlb/yankees/news/babe-ruth-day-exclusive-video-stories-from-new-york-sports-tours.

49. Louis Effrat, "58,339 Acclaim Babe Ruth in Rare Tribute at Stadium," *New York Times*, April 28, 1947, 1, 29; Mrs. Babe Ruth as told to William Slocum, "My Life with Babe Ruth," *Saturday Evening Post*, March 7, 1959, 79.

50. Ed Reddy, "Babe Ruth Arrives for Legion Game at Park Tonight," *Post-Standard*, June 5, 1947, 12; Bill Reddy, "'Glad to Be Back,' Says Bambino," *Post-Standard*, June 6, 1947, 19.

51. Lawrence K. Altman, "The Babe's Other Record: Cancer Pioneer," *New York Times*, December 29, 1988, F1.

52. Leavy, 448.

53. Hal Schram, "Bambino Sees Detroit Whip Suburban League All-Stars, 6–4," *Detroit Free Press*, June 23, 1947, 19; "Golfing Fans Desert Pros to See Babe," *Knoxville Journal*, June 22, 1947, 21.

54. "Ruth Takes Rest in Hospital," *New York Daily News*, June 25, 1947, 17.

55. Dick Young, "Dodgers' 9 Runs in 4th Rout Giants, 11–3; Gain 1st Place," *New York Daily News*, July 3, 1947, 41.

56. Felix R. McNight, "Babe Ruth Greets Texas Boys," *Dallas Morning News*, July 10, 1947, 1.

57. *Ibid.*

58. Mike Haikin, "Forest and Adamson Win Legion League Games," *Dallas Morning News*, July 10, 1947, 5.

59. United Press, "Babe Wishes He Could Begin Again," *Austin American*, July 11, 1947, 19.

60. Max Moseley, "Babe Ruth Here for Legion Game, Given Key to City," *Montgomery Advertiser*, July 25, 1947, 1, 11.

61. Fred Wilson, "Sport Shorts," *Delaware County Times*, July 29, 1947, 14; Art Morrow, "'Athletics' Rally Wins Inquirer Game, 7–6," *Philadelphia Inquirer*, July 29, 1947, 26.

62. "Babe Ruth Brings Cheer to Girl Paralysis Victim," *Paterson Evening News*, July 30, 1947, 1; "The Andrews Girls Deliver," *Paterson Evening News*, July 31, 1947, 33.

63. "Ruth and Young Hospital Patient Exchange Good Wishes," *Paterson Evening News*, August 14, 1947, 1; Bill Ford, "Cincinnati Shades Cleveland Legion, 2–1," *Cincinnati Enquirer*, August 5, 1947, 3C; Harold Harrison, "Lint, Castiglione Star as Indians Edge Out Brewers, 3–2," *Indianapolis Star*, August 6, 1947, 21.

64. James Segreti, "Youths to Play Today for Their Idol—Babe Ruth," *Chicago Tribune*, August 16, 1947, 18.

65. "Ruth Here, Hails Kid Ball Program," *Minneapolis Star*, August 19, 1947, 25.

66. "American Legion Junior Baseball Tournament Opens in City Today," *Billings Gazette*, August 20, 1947, 13; Don Jewell, "Billings Throng Greets Babe Ruth," *Billings Gazette*, August 20, 1947, 1, 8.

67. Curt Synness, "Driving Mr. Ruth," *Independent-Record* (Helena, MT), October 4, 2016: B1.

68. "San Diego and Omaha Score Wins in Legion Baseball Series," *Billings Gazette*, August 21, 1947, 12.

69. "Babe Ruth Happy with Kids; Still Baseball's No. 1 Idol," *Spokane Chronicle*, August 22, 1947.

70. Prescott Sullivan, "The Low Down: Babe Ruth Here for Kids' Game," *San Francisco Examiner*, August 23, 1947, 15.

71. Will Connolly, "Ruth Proves Keenest Fan of 'Em All," *San Francisco Chronicle*, August 24, 1947, 1H.

72. Bob Brachman, "12,000 Fans, Young and Old, Pay Tribute to Babe Ruth at Legion Games on Seal Lot," *San Francisco Examiner*, August 24, 1947, 25.

73. Braven Dyer, "The Sports Parade," *Los Angeles Times*, August 28, 1947, 8.

74. Dick Hyland, "Cincinnati Nine Captures Title," *Los Angeles Times*, September 1, 1947, 14.

75. Will Cloney, "Home Is the Home Run King," *Boston Herald*, September 13, 1947, 4.

76. Will Cloney, "6 N.E. Boys Win Grants to B.U.," *Boston Herald*, September 13, 1947, 9.

77. "Bearded Babe Ruth Cheers 50 Polio Kids at Yule Party," *New York Daily News*, December 11, 1947, 50.

78. Associated Press, "Ruth Arrives in Miami," *New York Times*, February 5, 1948, 29.

Chapter 15

1. Associated Press, "Babe Ruth Celebrates 53rd Birthday Twice," *Boston Globe*, February 7, 1948, 4.

2. "King Still Reigns," *Boston Globe*, March 15, 1948, 9.

3. Lawrence Ritter, introduction to Fred Lieb, *Baseball as I Have Known It* (Lincoln: University of Nebraska Press, 1996), 4; Leavy, 45–46.

4. Leavy, 451–452.

5. Bosley Crowther, "The Screen," *New York Times*, July 27, 1948, 18.

6. Mrs. Babe Ruth and Bill Slocum, 120.

7. John Rendel, "Ruth Gives 'Story' to Yale Library," *New York Times*, June 6, 1948, S1.

8. Mrs. Babe Ruth and Bill Slocum, 121.

9. W.C. Heinz, "Down Memory Lane with the Babe," *New York Sun*, June 14, 1948. Reprinted in *The Top of His Game: The Best Sportswriting of W.C. Heinz*. Ed. Bill Littlefield. (New York: Literary Classics of the United States, 2015), 57.

10. Mrs. Babe Ruth and Bill Slocum, 121.

11. Heinz, 57.

12. "25 Years of Glorious Deeds in the Stadium Revived by Babe Ruth and Host of Other Yankee Stars," *New York Times*, June 14, 1948, 26.

13. Leavy, 454.

14. Franz Wippold, "12,000 Kids Acclaim Ruth at Baseball School Here," *St. Louis Star-Times*, June 19, 1948, 13; Jack Herman, "Ruth Stops the Show as Over 12,000 Youngsters Cheer His Appearance," *St. Louis Globe-Democrat*, June 20, 1948, 41.

15. Grantland Rice, "Rice Calls Ruth Greater Than Ever, Forgetting Own Pain to Cheer Others," *Boston Globe*, March 24, 1948, 18.

16. *Ibid*.

17. Bill Bryson, "Babe Ruth Just a Tired Old Man Now," *Des Moines Register*, June 21, 1948, 12; Casler Stein, "Babe Ruth Pays Visit Here," *Sioux City Journal*, June 21, 1948, 3.

18. Associated Press, "4,000 Hear Babe Ruth at Spencer," *Waterloo Daily Courier*, June 22, 1948, 14.

19. "Mission from Mission," *Argus Leader*, June 23, 1948, 14.

20. John Ross, *Feeling Sports* (London: Minerva Press, 1998), 26.

21. Joe Hendrickson, "Sports Opinions: Interview We Won't Forget," *Minneapolis Star Tribune*, June 23, 1948, 20.

22. "The Best Sellers," *New York Times*, July 4, 1948, BR10.

23. "Babe Ruth Expected Here for Charity Baseball Game," *Baltimore Sun*, July 12, 1948, 14; Paul Menton, "City Owes Ailing Babe a Mighty Reception," *Baltimore Sun*, July 13, 1948, 22; "Ruth's Health May Bar Trip," *Baltimore Sun*, July 13, 1948, 9.

24. Walter Taylor, "Ruth Gets New Proof He's Still Fan Idol Here," *Baltimore Sun*, July 14, 1948, 42; "Ailing but Smiling, Babe Ruth Makes 3-Hour Visit to City," *Baltimore Sun*, July 14, 1948, 30, 19.

25. Leavy, 458.

26. Fran Rosa, "Ted Cheers Ruth Via Wire to Bedside," *Boston Globe*, July 25, 1948, 27.

27. Bosley Crowther, "Sic Transit Gloria," *New York Times*, August 1, 1948, XI; "Hear Ye! Hear Ye! It's Babe Ruth Day Here by Official Proclamation of Mayor O'Dwyer," *New York Times*, July 26, 1948, 19.

28. Pirone, 179.

29. "Ruth Sees Premier of Film on His Life," *New York Times*, July 27, 1948, 18.

30. "Of Local Origin," *New York Times*, July 26, 1948, 20.

31. Grantland Rice, "Ruth Is Dead; Greatest Name in Sports World," *Des Moines Tribune*, August 17, 1948, 1.

32. Tom Meany, "Why Babe Ruth Quit Baseball Here in '35," *Boston Globe*, August 19, 1948, 14.

33. Oscar Fraley, "Babe Ruth Dead Two Years but His Memories Live On," *Hastings Tribune* (Hastings, NE), August 16, 1950, 8.

34. Smelser, 528–529.

35. Rice, 1.

36. Fraley, 8.

37. "Mat Champ Supplies Dramatic Peak," *Minneapolis Star*, March 2, 1953, 32; William Johnson, "I Like It Here," *Minneapolis Tribune*, August 9, 1961, 16; "Overcoming Blindness to Teach School," *Minneapolis Tribune*, October 16, 1966, 174; Don Sulhoff, "Blindness Is No Handicap," *Cedar Rapids Gazette*, August 14, 1955, 4:2; Jim Byrne, "Blind Matman Ross Returns … as Coach," *Minneapolis Star*, January 6, 1967, 12B; Ralph Thornton, "Blind, Not Handicapped," *Minneapolis Star*, April 10, 1975, 2D; James Parsons, "Blind Himself, Minnesotan Starts Magazine for Blind Sports Fans," *Minneapolis Tribune* (Picture Magazine), June 29, 1975, 4–5.

38. Associated Press, "Blind Editor Has Background for the Job He Now Performs," *Fergus Falls Journal*, April 15, 1975, 8.

39. Robert T. Smith column, *Minneapolis Tribune*, June 1, 1975, 2B.

40. "History," *National Beep Baseball Association*. Retrieved January 9, 2022. nbba.org/history/.

41. *Ibid.*

42. "Judge Fuchs Feted by 300 at Dinner on 80th Birthday," *Boston Globe*, April 17, 1958, 8; Austen Lake, "Price of Sentiment," *Boston American*, June 29, 1960, 47.

43. Hy Hurwitz, "Judge Fuchs' Devotion to Game Great, Lasting," *Boston Globe*, December 6, 1961, 43.

44. "Judge Fuchs Dead at 83—Former Owner of Braves," *The Sporting News*, December 13, 1961, 26.

45. "Fuchs Lost Heavily, Kept Braves Afloat," *The Sporting News*, December 20, 1961, 10.

46. Austen Lake, "Goodbye to Old Friend," *Boston American*, December 9, 1959, 27; Francis Rosa, "B.U. Razing Braves Field," *Boston Globe*, December 8, 1959, 59.

47. Austen Lake, "Lurk in Vapors: Braves Ghosts Still Linger,' *Boston American*, April 1, 1956, 19.

Bibliography

Books

Abu-Lughod, Janet L. *From Urban Village to East Village: The Battle for New York's Lower East Side*. Cambridge: Blackwell, 1995.

Adomites, Paul, and Saul Wisnia. *Babe Ruth: His Life and Times*. Lincolnwood, IL: Publications International, 1995.

Alexander, Charles C. *Breaking the Slump: Baseball in the Depression Era*. New York: Columbia University Press, 2002.

Anbinder, Tyler. *City of Dreams: The 400-Year Epic History of Immigrant New York*. Boston: Houghton Mifflin Harcourt, 2017.

Barrow, Edward Grant, with James M. Kahn. *My Fifty Years in Baseball*. New York: Coward-McCann, 1951.

Barthel, Thomas. *Babe Ruth and the Creation of the Celebrity Athlete*. Jefferson, NC: McFarland, 2018.

Beatty, Jack. *The Rascal King: The Life and Times of James Michael Curley 1874–1958*. Reading, MA: Addison-Wesley, 1992.

Beim, George, with Julia Ruth Stevens. *Babe Ruth: A Daughter's Portrait*. Dallas: Taylor, 1998.

Bevis, Charlie. *Red Sox vs. Braves in Boston: The Battle for Fans' Hearts, 1901–1952*. Jefferson, NC: McFarland, 2017.

Boxerman, Burton A., and Benita W. Boxerman. *Jews and Baseball*. Jefferson, NC: McFarland, 2007.

Brother Gilbert, C.F.X. *Young Babe Ruth: His Early Life and Baseball Career, from the Memoirs of a Xaverian Brother*, edited by Harry Rothgerber. Jefferson, NC: McFarland, 1999.

Brown, Joe E., and Ralph Hancock. *Laughter Is a Wonderful Thing*. Chicago: Papamoa Press, 2019. Internet resource.

Caruso, Gary. *The Braves Encyclopedia*. Philadelphia: Temple University Press, 1995.

Creamer, Robert W. *Babe: The Legend Comes to Life*. New York: Penguin, 1986.

Crepeau, Richard C. *Baseball: America's Diamond Mind, 1919–1941*. Lincoln: University of Nebraska Press, 1980.

Cudahy, Brian J. *Change at Park Street Under: The Story of Boston's Subways*. Brattleboro, VT: Stephen Greene Press, 1972.

Durocher, Leo. *The Dodgers and Me, the Inside Story*. Chicago: Ziff-Davis, 1948.

Durocher, Leo, and Edward Linn. *Nice Guys Finish Last*. Chicago: University of Chicago Press, 2009.

Fuchs, Robert S., and Wayne Soini. *Judge Fuchs and the Boston Braves, 1923–1935*. Jefferson, NC: McFarland, 1998.

Heinz, W.C., and Bill Littlefield. *The Top of His Game: The Best Sportswriting of W. C. Heinz*. New York: The Library of America, 2015.

Hirshberg, Al. *The Braves: The Pick and the Shovel*. Boston: Waverly House, 1948.

Homberger, Eric. *The Historical Atlas of New York City: A Visual Celebration of Nearly 400 Years of New York City's History*. New York: Henry Holt, 2005.

Kaese, Harold. *The Boston Braves 1871–1953*. Boston: Northeastern University Press, 2004.

Kennedy, Lawrence W. *Planning the City Upon a Hill: Boston Since 1630*. Amherst: University of Massachusetts Press, 1992.

Leavy, Jane. *The Big Fella: Babe Ruth and the World He Created*. New York: HarperCollins, 2018.

Martin, Brian. *The Man Who Made Babe Ruth: Brother Matthias of St. Mary's School*. Jefferson, NC: McFarland, 2020.

McElvaine, Robert S. *The Great Depression: America, 1929–1941*. New York: Random House, 1984.

Meany, Tom. *Babe Ruth: The Big Moments of the Big Fellow*. New York: A.S. Barnes, 1947.

Montville, Leigh. *The Big Bam: The Life and Times of Babe Ruth*. New York: Anchor, 2006.

Nadel, Stanley. *Little Germany: Ethnicity, Religion, and Class in New York City, 1845–80*. Urbana: University of Illinois Press, 1990.

Nowlin, Bill. *Tom Yawkey: Patriarch of the Boston Red Sox*. Lincoln: University of Nebraska Press, 2018.

O'Toole, Andrew. *Fight For Old DC: George Preston Marshall, the Integration of the Washington Redskins, and the Rise of a New NFL*. Lincoln: University of Nebraska Press, 2016.

Pirone, Dorothy Ruth, with Chris Martens. *My Dad, the Babe: Growing up with an American Hero*. Boston: Quinlan Press, 1988.

Reisler, Jim. *A Great Day in Cooperstown: The Improbable Birth of Baseball's Hall of Fame*. New York: Carroll & Graf, 2006.

Ross, John. *Feeling Sports*. London: Minerva Press, 1998.

Ruth, Babe, and William R. Cobb. *Playing the Game: My Early Years in Baseball*. Mineola, NY: Dover, 2011.

Ruth, Babe, as told to Bob Considine. *The Babe Ruth Story*. New York: Signet, 1992.

Ruth, Mrs. Babe (Claire), with Bill Slocum. *The Babe and I*. Englewood Cliffs, NJ: Prentice-Hall, 1959.

Scheuer, Jeffrey. *Legacy of Light: University Settlement's First Century*. New York: University Settlement, 1985.

Smelser, Marshall. *The Life That Ruth Built: A Biography*. Lincoln: University of Nebraska Press, 1975.

Smith, Thomas G. *Showdown: JFK and the Integration of the Washington Redskins*. Boston: Beacon Press, 2011.

Stevens, Julia Ruth, and Bill Gilbert. *Babe Ruth: Remembering the Bambino in Stories, Photos & Memorabilia*. New York: Stewart, Tabori & Chang, 2008.

Stinson, Mitchell Conrad. *Deacon Bill McKechnie: A Baseball Biography*. Jefferson, NC: McFarland, 2012.

Stout, Glenn, and Dick Johnson. *Red Sox Century: The Definitive History of Baseball's Most Storied Franchise, Expanded and Updated*. New York: Houghton Mifflin, 2005.

Surdam, David George. *Wins, Losses, and Empty Seats: How Baseball Outlasted the Great Depression*. Lincoln: University of Nebraska Press, 2011.

Surdam, David George, and Michael J. Haupert. *The Age of Ruth and Landis: Economics of Baseball During the Roaring Twenties*. Lincoln: University of Nebraska Press, 2018.

Trout, Charles H. *Boston, The Great Depression, and the New Deal*. New York: Oxford University Press, 1977.

Tygiel, Jules. *Past Time: Baseball as History*. New York: Oxford University Press, 2000.

Wanczyk, David. *Beep: Inside the Unseen World of Baseball for the Blind*. Athens: Ohio University Press, 2018.

Wehrle, Edmund F. *Breaking Babe Ruth: Baseball's Campaign Against Its Biggest Star*. Columbia: University of Missouri Press, 2018.

Wolf, Thomas. *The Called Shot: Babe Ruth, the Chicago Cubs, and the Unforgettable Major League Baseball Season of 1932*. Lincoln: University of Nebraska Press, 2020.

Articles

Barton, Fred B. "How the First National Stores, Inc., is Cutting Its Overhead." *Chain Store Age* 2, no. 8 (August 1926): 14–16.

Cohen, Alan. "Babe Ruth's Final Legacy to the Kids." In *The Babe*, edited by Bill Nowlin and Glen Sparks. Phoenix: Society for American Baseball Research, 2019, 137–140.

_____. "80-Year-Old Ex-Cop Remembers Babe Ruth as a Boy." ridgelysdelight.org/PDFs/Cop-Story.pdf.

Kahn, Roger. "The Real Babe Ruth." *Esquire* 52, no. 2 (August 1959): 27–30.

Lamb, Chris. "Outside the Pale: The Exclusion of Blacks from the National Football League, 1934–1946." In *From Jack Johnson to LeBron James: Sports, Media, and the Color Line*. University of Nebraska Press, 2016, 117–147.

LeMoine, Bob. "Boston Braves Team Ownership History." SABR Team Ownership History Project. sabr.org/bioproj/topic/boston-braves-team-ownership-history/.

_____. "Judge Fuchs." SABR BioProject. sabr.org/bioproj/person/judge-emil-fuchs/.

Liebman, Bennett. "Dog Racing, Judge Fuchs and Babe Ruth: Boston Braves Baseball in 1935." *Entertainment, Arts and Sports Law Journal*, 26, no. 2 (Summer 2015): Albany Law School Research Paper No. 12 for 2015–2016, Available at SSRN: https://ssrn.com/abstract=2658692.

Linn, Ed. "Big Noise in Washington." *Sport*, November 1957.

Michaels, Will. "Babe Ruth the Humanitarian." *Northeast Journal*, March 15, 2017. northeastjournal.org/babe-ruth-the-humanitarian/.

"More Business Where it 'Isn't.'" *Business* 5, no. 6 (March 1924): 10–13.

Ross, J. Andrew "Hockey Capital: Commerce, Culture and the National Hockey League, 1917–1967." Doctoral Dissertation, University of Western Ontario, 2008. DOI: 10.13140/RG.2.1.4791.7685.

Online Resources

ancestry.com
baseball-reference.com
familysearch.org
geneaologybank.com
Google newspapers
newspapers.com
ProQuest Historical Newspapers
Retrosheet.org

Other Sources

Boston Braves Historical Association
Boston Public Library
Brady, Bob
Chicago History Museum
Cullum, Bob
Fuchs, Carolyn
Lent, Cassidy. Librarian, Giamatti Research Center, Baseball Hall of Fame
Leslie Jones Collection
Macalaster, Gretyl
Minnesota Historical Society
New York Public Library
Nowlin, Bill
Rochester (NH) Public Library
Society for American Baseball Research

Soini, Wayne
Tenement Museum, NYC
Williams, Phil

Interviews

Fuchs, Carolyn, March 25, 2019, and April 2, 2019
Soini, Wayne, March 25, 2019

Index

Numbers in *bold italics* indicate pages with illustrations